How to Use This Book

Decisions is a user-friendly guide to English grammer and composition, designed to help you find the information you need—fast. Try the following strategies to find help with error correction and to locate key terms and topics.

When you can't name a problem, use the Spotlight error correction system.

Sometimes you have a vague sense that your writing might be flawed, but you don't know enough about formal grammar and punctuation to name the issue. In these cases, use the Spotlight system, designed to help you check for and correct common errors.

First, check the chart on the inside back cover gatefold.

The nine sections in this chart cover over 90 percent of the most common sentence and punctuation errors. Look in these sections for sentence patterns and word forms that resemble what you have written. If any of the examples or explanations leads you to suspect an error in your work, follow the references to a numbered section in the text. Here is one example.

SPTLIGHT ON COMMON ERRORS

(1) FORMS OF NOUNS AND PRONOUNS

Apostrophes can show possession or contraction. Never use an apostrophe with a possessive pronoun.

FAULTY FORMS	REVISED
The scarf is *Chris*. It is *her's*.	The scarf is *Chris's*. It is *hers*.
Give the dog *it's* collar.	Give the dog *its* collar.
Its a difficult thing.	*It's* [it is] a difficult thing.

Choose a pronoun's form depending on its use. For pronouns connected by *and*, or with forms of the verb *be (is/are/was/were)*, decide which forms to use (*I/he/she/they* OR *me/him/her/them*).

FAULTY FORMS	REVISED
This is *him*. It was *me*. Is that *her?*	This is *he*. It was *I*. Is that *she?*
The ball landed between *she* and *I*.	The ball landed between *her* and *me*.
Her and *me* practice daily.	*She* and *I* practice daily.

• Also see the following **SPOTLIGHT** (1) sections: **20a, 20d, 20g, 30a–b.**

Next, check for the Spotlight symbol in the text.

The Spotlight symbols in the margin mark the places in the chapter that correspond to the Spotlight examples you found on the inside back cover. Read the section(s) marked by the symbol and then reread your sentence. Does your sentence match the guidelines provided in the text? If not, then make a decision about the best way to revise your sentence.

To find key terms and topics, use these information locators.

- *Inside front cover:* The brief contents provides an overview of each section.
- *Main Contents*—page vii: This detailed listing shows sections and pages for all topics and usage guidelines.
- *Index*—page I-1: This alphabetical listing shows the page numbers of every key term, word, and topic.
- *Tab guides*: Each of the nine tab part guides offers a brief contents of the material in each section.
- *Usage Glossary*—page 399: This handy reference section defines key terms, provides capsule usage guidelines, and directs you to text discussions.
- *Revision Symbols*—following the Index: This guide to common instructor markings directs you to corresponding sections of the text.
- *Spotlight on Common Errors*—back of book and inside gatefold: See page ii for a description and instructions on using this feature.
- *Critical Decisions boxes*—outer gatefold. A complete list of key topics.

To narrow your search, look for these features on each page.

Tab displays the section number of the topic discussed on that page. A *symbol* next to the tab shows the mark instructors typically use to refer to that topic.

Cross-references in many chapters direct you to related discussions elsewhere in the text.

Section number includes the chapter number and a letter that corresponds to a particular topic and heading.

Subsection number identifies subtopics within sections.

Explanations describe the how and why of processes and usage guidelines.

Examples show correct usage or identify common errors and provide effective revisions.

Boxed features—including examples, Critical Decisions and Computer Tips—highlight key information.

Footer corresponds to the *tab* and *symbol* at the top of the page; it briefly identifies the section topic covered on that page.

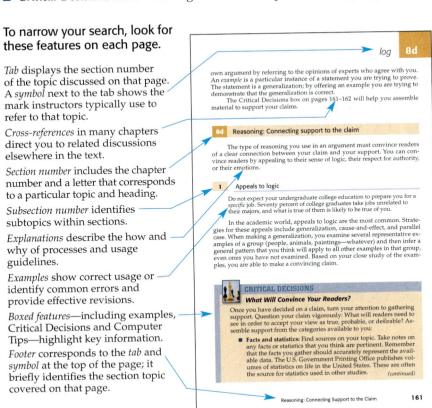

log **8d**

own argument by referring to the opinions of experts who agree with you. An *example* is a particular instance of a statement you are trying to prove. The statement is a generalization; by offering an example you are trying to demonstrate that the generalization is correct.

The Critical Decisions box on pages 161–162 will help you assemble material to support your claims.

8d Reasoning: Connecting support to the claim

The type of reasoning you use in an argument must convince readers of a clear connection between your claim and your support. You can convince readers by appealing to their sense of logic, their respect for authority, or their emotions.

1 Appeals to logic

Do not expect your undergraduate college education to prepare you for a *specific* job. Seventy percent of college graduates take jobs unrelated to their majors, and what is true of them is likely to be true of you.

In the academic world, appeals to logic are the most common. Strategies for these appeals include generalization, cause-and-effect, and parallel case. When making a generalization, you examine several representative examples of a group (people, animals, paintings—whatever) and then infer a general pattern that you think will apply to all other examples in that group, even ones you have not examined. Based on your close study of the examples, you are able to make a convincing claim.

CRITICAL DECISIONS

What Will Convince Your Readers?

Once you have decided on a claim, turn your attention to gathering support. Question your claim vigorously: What will readers need to see in order to accept your view as true, probable, or desirable? Assemble support from the categories available to you:

- **Facts and statistics:** Find sources on your topic. Take notes on any facts or statistics that you think are pertinent. Remember that the facts you gather should accurately represent the available data. The U.S. Government Printing Office publishes volumes of statistics on life in the United States. These are often the source for statistics used in other studies. *(continued)*

Reasoning: Connecting Support to the Claim **161**

CREDITS

Decisions

A Writer's Handbook

Second Edition

Leonard J. Rosen

New York   San Francisco   Boston
London   Toronto   Sydney   Tokyo   Singapore   Madrid
Mexico City   Munich   Paris   Cape Town   Hong Kong   Montreal

VICE PRESIDENT, EDITOR-IN-CHIEF	Joseph Opiela
MARKETING MANAGER	Christopher Bennem
SUPPLEMENTS EDITOR	Donna Campion
MEDIA SUPPLEMENTS EDITOR	Nancy Garcia
PRODUCTION MANAGER	Bob Ginsberg
PROJECT COORDINATION, TEXT DESIGN, AND ELECTRONIC PAGE MAKEUP	Pre-Press Company, Inc.
COVER DESIGN MANAGER	John Callahan
COVER DESIGNER	Maria Ilardi
COVER ILLUSTRATION	"Fork-in-the-Road" by Dennis Harms; courtesy of the Stock Illustration Source
MANUFACTURING BUYER	Lucy Hebard
PRINTER AND BINDER	Banta Book Group
COVER PRINTER	Lehigh Press, Inc.

For permission to use copyrighted material, grateful acknowledgment is made to the copyright holders on pp. iv, which is hereby made part of this copyright page.

Library of Congress Cataloging-in-Publication Data

Rosen, Leonard J.
    Decisions: a writer's handbook/Leonard J. Rosen.—2nd ed.
        p. cm.
    Includes index.
    ISBN 0-205-33935-2
    1. English language—Rhetoric—Handbooks, manuals, etc. 2. English language—Grammar—Handbooks, manuals, etc. 3. Report writing—Handbooks, manuals, etc. I. Title.

PE1408 .R6775 2002
808'.042—dc21   2001029747

Please visit our Web site at http://www.ablongman.com/rosen

ISBN 0-205-33935-2

1 2 3 4 5 6 7 8 9 10—BAT—04 03 02 01

CONTENTS

Tense

Voice

Mood

Misplaced Modifiers

Dangling Modifiers

PREFACE

The second edition of *Decisions: A Writer's Handbook* continues to be based on the premise that students at the college level must learn to think and read critically in order to write effectively. In all of their work across the disciplines, students must understand, respond to, and evaluate written material, ultimately synthesizing new information and ideas with old. At every level, they must make thoughtful decisions about what counts as important information, about the validity of an author's assumptions, and about connections among sources. And as readers who *write*, students must routinely decide how best to persuade an audience, structure a sentence, or address a problem with grammar. This handbook guides students through all of these decisions by helping them to master foundational skills.

Emphasis on Critical Thinking

Decisions gives more explicit coverage to critical thinking than any other brief handbook. Beginning with Chapter 1, "Critical Thinking, Reading, and Writing," students learn how to think and read strategically: to be alert to differences; to challenge and be challenged by a text; to appreciate broader contexts; to understand and write summaries; to evaluate and write critiques; and to integrate and write syntheses. Throughout the book, clear instructions, ample illustrations, and special features link thinking/reading skills to thinking/writing skills.

Emphasis on Writing in the Disciplines

In addition to providing extensive coverage of critical thinking, this handbook explains and illustrates what it means to think and write in discipline-appropriate ways. Composition instructors have long appreciated that students need to think critically about their reading and writing well beyond the introductory composition course. Students must be trained to reason like biologists, psychologists, and literary critics, and they learn to do so by reading and writing, with guidance, in their disciplines.

Decisions introduces students to the habits of mind and the topics they will encounter in writing assignments across the curriculum. Chapter 8, "Writing and Arguing in the Disciplines," begins with a discussion of the

Toulmin approach, which classifies the elements of argument as *claim, evidence,* and *reasoning.* The chapter goes on to analyze the ways in which claims, evidence, and reasoning change from one discipline area to the next, including sample papers from the humanities, social sciences, and sciences. *Decisions* also uses connected discourse from student and professional writings across the disciplines as the basis for many example sentences.

Thoughtful Coverage of the Writing Process

Chapters 2 and 3 on the writing process, including paragraph development, function as both a quick reference tool and a mini-rhetoric. With emphasis on *revision,* the discussion shows a student paper under development from initial brainstorming through final draft. The topic—the arrogant assumptions that nonsmokers make about smokers—is both timely and representative of topics that students choose for composition assignments. Because first-year college students often have difficulty formulating effective working theses, *Decisions* devotes considerable attention to this skill.

Comprehensive Treatment of the Research Process

Chapters 4–7, the research paper section of this handbook, build on and integrate the book's previous discussions of critical thinking and the writing process. The discussion on finding, evaluating, and integrating sources draws heavily on the critical thinking concepts introduced in Chapter 1. Advice on composing the paper amplifies writing process coverage in Chapters 2 and 3. The coverage of documentation in Chapter 7 includes four different conventions: the MLA and APA systems, with formats for electronic materials; the footnote style (based on the *Chicago Manual of Style);* and the CBE system used selectively in the sciences.

Extensive Coverage of Internet Sources

Decisions presents a thorough introduction to using Internet sources for research. Developed with the help of Rick Branscomb of Salem State College, the discussion in the research paper section encourages students to explore the wealth of material available on the Internet. Because much of this material is neither reviewed nor edited by any outside authority, Chapter 4 focuses on criteria for evaluating the validity of Internet sources, including the World Wide Web.

Guidelines and Choices in Sentence Revision

Any experienced writer knows that there is often more than one solution to a common sentence error. Therefore, when appropriate, *Decisions* discusses alternative solutions and encourages students to make choices as writers. However, when usage is a matter of strict convention, this handbook offers firm, clear guidelines for eliminating common errors and understanding key concepts of grammar, usage, and style.

New to This Edition

- **Greatly expanded numbers of "Critical Decisions" boxes** and **lead paragraphs focusing on the writer's critical decisions** at the head of many more chapters reinforce the centrality of critical thinking throughout the writing process.
- **Updated coverage of Web-based research, a new chapter on writing for the Web,** and **updated Web sites** (distributed as boxes throughout the text) ensure that *Decisions* provides students with current, practical advice on creating Internet documents and on evaluating and incorporating Internet sources into their work.
- **A new student research paper, "How computer-mediated communication affects interpersonal relationships,"** explores the promises and pitfalls of searching online for long-term relationships.
- **Expanded coverage of document design** and of **business writing (which now includes a discussion of e-mail)** broadens student awareness of the contexts in which they are expected to work as writers.
- **Important matters of grammar and usage, including ESL coverage,** receive heightened emphasis with a reorganization and expansion of chapters containing discrete coverage of each important topic.
- **Two new multimedia CD-ROMs** expand the ways in which students can use *Decisions. The Electronic Bookshelf,* which accompanies the text, includes a tutorial on avoiding plagiarism, and hundreds of interactive exercises in key topic areas. *Decisions: The Interactive Edition CD-ROM,* available in January 2002, will include the full text of the book, supplemented by video, hot-linked Web references, and contextually relevant interactive exercises.

Special Features That Reinforce Text Emphases

To highlight elements of its unique approach and to help students find and review key information quickly, *Decisions* includes the following features:

- **Spotlight on Common Errors** offers a quick reference system to help students identify and correct grammar and usage problems. First, the **Spotlight** chart on the inside back cover pinpoints error patterns and provides examples of faulty and revised sentences. Then, the chart directs students to portions of the text, identified with corresponding numbered icons, that provide detailed explanations and additional examples. See page ii for detailed instructions on using the **Spotlight** system.
- **Critical Decisions** boxes appear throughout the text, showing students how to analyze issues of content, organization, style, grammar, and mechanics in order to make sound choices for their writing.
- **Computer Tips**, appearing in many chapters, contain suggestions for using word processors and the Internet for writing and research.

Additional example boxes throughout the text trace the development of important issues or writing samples.

Comprehensive ESL Coverage

Students whose native language is not English have been entering mainstream composition courses in increasing numbers, with varying degrees of prior preparation from specialized English as a Second Language (ESL) courses. This handbook provides help for these students in a comprehensive three-chapter ESL Reference Guide, developed with the assistance of Will Van Dorp of Northern Essex Community College. This Guide summarizes troublesome features of English language usage in three functional areas: nouns, pronouns and articles; verbs and related structures; and modifying structures. Idioms and constructions with prepositions and particles—especially troublesome forms for international students—are treated in appropriate sections.

Acknowledgments

I am indebted to the people who provided helpful critiques of the manuscript for *Decisions*: Virginia Carroll, Kent State University; Scott Leonard, Youngstown State University; Charles Hill, University of Wisconsin Oshkosh; Dianne Fallon, York County Technical College; Sheryl McGough, Iowa State University; Donald F. Andrews, Chattanooga State Technical College; Diana Ashe, Texas A&M University; Larry Beason, Eastern Washington University; Robert Funk, Eastern Illinois University; Julie Hagemann, Purdue University, Calumet; Paul Heilker, Virginia Tech; Maureen Hoag, Wichita State University; Lisa McClure, Southern Illinois University at Carbondale; John Olson, ECPI College of Technology; Ken Risdon, University of Minnesota, Duluth; and Cheryl Ruggiero, Virginia Tech.

I thank those who contributed their comments and insights to develop the four editions of the *Allyn & Bacon Handbook,* from which I adapted much of the material for *Decisions*: John Clark, Bowling Green State University; Michel deBenedictis, Miami Dade Community College; Kathryn Fitzgerald, University of Utah; Nancy Jermark, Hutchinson Community College; Todd Lundberg, Cleveland State University; Kevin Morris, Greenville Technical College; Ruth Morris, Greenville Technical College; Donna Nelson, Bowling Green State University; Carol Scheidenhelm, Northern Illinois University; Nancy Schneider, University of Maine, Augusta; Margaret Shaw, Kent State University; Laura Yowell, Hutchinson Community College; and Trudy Zimmerman, Hutchinson Community College. Reviewers of the fourth edition reminded us that a widely used handbook is always a candidate for improvement. We wish to thank Anne Bliss, University of Colorado; Eric Branscomb, Salem State College; Jane Dugan, Cleveland State University; Rima Gulshan, University of Maryland, Eastern Shore; Julie Hagemann, Purdue Calumet; Bill Lalicker, West Chester University; Roake Mulligan, Christopher Newport University; Steven Szilagyi, University of Alabama Huntsville; Marilyn Valentino, Lorain County Community College; Lisa Williams, Jacksonville State University; and Lynn Zimmerman, Kent State University. Also: Tim Anderson, Bentley College; Bruce Appleby, Southern Illinois University; Phillip Arrington, Eastern Michigan University; Christy Bell, Bentley College; Linda Bensel-Myers, University of Tennessee; Anne Bliss, University of Colorado; Eric Branscomb, Salem State College; Melody Brewer, University of Toledo; Burke Brown, University of Southern Alabama; Therese Brychta, Truckee Meadow Community College; Christopher Burnham, New Mexico State University; Kathleen Shine Cain, Merrimac College; Patsy Callaghan, Central Washington University; Peter Carino, Indiana State University; Lindsey Carpenter, Bentley College; Barbara Carson, University of Georgia; Luigi Cassetta, Bentley College; John Clark, Bowling Green State University; John Clarke, University of Vermont; Thomas Copeland, Youngstown State University; Robert Crooks, Bentley College; Neil Daniel, Texas Christian University; Michel deBenedictis, Miami Dade Community College; Virginia Draper, Stevenson College; Jane Dugan, Cleveland State University; Ray Dumont, University of Massachusetts, Dartmouth; Nancy Esposito, Bentley College; Kathy Evertz, University of Wyoming; Kathryn Fitzgerald, Utah State University; Sallyanne Fitzgerald, University of Missouri, Saint Louis; Barbara Gaffney, University of New Orleans; Carol Gibbens, University of California, Santa Barbara; Dale Gleason, Hutchinson Community College; Eric Godfrey, Ripon College; Donna Gorrell, St. Cloud State University; Barbara Gottfried, Bentley College; Patricia Graves, Georgia State University; Ruth Greenberg, Jefferson Community College; Rima Gulshan, University of Maryland, Eastern Shore; Julie Hagemann, Purdue Calumet; Stephen Hahn, William Paterson College; John Hanes, Duquesne University; Kristine Hansen, Brigham Young University; Sherman Hayes, Bentley College; Tom Heeney, Bentley College; Kathleen Herndon, Weber State University; Bruce Herzberg, Bentley College; Vicki Hill, Southern Methodist University; Maureen Hoag, Wichita State University; Jeriel Howard, Northeastern Illinois State University; Clayton Hudnall, University of Hartford; Clarence Ivie, University of Southern Alabama; Ralph Jenkins, Temple University; Nancy Jermark, Hutchinson Community College; David Joliffe, University of Illinois at Chicago; Rodney Keller, Ricks College; Kate Kiefer, Colorado State University; Judith Kohl, Dutchess Community College; Douglas Krienke, Sam Houston State University; Richard Kyte, Bentley College; Nevin Laib, Franklin and Marshall University; Bill Lolicker, West Chester University; John Laucus, University Librarian, Boston University; William Leap, The American University; Todd Lundberg, Cleveland State University; Barry Maid, University of Arkansas at Little Rock; Thomas Martinez, Villanova University; Wendell Mayo, Indiana University-Purdue University Fort Wayne; Mary McGann, University of Indianapolis; Donald McIntyre, Bentley College; Kathy Meade, Bentley College; Charles Meyer, University of Massachusetts, Boston; Walter Minot, Gannon University; Kevin Morris, Greenville Technical College; Ruth Morris, Greenville Technical College; Roarke Mulligan, Christopher Newport University; Joan Mullin, University of Toledo; Patricia Murray, California State University, Northridge; Donna Nelson, Bowling Green State University; Richard Nordquist, Armstrong State University; Jack Oruch, University of Kansas; Twyla Yates Papay, Rollins College; Jon Patton, University of Toledo; Randall Popken, Tarleton State University; George Radford, Bentley College; Richard Ramsey, Indiana/Purdue University at Fort Wayne; Kirk Rasmussen, Utah Valley Community College; Sally Barr Reagan, University of Missouri; Larry Renbaum, Georgetown University Law School; David Roberts, Samford University; Annette Rottenberg, University of Massachusetts, Amherst; Carol Scheidenhelm, Northern Illinois University; Carol G. Schneider, Association of American Colleges; Nancy Schneider, University of Maine, Augusta; Mimi Schwartz, Stockton State College; Margaret Shaw, Kent State University; John Shea, Loyola University; Louise Smith, University of Massachusetts, Boston; Margot Soven, La Salle University; Sally Spurgin, Southern Methodist University; Judith Stanford, Rivier College; Barbara Stout, Montgomery College; Ellen Strenski, University of California, Los Angeles; Steven Szilagyi, University of Alabama Huntsville; Ann Taylor, Salem State College; Elizabeth Tentarelli, Merrimack College; Christopher Thaiss, George Mason University; Alison Tschopp, Boston University Law School; Marilyn Valentino, Lorain County Community College; Michael Vivion, University of Missouri, Kansas City; Barbara Weaver, Ball State University; Arthur White, Western Michigan University; Lisa Williams, Jacksonville State University; Laura Yowell, Hutchinson Community College; Richard Zbaracki, Iowa State University; Lynn Zimmerman, Kent State University; and Trudy Zimmerman, Hutchinson Community College .

I would also like to thank Joe Opiela, Vice President and Editor-in-Chief for English at Longman, who helped to shape the vision for this book. Allen Workman helped me transform that vision into reality, both in *Decisions* and in the *Allyn & Bacon Handbook*. Mark Gallaher ably assisted in preparing the second edition. Finally, I owe much to Elsa van Bergen, production coordinator for this book, and to Bob Ginsberg, Production Administrator, who ably shepherded the manuscript through the production process.

PART I
Reading, Thinking, and Writing

CHAPTER 1

Critical Thinking, Reading, and Writing

Success as a writer often requires that you be an effective, critical reader. "Critical" in this sense does not refer to negativity but, rather, to reading that is *active* and *alert*. You will need, for example, to make decisions about similarities and differences among sources; about what, exactly, a writer is saying and how you, as a reader, respond; about the broader context of an issue; and about your own opinions. Such decisions are key to thinking critically about the source materials that will provide the basis for much of your writing—both in college and beyond.

WWW

http://www.sonoma.edu/cthink/

The Center for Critical Thinking, a repository of information about the theory and practice of critical thinking.

CRITICAL DECISIONS

Determining a Writer's Purpose

There is one basic question any critical reader must ask of a text: What is the writer's primary purpose in this piece of writing? While multiple purposes may come into play, a writer will almost always have a dominant purpose for the piece of writing. Is it to share personal experience or explore the personal significance of some event? to provide readers with information or help them better understand a topic? to persuade readers to change their minds or see an issue in a new light?

Writers often provide readers with information about an issue with the larger purpose of *persuading* them to accept a particular position on that issue. Even personal writing can have as its underlying purpose to inform or to persuade.

To read critically, you must make such distinctions clearly. A good way to do so is to identify the writer's thesis. (For more on the thesis, see pages 26–29.)

Active, Critical Reading

Determining and questioning similarities and differences

Two or more sources on a particular topic will nearly always present similarities and differences in terms of facts, interpretations of facts, value judgments, or the policy each writer thinks ought to be pursued. With practice, you can discover such similarities and differences using questions that get you thinking critically.

1 ### Question similarities.

If two statements look alike, ask yourself *why*.

- Are the facts the same?
- Are the interpretations of facts the same?
- Have facts been established in the same way?
- If authors share the same view, is their reasoning or value system necessarily the same?
- What social conditions might explain the similarities?

Other questions are possible. The point is that your awareness of similarity marks a *beginning* point for your thinking.

The box below contains two selections on the topic of saving the world's tiger population. Think of these selections as sources you might read for class or discover in your research process. The discussion that follows on differing aspects of critical thinking will refer to these selections. As you read them for the first time, think about their similarities and differences.

To Save—or Not to Save—the Tiger

"Tiger Conservation Meeting
in Thailand"

UPI January 24, 1996

Conservation experts from around the world gathered in Thailand Wednesday to devise a united strategy to save Asia's dwindling number of tigers from extinction. Opening the Second International Conference to Assess the Status of Tigers, Yanjong Thanompichai, director-general of Thailand's Forestry Department, said he hoped

"Saving the Tiger
by Letting Him
Die with Dignity"

Bharat Jhunjhunwala
Baltimore Sun November 29, 1996

The Hindus believe in assisting every being to its highest potential. . . . What . . . is the highest potential of the tiger? The tiger used to rule the jungle. It no longer does. Man rules the jungle now. The tiger used to decide whether man will enter the

---

the meeting would serve to draw attention to the plight of tigers. . . .

The three-day meeting in Bangkok and central Thailand's Khao Yai National Park is a follow-up to the first such conference held in October 1994 in Thailand's Huai Kha Khaeng National Park and another in March 1995 in Hanoi, Vietnam. "The goal of this meeting is to ensure that tigers will continue to exist throughout Asia into the next millennium by fostering cooperation among and action by the tiger range countries," he said. He said participants hoped to accomplish five objectives at the conference, including—To map the extent of each tiger population in the region so that plans can be developed for conserving all the forest ecosystems in which tigers reside.—To develop an ecosystem approach to land management that integrates conservation and sustainable development objectives.—To integrate conservation efforts with an appreciation of human values and needs.—To plan a region-wide campaign to educate the public about tigers and the need to reduce the use of tiger products.—To let the world know about our region's unique biodiversity and our efforts to conserve it.

jungles. Now man decides whether [the] tiger will move out of it.

Today the tiger cannot attain its highest potential of ruling the jungles. To "conserve" it, even in its wild habitat, would amount to denying it its highest potential and reducing it to an item of exhibition. . . . Let us love the tiger by helping him realize his highest potential and administering euthanasia. To force him to live in unnatural conditions, albeit better than those in zoos and safaris, is not compassion for the tiger, but an insult to him. The "dominion of man" must be compassionate by allowing the tiger to become extinct.

That raises the question of conservation of species. Nature has lived with change. The dinosaurs became extinct but nature did not collapse. The Ganges Valley was once full of jungles, now it sustains millions of human beings. The tiger was extirpated in China in the 1970s. The jungles and wildlife of the Americas have been sacrificed to build a powerful economy. Nature wants the tiger to become extinct, but man is working at cross purposes.

---

2   Question differences.

When authors disagree about facts or hold differing opinions, you should also ask *why.*

- Do methods of determining facts differ?
- Which presentation of facts seems more authoritative?
- What logic, what values, underlie differing opinions?
- Why do writers disagree over what policies we should follow? Do their analyses of problems differ?
- Do their assumptions about correct or ethical behaviors differ?

Your awareness of similarities and differences should lead to more specific questions as well. The following box suggests some examples of such questions.

Questioning Similarities and Differences

When you encounter two sources such as the two articles on tiger conservation, it is helpful to formulate questions to pursue later. Here are some examples based on a careful reading of both articles.

Question similarities

Both articles agree that the tiger is endangered or, worse, becoming extinct. The facts of the situation are clear. However, the following are open to question:

- What are the conditions that lead to the threat of extinction?
- How is it that people who agree that a problem exists can disagree so sharply on solutions?
- To what extent does the apparent agreement that tigers are threatened actually rest on a *dis*agreement about the causes of the threat?

Question differences

The mission of the international meeting in Thailand was to save tigers. All participants likely agreed before attending that tigers *should* be saved. Jhunjhunwala, however, disagrees. The disagreement raises the following questions:

- Do protectors want to save tigers for the tigers' sake or for the sake of humans (so humans get the pleasure of watching tigers in zoos)?
- Is it degrading or unfair to tigers to keep them alive only in zoos and natural preserves?

1b   Challenging and being challenged by sources

Beyond searching for similarities and differences, try to maintain a questioning attitude when you read. Some questions you can direct to a source; others, to yourself. In both cases, your goal is to begin exploring the source and the issues it raises.

1   Challenge the author: Ask questions of the source.

WWW
http://www.kcmetro.cc.mo.us/
longview/ctac/reading.htm

How to apply critical thinking skills to reading.

Every reading invites specific questions, but the following basic questions can get you started in your effort to read any text critically:

- What central problem, issue, or subject does the text explore? If a problem, what are the reasons offered for it? What are its effects?
- What is the most important, or the most striking, statement the author makes? Why is it important or striking?
- Who is the author, and what are the author's credentials for writing on this topic? What is the author's stake in writing this? What does the author have to gain?

2   Challenge yourself: Ask questions of yourself.

The questions you ask about what you read can prompt you to investigate your experience, values, and opinions. As part of any critical reading, allow the issues that are important to the text to *challenge* you. Question yourself and respond until you know your views about a topic, using the following:

- What can I learn from this text? Will this knowledge change me?
- What is my background on this topic? How will my experience affect my reading?
- What is the origin of my views on the topic?
- What new interest, or what new question or observation, does this text spark in me?
- If I turned the topic of this selection into a question on which people voted, how would I vote—and why?

See the box below for examples of more specific challenges.

Challenging Yourself and the Source

Fruitful questions and reflections follow from challenging an author—and by letting an author's work challenge you. Jot your questions down; later, one (or more) may help you while writing a paper or conducting research. Here are some examples based on the articles concerning tigers on pages 2–3:

Challenging "Letting the Tiger Die with Dignity"

- How does Jhunjhunwala determine the tiger's "highest potential"? Is his reasoning logical?
- Is it possible for a being's—a tiger's—"highest potential" to change over time?
- Why isn't keeping a tiger alive a worthy goal in and of itself?
- How would letting the species become extinct help the tiger "realize his highest potential"?

continued

Challenging Yourself and the Source, continued

Challenging Yourself

■ Does my satisfaction from going to a zoo come at the expense of the animals there?

■ What is *my* position on saving tigers?

COMPUTER TIPS

Electronic Democracy at Its Best . . . and Worst

Usenet newsgroups represent perhaps the pinnacle of democracy and free speech. The exchanges in this new medium can be uninhibited, unrestrained, and uncensored. But that free flow of information increases the critical thinking challenge for researchers. Everybody from world-renowned experts in a field to ignorant, malicious crackpots has equal access to the medium, and it may be difficult to tell one from the other. Be careful when using a Usenet posting as evidence in your writing. If possible, try to verify the information first in another, more reliable source.

1c | **Setting issues in a broader context**

Whenever possible, identify the issues and questions that are important to a single reading selection and then think large: Assume that every issue, concern, or problem that you read about exists in a larger context—a larger cluster of related issues, concerns, or problems. This larger context will not always be obvious. Often, you will have to work to discover it. Here is a set of techniques for doing so:

WWW

http://www.colostate.edu/Depts/
WritingCenter/references/reading/
toulmin/pagel.htm

A Web site devoted to philosopher Stephen Toulmin's model of critically analyzing texts.

■ Begin by identifying one or more issues that you feel are important to a text.

■ Assume that each issue is an example of something larger. Your job is to speculate on this larger something.

■ Write the name of the issue at the top of a page, or on the computer screen. Below this, write a question: "What is this a part of?" Then write a one-paragraph response.

■ Reread your response, and briefly state the broader context.

- Use this broader context to stimulate more thought on the reading selection and to generate questions about issues of interest.
- Option: Begin an investigation. Find new reading selections about the issues you've defined.

Setting Issues in a Broader Context

Placing the topic you're reading about into a larger context helps you to "think large"—to go beyond the details of a particular case and to see broader patterns. Here is how you might view the selections on pages 2–3 in a range of broader contexts.

What Is "Saving Tigers" a Part of?

- Protecting different species from extinction—conservation
- Maintaining diversity of life on this planet
- Understanding evolution—the place of large mammals and humankind in nature
- Showing how one issue can bring nations together in a cooperative effort
- Illustrating how a complex problem can be approached from different perspectives: political, ecological, philosophical, agricultural
- Showing how apparent agreement (tigers are dying out) can sometimes rest on disagreements about outcomes

1d Forming and supporting opinions

To read critically, you need to know what you think about what you read. Form an opinion and be able to support it. Opinions generally follow from responses to questions such as these:

- Has the author explained things clearly?
- In what ways does this topic confuse me?
- Has the author convinced me of his or her main argument?
- What is my view on this topic?
- Would I recommend this source to others?

Whatever your opinion, be prepared to support it with details based on what you have experienced or read. Later in this chapter you will learn techniques for reading to evaluate a source and techniques for writing an evaluation—a type of writing in which you formally present your opinions and give reasons for holding them. A second type of writing in which you will express opinions is an argument. See Chapter 8, which is devoted entirely to argumentation.

It is not practical or necessary for you to develop a formal response (oral or written) to every source you read. Just the same, as a critical and active thinker, you should be able to offer reasons for believing as you do.

COMPUTER TIPS

Use a Scratchpad for Thinking

When you're writing, or when you're reading online material, it's useful to keep a second file window open for jotting down thoughts, ideas, and questions. If you have a big enough computer screen, you can even keep both windows visible at the same time and just switch between them. Some computers have small notepad utilities that simplify this process. Use this second file to record questions you may have, tangential material you think of, or bibliographic citations and URLs you need to remember. Be sure to save this file each time you enter something, if it doesn't have an auto-save feature. If your computer doesn't keep multiple windows open, embed your comments, questions, and off-topic musings in the text, surrounded by some kind of marker (like *** or —-). Later, when you need them or want to delete them, a simple search for the marker will locate each entry.

Components of a Close, Critical Reading

Thinking critically about what you read does not necessarily lead to formal statements on your part about the materials you encounter. However, when teachers and, later, employers ask you to read and use source materials as a basis for writing, you *will* need to formalize and systematize your critical thinking skills. The following discussion suggests ways to read purposefully—to understand, evaluate, and synthesize as appropriate to your task. You will learn, as well, the forms of writing associated with close reading—summary, evaluation, and synthesis.

1e   Reading to understand / Writing a summary

1   Reading to understand

You can use a source only when you understand it. When you know that you must base later writing on a source you are reading, you should consciously adopt a system for reading to understand. There are many systems you can follow, but each commonly entails reading in three stages:

PREVIEW   Skim the text, reading quickly both to identify the author's purpose and to recall what you know about the topic.

READ   Read with pen in hand, making notes (on separate sheets or on photocopied pages) about the content and the structure of the text. Stop periodically to monitor your progress.

REVIEW   Skim the text a second time to consolidate your notes: jot down questions and highlight especially important passages.

CRITICAL DECISIONS

Understanding Sources

To guide your notetaking during the process of reading a text for understanding, keep in mind the following goals:

- ■ *Identify the author's purpose.* This will likely be to inform or argue.
- ■ *Identify the author's intended audience.* The text will be written with particular readers in mind. Determine if you are the intended audience.
- ■ *Locate the author's main point.* Every competently written text has a main point that you should be able to express in your own words.
- ■ *Understand the structure of the text.* If the author is arguing, locate the main point and supporting points; if the author is explaining, locate the main point and identify the stages into which the presentation has been divided.
- ■ *Identify as carefully as possible what you do not understand.*

2   Writing a summary

Fundamental to working with sources in any academic setting is the **summary,** a brief, neutral restatement of a text. Before you can comment on sources or otherwise put them to use, you must first understand and be able to put into your own words what the authors are trying to communicate.

WWW

http://owl.english.purdue.edu/Files/31.html

Defines and illustrates quoting, paraphrasing, and summarizing.

Summary begins with an application of the skills you develop in reading to understand. First, make notes as you preview, read, and review a text. Then, you can use the following process to prepare for and write a summary:

1. Determine the purpose of the source—for instance, to inform, explain, argue, justify, defend, compare, contrast, or illustrate.

2. Summarize the thesis. Based on the notes you have made and the phrases or sentences you have highlighted while reading, restate

the author's main point in your own words. In this statement, refer to the author by name; indicate the author's purpose (e.g., to argue or inform); and refer to the title.

3. Summarize the body of the text.
   - STRATEGY 1: Write a one- or two-sentence summary of every paragraph. Summarize points important to supporting the author's thesis. Omit minor points and omit illustrations. Avoid translating phrase for phrase from sentences in the text.
   - STRATEGY 2: Identify sections (groupings of related paragraphs) and write a two- or three-sentence summary of each section.
4. Study your paragraph or section summaries. Determine the ways in which the paragraphs or sections work together to support the thesis.
5. Write the summary. Join your paragraph or section summaries with your summary of the thesis, emphasizing the relationship between the parts of the text and the thesis.
6. Revise for clarity and for style. Quote sparingly. Provide transitions where needed.

Example Summary

Here is a summary of the 236-word *UPI* selection on pages 2–3, "Tiger Conservation Meeting in Thailand." Notice that the summary is neutral as well as brief.

In January of 1996, Thailand hosted the Second International Conference to Assess the Status of Tigers. The goal of the conference was to coordinate efforts among "tiger range countries" so that tigers continue to survive in their natural habitats across Asia. Participants hoped to balance efforts to conserve the tiger's range with strategies for meeting the economic needs of people who would otherwise encroach on that range.

1f Reading to evaluate / Writing an evaluation

1 Reading to evaluate

Having understood a text, you are in a position to investigate its strengths and weaknesses—that is, to evaluate it. You will not find every text to be of equal value: equally accurate, useful, convincing, or well written. As a critical reader, you should determine the extent to which an author has succeeded or failed in presenting material; and you should be able to explain why you and the author agree or disagree.

When you are reading to evaluate, be alert to an author's use of *facts, opinions,* and *definitions,* and his or her *assumed views of the world.* You will also want to know if an author's purpose is primarily to inform or to argue, so that you can pose specific questions accordingly.

Distinguish facts from opinions.

WWW

http://www.gcse.com/teach/fo.htm

Useful tutorial on distinguishing fact from opinion.

Before you can evaluate a statement, you should know whether it is being presented to you as a fact or an opinion. A **fact** is any statement that can be verified.

New York lies at a more southerly latitude than Paris.

The construction of the Suez Canal was completed in 1869.

These statements, if challenged, can be established as true or false through research. As a reader evaluating a selection, you might question the accuracy of a fact or how the fact was shown to be true. An argument about facts is quickly settled by reference to agreed-upon sources.

An **opinion** is a statement of interpretation and judgment. Opinions are not true or false in the way that statements of fact will be. Opinions are judgments that are either well supported or not.

Identify the strongly stated opinions in what you read, and then write a **comment note:** In the margin, jot down a brief note summarizing your response to the opinion. Agree or disagree. Later, your note will help you crystallize your reactions to the selection.

CRITICAL DECISIONS

Distinguishing Facts from Opinions

In the following passage, what is fact? What is opinion?

> Professional athletes in America are among the most highly paid workers in the world, earning millions of dollars a year. That their jobs involve a high level of physical performance should not cloud the fact that they are entertainers paid to keep fans and sportswriters in their seats, marveling at displays of physical prowess.

The writer begins with a fact. Given the evidence, everyone could agree that professional athletes in America are among the highest paid workers in the world. Notice how the writer quickly moves to a second "fact": that athletes "are entertainers paid to keep fans and sportswriters in their seats." As a critical reader, determine for yourself (to the extent possible) what is and what is not factual. Ask: *Can the statement in question be established as true or false through research?*

continued

Distinguishing Facts from Opinions, continued

The statement classifying (or defining) athletes as entertainers is an opinion. Whereas there is solid evidence that athletes are highly paid, what they are labeled is a matter of how people define and attach meaning to terms. Calling professionals in the NBA or NFL *entertainers* might be a strategy to justify their earning as much as movie stars. Others might argue that, as people who play games with balls, NBA or NFL professionals are athletes who should be paid fairly but not extravagantly.

In a single paragraph, and sometimes within a single sentence, you are likely to find a mingling of facts and opinions. Read critically and make distinctions.

Distinguish your assumptions from those of an author.

An **assumption** is a fundamental belief that shapes people's views. If your friend says that a painting is "beautiful," she is basing that statement, which is an opinion, on another, more fundamental opinion—an assumed view of beauty. Whether or not your friend directly states what qualities make a painting beautiful, she is *assuming* these qualities and is basing her judgment on them. If the basis of her judgment is that the painting is "lifelike," this is an assumption. So, too, would be your assumption that a "good" painting must be abstract. The opinions that people have (if they are not direct expressions of assumptions themselves) can be better understood by identifying their underlying assumptions.

Evaluating Assumptions

Differences over a single assumption can explain why people agree or disagree. The example selections on tigers (pages 2–3) underscore the importance of identifying underlying assumptions as you read.

Jhunjhunwala's assumption: A being's (a tiger's) highest potential *does not* change. Accepting this assumption, you could justify the killing of tigers as an act of "love": Since it is now impossible for the tiger to achieve its highest potential (as lord of the jungle), we should kill the tiger to preserve its dignity.

A different assumption: A being's (a tiger's) highest potential *can* change. Accepting this opposite assumption, you would help tigers to achieve their highest potential at a given moment in time. In the late twentieth century, helping tigers would mean preserving them in a wild habitat—which is exactly what the participants at the Tiger Conservation Meeting were trying to accomplish.

Distinguish your definitions of terms from those of an author.

Consider this statement: *Machines can explore space as well as and, in some cases, better than humans.* What do the words *as well as* and *better than* mean? In evaluating a source, identify the words that are important to the author's presentation. How does the author define these words? How do you? Differences regarding definitions can mark an excellent place to begin your evaluation of a source. Very often, conflicting definitions reveal differing assumptions about the way the world (or at least one small part of it) works.

Evaluating Definitions

Before you can agree or disagree with an author, you must know how he or she defines key terms. Very often, definitions are based on assumptions that can be challenged. This example relates to Bharat Jhunjhunwala's "Saving the Tiger by Letting Him Die with Dignity" on pages 2–3.

Jhunjhunwala writes: "Nature wants the tiger to become extinct." This sentence appears in a paragraph that presents several supposedly parallel cases of extinction: the dinosaurs, jungles in the Ganges Valley, jungles and wildlife in the Americas, and the tiger in China.

Examine the definition: In order to understand Jhunjhunwala, you must understand how he defines the key word "wants." As a critical reader, you might ask: In what way can Nature be said to *want* anything? Jhunjhunwala seems to say that Nature has a purpose, or guiding plan, and that a natural act (even extinction) has a reason for occurring even if we don't understand it.

Challenge the definition: You might believe that Nature does *not* act with a purpose and has no guiding plan. If this is your view, then Nature cannot be said to *want* anything, and humans cannot logically work at "cross purposes" with Nature (as Jhunjhunwala believes). You would likely disagree with Jhunjhunwala, who argues that we should permit tigers to become extinct since this is what Nature *wants*.

Question sources that explain and sources that argue.

Outside of the literature classroom, you will read sources that are written primarily to inform or to argue. As a critical reader engaged in evaluating a source, determine the author's primary purpose and pose questions accordingly.

Sources that explain

When a selection asks you to accept an explanation, a description, or a procedure as accurate, pose—and respond to—these questions:

- For whom has the author intended the explanation, description, or procedure? The general public—nonexperts? Someone involved in the same business or process? An observer, such as an evaluator or a supervisor?

- What does the text define and explain? How successful is the presentation, given its intended audience?

- How trustworthy is the author's information? How current is it? If it is not current, are the points being made still applicable, assuming more recent information could be obtained?

- If the author presents a procedure, what is its purpose or outcome? Who would carry out this procedure? When? For what reasons? Does the author present the stages of the procedure?

Sources that argue

When a selection asks you to accept an argument, pose—and respond to—these questions:

- What conclusion am I being asked to accept?

- What reasons and evidence has the author offered for me to accept this conclusion? Are the reasons logical? Is the evidence fair? Has the author acknowledged and responded to other points of view?

- To what extent is the author appealing to logic? to my emotions? to my respect for authorities?

The box below shows how to examine a claim in an argument.

Evaluating Sources That Argue

As you read a source with strong viewpoints, such as the selection by Jhunjhunwala on pages 2–3, try to outline (mentally, at least) the author's arguments—the large claims and the smaller, supporting ones. Examine each claim to determine the degree to which it is logical and well supported.

Identify (a part of) an author's argument

In his final paragraph, Jhunjhunwala claims that throughout history Nature has acted in ways that have led to extinction. He offers four examples: dinosaurs, the Ganges Valley, tigers in China, and jungles and wildlife in the Americas. You might examine the claim by posing these questions:

---

1. Do all four examples parallel the case of tigers being endangered today?

   [No: human expansion caused the extinction of jungles in the Ganges Valley, tigers in China, and certain wildlife in the Americas, but humans did not cause the extinction of the dinosaurs.]

2. Of the cases that are parallel, is the fact that certain events led to extinctions in the past a reason to accept the assumption that similar events will lead to extinctions today?

   [If you answer *yes*, then you agree that tigers, too, will die out and that this is a part of Nature's cycle of life and death. If you answer *no*, then you might argue that our past mistakes do not constitute an excuse for present mistakes, especially correctable ones. We should avoid repeating our mistakes by saving, not killing, the tiger.]

2   Writing an evaluation

Once you have prepared for writing an evaluation by making notes based on questions you've posed, review your material and try to develop an overall impression of the reading. In writing an evaluation, you will have enough space to review at least two, but probably not more than four or five, aspects of an author's work. Therefore, be selective in the points you choose to evaluate. As with any piece of formal writing, plan your evaluation carefully. If you are going to discuss three points concerning a selection, do so in a particular order, for good reasons.

Students find these steps helpful in preparing evaluations:

1. Introduce the topic and author: one paragraph. One sentence in the introduction should hint at your general impression of the piece.

2. Summarize the author's work: one to three paragraphs. If brief, the summary can be joined to the introduction.

3. Briefly review the key points in the author's work that you will evaluate: one paragraph.

4. Identify key points in the author's presentation; discuss each in detail: three to six paragraphs. If you are evaluating the quality of the author's presentation, state your criteria for evaluation explicitly; if you are agreeing or disagreeing with opinions, try to identify the underlying assumptions (yours and the author's).

5. Conclude with your overall assessment of the author's work.

The order of parts in the written evaluation may not match the actual order of writing. You may be unable to write the third section of the evaluation without first evaluating the author's key points—the next section. The evaluation will take shape over multiple drafts.

At times you may write a paper devoted exclusively to evaluation—as would be the case if you were reviewing a book or an article; at other times you may write an evaluation that forms part of a larger effort, perhaps a research paper. In either case, remember to summarize any point you evaluate and to provide clear, logical reasons in support of your responses

1g Reading to synthesize / Writing a synthesis

1 Reading to synthesize

Once you have understood and evaluated a single source, you are in a position to link that source with others. By establishing links between one author and others (including yourself), you achieve a synthesis: an *integration* of sources. Synthesis is the third, and in some ways the most complex, component of close, critical reading. It requires that you read, understand, and evaluate all of your source materials.

When you are reading to synthesize, you want to be alert to the ways in which various sources "talk to" each other concerning a particular topic. Seek out relationships among sources. Be sure to consider yourself as a valuable source.

Students find the following plan helpful when reading to synthesize:

■ *Read, respond to, and evaluate multiple sources on a topic.* It is very likely that the authors will have different observations to make. Because you are working with the different sources, you are in a unique position to draw relationships among them.

■ *Subdivide the topic into parts and give each a brief title.* Call the topic that the several authors discuss *X*. What are all the parts, or the subdivisions, of *X* that the authors discuss? List the separate parts, giving each a brief title.

■ *Write cross-references for each part.* For each subdivision of the topic, list *specific* page references to whichever sources discuss that part. This is called **cross-referencing.** Once you have cross-referenced each of the topic's parts, you will have created an index to your reading selections.

■ *Summarize each author's information or ideas about each part.* Now that you have generated cross-references that show you which authors discuss which parts of topic *X*, take up one part at a time and reread all the passages you have cross-referenced. Summarize what each author has written on particular parts of the topic.

■ *Forge relationships among reading selections.* Study your notes and try to link sources. Relationships that you might establish include example, definition, comparison, contrast, and cause and effect (see 3c).

2 Writing a synthesis

A **synthesis** is a written discussion in which you gather and present source materials according to a well-defined purpose. In the process of writing a synthesis you answer these questions: (1) Which authors have written on my topic? (2) In what ways can I link the work of these authors to one another and to my own thinking? (3) How can I best use the material I've gathered to create a discussion that supports *my* views? The following assignment calls for synthesis:

SOCIOLOGY   This semester we have read materials on the general topic of marriage: its legal, religious, economic, and social aspects. In a five-page paper, reflect on these materials and discuss the extent to which they have helped to clarify, or confuse, your understanding of this "sacred institution."

The word *synthesis* does not appear in this assignment; nonetheless, the instructor is asking students to gather and discuss sources. Note the importance of the writer here. Given multiple sources, a dozen students working on this sociology assignment would produce a dozen different papers. The *particular* insights of each student would distinguish one paper from the next and make each uniquely valuable. You are the most important source in any synthesis. However much material you gather into a discussion, your voice should predominate.

No synthesis is possible without a critical, comprehensive reading of sources. A synthesis will draw on all of your critical reading and writing skills. It represents some of the most sophisticated and challenging writing you will do in college. The following box lists "danger" signs that show when you have become invisible in your papers.

Do Not Become Invisible in Your Paper

The DANGER signs:

1. Your paragraphs are devoted wholly to the work of the authors you are synthesizing.
2. Virtually every sentence introduces someone else's ideas.
3. The impulse to use the first-person *I* never arises.

Many students find the following guidelines helpful when synthesizing source materials:

- Read sources on the topic; subdivide the topic into parts and infer relationships among parts, cross-referencing sources when possible.
- Clarify relationships among authors by posing questions (e.g., Which authors agree? Which authors disagree? etc.).

- Write a thesis (see 2c) that ensures your voice is heard and that allows you to develop sections of the paper in which you refer to sources.

- Sketch an outline of your paper (see 2c-4), organizing your discussion by *idea*, not by summary. Enter the names of authors into your outline along with notes indicating how these authors will contribute to your discussion.

- Write a draft of your paper and revise, following strategies discussed in Chapters 2 and 3.

Every research paper you write, indeed any effort in which you combine ideas from multiple sources according to your unique insights, involves an act of synthesis. See pages 114–120, a research paper about on-line relationships, for an illustration.

CHAPTER 2

Planning, Writing, and Revising a Draft

There may be as many strategies for planning, writing, and revising a draft as there are writers. Just the same, the act of writing is always a decision-making process. Writers must decide on a topic to write about and on their purpose for writing. They must find effective ways to generate ideas and then choose among those ideas. They must then determine a thesis and an organizational plan. Drafting an essay is, of course, a series of decisions, small and large, while the choices made while revising—what to leave in, what to cut,

WWW
http://dlc.tri-c.cc.oh.us/wb/write/docs/
process.htm

A hyperlinked map of the steps of the writing process, with a discussion of each.

where additions need to be made, as well as matters of style, punctuation, and mechanics—are crucial to the success of any piece of writing.

Moreover, a writer's thoughts take shape through the act of writing and revising. By clarifying, expanding, and refining their ideas, writers are able to produce a finished piece of writing that communicates something significant to readers.

CRITICAL DECISIONS

Discovering a Productive Writing Process

Broadly speaking, the three stages of writing are preparing to write, drafting, and revising, and they generally unfold in that order. Experienced writers, however, often find themselves looping backward and forward through the stages—engaging in further planning when they find themselves stuck while drafting, for example, or revising a section before they've completed a first draft. In fact, no two writers work in exactly the same way; we each must decide what works best for us.

What follows are some guidelines for working through the process of preparing to write, drafting, and revising. You are encouraged to experiment as thoroughly as possible with this material as you work on several papers. By doing so, you should be able to discover a writing process that allows you to work both productively and successfully.

2a Discovering your topic, purpose, and audience

1 Understanding your topic

In both college and business, you can expect to be assigned topics for writing and to define topics for yourself. In either case, you will write most efficiently, and with greatest impact, when you write about what you know (or what you can learn in a reasonably brief time). Students find the following sequence helpful as they investigate and refine their topics:

Read: If you do not know a topic well, read sources and gather information: letters, articles, lecture notes—whatever is pertinent. Read until you understand all the aspects of your topic that you will be writing about.

Interview: Locate people who are knowledgeable about your topic and interview them. Read sufficiently before the interview so that you do not pose questions that can be answered with basic research. Develop pointed questions that yield information and ideas unique to this source.

Reflect: Investigate your personal commitment to the topic. What experiences have you had that influence your thinking? How has your point of view been shaped by these experiences? Issues on which you might write may require that you take a stand. Know your position.

Restrict and define your topic.

Know how long your document is expected to be, and limit your writing accordingly. Avoid the frustration of choosing a broad topic (for example, the controversy over affirmative action) for a brief paper or report—a mistake that will guarantee a superficial product. Instead, choose a sharply focused topic that you can manage in a short document.

CRITICAL DECISIONS

Restricting Your Topic

Students find the following guidelines helpful as they decide how best to limit their topics:

- *Divide the topic into constituent parts.* Ask yourself: What are the component parts of this topic? What parts (or subtopics) do I know the most about? Can I link subtopics together in meaningful ways? In which subtopic am I most interested?

- *Ask a journalist's questions.* To restrict a topic and focus on a subtopic that interests you, pose questions, as appropriate: *who, what, where, when, why, how?* Often, a response to one or more of these questions can become the focus of a paper.

---

2   Identifying your purpose

Think of an object, an idea, an emotion, a relationship, or an institution. Think of anything at all and you can probably explain it, argue about it, or reflect on its significance. In college-level work, these efforts are typically expressed in papers that inform or persuade.

Informative writing

When writing to *inform,* your job is to present a topic and to explain, define, or describe it so that the reader understands its component parts, its method of operation, its uses, and so on. The following assignments call for informative writing:

LITERATURE   Cite three examples of metaphor in *Great Expectations* and explain how each works.

CHEMISTRY   Explain the chemical process by which water, when boiled, becomes steam.

PSYCHOLOGY   What is "cognitive dissonance" and in what ways does it contribute to the development of personality?

Persuasive writing

When you write to *persuade,* your job is to change a reader's views about a topic. As with informative writing, the persuasive writer must carefully consider the reader's prior knowledge in order to provide the background information necessary for understanding. (See Chapter 8, which is devoted entirely to argumentation.) The following assignments call for persuasive writing.

ASTRONOMY | Given limited government money available for the construction and updating of astronomical observatories, which of the projects discussed this semester deserve continued funding? Argue for your choices based on the types of discoveries you expect the various projects to make within the next five years.

SOCIOLOGY | You have read two theories on emotions: the Cannon-Bard theory and the James-Lange theory. Which seems the more convincing to you? Why?

MARKETING | Select three ads that describe similar products. Which ad is most effective? Why?

Purposes for writing may overlap: in a single essay, you may inform and persuade a reader. But if an essay is to succeed, you should have a *primary* purpose for writing. Otherwise, you risk creating a document that tries to do all things but does none well.

3   Defining your audience

What you write should be determined by your readers. For readers who understand your topic, you can assume a common base of knowledge and terminology and move directly into your effort to inform or persuade. With readers who are unfamiliar with your topic, you will need to use nonspecialized language and provide considerable background information before you explain or persuade. Questions that you ask about an audience *before you write a first draft* can help you make important decisions concerning your paper's content and use of language.

CRITICAL DECISIONS

Defining Your Audience

Pose these general questions, regardless of your purpose:

- Who is the reader? What is the reader's age, sex, religious background, educational background, and ethnic heritage?
- What is my relationship with the reader?

continued

Defining Your Audience, continued

- How will the reader determine my presentation—choice of words, level of complexity, and choice of examples?
- Why will the reader be interested in my paper? How can I best spark the reader's interest?

If you are writing to inform, pose these questions as well:

- What does the reader know about the topic's history?
- How well does the reader understand the topic's technical details?
- What does the reader need to know? want to know?
- What level of language and content will I use in discussing the topic, given the reader's understanding?

If you are writing to persuade, pose both sets of questions above as well as the following:

- What are the reader's views on the topic? Given what I know about the reader, is the reader likely to agree with my view on the topic? to disagree? to be neutral?
- What factors are likely to affect the reader's beliefs about the topic? What special circumstances (work, religious conviction, political views, etc.) should I be aware of that will affect the reader's views?
- How can I argue to gain the reader's support, given her present interest, understanding, and beliefs?

2b Generating ideas and information

Even when you are clear about your topic, purpose, and audience, it is not always easy to generate ideas for a paper. In most academic writing, a combination of efforts is usually needed. Below are six proven strategies for generating ideas and information. Combine or modify them to develop a strategy that works best for you.

WWW

http://www.gsu.edu/~wwweng/rh/invention.htm

In classical rhetoric, the term for generating ideas and information was "invention."

1 Reading

Even if you do not plan to depend heavily on sources in a paper, reading about your topic will help you to generate ideas. Source materials may present compelling facts or strongly worded opinions with which to agree or disagree. Above all, use the suggestions in Chapter 1 and be alert to your responses. Jot them down; they may later become important to your paper.

- If you will be referring to any sources, as in a research report, realize that you will need to cite and document those sources (see Chapter 7).

2 Brainstorming/listing

The object of **brainstorming** is to generate as many ideas as possible in a short time. When you brainstorm, write quickly; once you are finished, you can return to your work with a critical eye. Place your topic at the top of a page, and then list any related phrase or word that comes to mind. Set a time limit of five or ten minutes, and list as many items as you can. All items are legitimate for your list, since even bad ideas can spark good ones.

After you have generated your list, group related items and set aside those that do not fit into a grouping. Groupings with the greatest number of items indicate areas that should prove fertile in developing your paper. Save the results of your brainstorming session for your next step in the planning process: selecting, organizing, and expanding information.

Here's an illustration of brainstorming on the topic of nonsmokers' attitudes toward smokers.

```
                    Nonsmokers on Smokers

smoking makes me sick--can't eat food near smokers
billboards show healthy smokers--irresponsible!
smokers are somehow "bad" or dangerous people--crazy!
Uncle Enrique--died early; widow and three kids
the party, meeting Daniel's fiancee; she changed my thinking
Henry!! 6 yrs old and I'm just like him, running away from
smokers
why the distrust?
smoking policies on campus
why do people smoke?
number of smokers I know
get cancers stats + when people start to smoke
start at young age, to fit in
billboards, tv, movies--everybody's healthy
healthy people are somehow good people--I think the society
believes it
I'm not superior but thought I was
I've changed
```

The list can be grouped as follows. The question mark denotes the "left over" category, which includes items the writer did not know how to group.

<pre>
              Nonsmokers on Smokers

My reactions
physical: smoking makes me sick--can't eat food near smokers
smokers are somehow "bad" or dangerous people--crazy!
Uncle Enrique--died early; widow and three kids
Henry!! 6 yrs old and I'm just like him, running away from
smokers
why the distrust?

Smokers in society
billboards show healthy smokers--irresponsible!
why do people smoke?
billboards, tv, movies--everybody's healthy
healthy people are somehow good people--I think the society
believes it
start at young age, to fit in

My changing attitudes
the party, meeting Daniel's fiancee; she changed my thinking
I'm not superior but thought I was
I've changed

?
get cancers stats + when people start to smoke
smoking policies on campus
number of smokers I know
</pre>

3 Freewriting

Freewriting is a technique to try when you are asked to write but have no topic. Choose a broad area of interest and then start writing for some predetermined amount of time—say, five or ten minutes. As you write, do not stop to puzzle over word choice or punctuation. Freely change thoughts from one sentence to the next, if this is where your thinking takes you. Once you have reached your time limit, read over what you have done. Circle ideas that could become paper topics. To generate ideas about one of these specific topics, you may then try another freewrite, following the same general procedure. Many writers also find that freewriting helps them overcome writer's block later in the drafting process. If you get stuck, try choosing one idea and repeating the freewriting process.

COMPUTER TIPS

Writing in the Dark

If you're a fairly speedy typist, one interesting use of your computer is to turn off the monitor and just type. You can either freewrite or compose a rough draft in this manner. It removes the fear of making mistakes, the urge to reread at inappropriate times, and the hypnotic effect of your words on the screen. Just type, then turn on the monitor to see what you have. You have no idea how liberating it can be, especially if you're stuck with writer's block.

4   The journalist's questions

You have read or heard of the journalist's questions: *who, what, when, where, why,* and *how.* In answering these questions, you can define, compare, contrast, or investigate cause and effect. The assumption is that by thinking about the parts of a topic you will have more to write about than if you focus on a topic as a whole. The journalist's questions can help you to restrict and define a topic, giving you the option to concentrate, say, on any three parts of the whole: perhaps the *who, what,* and *why* of the topic.

5   Mapping

If you enjoy thinking visually, try **mapping** your ideas. Begin by writing your topic as briefly as possible. Circle the topic and draw three, four, or five short spokes from the circle. At the end of each spoke, place one of the journalist's questions, making a major branch off the spoke for every answer. Now, working with each answer individually, pose one of the six journalist's questions. After you have completed the exercise, you will have a page that places ideas in relation to one another. Notice how the "map" on page 26 distinguishes between major points and supporting information.

6   The "many parts" strategy[1]

Another method for generating ideas about a topic is to list its parts. Number the items on your list. Then ask: "What are the uses of Number 1?

---

[1] This strategy is adapted from John C. Bean and John D. Ramage, *Form and Surprise in Composition: Writing and Thinking Across the Curriculum* (New York: Macmillan, 1986) 170–71.

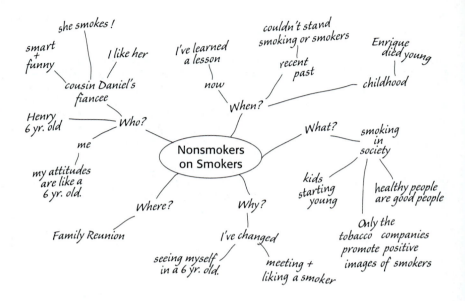

she smokes!

smart + funny

I like her

cousin Daniel's fiancee

Henry 6 yr. old

me

my attitudes are like a 6 yr. old.

Who?

Where?

Family Reunion

I've learned a lesson

now

When?

couldn't stand smoking or smokers

recent past

Enrique died young

childhood

What?

smoking in society

kids starting young

healthy people are good people

Why?

I've changed

seeing myself in a 6 yr. old.

meeting + liking a smoker

Only the tobacco companies promote positive images of smokers

Nonsmokers on Smokers

Number 2? Number 3?" and so on. If *uses of* does not seem to work for the parts in question, try *consequences of:* "What are the consequences of Number 1?" The *many parts* strategy lets you be far more specific and imaginative in thinking about the topic as a whole than you might be ordinarily. Once you have responded to your questions about the uses or consequences of some part, you might pursue the one or two most promising responses.

2c   Writing a thesis and devising a sketch

A **thesis** is a general statement you make about your topic, usually in the form of a single sentence, that summarizes the controlling idea of your paper. You cannot produce a fully accurate **final thesis** until you have written a complete draft. When sitting down to a first draft, you will at best have a **working thesis:** a statement that, based on everything you know about your topic, should prove to be a reasonably accurate summary of what you will write.

www

http://www.indiana.edu/~wts/wts/thesis.html

An extended look at the process of composing and revising a thesis statement.

Like any sentence, a thesis consists of a subject and a predicate—that is, a verb and its associated words. The *subject* of a thesis statement identifies the *subject* of your paper. The *predicate* represents the claim or assertion you will make about that subject.

Realize that your ideas for a paper develop and change as your paper develops. Use your working thesis to get started, but recognize that it *will* change.

1 Focusing on the subject of your thesis

As much as possible, you want the subject of your thesis statement to name something that is relatively specific and well defined; you want to discuss your subject thoroughly within the allotted number of pages. How should you focus your subject? One useful strategy is to pose a variation of the journalist's questions: *who, what, when, where,* and *which aspects?*

Subject (too broad): wilderness
Limiting questions: which aspects?
Focused subject: wilderness camping

2 Basing your thesis on a relationship you want to clarify

Once you have focused your subject, make an assertion about it; that is, complete the predicate part of your thesis. In examining the notes you have generated, ask yourself: What new statement can I make that helps to explain this material (if I am writing an informative paper) or to present my reactions to this material (if I am writing a persuasive paper)? Think of a relationship that ties all—or part—of your material together.

3 The thesis and your ambitions for a paper

Whether you intend to inform or persuade, the relationship that you assert in your thesis can be more or less ambitious. When the assertion is ambitious, your thesis and the paper that you build from it will be, too. What determines the ambition of a thesis is the complexity of the relationship you establish between the predicate part of the sentence and the subject. In the example theses that follow, the predicates are underlined.

LEAST AMBITIOUS THESIS

(1) Wilderness camping <u>poses many challenges</u>.
   – Challenge #1
   – Challenge #2, etc.
(2) Women <u>are not entering the field of computers in large numbers</u>.
   – Society tells them that computers are the domain of men.
   – Men are discriminating against women.

Each thesis requires little more than a summary of the topic's component elements. The writers make no attempt to forge relationships among these elements.

MODERATELY AMBITIOUS THESIS

(1) Like holding a mirror to your personality, wilderness camping <u>shows you to yourself—for better and worse</u>.
   - Wilderness camping described
   - The camper in the wilderness, described
   - Ways in which the wilderness elicits personal response, positive and negative

(2) Computers <u>have become the domain of men, who have developed a language about computers that excludes women</u>.
   - Society has long defined computing as an activity for men only.
   - Some men have patterned their lives and language around computers.
   - The development of computing as a male activity has caused women to avoid the field of computing.

Each thesis forges a relationship between two previously unrelated elements: between wilderness camping and self-reflection and between the domains of men and the language of computers. The writers will be reasoning with the facts, not merely presenting them in summary form. They will be making connections.

MOST AMBITIOUS THESIS

(1) Wilderness camping <u>teaches that we must preserve what is brutal in Nature, even at the expense of public safety</u>.
   - Rigors of wilderness camping
   - Potential danger to public
   - Paradox: dangers notwithstanding, wilderness must be maintained

(2) Since <u>women</u> are as capable as men in technology-related fields, they <u>need to participate in discussing computer technology on the same level as men do to succeed in the field</u>.
   - There are some significant differences in attitude between men and women about computers.
   - Men have often related to each other through talking about computers, while women have not.
   - In dealing with men who now dominate the computer field, women should learn the men's subtleties of language about technology.
   - Paradox: If women are as capable as men, why can't they use whatever language suits them?

Each thesis broadens the scope of the paper and creates interest through paradoxical opposites. Each thesis promises a paper that will be argumentative. In addition to making connections where none existed previously, each thesis shows a writer willing to take intellectual risks: That is, the writer is willing to expand the scope of the paper, widening its context in order to take up a broader, more complex, and (if executed well) more important discussion. A fully ambitious thesis will create a paradox, a tension among its parts, by setting opposites against each other.[2] In a thesis with tension, you often find the conjunctions *although* and *even if*. The writer's job is to navigate between paradoxical opposites. The reader, sensing tension, wants to know what happens and why.

What sort of paper are you writing?

As you create a working thesis, consider whether you are writing an ambitious, moderately ambitious, or an unambitious thesis. Sometimes you will understand the ambition of your paper before you set out to write it; at other times you will not have a clear sense of how "large" a paper you are writing until you get midway or most of the way through a draft and discover or challenge your ideas. Attempt to understand what sort of paper you are writing as you sit down to *revise* your first draft. Reread the draft and then determine how ambitious your final draft should be. You will write your final thesis and shape your final paper accordingly.

Generating a Working Thesis

1. Focus and restrict your subject so that you will be able to write specifically on it in the number of pages allotted.
2. Assemble the notes—arranged in categories—that you have generated for your paper.
3. Forge a relationship that clarifies the material you have assembled.
4. Devise a sentence—a working thesis—that links the relationship you have forged with your focused subject.
5. Determine how ambitious you will be with your thesis—and your paper.
6. Plan to let your thesis evolve as you develop and challenge your thoughts on your topic.

---

[2] The term *tension*, as it relates to the thesis statement, is borrowed from John C. Beam and John D. Ramage, *Form and Surprise in Composition: Writing and Thinking Across the Curriculum* (New York: Macmillan, 1986) 168-69.

CRITICAL DECISIONS

Quizzing or Making Comments about Your Thesis

Pose these and related questions and make these comments about your thesis in an effort to identify key sections of your paper. Practice this "quizzing" strategy with a draft in order to create a rough outline from which to work (see below). Practice the quizzing strategy after you have written a draft to check for unity and coherence (see pages 34–39).

Questions

how does/will it happen?	what has prevented/will prevent it
how to describe?	from happening?
what are some examples?	who is involved?
what are the reasons for?	what are the key features?
what is my view?	what are the reasons against?
compared to what?	how often?
what is the cause?	is it possible to classify types or parts?
are there any stories to tell?	what is the effect of this?
how?	which ones?
when?	

Comments

define	review the reasoning
review the facts	explain the contrast or paradox

---

4 Devising a sketch of your paper, or developing a formal outline

Look to your working thesis for clues about the ideas you will need to develop in your essay. For an academic paper to succeed, you must develop all directly stated or implied ideas in the thesis. To do so, try this strategy. Write the working thesis at the top of a page and circle its significant words. Then ask questions of, or make comments about, each circled element. (The Critical Decisions box above provides examples of questions you can ask.) If you are thorough in quizzing your thesis, you will identify most of its significant parts. (You may not discover some parts until you write a first draft.) Having identified these significant parts, briefly sketch the paper you intend to write.

Option: Sketch your paper.

Many writers feel that a rough sketch is sufficient for beginning the first draft of a paper. Here is a sketch that follows from a thesis that has been quizzed:

define "students' behalf" from students' and administration's point of view

THESIS   *review this reasoning*

By instituting a curfew and acting on what it believed was the students' be-half, the administration (undermined) the (moral and educational principles) it wanted to uphold.   *how?*   *define both*

SKETCH OF THE PAPER

– Review the reasoning: in setting a curfew, the administration said it was acting in the best interest of students
– Define "students' behalf" from student and administrative perspectives
– Define moral issues and educational principles at issue
– Explain the paradox: in mandating morality through a curfew, the administration denied students a chance to grapple with moral issues and reach mature decisions on their own. The administration undermined its own educational aims.

Option: Outline your paper.

Some writers prefer to work with an outline that delineates major and minor points. *Formal outlines* have several levels. The most common type employs a combination of Roman and Arabic numerals and letters.

I. Major topic
   A. Subtopic
      1. Minor subtopic
         a. sub-subtopic (or illustration)
            (a) illustration, example, explanation
            (b) illustration, example, explanation
         b. sub-subtopic (or illustration)
      2. Minor subtopic
   B. Subtopic
II. Major topic

Here is the second section of the formal outline for the student essay on pages 41–43.

Thesis statement: Smokers are not bad, or flawed, people because they smoke; if anyone is flawed, it is arrogant nonsmokers (like me) who think of themselves as superior.

   II. For years, I've been arrogant toward smokers.

      A. I have always disliked smoking.

      B. Uncle Enrique smoked cigarettes.

         1. He never went anywhere without his pack of cigarettes.

         2. He died young, leaving a widow and three children.

         3. My resentment of smokers can be traced to Enrique.

      C. I've equated good health with being a responsible person.

The parts of an outline are arranged in a logical order: Each major topic and each subtopic are divided into at least two constituent parts and each part is discussed separately.

Useful as an outline can be, you will still need to discover the important elements of your paper during the process of writing and, necessarily, your outline or sketch will change as the writing takes shape. Nonetheless, beginning with a plan is essential. See the box on pages 165–166 for two time-tested essay structures that you can adapt, as needed.

2d Writing a draft

The box below summarizes strategies for creating a draft of your paper.

Strategies for Drafting

Working yourself through the draft

1. Write *one* section of the paper at a time: Write a general statement that supports some part of your thesis, then provide details about the supporting statement. Once you have finished a section, take a break. Then return to write another section, working incrementally in this fashion until you have completed the draft.

   Alternately, write one section of the paper and take a break. Then reread and revise that one section before moving to the next. Continue to work in this fashion, one section at a time, until you complete the draft.

---

2. Accept *two* drafts, minimum, as the standard for writing any formal paper. In this way, you give yourself permission to write a first draft that is not perfect.

3. If you have prepared adequately for writing, then trust that you will discover what to write *as* you write.

4. Save substantial revisions concerning grammar, punctuation, usage, and spelling for later. In your first draft(s), focus on content.

The object of a first draft is to get ideas down on paper, to explore them, and to establish the shape of your paper. The object is *not* to produce anything that is readable to anyone other than yourself. Finished, readable documents come through revision.

1   Writing one section of your draft at a sitting

Unless you are writing an introduction, conclusion, or transition, every paragraph that you write will be situated in a grouping of paragraphs, or a section, that makes up part of the larger document. Think of your draft as a series of connected sections and set out to write at least one section at a sitting. Here is a strategy for doing so:

1. **Prepare to write.** Identify purpose and define audience; generate and organize ideas and information; and devise a working thesis.

2. **Identify sections of the paper.** Ask of your thesis: What parts must I develop in order to deliver on the promise of this statement? Your answer of perhaps three or four points will identify the sections you need to write to complete that statement.

3. **Plan to write one section of your paper at a sitting.** If a section is long, divide it into manageable parts and write one part at a sitting.

4. **Write individual paragraphs.** Each paragraph will be related to others in the section. As you begin a second paragraph, clearly relate it to the first; relate the third paragraph to the second, and so on until you finish writing the section. Then take a break.

5. **Write other sections, one at a time.** Continue writing, building one section incrementally on the next, until you complete your first draft.

2   Identifying and resolving problems in mid-draft

At some point in the writing process you may find yourself unable to steam ahead, one section after the next. You will encounter obstacles, which you can recognize as follows: You are aware that your work in one section of the paper is not as good as it is elsewhere, or you make several attempts at writing a section and find that you simply cannot do it. When you are feeling especially frustrated, stop. Step back from your work and decide how you will get past this obstacle. Ask: Why am I having trouble? Here are several possibilities—and suggested solutions:

■ You do not have enough information to write. You have not gathered enough information or, if you have, you may not thoroughly understand it.

  – *Solution: Stop writing and reread the materials you've gathered. Identify points you do not understand and speak with an authority (perhaps via a phone or e-mail interview) who can help you clarify each point. Identify gaps and return to the library for new information. Then return to writing.*

■ You do not understand the point you planned to make or its relation to the rest of your paper.

  – *Solution: Stop writing and begin a new freewriting session, with either of the following questions posted at the top of the page: What am I trying to say? What don't I understand? Let your response help clarify the obstacle you're facing. Circle a few useful sentences and return to your paper (or to the library if you need more information).*

■ The point you planned to make no longer seems relevant or correct, given what you have discovered about your subject while writing.

  – *Solution: If you lose confidence in your main point, consider the causes. Reread your draft and review research materials (if you are working from sources). Revise your position if need be.*

■ You recognize a gap in the structure of your paper, and you suddenly see the need to expand an existing section or to write an entirely new section.

  – *Solution: Pause to re-outline your paper. Then write the new section(s) or expand existing ones, as needed.*

■ The material in the section seems inappropriate for your audience.

  – *Solution: Conduct a new audience analysis (see 2a-3). Delete the section or rewrite it, altering the content, vocabulary, and style to fit the needs of your audience.*

■ You have said everything you need to in a page, but the assignment calls for six to ten pages.

  – *Solution: As you read, ask questions. Can you clarify or provide reasons for every statement (see a list of possible questions on page 30)? If you do not identify any sections that need additional writing, then re-examine your thesis. You will likely need to expand its scope or make a more ambitious claim.*

■ At the moment, you do not have the attention span to write.

  – *Solution: Stop writing. Begin again when you are rested and expect no distractions. Then write one section of your paper—perhaps five or six paragraphs. Take another break and then continue writing, one section at a time, until you've completed the draft.*

Each of these obstacles can frustrate your attempts at writing, and only you can know what is for you a normal or abnormal level of frustration. Frustration usually occurs for a good reason, so you should trust the reaction and then step away to name your problem and find a solution.

2e Revising a draft

Like a first draft, a revision is in its own way an act of creation. In a first draft you work to give a document potential: The writing may be incomplete, hurried, or inexact, but you are working toward an important, controlling idea. In your second and subsequent drafts, you work to make an earlier draft's potential *real:* You revise, and through revision—by adding, altering, or deleting sentences and paragraphs—you clarify your main point for yourself and, on the strength of that, for your reader. Think of revision as occurring in three stages—early, later, and final:

WWW

http//www.powa.org/revifrms.htm

Detailed view of revision from the Paradigm Online Writing Assistant.

Early revision: Reread your first draft and rediscover your main idea.

Later revision: Make all significant parts of your document work together in support of your main idea.

Final revision (editing): Correct errors at the sentence level.

COMPUTER TIPS

Don't Delete It—You May Want to Recycle It

Word processors have made the concept of discrete drafts obsolete. When handwriting or typewriting, it's always clear when a draft is finished and another one begins. Composing, revising, and editing on a word processor, however, is usually one long, seamless process. It is wise to save a version of your paper in a separate file (using the "Save As" function) from time to time, especially if you're embarking on some major changes. Later in the process, you may decide to restore a sentence or paragraph that you discarded.

1 Early revision: Rediscovering your main idea

Early revision involves adding, altering, or deleting entire paragraphs with the sole purpose of clarifying your main idea. First, ask: What is the main idea of this first draft?

- Underline one sentence in your draft in answer to this question; if you cannot find such a sentence, write one.
- Choose a title for your second draft. The title will help you to clarify your main idea.

Clarifying your main idea

Reread your first draft with care, looking for some sentence other than your working thesis that more accurately describes what you have written. Often, such a "competing" thesis appears near the end of the draft, the place where you force yourself to summarize. If you can find no competing thesis and are sure that your original working thesis does not fit the paper you have written, modify the existing working thesis or write a new one. Be prepared to quiz the new thesis as you did earlier. (See the box on page 30.)

The box on page 37 shows an example from one of Theresa Lopez's early revisions.

Reconsidering purpose and audience

Purpose

Reconsider your earliest reasons for writing. With your purpose firmly in mind, evaluate your first draft to determine the extent to which you have met that purpose. Alter your revision plans, if necessary, to satisfy your reason for writing.

- Identify the key verb in the assignment and define that verb with reference to your topic.
- If you have trouble understanding the purpose, bring your draft to a conference with your instructor and explain the direction you've taken.
- Once you identify the parts of a paper that will achieve a stated purpose, incorporate those parts into your plans for a revised draft.

Audience

Revisit your initial audience analysis. Take whatever conclusions you reached and use them as a tool for evaluating your first draft. You may find it useful to pose these questions:

- How will this subject appeal to my readers?
- Is the level of difficulty with which I have treated this subject appropriate for my readers? Are my choices of language and tone also appropriate?
- Are my examples interesting and of an appropriate complexity for my readers?

Make changes to your revision plans according to your analysis.

Early Revision

In reviewing the first draft of her essay, "Defending Smokers," Theresa Lopez could not locate and underline a single sentence that answered the question: "What is the main idea of this draft?" So her first task in early revision was to make certain she communicated a clear thesis statement to the reader. Here you'll find the original draft of her opening paragraph and, immediately following, a revision with the thesis statement underlined. Note that she decided to describe the incident in the first paragraph and then analyze it in the second.

FIRST DRAFT: ~~I'm so personally anti-smoking that I surprised myself recently when my six-year-old nephew ran away from my cousin's fiancee at a family gathering.~~ Henry ran to my sister, who feels about smoking the way I do, and pointed as if the woman in question were a criminal. In the child's eyes, she was; and I'm embarrassed to admit that I felt much the same way, until I introduced myself to the woman. I had an obligation to do so, since she's going to be a member of my family. What I discovered is that, aside from her smoking, she's bright (a college graduate) and very friendly.

Create more of a background

What else did I discover? Put the thesis here

SECOND DRAFT: Every year my extended family, on my father's side, gathers for a party. It's a two-day affair at which cousins from distant parts of the country show off their newborns and introduce prospective husbands and wives. At the most recent gathering last summer, Cousin Daniel walked in with his fiancee, who happened to be smoking. To our amazement, my six-year-old nephew, Henry, ran into his mother's arms, pointing at the cigarette in the woman's hand and glaring at her as if she were a criminal.

In my nephew's eyes, she was a criminal; and I'm embarrassed to admit that I felt much the same way until I introduced myself to Suzanne and got to know her. What I discovered was that, her smoking aside, she is bright (a college graduate) and very friendly. My larger discovery was that smokers are not bad, or flawed, people because they smoke; if anyone is flawed, it is arrogant nonsmokers (like me) who think of themselves as superior.

2	Later revision: Bringing your main idea into focus

Your first major revision of a draft will often require that you make fundamental changes in order to present a single idea clearly. Later revisions will not be as dramatic or far-reaching, and will require that you be able to systematically apply certain principles of organization. Two principles of organization important to a later revision are unity and coherence, which are discussed briefly below and then in detail in the next chapter.

Focusing the paper through unity

A paper is unified when the writer discusses only those elements of the subject implied by its thesis. **Unity** is a principle of logic that applies equally to the whole paper, to sections, and to individual paragraphs. In a unified paper, you discuss only those topics that can be anticipated by someone who reads your thesis. In addition, for each section of the essay, a general statement is used to guide you in assembling specific, supporting parts.

ESSAY-LEVEL UNITY	The thesis (the most general statement in the essay) governs your choice of sections in a paper.
SECTION-LEVEL UNITY	Section theses (the second-most general statements in the essay) govern your choice of paragraphs in a section.
PARAGRAPH-LEVEL UNITY	Topic sentences (the third-most general statements in the essay) govern your choice of sentences in a paragraph

See pages 45–47 for specific strategies on achieving unity in your essays. The box on page 39 shows an example from a later revision by Theresa Lopez.

Focusing the paper through coherence

Coherence describes the clarity of the relationship between one unit of meaning and another: between sections of a paper, between paragraphs within sections, and between sentences within paragraphs. Like unity, coherence is a principle of logic that applies equally to the whole paper, to sections, and to individual paragraphs.

ESSAY-LEVEL COHERENCE	Sections (groupings of related paragraphs) follow one another in a sensible order.
SECTION-LEVEL COHERENCE	Individual paragraphs that constitute a section follow one another in a sensible order.
PARAGRAPH-LEVEL COHERENCE	Individual sentences that comprise the paragraph follow one another in a sensible order.

At every level of a paper, you should establish coherence by building logical bridges, or transitions, between thoughts. (See pages 47–50 for a detailed discussion of coherence.)

Later Revision: Maintaining Unity

Theresa Lopez devoted a paragraph of her first draft to discussing smoking policies on campus, a topic she generated during a brainstorming session. Recall that in her early revision, Theresa added an explicit thesis statement to her draft. When she "quizzed" this thesis (see page 30) and generated a list of topics that she was committing herself to discuss, she discovered that campus smoking policies was not among them. Here is how she questioned her thesis.

Why did I believe this?

THESIS: My larger discovery was that smokers are not bad, or flawed,

Why do I think so? —— people because they smoke; if anyone is flawed, it is arrogant nonsmokers (like me) who think of themselves as superior.

Theresa then posed and answered these questions: *How did I change?*

> Why are smokers not bad, or flawed, because they
> smoke?
>> They've made an unhealthy decision--but we
>> all do; their decision has led to an addic-
>> tion; mine hasn't.
> Why have I thought of myself as superior?
>> I accepted the common belief that good
>> health equals virtue. I didn't explore my
>> own assumptions; I acted like my six-year-
>> old nephew. Memories of Uncle Enrique made
>> me sure that he, and all smokers, choose to
>> smoke and selfishly disregard their fami-
>> lies. I didn't consider how difficult addic-
>> tions can be to overcome.
> How have I changed?
>> Talking with Daniel's fiancee made me real-
>> ize I was being simple-minded. I no longer
>> assume smokers are bad people. They smoke--
>> that's all I can say with confidence. Beyond
>> that, they are individuals--some good, some
>> not: like everyone else.

When Theresa quizzed the thesis statement and reviewed her answers, she realized that a discussion of smoking policies on campus did not belong in the essay since that topic did not develop any part of her thesis. To maintain the essay's unity, therefore, she had to make a choice: either expand the thesis to allow for a discussion of policies, or cut that discussion entirely. In the end, Theresa cut the discussion, focusing instead on her own discovery—and finally on a resolution that would help her nephew.

COMPUTER TIPS

Break the Paper Habit

If you are in the habit of handwriting your first drafts, experiment with writing at the keyboard. There will be times when you need to print out a paper copy of your draft and edit it, but much of your revising, editing, and proofreading can (and should) be done quickly and efficiently on the screen. You may decide that preparing first drafts of one type of writing (for example, academic papers) works well at the keyboard, whereas drafting other types of writing (poetry) does not. Experiment and learn your preferences.

3 Final revision: Tending to details

Editing and proofreading

Editing is revision at the sentence level: the level at which you attend to style, grammar, punctuation, and word choice. Depending on their preferences, writers will edit (just as they revise) throughout the writing process, from the first draft through to the last. It would be misleading to state flatly that the process of sentence-level rewriting should wait until all issues of unity and coherence are resolved. Still, to the extent that you *can* hold off, save editing until the later drafts, once you are relatively confident that your paper has a final thesis and that the major sections of the paper are in order. In any event, don't allow sentence-level concerns to block your writing process early on—especially since the sentence you are fretting over may not even make it to the final draft. The box on page 41 shows how Theresa Lopez edited a late draft.

You can use the "Spotlight on Common Errors" feature on the inside back cover of this book to help you check for sentence-level problems.

Proofread your paper to identify and correct minor errors. If you have trouble spotting them, find a way to disrupt your usual pattern of reading so that the errors will become visible to you. One technique is to photocopy your work and have a friend read it aloud. You can read along and make corrections when you hear an error. Another technique is to read each line of your paper in reverse order, from the last word on the line to the first. This approach forces you to focus on one word at a time. Besides checking for minor errors, review your assignment one last time to make sure you have prepared your manuscript in an appropriate form. (See Chapter 12.) Pages 41–43 show

WWW

http://www.researchpaper.com/
writing_center/32.html

Proofreading strategies from an invaluable writer's resource: Researchpaper.com

Sentence-Level Revision

Although Theresa Lopez revised some sentences during the course of earlier revision, she resisted the urge to revise *every* sentence, knowing that she might delete or substantially change entire paragraphs to achieve unity and coherence. Once her essay's basic structure and development were sound, Theresa felt confident enough to begin polishing her sentences. Here's an example of her sentence-level revision:

> For as long as I can remember, I've disliked smoking and resented smokers ~~polluting~~ *for invading* the air *I breathe*. When I see a smoker I ~~see~~ *can picture* my Uncle Enrique~~. He~~ *, who* was ~~once~~ supposed to be quite a dancer, but ~~he~~ *who* never went anywhere without his cigarettes. Enrique died in his forties, *gasping for breath and unable to walk across a room. He left* ~~leaving~~ my father's sister *alone to support* ~~and~~ three kids. I never forgave him for smoking and getting lung cancer~~, and (with respect to smokers) I've been living with a chip on my shoulders ever since.~~

Here's the same section from the final draft:

> For as long as I can remember, I've disliked smoking and resented smokers for invading the air I breathe. When I see a smoker I can picture my Uncle Enrique, who was supposed to be quite a dancer, but who never went anywhere without his cigarettes. Enrique died in his forties, gasping for breath and unable to walk across a room. He left my father's sister alone to support three kids. I never forgave him for smoking and getting lung cancer.

```
                    Defending Smokers
                     Theresa Lopez
     Every year my extended family, on my father's side,
gathers for a party. It's a two-day affair at which cousins
from distant parts of the country show off their newborns
and introduce prospective husbands and wives. At the most
recent gathering last summer, Cousin Daniel walked in with
```

his fiancee, who happened to be smoking. To our amazement, my six-year-old nephew, Henry, ran into his mother's arms, pointing at the cigarette in the woman's hand and glaring at her as if she were a criminal.

In my nephew's eyes, she *was* a criminal; and I'm embarrassed to admit that I felt much the same way until I introduced myself to Suzanne and got to know her. What I discovered was that, her smoking aside, she is bright (a college graduate) and very friendly. My larger discovery was that smokers are not bad, or flawed, people because they smoke; if anyone is flawed, it is arrogant nonsmokers (like me) who think of themselves as superior.

For as long as I can remember, I've disliked smoking and resented smokers for invading the air I breathe. When I see a smoker I can picture my Uncle Enrique, who was supposed to be quite a dancer, but who never went anywhere without his cigarettes. Enrique died in his forties, gasping for breath and unable to walk across a room. He left my father's sister alone to support three kids. I never forgave him for smoking and getting lung cancer. Because of Enrique I developed a belief that responsible people try to take care of themselves through diet, exercise, and medical help. They read warning labels on cigarette cartons and at least try to stop smoking, which Enrique never did.

The opposite, I believed, was also true: that people who knowingly pollute their bodies (by smoking, for instance) are irresponsible and can't be trusted. For years, I would pass smokers on the street and think: These guys must be stupid. Do they want to die? I would actually avoid meeting people if they smoked. My biggest blind spot was that I confused the act of smoking with the person who smokes. I never saw that the act is *not* the person.

When I met Suzanne, I was forced to make the distinction. She was about to become a member of my family, so I had to look for her good points and accept her. Suzanne opened my eyes to the fact that smoking is a behavior, an addiction. Like many people who smoke, she began at a

young age when social pressures were high. Much later,
when she realized she was addicted, she couldn't stop.
That doesn't make Suzanne or others who smoke bad; it
makes them human.

All of us, on occasion, make less than healthy decisions about how to live. In my case I sometimes eat a pint
of ice cream at a sitting! The fact that my unhealthy habits
(which started when I was a kid) have not led to a damaging
addiction means only that I'm lucky--not that I'm smarter
than or morally superior to smokers. I needed to learn this
lesson and to pass it on to my nephew. If Henry can learn to
look beyond bad habits and to empathize with people who are
slaves to those habits, then he may not have to wait until
he grows up to discover that he, too, is human.

Theresa Lopez's completed essay on the attitudes of nonsmokers toward
smokers—the topic developed earlier in this chapter. Note how she achieved
unity, coherence, and precision through a series of drafts.

2f   Adapting your writing strategy for essay exams

Essay exams are a specialized case of the writing you will do in college.
In formal papers, you have the opportunity to research, draft, and revise before preparing a final version. In essay writing, the process is compressed:
whatever research you do comes in the form of studying previously assigned
texts and articles. In the exam, you will have little time, if any, to revise. Your
writing should be direct. It needs to demonstrate that you have read assigned material, have been an active listener in class, and can use what
you've learned to think independently.

Prepare

Ideally, you will have read your textbooks and assigned articles with
care *as* they were assigned during the period prior to the exam. Review these
materials and pay close attention to notes you have made in the margins.
Take new notes based on your original notes: highlight important concepts
from each assignment. Then reorganize your notes according to key ideas
that you think serve as themes or focus points for your course. Turn next to

your class notes (you may want to do this *before* reviewing reading assignments), and add information and comments to your lists of key ideas. Develop statements about each idea that you could, if asked, support with references to specific information. Try to anticipate your instructor's questions.

Read the entire exam before beginning to write.

Allot yourself a certain number of minutes to answer each essay question, allowing extra time for the more complex questions. As you write, monitor your use of time.

Adopt a discipline-appropriate perspective.

Essay exams are designed in part to see how well you understand particular ways of thinking in a discipline. If you are writing a mid-term exam in chemistry, for instance, appreciate that your instructor will expect you to discuss material from a chemist's perspective. You will need to demonstrate not only that you know your information but also that you can *use* it to think and reach conclusions in discipline-appropriate ways.

Adapt the writing process according to the time allotted for a question.

Assuming that you have thirty minutes to answer an essay question, spend at least five minutes of this allotted time in plotting an answer.

- Locate the assignment's key verb and identify your specific tasks in writing. Words such as *summarize, explain, compare, illustrate,* or *prove* provide important cues as to your instructor's expectations.
- List information you can draw on to develop your answer.
- Examine the information you have listed and develop a thesis that directly answers the essay question and demonstrates your understanding of key concepts.
- Sketch an outline of your answer. In taking an essay exam, you have little or no time for writing to discover. Know before you write what major points you will develop in support of your thesis and in what order.

Spend twenty minutes of your allotted time on writing your answer. Save five minutes to reread your work, check your logic, and correct minor errors.

CHAPTER 3

Developing the Paragraph and the Paper

It is easy enough to define a paragraph: a group of related sentences organized by a single, controlling idea and marked by an indented first word (typically five spaces from the left margin). More complicated, however, is determining what makes an effective paragraph. As this chapter will clarify, an effective paragraph is unified, coherent, and well developed. During the process of drafting and revising, you will need to make certain that each paragraph in your paper exhibits these qualities. Well-written paragraphs are so important to the development of a paper that discussion of paragraphs warrants its own chapter.

 CRITICAL DECISIONS

Determining Paragraph Length

A paragraph can be as brief as a sentence or as long as a page. Because there is no formula regarding paragraph length, writers must determine for themselves what is appropriate given their purpose, subject, and audience.

As you draft, concentrate on the content of your paragraphs. Save your concerns about paragraph length for the later stages of revision, when you are relatively satisfied with your work. Then think of your reader and the way your paragraphs appear on the page. Keep the following guidelines in mind:

- Consistently short paragraphs (two or three sentences) may send the signal that your ideas are not well developed. Do you need to combine paragraphs? Or do many of your paragraphs actually require further development?

- Consistently long paragraphs (nine or ten sentences) may give the impression that your writing is dense or that your ideas are not well differentiated. Think about dividing long paragraphs in a logical way. The new paragraph does not need its own topic sentence as long as it is clearly a continuation of the paragraph that precedes it.

- One-sentence paragraphs are rarely appropriate for academic writing. In other writing situations, however, a one-sentence paragraph may be useful to emphasize a point, to provide a transition, or to offer a summary.

3a Writing and revising to achieve paragraph unity

A unified paragraph will focus on, develop, and not stray from a paragraph's central, controlling idea or **topic sentence.** Recall that a *thesis* announces and controls the content of an entire essay. Just so, a *topic sentence* announces and controls the content of sentences in a single paragraph. Think of the topic sentence as a paragraph-level *thesis,* and you will see the principle of unity at work at *all* levels of the paper. At each level of the essay, a general statement is used to guide you in assembling specific, supporting parts.

Within a paragraph, a topic sentence can appear anywhere, provided that you recognize it and can lead up to and away from it with some method in mind—using, for instance, examples, reasons, statistics, facts, or descriptions. Well-written, unified paragraphs usually result from a combination of these techniques.

1 Placing the topic sentence at the beginning of a paragraph

Witold Rybczynski begins the following paragraph with a direct statement: *The college town is an American institution.* Every subsequent sentence focuses on and develops this topic sentence.

> The college town is an American institution. Throughout the 19th century, it was common practice to locate private colleges in small towns like Amherst in Massachusetts, Middlebury in Vermont and Pomona in California. The idea was that bucolic surroundings would provide the appropriate atmosphere for the pursuit of learning and (not incidentally) remove students from the distractions and temptations of the big city. The influence of the small college on its town was minimal, however, beyond providing a few local residents with service jobs.
>
> —WITOLD RYBCZYNSKI, "Big City Amenities"

2 Placing the topic sentence in the middle of a paragraph

In the following paragraph, Jack Shaheen's topic sentence is *There is, however, great diversity in Islam, a religion that covers one-seventh of the earth's inhabitable area and includes a sixth of its population.* Two sentences lead up to this topic sentence, preparing for it; three sentences follow and develop this topic sentence.

> A host of simple-minded cliches about Moslems and Islam exists. When the hostage crisis in Iran occurred, most Westerners began to view all Moslems, the followers of Islam, as Arab or Iranian militants seeking to return the world to the 14th century. There is, however, great diversity in Islam, a religion that covers one-seventh of the earth's inhabitable area and in-

cludes a sixth of its population. To judge all Moslems as the same is as futile as judging all Christians and Jews in the same way. Most of the world's 800 million Moslems are not fatalistic radicals. Like most Christians and Jews, they, too, devoutly believe in and respect God and seek to live a good life in peace with others.

—JACK SHAHEEN, "In Search of the Arab"

You can place a topic sentence at the end of a paragraph—especially when you want to provide readers with information or reasons that will incline them to accept your point. On relatively rare occasions, you can omit the topic sentence, provided that the paragraph remains as unified as it would be if a topic sentence were present.

3b Writing and revising to achieve paragraph coherence

When your paragraphs are coherent, readers will understand the logic by which you move from one sentence to the next, toward or away from your topic sentence. When writing the first draft of a paper, you may not have a plan to ensure paragraph coherence; you may not even have a clear idea of every paragraph's main point. Revision is the time when you sort out these matters, when you can make certain that each paragraph has a clear purpose and a clear, coherent plan for achieving that purpose. As you read the following descriptions of techniques for achieving coherence, keep in mind that experienced writers typically use these techniques in combination.

COMPUTER TIPS

Cut, Don't Delete

In freewriting, in early exploratory drafts, and in other initial stages of writing, you may find it useful not to delete information at first. If you've typed a paragraph that you decide you probably don't need, don't be hasty—you *may* need it later. Instead, use your word processor's *cut* function to remove the text. Unlike deleted text, cut text remains in your computer's memory in case you want it back. A word of caution: in nearly all word processors, only one chunk of cut text at a time can stay in memory. Cutting a second chunk of text automatically deletes the first chunk from memory forever. So before you cut a second chunk of text, use your computer's *paste* function to place the first one in some permanent location—perhaps at the very end of your paper or in another "notepad" file. Once your revisions are nearly finished and you're sure of the information you need, then you can delete material you haven't used.

1 Achieving coherence with cues

When sentences are arranged with care, you need only highlight this arrangement to ensure that readers will move easily through a paragraph. To highlight paragraph coherence, use **cues**: words and phrases that remind readers as they move from sentence to sentence (1) that they continue to read about the same topic, and (2) that ideas are unfolding logically. You may want to wait until the revision stage to add cues to a paragraph, when you are better able to discern the paragraph's shape. The following Critical Decisions box discusses further how to revise paragraphs.

CRITICAL DECISIONS

Revising Paragraphs for Coherence

As a writer, you probably have too much to do in a first draft to monitor the relationship among sentences and paragraphs or to develop coherence, the smooth flow of ideas. In a second or third draft, however, once you are settled on your final thesis and on the structure of your paper, you should evaluate your sentences in the broader context of paragraphs, and paragraphs in the broader context of sections (groupings of related paragraphs).

■ **Revise every paragraph within its section.** To revise an individual paragraph, examine it in relation to the ones that come before and after. Develop the habit of including transitional words at the beginning or end of paragraphs.

A section:
Paragraph _____
_____
_____

Paragraph _____
_____   **Coherence**
_____   Does each paragraph lead
_____   logically to, and follow
Paragraph _____   logically from, its neigh-
_____   boring paragraphs?
_____

■ **Revise every sentence within its paragraph.** Once you are sure of a paragraph's place in your paper, evaluate each sentence in relation to the sentences that come before and after. Use cues—pronouns, parallelism, repetition, and transitions—to help move the reader from one sentence to the next through a paragraph.

Pronouns

As the example below shows, the most direct way to remind readers that they continue to examine a certain topic as they move from sentence to sentence is to repeat the most important noun, or the subject, of your topic sentence.

The choice of Peter Hall to supply vigorous entrepreneurial leadership was logical. Only twenty-nine, he was already an eminent director. He had earned his credentials with the theatre work he began at Cambridge and continued with the Elizabethan Theatre Company, formed by Oxford and Cambridge students to tour Shakespeare plays. More impressive and attention-getting was his direction of the 1955 premiere at the London Arts Theatre of Samuel Beckett's *Waiting for Godot,* an event that alone would have entered Hall's name into theatre history.

—Roger Cornish and Violet Ketels, *Landmarks of Modern British Drama*

Repetition

While unintentional repetition can make sentences awkward, planned repetition can contribute significantly to a paragraph's coherence. Either repeat identically or use a substitute phrase to repeat an important word or words in a paragraph, as shown in the paragraph below.

Although the performance practices of the Church held considerable power and influence, the medieval audience was familiar with other types of performance events. The jongleurs and the troubadours of southern France were professional performers who glorified heroic life and courtly love in verse, often singing of love in rather earthy terms. In Anglo-Saxon England, such performers were called scops and gleemen; later, they were known as minstrels. Usually accompanying themselves with a harp, minstrels probably composed such literary texts as *Widsith, Doer's Lament,* and *Beowulf.* Just as important, each of these texts offers a picture of the minstrels' performance work.

—Ronald J. Pelias, *Performance Studies*

Parallelism

Chapter 23 is devoted entirely to a discussion of **parallelism:** the use of grammatically equivalent words, phrases, and sentences to achieve coherence and balance in your writing. A sentence whose structure parallels that of an earlier sentence has an echo-like effect, linking the content of the second sentence to the content of the first.

All students need to be aware of what some students know by instinct: that you can divert or reduce aggression with a quick apology or with humor. This is what social psychologists call reducing levels of arousal by introducing an incompatible response. Also, the school can implement Peer Mediation where if students feel a physical or emotional threat they can report it and discuss it with other students. Talking can show students that disagreements are not worth a trip to the emergency room or worth the legal problems or medical bills—the consequences of violence that movies and rap videos don't usually show. If more students would have used these simple measures at my high school, I'm convinced that at least several fights could have been avoided.

—JIM WALKER, *Student Writer*

2   Highlighting coherence with transitions

Transitions establish logical relationships between sentences, between paragraphs, and between whole sections of an essay. A transition can be a single word, a phrase, a sentence, or an entire paragraph. In each case it functions the same way: first, it either directly summarizes the content of a preceding sentence (or paragraph) or it implies that summary. Having established a summary, transitions then move forward into a new sentence (or paragraph), helping the reader anticipate what is to come. Notice how the highlighted words and phrases below move the paragraph forward.

> When we think about addiction to drugs or alcohol we frequently focus on negative aspects, ignoring the pleasures that accompany drinking or drug-taking. And yet the essence of any serious addiction is a pursuit of pleasure, a search for a "high" that normal life does not supply. It is only the inability to function without the addictive substance that is dismaying, the dependence of the organism upon a certain experience and an increasing inability to function normally without it. Thus people will take two or three drinks at the end of the day not merely for the pleasure drinking provides, but also because they "don't feel normal" without them.
>
> —MARIE WINN, "The Plug-in Drug"

The box on page 51 provides a useful list of transitional expressions.

3c   Writing and revising to achieve well-developed paragraphs

One important element of effective writing is the level of detail you can offer in support of a paragraph's topic sentence. To *develop* a paragraph means to devote a block of sentences to a discussion of its core idea. Sentences that develop will explain or illustrate and will support with reasons or facts. The various strategies presented here will help you to develop paragraphs that inform and persuade.

When writing the first draft of a paper, you may not stop to think about how you are developing the central idea of every paragraph. By the second draft, however, you will want to be conscious of developing your paragraphs.

Transitional Expressions

To SHOW ADDITION	additionally, again, also, and, as well, besides, equally important, further, furthermore, in addition, moreover, then
To SHOW SIMILARITY	also, in the same way, just as . . . so too, likewise, similarly
To SHOW AN EXCEPTION	but, however, in spite of, on the one hand . . . on the other hand, nevertheless, nonetheless, notwithstanding, in contrast, on the contrary, still, yet
To INDICATE SEQUENCE	first, second, third, . . . next, then, finally,
To SHOW TIME	after, afterwards, at last, before, currently, during, earlier, immediately, later, meanwhile, now, recently, simultaneously, subsequently, then
To PROVIDE AN EXAMPLE	for example, for instance, namely, specifically, to illustrate
To EMPHASIZE A POINT	even, indeed, in fact, of course, truly
To INDICATE PLACE	above, adjacent, below, beyond, here, in front, in back, nearby, there
To SHOW CAUSE AND EFFECT	accordingly, consequently, hence, so, therefore, thus
To CONCLUDE OR REPEAT	finally, in a word, in brief, in conclusion, in the end, on the whole, thus, to conclude, to summarize

The most common technique is **topical development,** that is, announcing your topic in the opening sentence; dividing that topic into two or three parts (in the case of chronological arrangement, into various *times*); and then developing each part within the paragraph. The pattern you choose for development should reflect the relationship among ideas expressed in your thesis.

Narratives

A narrative's main purpose is to recount for readers a story that has a point pertinent to the larger essay. Brief stories are often used as examples. Most often, narratives are sequenced chronologically and occur in an essay either as a single paragraph or as a grouping of paragraphs. The challenge in

CRITICAL DECISIONS

Developing Paragraphs: Essential Features

In determining whether a paragraph is well or even adequately developed, you should be able to answer three questions without hesitation:

- **What is the main point of the paragraph?**
- **Why should readers accept this main point?** (What reasons or information have you provided to convince a reader?)
- **Why should readers care about the main point?**

In answering each question, you should be able to point to one, or several, sentences. Remember: readers are busy. They will ignore what you write unless you give them ample reason to understand, to be convinced, and to care. Every paragraph enables you to do exactly this.

writing a narrative is to keep readers involved both in the events you are relating and in the people involved in those events. In the example that follows, *Time* magazine reporter David Van Biema's narration of a deliberately planned Amtrak derailment in Arizona adds vivid and chilling detail to his extended discussion of "diabolically elegant" criminals who model their crimes on those of the past:

> It was a chilly, 60 degree night in southern Arizona last Monday. The moon was full, and Amtrak's 12-car Sunset Limited, bearing 248 passengers and 20 crew members, was doing between 50 and 55 m.p.h. as it approached a gentle curve not too far from the tiny town of Hyder. It was 1:20 A.M., and most of the passengers on the train, which is especially popular among retirees traveling from Los Angeles to Miami and back, were in bed. Suddenly, they were not so much awakened as catapulted from sleep. Those who kept their wits about them remember a terrible, prolonged shriek of metal against metal. For others, their waking sensation was pain, as they smashed into a wall or a chair or a sink. The Limited's two diesel locomotives had safely crossed a 30-ft.-high trestle over a desert gulch. But the next five [sic] cars—a dormitory car for crew members, two sleeping cars for passengers and a dining car—had jumped the rails. One hit the ground below; the other three hung down from the trestle like beads in a giant's necklace.
>
> —DAVID VAN BIEMA, "Murder on the Sunset Limited"

Description

A writer who can evoke in us a clear sense of sight, feeling, smell, hearing, or taste earns our admiration. The following paragraph is a brief but poignant portrait of the homeless population of New York City:

There are more-visible people in need. There are the legions of homeless, lying on the benches in Grand Central Terminal, huddled in doorways against the cold, carrying their lives on their backs, trading subsistence for life. In soup kitchens they lean over their meals as though in prayer and use the broth to warm as well as feed them, and use their dinnertime to stoke their beaten souls as well as their empty stomachs.

—ANNA QUINDLEN, "A City's Needy"

Example

An example is a particular case of a more general point. After topical development, development by example is probably the most common method of supporting the core idea of a paragraph. Examples *show* readers what you mean. Several transitions are commonly used to introduce examples: *for example, for instance, a case in point, to illustrate.* In this paragraph, a counselor who advises high-school students on the college admissions process uses a funny story to illustrate a point about nervousness.

Nervousness [in a college interview] . . . is absolutely and entirely normal. The best way to handle it is to admit it, out loud, to the interviewer. Miles Uhrig, director of admission at Tufts University, sometimes relates this true story to his apprehensive applicants: One extremely agitated young applicant sat opposite him for her interview with her legs crossed, wearing loafers on her feet. She swung her top leg back and forth to some inaudible rhythm. The loafer on her top foot flew off her foot, hit him in the head, ricocheted to the desk lamp and broke it. She looked at him in terror, but when their glances met, they both dissolved in laughter. The moral of the story—the person on the other side of the desk is also a human being and wants to put you at ease. So admit to your anxiety and don't swing your foot if you're wearing loafers! (By the way, she was admitted.)

—ANTHONY F. CAPRARO III, "The Interview"

Sequential order/process

A paragraph that presents a process will show carefully sequenced events. You may want to use transitions that show sequence in time: *first, second, after, before, once, next, then,* and *finally.*

The first and simplest type of iron furnace was called a bloomery, in which wrought iron was produced directly from the ore. The ore was heated with charcoal in a small open furnace, usually made of stone and blown upon with bellows. Most of the impurities would burn out, leaving a spongy mass of iron mixed with siliceous slag (iron silicate). This spongy mass was then refined by hammering, reheating, and hammering some more, until it reached the desired fibrous consistency. During the hammering, the glasslike slag would be evenly distributed throughout the iron mass. This hammered slab of wrought iron, or "bloom," was then ready to forge into some usable object.

—ELIOT WIGGINTON, "Furnaces"

Definition

Writers use paragraphs of definition in informative writing to help readers learn the meaning of terms needed for understanding difficult concepts. In essays intended to persuade, writers define terms in order to establish a common language with the reader, an important first step toward gaining the reader's agreement. Once a term is defined, it can be clarified with examples, comparisons, or descriptions. The paragraph that follows is informative in character—more or less announcing its definition.

> Alzheimer's disease is a slow death of the brain in which the first disturbing symptom is increasing forgetfulness. People with AD can no longer recall recent events or assimilate new information and ideas. They constantly misplace objects and repeat questions that have just been answered. Eventually they develop aphasia (loss of language), agnosia (inability to recognize people and objects), and apraxia (inability to perform everyday actions). They search their minds for words they have always known. They have increasing difficulty in following a conversation; their own talk becomes disjointed and empty, their vocabulary impoverished and their language simplified. Their judgment declines, and they lose the capacity to generalize and classify. They start a routine action and no longer know how to finish it. They cannot find their way even in familiar places, or recall the day of the week or time of year. Cooking, driving, and using tools become too complicated for them. Toward the end they have difficulty in dressing and even using the bathroom and eating.
> —HARVARD MEDICAL SCHOOL, "Mental Health Letter"

Division and classification

Division (also called *analysis*) and classification are closely related operations. A writer who divides a topic into parts to see what it is made of performs an analysis.

A *classification* is a grouping of like items. The writer begins with what may appear at first to be bits of unrelated information. Gradually, patterns of similarity emerge, and the writer is able to establish categories by which to group like items. In the example that follows, Brian Fagan considers the various locations at which archaeological digs are made and then classifies or groups the digs according to common features.

> Archaeological sites are most commonly classified according to the activities that occurred there. Thus, cemeteries and other sepulchers like Tutankhamen's tomb are referred to as **burial sites.** A 20,000-year-old Stone Age site in the Dnieper Valley of the Ukraine, with mammoth-bone houses, hearths, and other signs of domestic activity, is a **habitation site.** So too are many other sites, such as caves and rockshelters, early Mesoamerican farming villages, and Mesopotamian cities—in all, people lived and carried out greatly diverse activities. **Kill sites** consist of bones of slaughtered game animals and the weapons that killed them. They are found in East Africa and on the North American Great Plains. **Quarry sites** are another type of spe-

cialist site, where people mined stone or metals to make specific tools. Prized raw materials, such as obsidian, a volcanic glass used for fine knives, were widely traded in prehistoric times and profoundly interest the archaeologist. Then there are such spectacular **religious sites** as the stone circles of Stonehenge in southern England, the Temple of Amun at Karnak, Egypt, and the great ceremonial precincts of lowland Maya centers in Central America at *Tikal,* Copán, and Palenque. **Art sites** are common in southwestern France, southern Africa, and parts of North America, where prehistoric people painted or engraved magnificent displays of art.

—BRIAN FAGAN, *Archaeology*

COMPUTER TIPS

Save Frequently

This is probably the most frequently given advice in all guides to writing with computers, and it's certainly the most ignored: **Save your writing frequently.** Everything that you've typed since the last save will be lost if there's a power failure or someone walks by and accidentally kicks the plug out of your computer. How long would it take you to reconstruct and retype all that material? It takes almost no time or effort to execute the keystroke combination necessary to save: get in the habit of doing it automatically, mindlessly, whenever you stop to think, to reread, to rest, to get up from the computer for any reason.

Newer word-processing software allows you even more options for protecting your work: It saves your work automatically at regular timed intervals, allows you to work with a copy of your document rather than the original, and provides automatic backups. However, with multiple versions of your papers such as copies and backups, you need to be careful when you resume work at your next session: be sure you're using the most current version of your paper.

Comparison/contrast

To *compare* is to discuss the similarities between people, places, objects, events, or ideas. To *contrast* is to discuss differences. The writer developing such a paragraph conducts an analysis of two or more subjects, studying the parts of each and then discussing the subjects in relation to each other. Specific points of comparison and contrast make the discussion possible.

Paragraphs of comparison and contrast should be put to some definite use in a paper. It is not enough to point out similarities and differences; you must *do* something with this information: three possibilities would be to classify, evaluate, or interpret. When writing your paragraph, consider two common methods of arrangement: by subject or point-by-point. Note that when a comparative discussion becomes relatively long, you have the option of splitting it into two paragraphs, as Stephen Jay Gould does in this example arranged by subject.

> Science works with testable proposals. If, after much compilation and scrutiny of data, new information continues to affirm a hypothesis, we may accept it provisionally and gain confidence as further evidence mounts. We can never be completely sure that a hypothesis is right, though we may be able to show with confidence that it is wrong. The best scientific hypotheses are also generous and expansive: they suggest extensions and implications that enlighten related, and even far distant, subjects. Simply consider how the idea of evolution has influenced virtually every intellectual field.
>
> Useless speculation, on the other hand, is restrictive. It generates no testable hypothesis, and offers no way to obtain potentially refuting evidence. Please note that I am not speaking of truth or falsity. The speculation may well be true; still, if it provides, in principle, no material for affirmation or rejection, we can make nothing of it. It must simply stand forever as an intriguing idea. Useless speculation turns in on itself and leads nowhere; good science, containing both seeds for its potential refutation and implications for more and different testable knowledge, reaches out.
>
> —STEPHEN JAY GOULD, "Sex, Drugs, Disasters"

In the next paragraph, student Michele Pelletier uses a point-by-point arrangement to compare and contrast two types of armies of the fifteenth and sixteenth centuries.

> Armies of volunteers and conscripts are today's versions of the militias and mercenary forces that existed in the 15th and 16th centuries. Militias were armies made up of citizens who were fighting for their home country. Mercenaries were professional soldiers who, better trained than militia men (they were always men), were hired by foreign countries to fight wars. Mercenaries had no cause other than a paycheck: if the country that hired them did not pay, they would quit the battlefield. Mercenaries may have been fickle, but technically they were good fighters. Militia men may not have been as technically proficient as mercenaries, but they had the will to fight. Both of these traditions—fighting for a cause and fighting for money—have found their way into American military history of the past thirty years.

Analogy

An **analogy** is a comparison of two topics that, on first appearance, seem unrelated. An analogy gains force by surprising a reader, by demonstrating that an unlikely comparison is not only likely but also illuminating.

> AIDS is a killer disease and any measures taken to prevent its transmission must be 100 percent effective. For condoms to be the answer to AIDS, they must be used every time and can never break or leak. Neither criterion

is ever likely to be met. Condoms may mean "safer" sex, but is "safer" acceptable for this deadly epidemic?

Suppose that, for unknown reasons, automobiles suddenly began to explode every time someone turned the ignition. Motorists were getting blown up all over the country. Finally, the government comes out with a solution. Just put this additive in the fuel, they say, and the risk of explosion will go down 90 percent. Would you consider the problem solved? Would you still keep driving your car? I doubt it. Then why do we accept condoms as the solution for AIDS?

—STEVEN SAINSBURY, "Condoms: Safer, But Not 'Safe' Sex"

Cause and effect

Development by cause and effect shows how an event or condition has come to occur. Inferring a causal relationship between events requires careful analysis. Causes are usually complex, and a writer must avoid the temptation to oversimplify.

The depression was precipitated by the stock market crash in October 1929, but the actual cause of the collapse was an unhealthy economy. While the ability of the manufacturing industry to produce consumer goods had increased rapidly, mass purchasing power had remained relatively static. Most laborers, farmers, and white-collar workers, therefore, could not afford to buy the automobiles and refrigerators turned out by factories in the 1920s, because their incomes were too low. At the same time, the federal government increased the problem through economic policies that tended to encourage the very rich to over-save.

—JAMES WATTS AND ALAN F. DAVIS, *Your Family in Modern American History*

Writers often combine methods of developing a paragraph's core idea. The same paragraph that shows an example may also show a comparison or contrast. No firm rules constrain your choices. Let your common sense and an interest in helping your reader understand your subject be your guides.

3d   Writing and revising paragraphs of introduction and conclusion

The introduction and conclusion to a paper can be understood as a type of transition. The introduction moves the reader from the world outside of your paper to the world within; the conclusion moves readers from the world of your paper back to their own world.

1   Introductions

Writing an introduction is often easier once you know what you are introducing; for this reason many writers choose not to work seriously on an introduction until they have finished a draft and can see the overall shape and content of a paper. Other writers need to begin with a carefully written introduction. If this is your preference, remember not to demand perfection of a first draft, especially since the material you will be introducing has yet to be written. Once it is written, your introduction may need to change.

The following box provides some strategies for writing introductions.

Strategies for Writing Introductions

Very often, the most profitable time to write an introduction to your paper is *after* you have completed a draft. Once you know the main idea you want to introduce, try one of the strategies suggested in this chapter. Your overall strategy should be as follows:

1. Announce your topic, using vocabulary that hints at the perspective from which you will be writing and introduces the type of language, evidence, and logic you will use in your paper.

2. If readers lack the background needed to understand your paper, then provide this background. Define terms, present a brief history, or review a controversy.

3. If readers know something of your subject, then devote less (or no) time to developing background information and more time to stimulating interest. Raise a question, quote a source familiar to the reader, tell a story, or begin directly with a statement of the thesis.

4. Once you have provided background information and gained the reader's attention, gradually turn that attention toward your thesis, the last sentence of the introductory paragraph(s).

The introduction as a frame of reference

Introductions establish frames of reference. They let readers know the general topic of your paper, the disciplinary perspective from which you will discuss this topic, and the standards they should use in evaluating your work. Readers quickly learn from an introduction if you are a laboratory researcher, a field researcher, a theorist, an essayist, a reporter, a student with a general interest, and so on. Each of these possible identities implies for readers different standards of evidence and reasoning by which they will evaluate your work. Here is an example of an introduction to a literary analysis, written by a student.

James Joyce's "Counterparts" tells the story of a
man, Farrington, who is abused by his boss for not doing
his job right. Farrington spends a long time drinking
after work; and when he finally arrives home, he in turn
abuses—he beats—his son Tom. In eleven pages, Joyce
tells much more than a story of yet another alcoholic
venting failures and frustrations on family members.
In "Counterparts," Farrington turns to drink in order
to gain power—in much the same way his wife and
children turn to the Church.

Language of literary analysis

Evidence: based on close reading of a story

Logic: generalization

Thesis: drinking and church-going related to a need for power

---

2   Conclusions

One important job in writing a paper is to explain to readers what you
have accomplished and why your ideas are significant. Minimally, a conclusion will summarize your work, but often you will want to do more than
write a summary. Provided you
have written carefully and believe in what you have written,
you have earned the right to expand on your paper's thesis in
a conclusion. You can point the
reader back to the larger world
and suggest the significance of
your ideas in that world. Here is an example of a conclusion to a paper on
school violence:

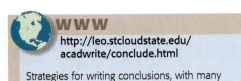

WWW

http://leo.stcloudstate.edu/
acadwrite/conclude.html

Strategies for writing conclusions, with many
examples.

> It will be in schools that students learn effective social and communica-
> tion skills that will help reduce the levels of aggression and divert the dam-
> age that rumors, confrontations, and fights cause. Talking about differences,
> talking through differences, and deflecting aggressive acts by apologizing
> and by our sense of humor will show by example that we have the heart to
> live together and have the courage and good sense to get along. We can
> break the cycle of violence by seeing weapons as part of the problem, not as
> the solution to the lethal levels of violence in our society.

A conclusion gives you an opportunity to answer a challenge that all
readers raise—*So what? Why should this paper matter to me? What actions should*

I take? A well-written conclusion will answer these questions and will leave readers with a trace of your thinking as they turn away from your paper and back to their own business.

Strategies for Writing Conclusions

1. **Summary.** The simplest conclusion is a summary, a brief re-statement of your paper's main points. Avoid conclusions that repeat exactly material presented elsewhere in the paper.

2. **Summary and Comment.** More emphatic conclusions build on a summary in one of several ways. These conclusions will
   - set ideas in the paper in a larger context
   - call for action (or research)
   - speculate or warn
   - raise a question
   - quote a familiar or authoritative source
   - tell a story

COMPUTER TIPS

Use the TAB Key for Paragraph Indentation

One major difference between word processors and typewriters is that the former uses a proportional font: each letter takes up a different amount of space. Typewriters use monospaced fonts: Each letter takes up exactly the same amount of space. Starting a paragraph with five taps on the typewriter space bar always gives you exactly the same indentation, but this is not true for a word processor. Depending on the font and size, typographical distinctions (boldface or italics), and the page justification setting, the amount of space taken up by five spaces varies quite a bit. Use the TAB key for paragraph indentations; it's one keystroke, it's absolutely consistent, and the command can be easily deleted.

In Chapters 1–3, you've been introduced to strategies for thinking, reading, and writing critically. The discussions have assumed that most of the writing you will do in college will be based on source materials. The next four chapters will present specific strategies for locating these materials and for using them in research papers.

PART II
Writing the Research Paper

CHAPTER 4

Researching Print and Electronic Sources

Research begins with a question, with a need to *know*. To succeed in writing an effective research paper, you have to do more than simply fulfill an assignment. You need to do everything you can to make the assignment your instructor gives you your own by formulating a question that you, personally, want to answer. Deciding on such a crucial question will ensure that you spend your time locating and examining sources because you are truly interested in your topic.

This is the first of five chapters devoted to research. This chapter provides the basic strategies for posing the questions that launch research and for seeking information, both print and electronic, that will help you to answer your questions in the form of a research paper. Chapter 5 discusses the ways you will actually *use* the source materials you find: by taking notes, summarizing, paraphrasing, and quoting. Chapter 6 provides guidance on arranging materials and writing your paper. Chapter 7 acquaints you with the process of documenting sources—acknowledging in your papers that you have drawn on the work of others. And Chapter 8 provides advice on writing research papers in courses across the curriculum.

CRITICAL DECISIONS

Think Actively: Adopting Strategies to Motivate Yourself as a Researcher

The best research is conducted by those who are fully interested in their topic. Interest will motivate you to look for sources, find connections among them, and evaluate in ways that will eventually lead to your research question. Interest and motivation are clearly functions of critical thinking, as discussed in Chapter 1:

- Read actively: Be alert to similarities and differences. See 1a.
- Challenge yourself and your sources. See 1b.
- Place particular events or ideas in a broader context. See 1c.
- Evaluate what you read. See 1f.

The process of conducting research takes time. If you are like most students, you are busy; so the research project you undertake should be worth your time and effort. What will make the investment worthwhile? In a word, *interest*. Any efforts you make at the beginning and through the early stages of the process to become truly interested in your work will pay handsome dividends. The box below describes strategies for developing your engagement with a topic.

Generating Personal Interest in a Topic

With a bit of effort, you can discover enthusiasm for many topics, even those that you do not choose yourself.

- **If you find a topic interesting:** If you are drawn to the topic, so much the better. Divide it into several well-defined parts. Ask: Which part do I want to learn more about? Use your answer to locate general sources. Then read.

- **If you react negatively to an assigned topic:** Try to understand your negative response. Negative reactions, as well as positive ones, can lead to an effective paper. Again, divide the topic into well-defined parts. Ask: What information could help me to understand my reaction? Use your answer to locate general sources. Then read.

- **If a topic leaves you feeling neutral:** At the beginning stages, you may not know enough about a topic to be interested. When you learn even a little about the topic, you may discover possibilities. So go to a general source—an encyclopedia or an introductory book—or try a general index (for example, the *Readers' Guide to Periodical Literature*) to locate two or three promising articles to read.

  1. Based on your reading, identify as many approaches to the topic as you can. Discovering an approach you never considered may spark your interest.

  2. Generate as many questions as you can, based on what you read. Perhaps one will become your research focus.

  3. Read in "hyper-alert" mode. Actively respond to multiple points in the article. Perhaps one response will become your research focus.

Evaluating your research question

As you read about your topic, you will sift through questions that occur to you. Eventually, you will arrive at one that interests you enough to pursue through still more research. This question must sustain you through the days of work that lie ahead, so you have a great deal to gain from making a good choice. How can you tell if your research question is a good one? Apply the criteria in the Critical Decisions below.

WWW

http://www.researchpaper.com/
Researchpaper.com

One of the best Internet resources for help with research papers. Check out the Idea Directory and Discussion Area for help getting started.

As you move from one discipline to another, the questions you pose as a researcher, your strategies for arguing, and

CRITICAL DECISIONS

Do You Have a Good Research Question?

As you reflect on what you think will be your main research question, consider the following:

- Have any of your sources answered the question completely and, in your view, comprehensively? If *no*, then your question is a good one—your research efforts will provide an answer that does not yet exist. If your sources *have* completely and comprehensively answered your research question, try to find some aspect of the question that is *not* yet answered, to ensure that your efforts are original.

- Does your question linger with you? Do you find yourself thinking about this question at odd times—on the way to the mailbox or the cafeteria? If *yes*, then stay with your question: It has engaged you. Frequently, it is in these "off" hours, when you are not formally working, that important insights occur. If *no*, then re-examine your question. Make sure it interests you sufficiently to continue letting it guide your research.

- Does investigating your question give you opportunities to make connections from one source to another—connections that the sources themselves don't seem to be making? If *yes*, then stay with your question: It is prompting efforts of *synthesis*—you are piecing elements of a puzzle together, which is what researchers do. If *no*, then re-examine your question. Make sure the question encourages you to forge connections.

your uses of evidence will change. Topics, too, will change. For instance, a paper on the incidence of alcoholism among student athletes would be suitable for a sociology course, but not for a literature or business course. A paper on the genetic factor in crack cocaine addiction would be suitable for a biology course, but not for a sociology course.

Be aware of strategies for writing arguments in different disciplines. See Chapter 8 for details on writing arguments in the humanities, the social sciences, and the sciences.

4c   Focusing your ideas

Many students keep track of their ideas in a research log. They write down their initial questions in this log and update it as often as possible. The log becomes a running record of all their inspirations, false starts, dead ends, second thoughts, breakthroughs, self-criticisms, and plans.

Many writers find freewriting or brainstorming useful at the outset of a project. See Chapter 2 for a description of these and other techniques for generating ideas.

Here are some initial ideas generated by a brief brainstorming session about computer-mediated communication, the topic on which you will see a student paper developed in this and succeeding chapters. Even though these ideas are in crude form, you can see a paper beginning to take shape here.

> communicating online—Internet has made online communication a part of our lives, people can keep in touch with friends and family online and also meet people through newsgroups and chat rooms, even start virtual romantic relationships. Possibilities are exciting, but are there any potential downsides to virtual communication? And what happens to FTF communication? Is the Internet going to fundamentally change the way we communicate?

Next, you may want to discuss your ideas with your instructor, who may help you sharpen your focus and direct you to sources of information. As you proceed with your research, keep your log updated. You will want to do this not just to preserve a record of your research (often valuable in itself), but also to allow you to return to initially discarded ideas, which, at a later stage in the paper, may assume new relevance or importance.

4d   Doing preliminary research

WWW
http://encyclopedia.com/

A free searchable site with more than 17,000 articles from the Columbia Concise Electronic Encyclopedia.

Effective search strategies often begin with the most general reference sources, like those listed in the box on the facing page. General sources are comprehensive in their coverage, but they review a subject in less depth than do specialized sources. So you'll want to read these sources early in your search. Their authors assume that readers have little or no prior knowledge of the subjects covered and of the specialized terminology used in the field. If they use specialized terms, they will define them.

WWW

http://www.s9.com/biography/

This searchable free online biographical dictionary includes more than 27,000 biographies.

The diagram on page 66 suggests an approach for conducting systematic preliminary research. Certainly, there are other avenues into the source materials you will discover. Whatever strategy you follow, your efforts at this stage will help you to focus your topic, restricting it to a manageable scope.

Using General Sources

- Use *encyclopedias* to get a broad overview of a particular subject.
- Use *biographical sources* for information about persons living or dead.
- Use *general dictionaries* to look up the meaning of particular terms.
- Use *guides to the literature* to locate sources in particular disciplines.
- Use *handbooks* to look up facts and lists of data for particular disciplines.
- Use *almanacs* to look up annually updated facts and lists of data.
- Use *yearbooks* to find updates of data already published in encyclopedias and other reference sources.
- Use *atlases* and *gazetteers* to find maps and other geographical data.
- Use *citation indexes* to trace references to a given published work.
- Use *book review indexes* to look up book reviews.
- Use *government publications* to look up recent and authoritative information in a given field.
- Use *bibliographic sources* to find books and articles on particular subjects.
- Use *electronic* searches to locate any of the information above.

A PRELIMINARY SEARCH STRATEGY

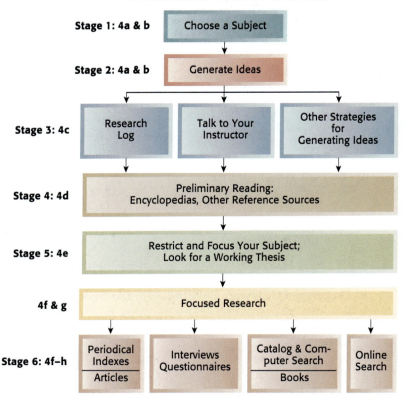

Stage 1: 4a & b — Choose a Subject

Stage 2: 4a & b — Generate Ideas

Stage 3: 4c — Research Log | Talk to Your Instructor | Other Strategies for Generating Ideas

Stage 4: 4d — Preliminary Reading: Encyclopedias, Other Reference Sources

Stage 5: 4e — Restrict and Focus Your Subject; Look for a Working Thesis

4f & g — Focused Research

Stage 6: 4f–h — Periodical Indexes / Articles | Interviews Questionnaires | Catalog & Computer Search / Books | Online Search

---

Devising a working thesis

1   Answering your research question

As you do your preliminary research, you begin to focus on a **research question.** Logan Kole, the student researcher whose paper is being developed in this chapter, asked: How will computer-mediated communication affect interpersonal relationships? As you continue to read about your subject, you should begin to develop your own ideas about it. Answer your research question, at least provisionally, and you will have a **working thesis** (see 2c): the clearest, most succinct statement thus far of your paper's main idea.

This thesis is *provisional.* It is subject to change as you come across new material and as your thinking about the subject develops. For now, however, this working thesis is the main idea that shapes your thinking and influences your subsequent research. By defining relevant areas and eliminating irrelevant ones, it will narrow the scope of your search for supporting evidence.

Let's examine four working theses. Here are four discipline areas and four narrowed topics:

> For a paper in the *humanities,* the topic is nineteenth-century literature about the potential excesses of science, for example, in *Frankenstein* and *Dr. Jekyll and Mr. Hyde.*
>
> For a paper in *business,* the issue is who owns the information contained in genetic algorithms.
>
> For a paper in the *social sciences,* the topic is social and ethical issues in technological intervention in human reproduction.
>
> For a paper in *science,* the topic is whether genetically altered food products are safe.

2   Taking a stand: The working thesis as a statement to be proven

So far, these are only *topics*—not theses. To develop a working thesis from each of these topics, you will need to make a *statement* about the topic (after surveying a good deal of source material). Here are four statements that could be used as working theses:

> *Humanities: Frankenstein* was perhaps the first in a long line of books to exploit people's nervousness about scientific progress.
>
> *Business:* Companies employing genetic engineers try to be diligent about patenting their discoveries.
>
> *Social Science:* Safeguards need to be strengthened to protect infertile couples who are promised "miracle cures" by doctors using expensive medical procedures.
>
> *Science:* Biotechnology promises to improve the *quantity* of food, but quantity will mean little unless we can guarantee the safety of genetically altered foods.

Note that the first two theses suggest an *informative* approach, whereas the second two suggest an *argumentative* approach. That is, in each of the first two cases, the thesis would be unlikely to generate strong emotions. In the latter two cases, however, the writer will argue one side of a fairly controversial issue. The stand you take in an argumentative thesis may depend on your ambition for the paper (see 2c-3), as well as on the materials available and the conditions that apply to your argument (see 8b-e). Use the questions in the Critical Decisions box on page 63 to test the soundness of your working thesis.

Once you have looked through a number of general sources and developed a working thesis, you have some basic knowledge about your subject and some tentative ideas about it. But there are limits to your knowledge because of the kinds of sources you have relied on so far. You need more specific information to pursue your thesis. When you return to the library to do more focused research, you will likely begin by using an online catalog.

CRITICAL DECISIONS

How Sound Is Your Working Thesis?

■ Is the subject of the thesis *narrow* enough in scope that you can write a detailed paper without being constrained by the page limits of the assignment?

■ Does the thesis communicate a relationship you want to clarify about your subject, based on your understanding of the information you have gathered?

■ Does the thesis clearly suggest the patterns of development you will be pursuing in your paper?

■ Does the thesis clearly communicate your ambitions for the paper?

1   Finding print materials in libraries

The following overview of available sources will help you focus on the

WWW

http://www.ipl.org/

The Internet Public Library is the first public library of the Internet.

ones that best address your working thesis. Periodical indexes are often preferable to the library's main catalog as a first step in conducting focused research.

General periodical indexes: Magazines

Periodicals are magazines and newspapers published at regular intervals—quarterly, monthly, daily. Periodical articles often contain information available from no other source and are generally more up-to-date than books published during the same period. You are probably familiar with the *Readers'*

Guide to Periodical Literature as a means of locating magazine articles in sources such as *Time, Newsweek,* and *The New Republic.* In addition, there are numerous other periodical reference guides to which a librarian can refer you.

These days, you will typically find periodical indexes computerized in your library's reference area. See section 4g for more information on the variety of electronic sources available. Here is a *Readers' Guide* entry for "Internet—social use," which provides a cross-reference to the further listing, "online dating."

INTERNET—*cont.* ———————————————————— Main heading

Subheading ——————————————— **Social use**

               See also

Related main ——————⌐ Foreign Affair (Web site)
headings   └ Online dating

      E-mail and mom. Touré. por *Essence* v29 no11 p66 Mr 1999

      Geeks [J. Dailey and E. Twilegar] J. Katz. il pors *Rolling Stone*   Includes
          no 811 p 48-50+ Ap 29 1999   picture

Title of   Home sweet virtual home. N. Gross. il *Business Week* no3649
periodical ——————   p 200+ O 4 1999

      Logging on. il *Fortune* special issue p29-30 Wint 2000

      The Net is a family affair. D. Brady. il map *Business Week*
          no3659 p EB80-EB82+ D 13 1999

      Turkish delight [M. Cagri] il por *People Weekly* v52 no21 p84 —— Volume, pages,
          N 29 1999   date of issue

      ONLINE DATING

      For a good man, click here [dating] S. Schlosberg. il *Health*
          (*San Francisco, Calif.: 1992*) v13 no7 p78+ S 1999

      They've got love [online dating leads to marriage] il *People*   Subject of
          Weekly v51 no6 p46-51 F 15 1999   article, if not

      Valley of the doll-less [Internet dating thrives in Silicon Valley]   clear from title

Author —————— B. Stone. il *Newsweek* v134 no7 p59 Ag 16 1999

      What do guys think about meeting girls over the Internet? il
          'Teen v43 no2 p36 F 1999

General periodical indexes: Newspapers

Most libraries have back issues of important newspapers on microfilm. The *New York Times Index* may be used to retrieve articles in the *Times* as far back as 1913. There are also indexes for the *San Francisco Chronicle*, the *Los Angeles Times,* and the *Wall Street Journal* (an important source of business news). The *Newspaper Index* lists articles from the *Chicago Tribune,* the *New Orleans Times-Picayune,* the *Los Angeles Times,* and the *Washington Post.*

The library catalog

Almost certainly, your library's catalog has been converted to electronic form, allowing you to search for items far more quickly than you could when they were filed on cards. You can search the catalog by *author,* by *title,* or by *subject.* Many library catalog terminals also allow access to magazine and newspaper databases such as MAGS and NEWS. In some cases, you can view (or print out) abstracts or even complete texts of particular items that you locate in such indexes. Electronic databases generally don't include information more than ten years old. You would still have to rely largely on print indexes for information about—for example—the Watergate scandal of the 1970s.

Shown below is an online catalog screen for *Life on the Screen: Identity in the Age of the Internet* by Sherry Turkle.

Computer display

Title:	Life on the screen: identity in the age of the Internet / Sherry Turkle.
Author:	Turkle, Sherry
Published:	New York: Simon & Schuster, 1997, c 1995.
Description:	347 p.; 25 cm.
Edition:	First Touchstone Edition, 1997.
Notes:	"A Touchstone Book"
	Includes bibliographical references (p. [271]-320) and index.
Subject:	Computers and civilization.
	Computer networks–Psychological aspects.
ISBN:	0684833484
DBCN:	AGR-4402

LOCATION	CALL NO.	STATUS
South Florida CC/MAIN/CIR	QA76.9.C66 T87 1997 (book)c.1	Available

The paper catalog card would include the same information, organized a bit differently.

4g Doing focused research: CD-ROM sources

Since a CD can store several years' worth of indexes, a CD search takes less time and effort than a search through several bound volumes. Many general-reference print materials, such as *The Oxford English Dictionary* and various encyclopedias, are currently available on CD-ROM—a format that allows users to make rapid cross-references and searches.

One important CD index is InfoTrac, which provides access to articles in over 1,000 business, technological, and general-interest periodicals, as well as the *New York Times* and the *Wall Street Journal.* Your reference librarian will have a listing of the CD-ROMs available at your library.

COMPUTER TIPS

The Library without Books

More and more, libraries are beginning to resemble computer labs rather than book repositories. Many of the indexes you may be used to consulting such as the *Readers' Guide to Periodical Literature* and many others, are now available electronically through your library's online subscription, the Internet, or CD-ROM. Often these electronic resources do more than find titles and brief descriptions of articles and other sources of information; they also allow you to retrieve the full text of the article. Ask your reference librarian for a listing of these electronic resources, and for instructions on how to access them and print out articles.

4h   Doing focused research: Online sources

As you are probably aware, the Internet holds a universe of searchable information that can enrich your research papers.

However, Internet-based research is a *supplement* to, and does not replace, print-based research. Only a fraction of the world's printed resources are available electronically. Unlike print libraries, the Internet is a decentralized, often chaotic environment in which to work. The search strategies that you use in libraries to locate sources must be adapted when you begin searching online. Finally, unlike the books and journal articles you find in your college library, resources on the Internet are not necessarily edited for fairness or accuracy—and you must take special care before using online sources in your papers.

The following general process of finding online resources will be familiar to you if you have searched for information in print-based libraries:

1. Begin by investigating broad topics.
2. Scan numerous sites, some of which will strike you as immediately promising.
3. Browse these sites and pursue links to other, related sites.
4. Narrow your search and locate Web pages on your specific topic.
5. Along the way, collect pertinent material—in this case not by photocopying articles or checking books out from the library, but by downloading computer files or taking notes electronically.

> ### Commercial and Professional Information Services
>
> Libraries often subscribe to professional and commercial information services. One of the largest of these is DIALOG, which provides access to more than 300 million items in over 400 separate databases in the humanities, the social sciences, the natural sciences, and business. Specialized databases include NEXIS and LEXIS, used for locating news and legal or government publications; PsycINFO, which references items in psychological journals; ERIC, which references educational journals; and Arts and Humanities Search. An especially useful commercial service is WILSONLINE, which provides electronic access to the printed indexes published by H. W. Wilson Co., including *Readers' Guide to Periodical Literature, Education Index,* and *Social Science Index.* If your school subscribes to these services, you will find them on a computer in your library's reference area.

1 What's on the Internet?

The Internet provides researchers with both *communication* and *information* tools that allow you to find and retrieve information stored on computers nearly anywhere in the world. A description of four of these tools follows.

E-mail

Definition E-mail, or electronic mail, is a communication tool. If you've used the Internet at all, it has probably been with e-mail—sending and receiving messages to and from friends and family. But e-mail can benefit you as a researcher as well. More and more authorities (university and private researchers, journalists, government officials) have and regularly use e-mail. Many (not all, of course) would welcome an inquiry from a student and would respond positively for a request for an interview, or a request to see the current draft of a new project or an old, unpublished conference paper.

WWW
http://www.fau.edu/netiquette/
netiquette.html

The Netiquette Home Page at Florida Atlantic University, from Arlene H. Rinaldi, who insists she's not Miss Manners of the Internet.

Reliability Judge the reliability of an e-mail source as you would that of any person you've interviewed. When referring to this source in your paper, provide some background context. Who is this person? What is his or her area of expertise? Why is he or she qualified to speak on your topic?

Access How do you find e-mail addresses of people with whom you would like to correspond?

- Simply ask them. Keep a list of e-mail addresses for people you know.
- Save one or two messages from people who contribute to newsgroups and discussion lists (see description below), and you will have their addresses.
- Use an Internet e-mail directory such as Bigfoot (http://www.bigfoot.com) or Whowhere (http://www.whowhere.com)

Usenet Discussion Groups or "Newsgroups"

Definition   A Discussion Group is a communication tool. The easiest way to visualize a newsgroup is to think of a standard cork bulletin board hanging on a wall. Anyone can walk by and tack up a message, and anyone else can come by and read the message, respond to it, or put up a new message. Newsgroups on the Internet are electronic versions of that cork bulletin board. Anyone with an Internet account can use a newsreader to follow a continuing discussion, read the current messages, and post a reply or a new message. Newsgroups can provide an excellent forum for trying out your ideas on others before you commit to these ideas in your paper.

Reliability   Because they are a radically democratic forum in which everyone—the unknowing and the expert—can offer an opinion, newsgroups vary in reliability. Use material gathered from this resource with caution. If you want to refer to a newsgroup posting in a paper, first try to confirm from other sources the reliability of that information. You may also want to interview the person who posted the message by e-mail.

Access   If your school subscribes to a newsfeed, a central computer where all the messages are stored and fed to other providers, you will have access to a newsreader and will be able to choose which newsgroups to follow (remember, there are well over 10,000).

You can also search Usenet for postings on any topic by accessing DejaNews on the World Wide Web (http://www.dejanews.com/). Newsgroup addresses read hierarchically, in a series of units separated by dots. For example, the newsgroup address "rec.music.bluenote.blue" is read as follows:

Its type is "recreation."
Its subtype is "music."
Its particular category is "bluenote."
Its topic is "blue."

WWW

http://tile.net/listserv/

To find listservs on your chosen topics, check out this searchable listing of e-mail discussion groups.

That is, "rec.music.bluenote.blue" is a discussion group about blues music. When you join in on the conversation of a newsgroup, you will be able to read and reply to messages, just as you can with e-mail. However, keep in mind that what you write is public.

Discussion lists or "listservs"

Definition Academic discussion lists are similar to newsgroups, with one significant difference: you must actively subscribe to the list, and then you receive the messages directly as individual e-mail messages. The mailing of the discussions is essentially managed by automated computer programs that receive all incoming messages and immediately forward them to everyone who subscribes to the list; one of the most common of these automated programs is called "Listserv."

Reliability Lists usually stick to their stated topics; although theoretically anyone can subscribe to any discussion list, usually contributors are serious about their commitment to the topic. They tend to be knowledgeable—though, as with any source, you will want to verify information before citing it as credible. The mere appearance of information on a discussion list does not ensure its reliability.

Access To find a listing of currently active academic listservs, use your WWW browser to access the URL http://www.liszt.com. If you find a list to which you would like to subscribe, address an e-mail message *to the listserv* (the machine that manages the list), not to the list itself. The machine will ignore the "subject" line of the e-mail box and read only the message, which must contain the following information:

- Type the word "subscribe". Don't use the quotation marks. Simply type the word as the first word in an e-mail message.
- Next, type the name of the list to which you want to subscribe.
- Finally, type your first name, followed by your last name.

COMPUTER TIPS

Searching versus Browsing

There are two methods of finding information on the Internet: searching and browsing. Searching involves actively looking for particular information that you have described using keywords. This is most useful when you know what you're looking for. Browsing involves looking at Web sites that have been arranged into categories, just to see what is there. It is most useful when you have a general topic to explore but don't yet know exactly what information you're looking for.

The message must contain absolutely nothing else. (Added words can confuse the machine.) For example, if your name were Mary Rose, you would send the basic message "subscribe deos-1 Mary Rose" (again, no quotation marks) to the listserv's address to subscribe to the Distance Education list. After you have subscribed, you will receive further instructions about using the list and posting to it.

World Wide Web

Definition   Currently the most popular information tool for browsing and searching the Internet is the World Wide Web. Its popularity derives both from its hypertext interface (clicking on the screen brings you to a new page of information) and its ability to display color and graphics. Here are some key terms worth knowing:

- *Webservers:* specially configured computers, worldwide, on which information for the WWW is stored.
- *Web page or home page* (or simply page): individual documents on the WWW.
- *Web site or site:* a collection of pages.
- *URL:* the acronym (for Uniform Resource Locator) that designates particular characters used to locate a Web site. The URL is a Web site's "http://" address.
- *Hypertext:* links from information on one Web page to related information on another Web page—perhaps located on another Web server in a different school, country, or continent. Hypertext links are usually underlined in blue. If you see something on a Web page that you'd like to explore further and it's underlined in blue, click your mouse or press the appropriate key—and you're there.
- *Browsing:* linking from one Web document to another, following your interests. Software such as Netscape or Microsoft Explorer are used as browsing tools, or "browsers."
- *Downloading:* Some links on a Web page may not be hypertext links but, rather, links that prompt you to download a file—that is, to transfer a file from the Web server (the machine on which the Web page resides) to your computer. Click on the link and the browser will display a message box asking if you would like to save the file.
- *Search engines.* The Web has many different search engines, but all work on the keyword search principle. You type a word or phrase into the search engine's subject box and the engine scans the Internet for Web pages that have your word(s) listed as a keyword by the creator of the page. Some engines search entire Web pages for occurrences of your word(s). Different engines follow various protocols and specialize in finding particular types of information on the Web. So it is best,

when searching for information, to conduct several searches using different engines. The next section, 4h-2, offers extensive guidance on using Internet search engines to find what you want online.

Reliability   The quality and reliability of information you find on the Web will vary considerably. Individuals, commercial operations, and organizations create their own Web sites. So, while you may find research reports and government documents and online medical journals, you may also find unsubstantiated opinion, self-serving advertisements, and propaganda. Judge your materials carefully—and see section 4h-3 for extensive guidance on evaluating Web-based sources.

Access   Most likely, you will gain access to the Web through a browser such as Netscape Navigator or Microsoft Internet Explorer. You will move from document to document on the Web by following hypertext links. If the trail you follow begins to seem fruitless, you can back out of it by clicking the mouse on the "back" key (the left-pointing arrow near the top of the screen) in your browser. With enough backward steps like this, eventually you'll return to where you entered, for a fresh start.

2   Constructing effective Internet searches[1]

The most frustrating aspect of the Internet for those seeking information is the difficulty of locating the information they're looking for. Typically, people will type in a query to one of the search services and then find themselves deluged with possible sites. As an online researcher, *you* must provide the judgment that search engines lack. The way you express this judgment is to construct a precise query—the single most important key to a successful search. Good queries yield good results; poor queries yield poor results. This section will help you to devise good, focused search queries.

Choose appropriate search tools

When conducting online searches, approach your task not as a single search but as a *series of related* searches—each focusing on *different* sources of information. Web search tools are classified into two types: subject directories and search engines.

---

[1] Section 4h-2 is based on our adaptations of two excellent sources on conducting Internet searches: Keith Gresham's "Surfing with a Purpose" from the September/October 1998 issue of *Educom Review* and "Guide to Effective Searching of the Internet," a tutorial prepared by Michael Bergman of The Web Tools Company at www.theWebtools.com. Suggestions for Web links were provided by Prentiss Riddle, Web Master for Rice University. Visit and launch searches from the Rice University Internet Page at www.riceinfo.rice.edu/Internet to get updated advice on the best Internet search tools as they become available.

A Process for Conducting Research on the Internet

We recommend the search process devised by instruction librarian Keith Gresham (University of Colorado at Boulder). The section that follows this summary box is organized around Gresham's four-step process:

1. **Determine the type of information you need; choose appropriate search tools.** Do you need news? Government reports? Industry statistics? Journal articles? Magazines? Choose carefully among general search engines, specialty search engines, and subject directories.
2. **Create a list of search terms.** Search terms are those specific words or phrases that best describe the major concepts of your topic.
3. **Construct a search statement and conduct your search.** Depending on the search tool you are using, search by individual key words, by exact phrases, or by Boolean search expressions.
4. **Evaluate search results and revise the query (if needed).** Even carefully constructed searches retrieve irrelevant results or result lists with thousands of hits. If you don't locate useful information within the first fifteen retrieved sites, revise the query. Construct new search statements using different combinations of search words or phrases.

Subject directories

Directories classify Web pages into types, according to a subject breakdown. For example, *Yahoo*, the most well-known directory, classifies Web sites into categories such as Arts and Humanities, Business and Economy, Education, and Science. Each category is divided into subcategories: for example, Science includes sites on Astronomy, Biology, and Oceanography. Oceanography is further subdivided into sites such as Coral Reefs, Marine Biology, and Meteorology. The subdividing continues (for example, "seagrasses" is a subdivision of Marine Biology) until there are no more subclassifications, at which point Yahoo provides hyperlinks to one or more relevant sites. Here are the URLs for several popular directories:

Argus Clearinghouse	http://www.clearinghouse.net
Internet Public Library	http://ipl.sils.umich.edu/index.text.html
LookSmart	http://looksmart.com/
About.com	http://www.about.com/

WWW Virtual Library	http://conbio.rice.edu/vl/database/ (for browsing)
	http://www.vlib.org/ (for general subject directory)
Yahoo	http://www.yahoo.com/

COMPUTER TIPS

Carriage Returns, Linefeeds, and Formatting Problems

Each major type of computer system used in schools, businesses, and on the Internet has a different method for breaking lines on the screen and for printing. As a result, what looks like perfectly formed text on one machine may wind up looking like a series of short, choppy little lines or perhaps like a long line trailing off the screen. When you retrieve text from the Internet, be prepared for such short or long lines, added spaces, and other strange formatting problems. Take time to reformat as you work, using your delete function and format menu.

Search engines

Search engines index words and terms in Web pages and feature "spiders" or "robots" to retrieve documents containing these terms. The number of keywords queried by search engines is virtually unlimited, as opposed to the finite number of classifications used by directories (Yahoo has about 1,400). If a Web page's topic doesn't easily fall into one of the pre-established classifications, it may not be accessible through the directory. But the relatively smaller number of sites located through a directory may be an advantage in researching topics that are easily classifiable by the directory.

Many search services are hybrids: Yahoo allows users to search by keywords, and Excite has some features associated with directories. Here are URLs for some of the most highly used general search engines.

General search engines

AltaVista	http://www.altavista.digital.com/
Excite	http://www.excite.com/
Hotbot	http://www.hotbot.com/
Infoseek	http://www.infoseek.com/

Lycos	http://lycos.com/
Northern Light	http://www.nlsearch.com/
WebCrawler	http://Webcrawler.com/WebCrawler/ WebQuery.html

As a rule of thumb, remember: Use *several* search services—a variety of search engines and subject directories—in any given search to assure that you don't miss important sites and sources of information.

Depending on your need for specific types of information, you may want to use more specialized search engines, as follows.

Searching to access multiple WWW indexes

Dogpile	http://www.dogpile.com/
MetaCrawler	http://www.metacrawler.com/
MetaFind	http://metafind.com/
Savvy Search	http://www.cs.colostate.edu/~dreiling/ smartform.html

Searching for news

WWW

http://www.askjeeves.com/

This unique meta-search engine allows you to enter your query in plain English in the form of a question.

When you are searching a topic of current interest in the news, consider using search engines that query news sources, exclusively. The following tools will help you to search a variety of news sources.

CNN	http://www.cnn.com/
Ecola Newsstand	http://www.ecola.com/
NewsBot	http://www.newsbot.com/
NewsIndex	http://www.newsindex.com/
TotalNews	http://totalnews.com/

And you may want to register at the *New York Times* site http://www.nytimes.com/ for free access to the last year's *Times* online.

Searching mailing lists and Usenet news groups

| Browse Usenet Archive | http://www.reference.com/cgi-bin/ pn/go?choice=browse_newsgroups |

Browse Usenet Groups with FeedMe	http://www.feedme.org/
DejaNews	http://www.dejanews.com/
Liszt Directory of E-Mail Discussion Groups	http://www.liszt.com/
Newsgroups Info Center	http://sunsite.unc.edu/usenet-i/search.html
Scholarly and Professional E-Conferences	http://n2h2.com/KOVACS/Sindex.html
WWW forums	http://www.forumone.com/

Searching for people

Anywho Reverse Telephone Search	http://www.anywho.com/telq.html
Bigfoot	http://www.bigfoot.com/
Finger (by Internet Site)	http://www.cs.indiana.edu/finger/gateway
Personal Web Pages	http://www.utexas.edu/world/personal/
Student Home Pages	http://www.student.net/homepages
Switchboard	http://www.switchboard.com/bin/cgiqa.dll
WhoWhere?	http://www.whowhere.lycos.com/
Yahoo! People Search	http://people.yahoo.com/

Searching for discussion lists

If you are searching a topic that is likely to generate an ongoing Internet discussion, use one of these search engines to locate the discussion.

DejaNews	http://www.dejanews.com
ForumOne	http://www.forumone.com

The Internet Domain Name System

The Domain Name System allows for each computer on the Internet to have its own address. Internet addresses are composed of units separated by the symbol "." (pronounced "dot"). The Internet address "www.gsfc.nasa.gov" is read as follows:

- The abbreviation "gov" means this Internet site is located at a government agency;
- The particular agency is "nasa";
- The particular computer where the Internet service resides is named "gsfc"; and
- The service provided is particular to the World Wide Web ("www").

The major domain names are as follows:

com—companies and commercial sites
edu—educational institutions
gov—government organizations
mil—military organizations
net—Internet service providers and users
org—nonprofit institutions

Create a list of search terms.

This section will help you to select keywords, which you can then combine in various ways into a search statement (step 3, below). We'll dramatize the process of formulating queries by presenting a scenario. Jan, an office worker, notices that the fingers of her right hand feel strained when she bends them and that her wrist is stiff. She decides to do some investigating on the Web.

WWW
http://www.monash.com/spidap.html

Detailed explanations of how search engines work and how to get the most out of them.

An Index to Keywords

To select keywords

1. Ask the five Ws and generate a list.
2. Strip out prepositions, articles, etc.
3. Classify the words remaining: nouns, actions, modifiers.
4. Focus on a noun: a person, place, or thing.
5. Narrow the search with a modifier to create a phrase.
6. Find synonyms.
7. Find the right level of generality.

Ask the five Ws.

A good way to begin formulating an accurate query is to jot down the *who, what, where, when, how,* and *why.* Considering her mystery ailment, Jan jots down the following:

- ■ Who/What?—sore fingers, stiff wrist, injury
- ■ Where?—workplace, on-the-job pain
- ■ When?—during typing
- ■ How?—when I bend, painful fingers and wrist
- ■ Why?—related to work at a keyboard? typing? safety?

Strip out prepositions, articles, and so on.

The next step is to break down the query by identifying key words. Note that common words such as *and, about, the, of, an, in, as, if, not, is,* and *it* are ignored by search engines since they appear so frequently in connection with any subject. Eliminating such words leaves

sore	workplace	painful
fingers	job	keyboard
stiff	pain	safety
wrist	typing	
injury	bend	

Classify words.

Now let's further classify these terms by arranging them into three categories: *nouns (persons/places/things), actions,* and *modifiers.*

PERSON/PLACE/THING		ACTIONS	MODIFIERS
fingers	job	typing	stiff
wrist	pain	bend	sore
workplace	keyboard		painful
injuries	safety		

Focus on a noun: a person, place, or thing.

The most important terms in your query should be *objects*—that is, tangible "things." The thing (or person or place) you want to learn more about becomes the center of your search: your subject.

In the example search, there are eight potentially useful keywords:

fingers, wrist, workplace, job, pain, injuries, keyboard, safety

Selecting a single keyword will not (in most cases) be sufficient for getting the results you want. You need to qualify your search term with a modifier.

Narrow the search with a modifier to create a phrase.

When you qualify your search terms by combining them in meaningful ways, Internet searches become more useful. For instance, narrowing the keyword "wrist" by converting it to a modifier that qualifies the noun "pain" yields the new search term "wrist pain." Focusing the keywords in these ways had impressive results:

HotBot search on "wrist": 27,680

HotBot search on "wrist pain": 9,834

Narrowing a search by using a modifier can help in two ways:

1. The narrowed search may directly yield the information you want.
2. The narrowed search may yield information that enables you to focus the search still further, bringing you that much closer to the information you want.

To illustrate: the first returned hit on the Hotbot search of "wrist pain" listed a Web site for a product that relieved wrist pain—particularly "carpal tunnel syndrome" and "repetitive stress injuries." As it turned out for Jan, who was doing research on her wrist ailment, she suffered from what she suspected was carpal tunnel syndrome. A search on that term brought her to a wealth of pertinent information.

Using quotation marks You may want to make sure that a search engine regards the words you have entered as an exact phrase or text string, rather than as individual words. You can instruct a search engine to treat words as an exact phrase by enclosing the words within quotation marks. Thus, you would type "workplace injuries" into the query box. (Note that not all search engines recognize quotation marks as a means of defining phrases.)

Find synonyms.

Spend a few moments thinking of synonyms for your keywords. If you're having trouble thinking of synonyms, use a thesaurus (available on most word processors—check under "tools," where you'll also find spell checkers). Synonyms allow a search engine a greater chance to identify sources related to your query. In constructing a search relating to her stiff fingers and wrist, Jan settled on the synonym "occupation" and "occupational" for "job" and "work." She settled on the synonym "accident" for "injury"— not an exact synonym but an approximation she thought might yield more results.

Find the right level of generality.

One key to effective searching on the Internet is to search at the level of generality that will yield useful results. Recall our earlier discussion of directories, when we saw how Yahoo subdivides one of the disciplinary areas of science as follows:

Science
    oceanography
        marine biology
            seagrasses

If you are using a keyword or phrase and the search returns too many or too few documents, shift your level of generality up or down, accordingly. When you are overwhelmed with hits in the tens of thousands, shift the level of generality *down* by experimenting with different modifiers that will limit the keyword. When you have the opposite problem—*no* hits—broaden the search term.

Construct the search statement and conduct your search.

Depending on the search engine you use, you can refine your key words and phrases further in an effort to improve your search results. Search engines are increasingly providing a "refine" function—sometimes called "advanced" search tools or "power" searches—that refine function allows you to narrow searches by date, type of publication, and type of Web site. For instance, you might instruct the engine to search only organizations, government, or military sites. Refining your searches is easy: locate the advanced feature set and fill in (or, in some cases, click to check) a box.

Beyond using these "refine" functions, you can refine your queries in two additional ways: Use "wildcards" on word stems and use Boolean connectors between keyword terms.

Use "wildcards" on word stems.

You want to be able to select relevant documents containing *work,* but you also want to select documents containing *workplace.* To avoid having to use two similar keywords for the same concept (since it's best to limit the number of keyword terms to about three), you can "truncate" (cut off) the keyword to its stem—in this case *work.* Adding an asterisk to the stem produces *work**. Your search engine can now look for documents containing variants of the keyword—including variant spellings.

Remember this important tip for effective Internet searching: Once you have settled on a topic, search the Internet *multiple* times, using different search tools. Here are two Web sites on carpal tunnel syndrome, found in different searches using different search tools:

A general search of the Web using the AltaVista search engine located a site on carpal tunnel syndrome prepared by the American Academy of Family

Physicians. Besides defining the condition, this page has an illustration showing the ligament that causes the condition.

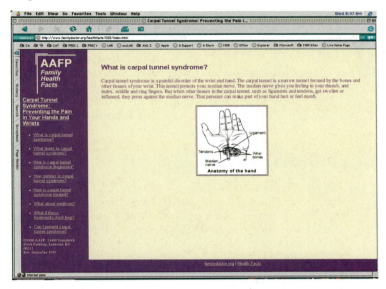

A second search found the Carpal Tunnel Syndrome home page, a vast resource of Web links on defining, preventing, discussing, and treating the disorder.

Use Boolean connectors between keyword terms.

One of the most effective ways to narrow your search is to use Boolean connectors between keywords. (The name comes from George Boole, a nineteenth-century mathematician and logician, who developed

WWW
http://www.exo.net/uce/
uce6_boolean.html

A basic introduction to Boolean logic.

Boolean algebra.) Such terms are called *operators*, and the way they are used to connect keywords is called *syntax*. The main Boolean operators are listed in the following box.

Using Boolean Logic

- **AND**   Terms on both sides of this operator must be present somewhere in the document to be scored as a result. **AND** may be used more than once in a query to narrow a search: thus, using "**London AND Big Ben AND Buckingham Palace AND Trafalgar**" would yield only documents containing all four terms.

- **OR**   Terms on EITHER side of this operator are sufficient to be scored as a result. **OR** means that the document may contain either term, but not necessarily both. In most cases, then, **OR** will yield too many results. It is mainly useful at the introductory stages of a search.

- **AND NOT**   Documents containing the term that occurs AFTER this operator are rejected from the results set. (For instance, you might search on "Queen Elizabeth AND NOT ship.") **AND NOT** is a means of weeding out irrelevant documents. *Note:* Only one instance of an unwanted term is sufficient to eliminate a document from consideration.

- **NEAR**   Similar to AND, only both terms have to occur within a specified word distance from one another to be scored as a result. You might search on "Diana NEAR Wales" or "Diana NEAR Charles."

- **BEFORE**   Similar to NEAR, only the first (left-hand) term before this operator has to occur within a specified word distance *before* the term on the right side of this operator in order for the source document to be scored as a result.

- **AFTER**   Similar to NEAR, only the first (left-hand) term before this operator has to occur within a specified word distance *after* the term on the right side of this operator in order for the source document to be scored as a result.

Using the keywords and phrases you have generated and, given the capabilities of the search engines you are using, conduct your searches. Notice the plural form of the term. The consistent message of this section that you approach your task of finding information on the Internet not as a single search but as a series of related searches—with each focusing on *different* sources of information, using different search tools.

3   Evaluating Internet sources

How do you assess the accuracy, reliability, and overall quality of information you find on the Web? In general, the same criteria that apply to print information (see 1f) also apply to Web-based information. Most major print journals, magazines, and newspapers have Web sites that post current and archived articles, and evaluating articles on these sites presents the same challenges as evaluating a printed article. However, a good deal of information on the Internet presents an additional set of challenges for evaluation primarily because anyone can "publish" on the Web.

Writers usually can't get an article into print unless a publisher reviews the piece to check, or at least to question, what is written in order to avoid responsibility for obvious misstatements of fact, inflammatory or potentially libelous statements, or just plain bad writing. No such barriers exist on the Internet. Anyone with an ax to grind, anyone who imagines his or her words are worth broadcasting to the world, can do so with relatively little effort and expense, and with no outside review.

Moreover, self-published Internet authors may post their sites anonymously. Academic research is premised on the reader's ability to check facts and verify methods. Thus, when you encounter anonymously published Web sites, you face the task not only of determining the accuracy and fairness of the material, but also of inferring clues about the author's credibility. Students who refer to such sites in their research run the risk of using sources that are not valid. You should, therefore, avoid quoting from anonymously published sites unless you are instructed to view them as part of your coursework.

Evaluating Web pages

You will find a great deal of value on the Web. But as a researcher you should approach Web-based sources with caution—both for the above-mentioned reasons and because of the distinctive nature of electronic information on the Internet: Web search engines frequently retrieve irrelevant or questionable pages. Subsidiary pages may also be retrieved out of context, that is, apart from their "home" pages. Web pages that appear to be informational may actually be "infomercials" for products or services. Web pages may not be regularly updated, and may become outdated. Page hyperlinks may be outdated or inactive. Hyperlinks in otherwise reliable

Web pages may lead to pages of doubtful reliability or accuracy at other sites. Web pages are inherently unstable; they can change or even disappear without warning. And outdated browser software, or software without necessary "add-ons" or "plug-ins," may not allow you to view certain Web pages accurately.

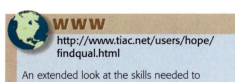

www

http://www.tiac.net/users/hope/findqual.html

An extended look at the skills needed to evaluate Internet information critically.

A highly useful approach to evaluating information on the Web has been provided by Jan Alexander and Marsha Tate, reference librarians at the Wolfgram Memorial Library at Widener University. Alexander and Tate categorize Web pages into five major types. Following their explanation of these types, you will find questions to pose of each.

■ **Advocacy Web Page:** "one sponsored by an organization attempting to influence public opinion (that is, one trying to sell ideas). The URL address of the page frequently ends in .org (organization)."[2] *Examples:* National Abortion and Reproductive Rights Action League (www.naral.org), The National Right to Life Committee (www.nrlc.org).

– What is the site advocating? Is the advocacy reasonable in tone?

– What does the organization have to gain through its advocacy?

– How does the organization characterize its opponents?

■ **Business/Marketing Web Page:** "one sponsored by a commercial enterprise (usually it is a page trying to promote or sell products). The URL address of the page frequently ends in .com (commercial)." *Examples:* Adobe Systems, Inc. (www.adobe.com), Coca Cola Co. (www.cocacola.com).

– Is advertising clearly differentiated from content?

– How does the commercial sponsor profit from the content on the site?

– Is the validity of the information compromised by commerce?

■ **News Web Page:** "one whose primary purpose is to provide extremely current information. The URL address of the page usually ends in .com (commercial)." *Examples: USA Today* (www.usatoday.com), *Washington Post* (www.washingtonpost.com).

---

[2] This section is taken in large part from the Web site "Evaluating Web Resources" (http://www2.widener.edu/Wolfgram-Memorial-Library/webeval.htm, copyright 1996–1999) which complements the book *Web Wisdom: How to Evaluate and Create Information Quality on the Web* (1999) by Janet Alexander and Marsha Ann Tate.

- Could you verify the news on the site from a print source?
- Are sources of information clearly listed so that you can verify them?
- How current is the page? When was it last revised?
- Are editorial opinions clearly distinguished from news items?

■ **Informational Web Page:** "one whose purpose is to provide factual information. The URL address frequently ends in .edu or .gov, as many of these pages are sponsored by educational institutions or government agencies." *Examples:* U.S. Census Bureau (www.census.gov/), dictionaries (work.ucsd.edu:5141/cgi-bin/http_Webster).

- How current is the information? When was it last revised?
- Can you verify the information?
- How reputable are the sources of information?

■ **Personal Web Page:** "one published by an individual who may or may not be affiliated with a larger institution. Although the URL address of the page may have a variety of endings (e.g., .com, .edu, etc.) a tilde (~) is frequently embedded somewhere in the URL."

- Does the individual have any obvious biases?
- Is the site free of obvious errors in grammar, punctuation, and usage?
- On the basis of what experience does the individual publish on the Web?

The first step in evaluating a Web site is to understand its type, and to then pose appropriate questions—some of which have been suggested above. You will find a more complete set of questions in Chapter 1, which is devoted to critical thinking.

Evaluating Usenet postings

Usenet postings present the greatest challenge to your critical evaluation skills because of the amount of "noise" you have to filter through to get information. Usually, Usenet posters are just average people expressing their opinions—informed, misinformed; rational, biased; thoughtful, off-the-cuff. Occasionally there will be a posting by experts in a particular field who have substantial information to offer, but this is not common. Ultimately, recognizing misleading, inaccurate, or useless postings is a matter of skill, experience, and taste, but here are some guidelines that may help as you gain experience in the Usenet world:

1. Consider your first impulse if the posting you're reading appears to contradict what you believe, what you've seen and heard firsthand, or what most other posters in the group are saying. Start with your gut feeling.

2. What are the motivations, biases, and outright prejudices of the poster?
3. This is the hardest part: If you agree with the poster, or most other authorities you've read appear to agree, put yourself in the position of someone who disagrees with you. How would that person react to this particular posting?
4. Try to verify with a second source any information you get from Usenet. How much of what a poster writes is verifiable fact, how much is well-considered opinion, and how much is just mindless ranting and raving?
5. Does the poster use inflammatory or blatantly prejudiced language?
6. Who is the poster? What do you know about him or her? A poster who signs herself as an employee of the Environmental Protection Agency has at least a head start on authority and believability compared with one who signs himself as a member of "Free Americans to Eliminate Government."

4 URLs for researchers

Below is a list of URLs for sites that are of special interest to writers and researchers in all disciplines. Given the changing nature of the Internet, by the time this book is printed, some of these sites may either have changed or vanished. Visit each site before entering it in your bookmark list.

General research sites

Berkeley Digital Library	http://sunsite.berkeley.edu/
The Best Information on the Net (Librarians of St. Ambrose University)	http://www.sau.edu/CWIS/Internet/Wild/index.htm
Blue Web'n Online ("a library of Blue Ribbon learning sites on the Web")	http://www.kn.pacbell.com/wired/bluewebn/#table
Complete Reference to Usenet Newsgroups	http://www.tile.net/tile/news/index.html
Ecola Newstand	http://www.ecola.com
ERIC Clearinghouse on Information and Technology	http://ericir.syr.edu
The Internet Public Library	http://www.ipl.org/
Internet Subject Guides (University of Alberta)	http://www.ualberta.ca/~slis/guides/guides.html

Libweb: Library Servers via WWW	http://sunsite.Berkeley.EDU/Libweb/
Listserv Lists Search	http://tile.net/listserv/
Needle in a CyberStack: The InfoFinder	http://home.revealed.net/~albee/index.html
Study Web (70,000 Research Quality Web sites, all disciplines)	http://www.studyweb.com/
Supreme Court Decisions	http://www.law.cornell.edu/supct/
The Universal Library (Carnegie Mellon University)	http://www.ul.cs.cmu.edu/first.htm
University of California InfoMine	http://lib-www.ucr.edu/
Vincent Voice Library (Michigan State University)	http://web.msu.edu/vincent/
WebGems: A Guide to Substantive Web Resources (all disciplines)	http://www.fpsol.com/gems/webgems.html
Webliography (Louisiana State University)	http://www.lib.lsu.edu/hum/lit.html
WWWVirtual Library (All disciplines)	http://vlib.stanford.edu/Overview.html

Desktop references

Acronym and Abbreviation List   (http://www.ucc.ie/info/net/acronyms/)
Searchable list of acronyms; also reversible to search for acronym from a keyword.

The Alternative Dictionaries   (http://www.notam.uio.no/~hcholm/altlang/)
Dictionary of slang and expressions you most likely won't find in a normal dictionary; all entries are submitted by users.

CIA World Factbook   (http://www.odci.gov/cia/publications/95fact/index.html)
Every hard fact about every country in the world.

Computing Dictionary   (http://wombat.doc.ic.ac.uk/)
Dictionary of computing terms; often technical.

Hypertext Webster Interface   (http://c.gp.cs.cmu.edu:5103/prog/webster)
A searchable dictionary

Quotations page   (http://www.starlingtech.com/quotes/)
Enables searches for quotations by keyword.

Roget's Thesaurus   (http://humanities/uchicago.edu/
forms_unrest/ROGET.html)
An online searchable version of the venerable book of synonyms.

Scholes Library Electronic Reference Desk   (http://scholes.alfred.edu/
Ref.html)
An index of "ready reference" sources.

Writing help

Critique Partner Connections   (http://www.geocities.com/
TheTropics/8977/)
A place to find a writing partner for help by e-mail.

Dakota State University Online Writing Lab (OWL)   (http://www.
dsu.edu/departments/liberal/cola/OWL/)
An online writing lab that provides writing help via e-mail.

An Elementary Grammar   (http://www.hiway.co.uk/~ei/intro.html)
Twenty-two sections of moderately technical discussions of grammatical topics from The English Institute.

Elements of Style   (http://www.cc.columbia.edu/acis/bartleby/
strunk/)
Will Strunk's 1918 classic.

English Grammar FAQ As Posted to alt.usage.english   (http://www.lsa.
umich.edu/ling/jlawler/aue/)
Answers to common grammar questions from linguist John Lawler.

English as a Second Language   (http://www.lang.uiuc.edu/r-115/esl/)
Bills itself as the starting point for learning English as a second
language online. Includes visual and auditory resources, as well as a
24-hour help center.

The "It's" vs. "Its" page   (http://www.rain.org/~gshapiro/its.html)
The difference between the two homophones.

The King's English   (http://www.columbia.edu/acis/bartleby/
fowler/)
Full text of H. W. Fowler's 1908 classic on English, Victorian style.

Non-Sexist Language   (http://mickey.la.psu.edu/~chayton/eng202b/
nonsex.htm)
Tips for avoiding sexist language, based on National Council of
Teachers of English guidelines.

Purdue On-Line Writing Lab   (http://owl.english.purdue.edu/)
An extensive source of online help for writers, including professional
help to specific questions by e-mail. Links to other OWLs worldwide.

University of Michigan OWL   (http://www.lsa.umich.edu/ecb/
OWL/ owl.html)

Receive advice about your writing via e-mail, link to other writing resources, or, if you're in Ann Arbor, make an appointment for a face-to-face tutoring session.

The Word Detective   (http://www.word-detective.com/)
Online version of the newspaper column answering questions about words.

Humanities resources on the World Wide Web

General sites

American Communications Association Humanities Gateway
(http://www.uark.edu/depts/comminfo/www/books.html)

American Studies Web
(http://www.georgetown.edu/crossroads/asw)

Arts and Humanities Data Service (gateway to history and literature archives)
(http://ahds.ac.uk/)

Biographies
(http://www.biography.com/find/find.html)

Chorus: New Media in the Arts and Humanities
(http://www.writing.berkeley.edu/chorus/)

Creative Impulse: The Artists' View of History and Western Civilization
(http://history.evansville.net/)

H-Net: Humanities and Social Sciences Online (University of Michigan)
(http://h-net2.msu.edu/)

Humanist Discussion Group (Princeton University)
(http://www.princeton.edu/~mccarty/humanist/humanist.html)

Institute for Advanced Technology in the Humanities
(University of Virginia)
(http://jefferson.village.virginia.edu/home.html)

Modern Language Association Online
(http://www.mla.org/)

Oxford University Humanities Gateway
(http://users.ox.ac.uk/~humbul/)

Scholarly Sites (in the Humanities)
(http://www.wam.umd.edu/~mlhall/scholarly.html)

University of California at Santa Barbara Humanities Gateway
(http://humanitas.ucsb.edu/shuttle/general.html#metapages)

Voice of Shuttle Highlights (access to humanities Web links)
(http://humanitas.ucsb.edu/shuttle/hilights.html#general)

Worldwide Arts Resources (Museums, etc.)
(http://wwar.world-arts-resources.com)

Literature

Alex database (University of California, Berkeley)
(http://sunsite.berkeley.edu/alex/)

Film and Folklore Links
(http://www.hsu.edu/faculty/beggsm/advcomp/links.html)

Literary Resources on the Internet (University of Pennsylvania)
(http://www.english.upenn.edu/~jlynch/Lit/)

Malaspina College Great Books Home Page
(http://www.mala.bc.ca/~mcneil/template.htx)

The On-Line Books Page (7,000 books online)
(http://www.cs.cmu.edu/books.html)

Shakespeare Glossary
(http://english-server.hss.cmu.edu/langs/shakespeare-glossary.txt)

University of Pennsylvania Gateway to Sources on Comparative
Literature and Theory
(http://ccat.sas.upenn.edu/Complit/Eclat/)

The Western Canon
(http://www.geocities.com/Athens/Acropolis/6681/index.html)

History

British Broadcasting Corporation History site
(http://www.bbc.co.uk/education/modern/)

History Gateway (Kansas State)
(http://history.cc.ukans.edu/history/WWW_history_main.html)

History Gateway (Mississippi State)
(http://www.msstate.edu/Archives/History/index.html)

History Time Line
(http://www.smokylake.com/Christy/ultimate.htm)

Media History Project
(http://www.mediahistory.com)

U.S. Civil War Center
(http://www.cwc.lsu.edu/civlink.htm)

Virginia Antiquities Home Page
(http://www.apva.org/)

Philosophy and religion

The Bible Online
(http://www-writing.berkeley.edu/chorus/bible/index.html)
(http://etext.virginia.edu/kjv.browse.html)

Business Ethics on the Web
(http://www.hsu.edu/faculty/beggsm/advcomp/links.html)

The Holy Qur'an
(http://www.utexas.edu/students/amso/quran_html)

The Internet Encyclopedia of Philosophy
(http://www.utm.edu/research/iep/)

Medical Humanities (New York School of Medicine)
(http://endeavor.med.nyu.edu/lit-med/)

Philosophy and Religion (Georgetown University American Studies page)
(http://www.georgetown.edu/crossroads/asw/philos.html#philo)

Philosophy Sites
(http://scout18.cs.wisc.edu/sosig_mirror/roads/cgi/browse.pl?section=philos&area=World)

Religion Resources Online
(http://www.utoronto.ca/stmikes/theobook.htm)

Social sciences resources on the World Wide Web

General sites

General Sociological Links
(http://www.trinity.edu/~mkearl/resource.html)

Information Resources for Social Sciences (University of California, Santa Barbara)
(http://www.library.ucsb.edu/subj/social.html)

National Center on Addiction and Substance Abuse
(http://www.casacolumbia.org)

Social Science Gateway
(http://sosig.esrc.bris.ac.uk/)

Social Science Information Gateway
(http://scout.cs.wisc.edu/scout/mirrors/sosig/)

Social Sciences Data Center (University of Virginia)
(http://www.helsinki.fi/WebEc/aboutweb.html)

Sociological Research Online
(http://www.socresonline.org.uk/socresonline/welcome.html)

Sociological Subject Areas (University of Amsterdam)
(http://www.pscw.uva.nl/sociosite/TOPICS/index.html)

Suicide Information and Education Center
(http://www.siec.ca/)

University of California's GPO Gate—access to U.S. government information
(http://www.gpo.ucop.edu/)

Anthropology

Anthropology Page, Voice of the Shuttle (University of California, Santa Barbara)
(http://humanitas.ucsb.edu/shuttle/anthro.html)

Anthropology Web Sites (University of California, Santa Barbara)
(http://www.anth.ucsb.edu/netinfo.html)

Human Languages Page
(http://www.june29.com/HLP/)

Economics

Economics and Business
(http://www.library.ucsb.edu/subj/economic.html)

Economics WebEc
(http://www.helsinki.fi/WebEc/aboutweb.html)

Education

AskERIC
(http://www.askeric.org/)

The Chronicle of Higher Education
(http://chronicle.com)

Information Resources for Education
(http://www.library.ucsb.edu/subj/educatio.html)

United States Department of Education Databases
(http://www.ed.gov/databases/ERIC_Digests/index/)

United States Department of Education, Topics from A to Z
(http://www.ed.gov/topicsaz.html)

Yahoo! Education
(http://www.yahoo.com/Education/Organizations/)

Yahoo! Education (News and Media)
(http://www.yahoo.com/Education/News_and_Media/)

Political science

Federal Government Resources (Legislative Branch)
(http://www.lib.umich.edu/libhome/Documents.center/
fedlegis.html#cdd)

General Political Science Web Sites (University of California,
Santa Barbara)
(http://www.library.uscb.edu/subj/politica.html)

Information Resources for Sociology (University of California,
Santa Barbara)
(http://www.library.ucsb.edu/subj/sociolog.html)

Political Science Resources on the Web (University of Michigan)
(http://www.lib.umich.edu/libhome/Documents.center/polisci.html)

Thomas (Bills before Congress)
(http://Thomas.loc.gov)

Richard Kimber's Political Science Resources
(http://www.psr.keele.ac.uk/)

Yahoo! Politics
(http://www.yahoo.com/government/politics)

Psychology

American Psychoanalytic Association
(http://apsa.org/)

American Psychological Association
(http://www.apa.org/)

Classics in the History of Psychology
(http://www.yorku.ca/dept/psych/classics/)

Cognitive and Psychological Sciences on the Internet
(http://www.psych.stanford.edu/cogsci/)

Electronic Journals in Psychology (Armin Gunther)
(http://www.psywww.com/resource/journals.htm)

Electronic Journals in Psychology (Hanover College)
(http://psych.hanover.edu/Krantz/journal.html)

FreudNet (Abraham Brill Library at the New York Psychoanalytic
Institute)
(http://plaza.interport.net/nypsan/)

Information Resources for Psychology (University of California,
Santa Barbara)
(http://www.library.ucsb.edu/subj/psych.html)

JungWeb
(http://www.psych.stanford.edu/cogsci/)

PsychJournal Search (an index to 1450 electronic journals in psychology)
(http://www.cmhc.com/journals/)

Psychology Virtual Library (WWWVirtual Library)
(http://www.psych.stanford.edu/cogsci/)

Psych Web
(http://www.psywww.com/)

Yahoo! Psychology
(http://www.yahoo.com/Social_Science/Psychology/)

Sociology

American Sociological Association
(http://www.asanet.org/)

Demography and Population Studies (WWWVirtual Library)
(http://coombs.anu.edu.au/ResFacilities/DemographyPage.html)

Inter-University Consortium for Political and Social Research
(http://www.icpsr.umich.edu/)

Research Resources for Social Scientists
(http://www.socsciresearch.com/)

Selected Internet Resources in Sociology (University of Illinois at Urbana-Champaign)
(http://www.library.uiuc.edu/edx/elecsoc.htm)

Substance Abuse and Mental Health Data Archive
(http://www.icspr.umich.edu/SAMHDA/)

Yahoo! Sociology
(http://www.yahoo.com/Social_Science/Sociology/)

Science resources on the World Wide Web

General sites

Cornell Math and Science Gateway
(http://www.tc.cornell.edu/Edu/MathSciGateway/)

Ecola Newsstand Science (Electronic Magazines)
(http://www.ecola.com/news/magazine/science/)

Electronic Journals in the Sciences (and other disciplines)
(http://ejournals.cic.net/toc.Topic.html)

Information Resources for the Sciences (University of California, Santa Barbara)
(http://www.library.ucsb.edu/subj/sciences.html)

National Science Foundation
(http://www.nsf.gov/)

UniScience Science News Online (Weekly news updates and searchable archive)
(http://unisci.com/)

Yahoo! Science
(http://dir.yahoo.com/Science/)

Astronomy

AstroWeb
(http://www.cv.nrao.edu/fits/www/astronomy.html)

Earth from Space: An Astronaut's Views of the Home Planet
(http://earth.jsc.nasa.gov/)

Indexes and Gateways to Astronomical Resources on the Internet Sciences (University of California, Santa Barbara)
(http://www.library.ucsb.edu/subj/astronom.html)

Biology

Biodiversity and Biological Collections Web Server
(http://biodiversity.uno.edu)

Entomology
   (http://www.ColoState.edu/Depts/Entomology/ent.html)

The Genome Database
   (http://gdbwww.gdb.org)

Human Body Image Browser
   (http://www.vis.colostate.edu/cgi-bin/gva/gvaview)

Indexes and Gateways to Biology and Aquatic Science Sources on the
   Internet Sciences (University of California, Santa Barbara)
   (http://www.library.ucsb.edu/subj/astronom.html)

Chemistry

Chemical Information Resource Shelf
   (http://www.umsl.edu/divisions/artscience/chemistry/books/
   welcome.html)

Information Resources for Chemistry (University of California,
   Santa Barbara)
   (http://www.library.ucsb.edu/subj/chemistr.html)

ChemWeb
   (http://chemweb.com/home/home.exe)

Science Hypermedia, Inc.
   (http://www.scimedia.com)

Environmental studies

Environmental Protection Agency
   (http://www.epa.gov/)

Geologylink
   (http://www.geologylink.com/hot)

Marine Watch
   (http://www.marinewatch.com/)

United States Department of the Interior
   (http://www.doi.gov/)

The Weather Processor
   (http://wxp.atms.purdue.edu/)

Physics

Albert Einstein: Images and Impact
   (http://www.aip.org/history/einstein/)

European Laboratory for Particle Physics
   (http://www.cern.ch/)

The Galileo Project
   (http://es.rice.edu/ES/humsoc/Galileo/)

Physics resources (WWWVirtual Library)
(http://www.fisk.edu/vl/Physics/Overview.html)

COMPUTER TIPS

Remember Those URLs

When you find a site on the Internet that might be useful for your research paper, be sure to note the URL ("Uniform Resource Locator," which serves as an address for the site) and the date you visited the site. You'll need the information for your bibliography. Also, consider adding the site to the list of "bookmarks" stored in your Web browser.

4i   Bringing your research to an end

You should recognize that any description of gathering sources for a research paper makes these processes look neater than they generally are. In practice, they are often considerably less systematic, because writing is such a layered, looping process. It is crucial to keep in mind the kinds of resources and procedures that are available to you, and—given the constraints on your time—to use as many as you can.

As you proceed, you will discover that research is to some extent a self-generating process. That is, one source (whether print or electronic) will lead you—through references in the text, citations, and bibliographic entries—to others. Authors will refer to other studies on the subject. Frequently, they will indicate which ones they believe are the most important, and why. At some point you will realize that you have already looked at most of the key research on the subject. Then you can be reasonably assured that the research stage of your project is nearing its end. Chapter 5 will show you how to use effectively the sources you have found.

CHAPTER 5

Using Sources

Writing an effective research paper requires making careful decisions about how to use the sources you discover. To make such decisions, you need to read your sources critically: first to understand them and respond to them, next to evaluate what you read and to forge relationships among your sources. If necessary, review Chapter 1, where critical reading is covered in detail.

CRITICAL DECISIONS

Writing Research Papers in Specific Subject Areas

Expectations about research and writing vary from the humanities to the social sciences to the sciences, and even among the more specific disciplines within these areas. Be aware that your instructors will be looking for evidence in your writing and research that you are thinking like a biologist or historian or sociologist. To understand the expectations of the discipline in which you are working, you need to pay close attention to the examples you are reading within that discipline. Then, you can determine how to approach your sources accordingly. See Chapter 8 for an extended discussion on how thinking and writing change as you move from one discipline to another.

5a   Creating a working bibliography

As you do the research for a paper, you should keep a **working bibliography,** a list of all of the sources you locate. This includes books, articles, entries from biographical sources, handbooks, almanacs, electronic sources, and various other kinds of sources. The bibliography should also include sources you locate in indexes that you intend to check later. A working bibliography is more comprehensive than your **final bibliography,** which consists only of those sources that you actually use in writing the paper.

COMPUTER TIPS

Bookmarks

One of the most convenient time savers for using the Internet is the "bookmark," a record of a URL that you'd like to remember. URLs are often complex and unwieldy, so to copy them down and later type them in again by hand invites mistakes. Instead, let your Web browser keep a list of them for you. In the course of your research, when you access a Web page from which you use information or one that you think you may need to access again, add a bookmark to your list. Then, when you need to return to the page, all you have to do is click on that bookmark. Most browsers let you examine your bookmarks, so your list can function as a readily accessible record of the URLs you'll need for your bibliography.

As you consult each new source, carefully record the following key information on 3" × 5" index cards or in a computer file:

1. full name of author (last name first)
2. title (and subtitle)
3. publication information:
   a. place of publication
   b. name of publisher
   c. date of publication
4. inclusive page numbers
5. call number

When the time comes to prepare your final bibliography, you can simply arrange the cards (or the entries) for the sources you used in alphabetical order and type up the pertinent information as a list. Here's a sample bibliography record for a book:

---

⑤   Turkle, Sherry. _Life on the Screen: Identity in the Age of the_   QA
     Internet. New York: Simon & Schuster, 1995.   769.9
     .C66
     T87
     pages 228-231: discusses the ease with which one can be deceptive in   1997
     online relationships

Here is a sample bibliography record for an article:

---

⑧   Branscum, Deborah. "Life at High-Tech U." _Newsweek_ 27 Oct. 1997: 78-80.

     makes point that a study of first-year college students found that ordinarily reserved
     students were more comfortable joining into classroom debates online

---

5b   Taking notes: Summarizing and paraphrasing

WWW

http://www.wisc.edu/writing/
Handbook/QuosuccessfulSummary.html

Detailed explanations and examples of using
quotes, paraphrases, and summaries.

Use your computer's note-taking software or 4" × 6" cards for taking notes. Any system will work as long as you are able to (1) clearly identify the source from which the note is taken and (2) sort through and rearrange notes with ease.

Researchers use various formats for recording their notes, but the following elements are most important:

1. a *code number* corresponding to the code number on your bibliography record *or* the bibliographic reference itself;
2. a *topic* or *subtopic* label (these enable you to easily arrange and rearrange your records in topical order);
3. the *note* itself; and
4. a *page reference.*

Do not attempt to include too much information in a single note record. For example, do not summarize an entire article or chapter in one record, particularly if you are likely to use information from a single record in several places throughout your paper. By limiting each note to a single point or illustration, you make it easier to arrange the records according to your outline, and to rearrange them later if your outline changes. Here is a sample note for *Life on the Screen,* by Sherry Turkle.

Deception in online relationships ⑤

Relationships online allow people an opportunity to pretend to be someone very different from who they really are. While some may regard this as deception, others believe that creating a separate online identity is all part of the fun, that there are no rules requiring one to be honest. So if someone gets hurt when the deception is found out, opinion differs as to who is responsible. (228)

There are three methods of notetaking: **summarizing, paraphrasing,** and **quoting.** These methods can be used either individually or in combination with one another. Your choice of method will depend on how significant the ideas are and how you may want to use them in your paper. The Critical Decisions box on the next page will help you make the right choice.

1   Summarizing sources

A *summary* is a relatively brief, objective account, in your own words, of the main idea in a source passage. You summarize a passage when you want to extract the main ideas and use them as background material in your own paper. Here is a section of an article by Ron Kling, which Logan Kole discovered while researching a paper on computer-mediated communication (CMC):

> In the United States, communities seem to be deteriorating from a complex combination of causes. In the inner cities of big urban centers, many people fear street crime and stay off the streets at night. In the larger suburban and

CRITICAL DECISIONS

Deciding Whether to Summarize, Paraphrase, or Quote from a Source

Summarize when you want to

- present the main points from a relatively long passage
- condense information essential to your discussion

Paraphrase when you want to

- clarify complex ideas in a short passage
- clarify difficult language in a short passage

Quote when

- the language of the source is particularly important or effective
- you want to enhance your credibility by drawing on the words of an authority on the subject

post-suburban areas, many people hardly know their neighbors and "latch key" children often have little adult contact after school. An African proverb which says that "it takes a whole village to raise a child" refers to a rich community life with a sense of mutual responsibility that is difficult to find in many new neighborhoods. Some advocates believe that computer technology in concert with other efforts could play a role in rebuilding community life by improving communication, economic opportunity, civic participation, and education.

> —RON CLING, "Social Relationships in Electronic Forums: Hangouts, Salons, Workplaces, and Communities." *CMC Magazine,* July 22, 1996.

Here is a sample summary of this source:

> CMC is potentially so powerful a medium of exchange that some believe it can promote dialogue within communities that are declining. A community, after all, is built on people acting in the interests of their neighbors for the common good. Via e-mail, online newsgroups, and e-forums, neighbors will have new ways of looking out for one another.

2   Paraphrasing sources

A paraphrase is a restatement, in your own words, of a passage of text. Paraphrases are sometimes the same length as the source passage, sometimes shorter. In certain cases, particularly if the source passage is written in densely constructed or jargon-laden prose—the paraphrase may even be longer than the original.

You paraphrase a passage when you want to preserve all the points of the original, major and minor, and when—perhaps for the sake of clarity— you want to communicate the ideas in your own words. Keep in mind that only an *occasional* word (but not whole phrases) from the original source should appear in the paraphrase, and that the paraphrase's sentence structure should not reflect that of the source.

Original passage:

Parents need to be able to talk to their children about where they are going and what they are doing. This same commonsense rule applies to their children's lives on the screen. Parents don't have to become technical experts, but they do need to learn enough about computer networks to discuss with their children what and who is out there and lay down some basic safety rules.

—SHERRY TURKLE, *Life on the Screen: Identity in the Age of the Internet,* page 227.

Paraphrase:

Just as parents should make sure they know their children's whereabouts and activities in real life, so should they monitor their children's online activities. Without having to master the complexities of these new technologies, they can still become familiar enough with online systems to talk with their children about their online activities. In doing so, they should also establish guidelines for their children to follow. (227)

This paraphrase is as long as Turkle's original passage, with roughly the same level of detail.

5c Quoting sources

You may decide to quote from a passage when the author's language is particularly well chosen, lively, dramatic, or incisive, and when you think you could not possibly express the same idea so effectively. Or you may decide to quote when you want to bolster the credibility of your argument with the reputation of your source.

1 Deciding what to quote

When you quote a source, you need to record the author's wording *exactly.* The conventions for altering quotations with ellipses and with bracketed words (that you provide) are discussed in 5c-2. Here is a passage from Brittney G. Chenault, "Developing Personal and Emotional Relationships Via Computer-Mediated Communication" (*CMC Magazine,* May 1998):

People meet via CMC every day, exchange information, debate, argue, woo, commiserate, and support. They may meet via a mailing list or newsgroup, and continue the interaction via e-mail. Their relationships can range from the cold, professional encounter, to the hot, intimate rendezvous.

What you consider to be quotable depends on the purpose of your research. A student researcher read this section of Chenault's article to investigate the ways computer-mediated communication will affect the way we communicate and the quality of our relationships. For this reader, the following quotation was most useful:

<u>Kinds of online relationships</u>

"People meet via CMC every day, exchange information, debate, argue, woo, commiserate, and support.... Their relationships can range from the cold, professional encounter, to the hot, intimate rendezvous."

Note that this writer has used an ellipsis in the place of a deleted sentence. Ellipses are discussed in the next section.

COMPUTER TIPS

Read Online or Download?

According to conventional wisdom, you should take notes from your sources rather than make photocopies as you conduct research. But the ease of downloading text files from the Internet has made that advice outmoded. Now, you can use your Web browser to download files and open them later with text-processing software. Then you can simply cut and paste quoted material into your drafts. This process is easier than retyping from your notes, and it guarantees accuracy. However, some files on the Internet are enormous. If you plan to use only a small bit of information, then it would probably be more efficient to take notes from such a file. Software programs are available for online notetaking.

2 Using brackets and ellipses in quotations

Sometimes for the sake of clarity, conciseness, or smoothness of sentence structure, you will need to make additions, omissions, or changes to quotations. For example, suppose you wanted to quote a passage beginning with the following sentence: "In 1979, one week after receiving a 13.3% pay raise, she was called on the carpet." To clarify the pronoun *she,* you would need to replace it with the name of the person in question enclosed in a pair of brackets: "In 1979, one week after receiving a 13.3% pay raise, [Virginia Rulon-Miller] was called on the carpet."

Suppose you also decided that the 13.3% pay raise was irrelevant for your purpose in quoting the material. You could omit this phrase and indicate the omission by means of an *ellipsis*—three spaced periods: "In 1979 . . . [Virginia Rulon-Miller] was called on the carpet." Note that when using brackets, you do not need to use the ellipsis to indicate that the pronoun (*she*) has been omitted.

Sometimes you need to change a capital letter to a lowercase one in order to smoothly integrate the quotation into your own sentence. For example, suppose you want to quote the following sentence: "Privacy today matters to employees at all levels, from shop-floor workers to presidents." You could smoothly integrate this quotation into your own sentence by altering the capitalization, as follows.

> The new reality, as John Hoerr points out, is that "[p]rivacy today matters to employees at all levels, from shop-floor workers to presidents."

3   Smoothly integrating quotations into your sentences

Using attributive phrases to introduce quotations

Whether or not you alter quotations by means of ellipses or brackets, you should strive to integrate them smoothly into your own sentences. Use attributive phrases (phrases that specify the origin of the quoted source). Here is a quotation from an interview with Richard Marks, the chairman of the Environmental Subcommittee for the International Council of Shopping Centers.

> Malls are designed to maximize profits. They were not built as a replacement for Main Street. If intimacy encourages sales, there will be intimacy.

The quotation can be integrated in the text of a paper in any of several ways. When you attribute a quotation to someone, use verbs in the present tense (Smith *claims* or Smith *adds*).

1. According to the chairman of the Environmental Subcommittee for the International Council of Shopping Centers, "Malls are designed to maximize profits. They were not built as a replacement for Main Street. If intimacy encourages sales, there will be intimacy" (Marks).

Because the source of the quotation is an unpublished interview, there are no page references in the parenthetical citation. Most sources require page references as follows: "Malls offer no community" (Jones 8).

2. "Malls are designed to maximize profits," according to Richard Marks.
3. "If intimacy encourages sales," says Richard Marks, "there will be intimacy."
4. "Malls are designed to maximize profits," says the chairman of the Environmental Subcommittee for the International Council of Shopping Centers. "They were not built as a replacement for Main Street" (Marks).
5. According to Richard Marks, malls "were not built as a replacement for Main Street."

The list below suggests words you can use to vary attributive phrases.

adds	concedes	disagrees	maintains	says
agrees	concludes	disputes	notes	sees
argues	condemns	emphasizes	observes	shows
asks	considers	explains	points out	speculates
asserts	contends	finds	rejects	states
believes	declares	holds	relates	suggests
claims	defends	illustrates	reports	thinks
comments	denies	implies	responds	warns
compares	derides	insists	reveals	writes

4 Using block quotations

You should integrate most quotations into your paragraphs, using quotation marks. If a quotation runs longer than four lines, however, you should set it apart from the text by indenting it ten spaces from the left margin. Quotation marks are not required around block quotations, which should be double spaced, like the rest of the text. See 7a-1 for details on using block quotations.

5d Avoiding plagiarism

In its most blatant form, **plagiarism** is an act of conscious deception, an attempt to pass off the ideas or words of another as your own. The penalties for plagiarism can be severe—including a failing grade in a course or even suspension from school.

Much plagiarism is unintentional, but the consequences may be the same, so you'll want to avoid the problem. Here are two general rules to help you avoid unintentional plagiarism:

1. Whenever you *quote* the exact words of others, place these words within quotation marks and properly cite the source.

2. Whenever you *paraphrase* or *summarize* the ideas of others, do not use whole phrases, or many of the same words, or sentence structures similar to those in the original. You must identify the source of the paraphrased or summarized material. Do not assume that you are under no obligation to credit your source if you simply change the wording of the original statement or alter the sentence structure.

Determining What Is Common Knowledge

The only exception to the second rule stated on page 108 is if the information summarized or paraphrased is considered common knowledge. For example, you need not cite the source of the information that General Lee commanded the Confederate forces during the Civil War, or the fact that Mars is the fourth planet from the sun, or the fact that Ernest Hemingway wrote *The Sun Also Rises*. If, on the other hand, you are summarizing one particular theory about why Lee's forces faced almost certain defeat, or the geological composition of the Martian surface, or how the critical assessment of Hemingway's *The Sun Also Rises* has shifted over the years, then you are obliged to cite the sources of your information or ideas, whether or not you quote them directly.

The key issue is whether readers may mistakenly think that a certain idea or item of information originated with you when, in fact, it did not. If there is *any* chance of such a mistake occurring, you should cite the source.

---

1   Identifying forms of plagiarism

The examples below will illustrate what can happen when source ideas undergo several possible levels of intentional or unintentional plagiarism. The passage is from Steven F. Bloom's "Empty Bottles, Empty Dreams: O'Neill's Use of Drinking and Alcoholism in *Long Day's Journey into Night*," which appears in *Critical Essays on Eugene O'Neill*, edited by James J. Martine (Boston: G. K. Hall, 1984).

> In *Long Day's Journey into Night*, O'Neill captures his vision of the human condition in the figure of the alcoholic who is constantly and repeatedly faced with the disappointment of his hopes to escape or transcend present reality. As the effects of heavy drinking and alcoholism increase, the alcoholic, in his attempt to attain euphoric forgetfulness, is repeatedly confronted with the painful realities of dissipation, despondency, self-destruction, and ultimately, death. This is the life of an alcoholic, and for O'Neill, this is the life of modern man.

Here is a plagiarized student version of this passage.

> *Long Day's Journey into Night* shows O'Neill's vision of the human condition in the figure of the alcoholic who is constantly faced with the disappointment of his hopes to escape. As the effects of heavy drinking and alcoholism increase, the alcoholic, in his attempt to attain forgetfulness,

is repeatedly confronted with the painful realities of dissipation, self-destruction, and, ultimately, death. This is the life of an alcoholic, and for O'Neill, this is the life of modern man.

This is the most blatant form that plagiarism can take. The student has copied the passage almost word for word and has made no attempt to identify the source of either the words or the ideas. Even if the author *were* credited, the student's failure to use quotation marks around quoted material would render this version unacceptable.

Here is another version of the same passage.

The figure of the disappointed alcoholic who hopes to escape reality represents the human condition in *Long Day's Journey into Night*. Trying to forget his problems, the alcoholic, while drinking more and more, is confronted with the realities of his self-destructive condition, and, ultimately, with death. For Eugene O'Neill, the life of the alcoholic represents the life of modern man.

In this version, the writer has attempted to put the ideas into his own words; but the result still so closely resembles the original in sentence structure, in the sequence of ideas, and in the use of key phrases ("confronted with the realities") that it is also unacceptable. Note that this would hold true even if the author *were* credited; that is, had the first sentence begun, "According to Steven F. Bloom, . . . " The student may not have intended to plagiarize—he may, in fact, believe this to be an acceptable rendition—but it would still be considered plagiarism.

2   Making legitimate use of a source

The following use of the source passage is entirely acceptable:

According to Steven F. Bloom, alcoholism in *Long Day's Journey into Night* is a metaphor for the human condition. The alcoholic drinks to forget his disappointments and to escape reality, but the more he drinks, the more he is faced with his own mortality. "This is the life of an alcoholic," asserts Bloom, "and for O'Neill, this is the life of modern man" (177).

The student has carefully attributed both the paraphrased idea (in the first part of the passage) and the quotation (in the second part) to the source author, Steven Bloom. The student has also taken special care to phrase the idea in her own language.

Of course, you cannot avoid keeping *some* key terms. Obviously, if you are going to paraphrase the ideas in this passage, you will need to use words and phrases such as "alcoholic," "heavy drinking," "the human condition," and so on. However, what you say *about* these terms should be said in your own words. When you do quote material directly, be certain that you quote it accurately, introducing no word changes, however minor.

CHAPTER 6

Writing the Research Paper

Because the *process* of writing a research paper is in many respects similar to that of writing an essay, the discussion of process here will be brief. See Chapters 1–3 for additional advice on thinking critically about your sources, and about planning, writing, and revising a draft.

CRITICAL DECISIONS

Developing a Tentative Thesis and Outline

You have conducted systematic research on your subject, and you have accumulated a stack of notes in which you have summarized, paraphrased, and quoted relevant material. Now, before you begin drafting, you need to return to your working thesis and revise it in light of what you have discovered over the course of your research. Such revision may be quite extensive; in fact, you may find that your research has led you to a new thesis that is entirely different from the one you started with. Based on this revised thesis, you will also need to prepare a careful sketch or outline that you can use to organize your notes. (See 2c for a discussion of writing a thesis and developing a sketch.) Deciding on your main idea for your paper and on a tentative structure is a crucial first stage for drafting.

6a Writing a draft

At this point, if your research has been successful, you have become something of an expert on your subject. Now it is time to write a rough draft that will be seen by no one but yourself (and possibly some friends whose advice you trust). You will have plenty of opportunity to revise this rough draft.

To avoid overreliance on sources, as well as to clarify the main lines of a paper's argument, some researchers write their first drafts referring only to their outlines—and not to their source notes. As they write, they mark the places where source material (in summarized, paraphrased, or quoted form) will later be inserted. Drafts written in such a manner are simply skeletons or scaffolds. But by examining the skeleton, you can see whether the logic of your paper is sound. Does the argument make sense to you? Does one part logically follow from another? It should, even without the material from your notes. Remember your purpose and your audience: tell readers, as if you were having a conversation, what they should know about your subject and why you believe as you do.

At some point in the drafting process, you will need to turn to your notes and consider how to let your sources help to advance your ideas. Here are some considerations:

- Try arranging source notes in the order in which you intend to use them, but avoid simply transcribing your notes onto your rough draft.

- If you think you have made your point, move on, and skip any additional, unused notes on the topic or subtopic.

- Once you have completed a draft, you can revisit your notes and decide to substitute particularly effective unused notes for less effective ones used in the draft.

If you used cards rather than a computer file to store your notes, then to avoid having to transcribe lengthy quotations from your notes onto your draft, consider taping or stapling these notes (or photocopies of the quotations) directly onto the appropriate spots on the draft. When you do incorporate sources, remember to transfer bibliographic codes and page numbers, so that later you can enter the correct citations.

COMPUTER TIPS

Online Sharing of Drafts and Materials

Researchers and scholars all over the world are using the Internet to share their writing quickly and easily with people at distant locations. If you have trusted friends or colleagues in other classes or even at other schools, you can ask for their feedback via e-mail as you begin to revise a paper. If your particular Internet connection and computer system allow you to send "attached files," then you can compose a brief message and attach the whole word-processed file for the other person to download into his or her own file system. If you cannot easily attach files to your e-mail messages, then just copy your paper, paste it into the body of your message, and then send it as you would any other e-mail message.

6b   Revising and editing

In Chapter 2, you will find a discussion on revising and editing. Keep in mind that revision literally means "re-seeing." You should not consider revision simply a matter of fixing punctuation and spelling errors and improving a word

WWW
http://www.researchpaper.com/
writing_center/111.html

Covers the priorities in revising: Begin with the higher-order concerns, the aspects of writing most responsible for the quality of the paper.

or phrase here and there. Instead, look at the whole paper from top to bottom and try to determine whether you have presented material effectively. Revising a research paper is similar to revising other kinds of essays. Be sure to include the following steps.

1 Arrive at a final thesis

After writing a complete draft, you will probably need again to revise your thesis. Ask yourself these questions as you reread your work:

- What is the main question of this research project?
- Is the question suitably complex for the subject I've defined?
- Is my *answer* to this question—my thesis—clear?
- Have I *stated* my thesis clearly in the draft?

Responding to these questions, and making corresponding adjustments in your paper, will help you formulate a final thesis that accurately reflects your focus.

2 Work with feedback from readers and peer editors

When revising your paper, get as much feedback as possible from others. It is difficult even for professional writers to get perspective on what they have written immediately after they have written it. You are likely to be too close to the subject, too committed to your outline or to particular words, to be very objective at this point. Show your draft to a friend or classmate whose judgment you trust and to your instructor. Obtain reactions on everything from the paper as a whole to the details of word choice.

COMPUTER TIPS

Help Online

Online Writing Labs (OWLs) are beginning to proliferate on the Internet. These resource centers offer writing services ranging from standard handbook information to reviewers who will actually read a draft and offer suggestions. Most provide help with specific questions on composition, research, grammar, and style. The most popular OWL is located at Purdue University, but you can find a frequently updated list of OWLs at Writing Centers Online (http://www2.colgate.edu/diw/NWCAOWLS.html).

The research paper on pages 114–120 reflects the process of research and writing discussed in this and the two preceding chapters. The student writer chose to direct his efforts toward answering a key research question: "How will computer-mediated communication affect interpersonal relationships?" This question led to a working thesis and then to a refined thesis. Logan retained the question as the focal point for the paper.

This paper conforms to Modern Language Association (MLA) documentation style. For complete coverage of this and other documentation styles, see Chapter 7.

Cover-page format

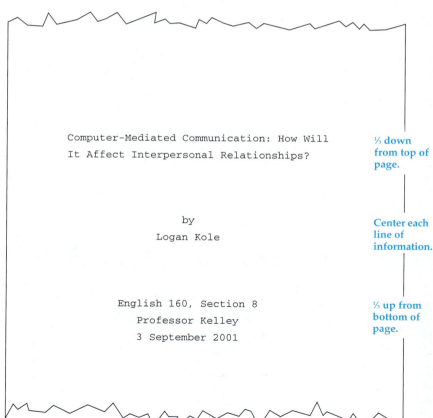

```
Computer-Mediated Communication: How Will
It Affect Interpersonal Relationships?
```
⅓ **down from top of page.**

Center each line of information.

```
                    by
              Logan Kole
```

```
        English 160, Section 8
           Professor Kelley
           3 September 2001
```
⅓ **up from bottom of page.**

Kole 1

Computer-Mediated Communication:
How Will It Affect
Interpersonal Relationships?

From the home, to the workplace, to the classroom, the Internet has clicked its way into our
everyday lives. Today's students can e-mail as file
attachments their end-of-term papers to their professors and can then turn around and use e-mail to
gather a group of friends for a party or to celebrate
the term's completion. These online exchanges, called
CMC (or computer-mediated communication) sound fairly
commonplace at the turn of the millennium. But what
we have yet to discover is how CMC might change both
the ways we communicate and the quality of our relationships. While many praise CMC's potential to
bridge barriers and promote meaningful dialogue,
others caution that CMC is fraught with dangers.

Very soon, half of America will communicate
via e-mail, according to analysts (Singh 283). We
can only assume that figure will grow--rapidly--as
children who have matured in the Internet era move
to college and into careers. With e-mail becoming
an increasingly common form of communication, people
are discovering and conversing with one another in a
variety of ways that bring a new twist to old, familiar patterns. Using e-mail, people meet "to
exchange pleasantries and argue, engage in intellectual discourse, conduct commerce, exchange knowledge, share emotional support, make plans, brainstorm, gossip, feud, [and] fall in love" (Chenault).
That is, through e-mail people do what they have always done: communicate. But the medium of that communication has changed, which excites some people
and concerns others.

Advocates argue that the Internet has not only
made existing types of communication faster, more

Thesis

Information cited from source; reference to "Works Cited" list

Common knowledge: no citation needed

convenient, more efficient, and less expensive; it
has also made possible "new forms of community
life," such as chat rooms and discussion lists, in
which people from all over the country, and world,
gather to share information and exchange points of
view (Kling). CMC is potentially so powerful a
medium of exchange that some believe it can promote
dialogue within communities that are declining. A
community, after all, is built on people acting in
the interests of their neighbors for the common
good. Via e-mail, online newsgroups, and e-forums,
neighbors will have new ways of looking out for one
another (Kling).

   Still, skeptics aren't convinced that electronic communication can provide the basis of lasting personal relationships, primarily because
relationships initiated on a cathode ray tube lack
immediacy and physical presence. What may be missing in the electronic village say the critics is
"an essential core of humanity" (Maasik and Solomon
701):

   The unreal world of virtual culture [...] is
   being substituted for a social reality made up
   of real human beings. And such a world, based
   entirely on the transmission of electronic
   signals, is potentially a world in which human
   beings will be unable to conceive of others as
   human beings. When all interaction is electronic, [the critics] ask, where is the ground
   for true human empathy and related-ness?
   (Maasik and Solomon 701)
The fact that people communicate--via e-mail, snail
(written) mail, or in person--does not guarantee that
their exchanges lead to community. Members of a community trust and care for one another; they extend
themselves and offer help (Kling). Critics of CMC

**Section 1:
Pros and
cons on on-
line com-
munities**

**If no pagi-
nation in a
www
source, then
no pagina-
tion in a
parentheti-
cal reference**

**Paraphrase:
See original
source**

**Quotation
altered with
ellipses and
brackets**

**Reference
set outside
end punctu-
ation in
block quo-
tation**

argue that the supporters gloss over this important distinction when they assume that electronic forums are "building new forms of community life" (Kling). Talking, electronically or otherwise, marks only the beginning of a process. Community building is hard work and takes time.

Notwithstanding these concerns, proponents of CMC confidently point to examples in which the new technologies of communication bring people together in meaningful, healthy ways. In a study of first-year college students, researcher Richard Holeton of Stanford University found that students who were or-dinarily reserved were able to come out of their shells and participate in Internet debates (Branscum 79). Similarly, the Internet can serve as a way for people who are having trouble dating to find part-ners. For instance, Tom Buckley of Portland, Oregon met his wife after signing up with Match.com. Buck-ley noted that the Internet helped him to meet his wife because "neither one of us was the type to walk up to someone in the gym or a bar and say, 'You're the fuel to my fire'" (qtd. in Morris). Holeton's research and Buckley's experience suggest that the Internet may provide a way for otherwise timid individuals to express themselves.

Beyond simply providing a safe and lower-stress place to meet, the Internet may actually promote honest communication. An Ohio State sociologist, An-drea Baker, concluded from her research that indi-viduals who begin their romance online can be at an advantage: writing via e-mail can promote a "better and deeper" relationship than one begun in person because writing itself promotes a frank, honest ex-change (qtd. in Wolcott). Certainly this was the ex-perience of John Dwyer, a Californian who tired of meeting women in bars and decided instead to post an

Section 2: pros and cons on on-line rela-tionships

Summary of two sources

advertisement online. He eventually met the woman who would become his wife, Debbie, who said: "If you are honest when talking online, you can strip away all the superficial stuff and really get to know someone" (qtd. in Wolcott). When it works, CMC can promote a sincere exchange among those looking for lasting relationships.

> **Shows that Morris is the source of the Buckley quotation**

Yet, as MIT professor Sherry Turkle notes, on-line relationships allow people an opportunity to pretend to be someone very different from who they really are; in fact, some see creating a separate online identity as all part of the fun (228). Obviously, such deception can lead to emotional or financial betrayal. Take, for instance, the experience of Robert Spradling. He met and formed a romantic attachment to a Ukrainian woman online. She encouraged the romance via e-mail and eventually asked for money to set up a business. He sent $8,000 and later, again online, asked her to marry him. She agreed, they met in Kiev, and after Spradling returned home she disappeared--his money gone and his heart broken (Morris). Perhaps Spradling was one of the Internet romantics for whom it is wiser to avoid face-to-face meetings. That way, he could have enjoyed the interactive fantasy of a "cyber-lover" without ever having to ruin the fun with the uncomfortable truths of real life (Suler).

> **Source author's name is in the sentence, so citation omits name.**

> **Summary of the Spradling example; paraphrase would be too long**

It is far from certain, then, that all or even most relationships begun online develop positively. Closer to the truth is that both online and offline, some relationships begin--and end--in deceit while others blossom. Experts do not yet know whether computer-mediated communication, because of its electronic format, alters relationships as they are forming or, rather, is simply a new territory in

> **Conclusion**

which to find others. Time will tell. In the mean-
time, the advice that loved ones give us when we set
off to find new friends--Be careful!--makes sense
whether we are looking in the virtual world or down
the street.

Works Cited

Branscum, Deborah. "Life at High-Tech U." Newsweek
27 Oct. 1997: 78-80.

Chenault, Brittney G. "Developing Personal and Emotional Relationships Via Computer-Mediated Communication." CMC Magazine May 1998. 8 Aug. 2000
<http://www.december.com/cmc/mag/1998/
may/chenault.html>.

Kling, Rob. "Social Relationships in Electronic Forums: Hangouts, Salons, Workplaces and Communities." CMC Magazine July 1996. 12 Sept. 2000
<http://www.december.com/cmc/mag/1996/jul/
kling.html>.

Maasik, Sonia, and Jack Solomon, eds. Signs of Life
in the USA. Boston: Bedford Books, 1997.

Morris, Bonnie R. "You've Got Romance! Seeking Love
Online: Net-Based Services Change the Land-
scape, If Not the Odds, of Finding the Perfect
Mate." New York Times Online 26 Aug. 1996. 8
Aug. 2000 <http://oak.cats.ohiou.ed/
~bakera/ArticleE.htm>.

Singh, Sanjiv N. "Cyberspace: A New Frontier for
Fighting Words." Rutgers Computer & Technology
Law Journal 25.2 (1999):283.

References
list. See
Chapter 7
for details.
Magazine
entry

Electronic
publication

Journal

Kole 7

Suler, John. "Cyberspace Romances: Interview with
        Jean-Francois Perreault of Branchez-vous." The
        Psychology of Cyberspace Dec. 1996. 14 Aug. 2000
        <http://www.rider.edu/users/suler/psycyber/
        psycyber.html>.

Turkel, Sherry. Life on the Screen: Identity in the
        Age of the Internet. New York: Simon & Schus-
        ter, 1995.

Wolcott, Jennifer. "Click Here for Romance." The
        Christian Science Monitor 13 Jan. 1999.
        23 Feb. 2000 <http://www.csmonitor.com/
        archive/archives.html>.

Internet
Web site

Book entry

CHAPTER 7
MLA, APA, CMS, CBE

CHAPTER 7

Documenting the Research Paper

Responsible writers credit their sources. The box below summarizes the reasons why they do so. Several systems of documentation have been established for crediting sources. Your choice will depend on the discipline in which you are writing—social sciences, humanities, science and technology, or business—or on the preferences of your audience.

Documenting sources is a two-part process:

1. Cite the source *in your paper* to identify it and give credit immediately after its use. This is called an *in-text* citation.
2. Cite the source *at the end of your paper,* in the form of a list of references that readers can pursue in more detail.

Using Documentation to Give Fair Credit and to Assist Your Reader

Why go to the trouble of documenting your sources?

- *To give credit where it is due.* Ethical practice demands that the originators of ideas and information be credited.
- *To allow readers to gauge the accuracy and reliability of your work.* Any research paper will stand or fall according to how well (how perceptively, accurately, or selectively) you use sources.
- *To avoid charges of plagiarism.* You certainly do not want to give readers the impression that you are claiming credit for ideas or words that are not your own.
- *To allow interested readers to follow up on a point.* Readers will sometimes want to pursue a point you have raised by going to your sources. Therefore, give readers the clearest possible directions for where to look.

For three of the four documentation systems reviewed in this chapter, MLA, APA, and CBE—in-text citations are usually placed within parentheses. For the CMS—footnote and endnote—system, in-text citations are made with a small superscript numeral, and references are listed in notes.

It is important to document *all* of the information and ideas that you take from sources, not just direct quotes. Summaries or paraphrases also require acknowledgment. The only exception to this rule is that *common knowledge*—as determined in part by your audience's level of expertise—need not be documented. The Critical Decisions box below will help you determine what is considered to be common knowledge.

CRITICAL DECISIONS

What Is Common Knowledge?
Deciding When Not to Cite a Source

The question of what information and ideas count as common knowledge and what should be attributed to a source is complicated. Partly, the issue depends on audience. A great deal of technical information could be considered common knowledge, if you are addressing an expert audience. For an audience of nonspecialists, who might mistake the information for your own ideas, you would need to cite the source.

Assume that in a paper on drug abuse in the workplace, you wrote that "6.6 million working Americans are alcoholics." If you were writing the paper for an audience of industrial psychologists well versed in the statistics on workplace alcoholism, this figure would likely be well known and considered common knowledge. Readers would not need, or expect, a citation.

On the other hand, if you were presenting the same information to an audience unfamiliar with the extent of alcoholism in the workplace—your classmates, for instance—you would need to cite your source. Strictly speaking, if three or more sources provided the same 6.6 million figure, you could reasonably claim that it was common knowledge and omit the citation—provided you were not quoting. But to avoid any hint of impropriety, you would be wise to cite information that your audience might not recognize as common knowledge. Otherwise, they could reasonably claim that you used the statistic without proper credit and you would be open to the charge of plagiarism. Remember: whenever you quote a source, you must cite it.

The remainder of this chapter discusses guidelines for four widely used documentation systems. For more detailed information on the conventions of style in the humanities, social sciences, business disciplines, and sciences, refer to these style manuals:

- Gibaldi, Joseph. *MLA Handbook for Writers of Research Papers.* 5th ed. New York: MLA, 1999.

- *Publication Manual* (of the American Psychological Association). 4th ed. Washington, DC: APA, 1994.

- *Chicago Manual of Style.* 14th ed. Chicago: University of Chicago Press, 1993.

- *CBE Style Manual.* 5th ed. Bethesda: CBE, 1983.
- Li, Xia, and Nancy B. Crane. *Electronic Styles: An Expanded Guide to Citing Electronic Information.* Westport: Meckler, 1996.

7a Using the MLA system of documentation

The Modern Language Association (MLA) publishes a style guide that is widely used for citations and references in the humanities. This section gives detailed examples of the MLA parenthetical reference system for in-text citation. Section 7c will discuss an alternate MLA system that uses footnotes or endnotes.

The MLA system calls for a list of references at the end of a paper titled "Works Cited." Keep in mind that the complete information provided in this list will be the basis of your in-text citations. The parenthetical form provides minimal information and sends the reader to the list of references to find the rest.

1 Making in-text citations in the MLA format

When you make a parenthetical in-text citation, you assume that your reader will look to the list of "Works Cited" for complete information on the author, title, and facts of publication. Within your paper, a parenthetical citation may refer either to the entire source or to a specific page within that source. Here is an example of an MLA in-text citation referring to a story as a whole.

```
In "Escapes," the title story of one contemporary author's book of
short stories, the narrator's alcoholic mother makes a public
spectacle of herself (Williams).
```

The next example refers to a specific page in the story. In the MLA system, no punctuation is placed between a writer's last name and a page reference.

```
In "Escapes," a story about an alcoholic household, a key moment
occurs when the child sees her mother suddenly appear on stage at
the magic show (Williams 11).
```

Here is how the same story would appear in the list of references or "Works Cited."

```
Williams, Joy. "Escapes." Escapes: Stories. New York: Vintage,
1990. 1-14.
```

Deciding where to insert a source citation and what information to include is often a judgment call. Use common sense. Introduce the parenthetical reference at a pause in your sentence, at the end if possible. Place it as close to the documented point as possible, so that the reader can tell exactly what it refers to. When the in-text reference is incorporated into a sentence of your own, always place the parenthetical reference *before* any enclosing or end punctuation.

```
In Central Africa in the 1930s, a young girl who comes to town
drinks beer with her date because that's what everyone does
(Lessing 105).

In a realistic portrayal of Central African city life in the 1930s
(Lessing), young people gather daily to drink.
```

When a quotation from a work is incorporated into a sentence of your own, the parenthetical reference *follows* the quotation marks, yet precedes the enclosing or end punctuation.

```
At the popular Sports Club, Lessing's heroine finds the "ubiqui-
tous glass mugs of golden beer" (135).
```

Exception   When your quotation ends with a question mark or exclamation point, keep these punctuation marks inside the end quotation marks; then give the parenthetical reference, and end with a period.

```
Martha's new attempts at sophistication in town prompted her to
retort, "Children are a nuisance, aren't they?" (Lessing 115).
```

Naming an author in the text

When you want to emphasize the author of a source you are citing, incorporate that author's name into your sentence. Unless you are referring to a particular place in that source, no parenthetical reference is necessary in the text.

```
Biographer Paul Mariani understands Berryman's alcoholism as one
form of his drive toward self-destruction.
```

Naming an author in the parenthetical reference

When you want to emphasize information in a source but not especially the author, omit the author's name in the sentence and place it in the parenthetical reference.

```
Biographers have documented alcohol-related upheavals in John
Berryman's life. For example, when he learned that Dylan Thomas
was dying in an alcohol-induced coma, Berryman himself drank to
escape his pain (Mariani 273).
```

When you are referring to a particular place in your source and have already incorporated the author's name into your sentence, place only the page number in parentheses.

```
Biographer Paul Mariani describes how Berryman, knowing that his
friend Dylan Thomas was dying in an alcohol-induced coma, himself
began drinking to escape his pain (273).
```

Documenting a block quotation

For block quotations, set the parenthetical reference—with or without an author's name—*outside* of the end punctuation mark.

```
The story graphically portrays the behavior of Central African
young people gathering daily to drink:

          Perry sat stiffly in a shallow chair which looked as if
          it would splay out under the weight of his big body
          [ . . . ] while from time to time--at those moments when
          laughter was jerked out of him by Stella--he threw back
          his head with a sudden dismayed movement, and flung half
          a glass of liquor down his throat. (Lessing 163)
```

A work by two or three authors

If your source has two or three authors, name them all, either in your text or in a parenthetical reference. Use last names, in the order in which they are given in the source, connected by *and.*

```
One theory claims that the alcoholic wants to "drink his environ-
ment in" (Perls, Hefferline, and Goodman 193-94).
```

A work by four or more authors

For a work with four or more authors, name all the authors, or use the following abbreviated format with *et al.* to signify "and others."

```
Some researchers trace the causes of alcohol dependence to "flawed
family structures" (Stein et al. 318).
```

Reference to two or more sources with the same authorship

When you are referring to two or more sources written by the same author, include in your in-text citation a shortened form of each title so that references to each text will be clear. The following example discusses how author Joy Williams portrays the drinking scene in her fiction. Note that a comma appears between the author's name and the shortened title.

```
She shows drinking at parties as a way of life in such stories as
"Escapes" and "White Like Midnight." Thus it is matter of course
that Joan pours herself a drink while people talk about whether or
not they want to survive nuclear war (Williams, "White" 129).
```

Distinguishing two authors with the same last name

Use one or more initials to supplement references to authors with the same last name.

```
It is no coincidence that a new translation of Euripides's The
Bacchae should appear in the United States (C. K. Williams) at a
time when fiction writers portray the use of alcohol as a means of
escape from mundane existence (J. Williams).
```

Two or more sources in a single reference

Particularly in an introductory summary, you may want to group together a number of works that cover one or more aspects of your research topic. Separate one source from another by a semicolon.

```
Studies that confront the alcoholism of literary figures directly
are on the increase (Mariani; Dardis; Gilmore).
```

A corporate author

A work may be issued by an organization or government agency with no author named. In such a case, use the name of the organization or agency as if it were the author. If the name is long, try incorporating it into your text rather than using a parenthetical note. In this example, the author of the book is the organization Alcoholics Anonymous. The book will be listed alphabetically under "Alcoholics" in the "Works Cited" list.

```
Among publications that discuss how to help young people cope with
family problems, Al-Anon Faces Alcoholism, put out by Alcoholics
Anonymous, has been reissued frequently since 1974 (117-24).
```

A multivolume work

When citing a page reference to a multivolume work, specify the volume with an arabic numeral followed by a colon, a space, and the page number. The work cited in the example below is in four volumes.

```
Drunkenness was such a problem in the first decades of the eigh-
teenth century that it was termed "the acknowledged national vice
of Englishmen of all classes" (Trevelyan 3: 46).
```

A literary work

Well-known literary works, particularly older ones now in the public domain, may appear in numerous editions. When referring to such a work or a part of one, give information for the work itself rather than for the particular edition you are using, unless you are highlighting a special feature or contribution of the edition.

When citing an older play, for instance, instead of referring to a new edition's page numbers, supply act, scene, and line number in arabic numerals, unless your instructor specifies using roman numerals for act and scene (II. iv. 118–19). In the following example, the title of the literary work includes numerals referring to the first of two plays that Shakespeare wrote about Henry IV, known as parts 1 and 2.

Shakespeare's Falstaff bellows, "Give me a cup of sack, rogue. Is there no virtue extant?" (1 Henry IV 2.4.118-19).

To cite a modern editor's contribution to the publication of a literary work, adjust the emphasis of your reference. The abbreviation *n* stands for *note*.

Without the editor's footnote in the Riverside Shakespeare explaining that lime was sometimes used as an additive to make wine sparkle, modern readers would be unlikely to understand Falstaff's ranting: "[Y]et a coward is worse than a cup of sack with lime in it. A villainous coward!" (1 Henry IV 2.4.125-26n).

Material quoted in your source

Often you will want to quote and cite material that you are reading at second hand—in a work by an intermediate author. Quote the original material and refer to the place where you found it.

Psychoanalyst Otto Fenichel included alcoholics within a general grouping of addictive personalities, all of whom use addictive substances "to satisfy the archaic oral longing, a need for security, and a need for the maintenance of self-esteem simultaneously" (qtd. in Roebuck and Kessler 86).

An anonymous work

A work with no acknowledged author should be alphabetized in the "Works Cited" list by the first word of its title. Therefore cite the anonymous work in the same way in your parenthetical reference. The title in this example is *The Hidden Alcoholic in Your Midst*.

People who do not suffer from addiction often can be thoughtless and insensitive to the problems of those around them. That is the message of an emotional and thought-provoking pamphlet (Hidden), whose author writes anonymously about the pain of keeping his alcoholism secret.

2   Preparing a "Works Cited" list in the MLA format

Your "Works Cited" list should include every source you have referred to in your paper. Be aware that some instructors request a more comprehensive list of references—one that includes every source you consulted in preparing the paper. That list would be titled "Bibliography."

The examples in this section show how entries in the "Works Cited" list consist of three elements essential for a list of references: authorship, full title of the work, and publication information. In addition, if the work is taken from an electronic (online) source, consult 7a-3. The basic format for each entry requires the first line to start at the left margin, with each subsequent line to be indented five typed spaces from the left margin.

Not every possible variation is represented here. In formatting a complicated entry for your own list, you may need to combine features from two or more of the examples.

The MLA "Works Cited" list begins on a new page, after the last page of your paper, and continues the pagination of your paper. Entries in the list are alphabetized by the author's last name. An anonymous work is alphabetized by the first word in its title (but disregard *A, An,* and *The*).

COMPUTER TIPS

Citation Format Software

Software programs such as Daedalus, Inc.'s *BiblioCite* and others now on the market allow you to plug in standard bibliographic information (author's name, title, and so on) to generate a perfectly formatted "Works Cited" or "References" page. If you have access to such software, use it. Following the conventions of standard bibliographic formats is the kind of tedious organizational task at which computers excel. Be sure to check, however, to be sure that your program is set up to comply with the latest formats for Internet sources. If not, then be prepared to do some manual editing to update your citations.

Listing books in the MLA "Works Cited" format

A book with one author

The basic format for a single-author book is as follows:

Mariani, Paul. <u>Dream Song: The Life of John Berryman</u>. New York: Morrow, 1990.

A book with two or three authors

For a book with two or three authors, follow the order of the names on the title page. Notice that first and last name are reversed only for the lead author. Notice also the use of a comma after the first author.

Roebuck, Julian B., and Raymond G. Kessler. <u>The Etiology of Alcoholism: Constitutional, Psychological and Sociological Approaches</u>. Springfield: Thomas, 1972.

A book with four or more authors

As in the example under in-text citations (see 7a-1), you may choose either to name all the authors or to use the abbreviated format with *et al.*

Stein, Norman, Mindy Lubber, Stuart L. Koman, and Kathy Kelly.
   Family Therapy: A Systems Approach. Boston: Allyn, 1990.

Stein, Norman, et al. Family Therapy: A Systems Approach. Boston:
   Allyn, 1990.

A book that has been reprinted or reissued

In the following entry, the date 1951 is the original publication date of the book, which was reprinted in 1965.

Perls, Frederick, Ralph F. Hefferline, and Paul Goodman. Gestalt
   Therapy: Excitement and Growth in the Human Personality.
   1951. New York: Delta-Dell, 1965.

A dictionary or encyclopedia

If an article in a reference work is signed (usually by initials), include the name of the author, which is spelled out elsewhere in the reference work (usually at the beginning). The first example is unsigned. The second article is signed (F.G.H.T.).

"Alcoholics Anonymous." Encyclopaedia Britannica: Micropaedia.
   1991 ed.

Tate, Francis G. H. "Rum." Encyclopaedia Britannica. 1950 ed.

A selection from an edited book or anthology

For a selection from an edited work, name the author of the selection and enclose the selection title in quotation marks. Underline the title of the book containing the selection, and name its editor(s). Give the page numbers for the selection at the end of your entry.

Davies, Phil. "Does Treatment Work? A Sociological Perspective."
   The Misuse of Alcohol. Ed. Nick Heather et al. New York: New
   York UP, 1985. 158-77.

When a selection has been reprinted from another source, include that information, too, as in the following example. State the facts of original publication first, then describe the book in which it has been reprinted.

Bendiner, Emil. "The Bowery Man on the Couch." The Bowery Man. New
   York: Nelson, 1961. Rpt. in Man Alone: Alienation in Modern
   Society. Ed. Eric Josephson and Mary Josephson. New York:
   Dell, 1962. 401-10.

Two or more works by the same author(s)

When you cite two or more works by the same author(s), you should write the author's full name only once, at first mention, in the reference list. In subsequent entries immediately following, substitute three hyphens and a period in place of the author's name.

Heilbroner, Robert L. The Future as History. New York: Harper
     Torchbooks-Harper, 1960.

---. An Inquiry into the Human Prospect. New York: Norton,
     1974.

A translation

When a work has been translated, acknowledge the translator's name after giving the title.

Kufner, Heinrich, and Wilhelm Feuerlein. In-Patient Treatment for
     Alcoholism: A Multi-Centre Evaluation Study. Trans. F. K. H.
     Wagstaff. Berlin: Springer, 1989.

A corporate author

If authorship is not individual but corporate, treat the name of the organization as you would the author. This listing would be alphabetized under "National Center."

National Center for Alcohol Education. The Community Health Nurse
     and Alcohol-Related Problems: Instructor's Curriculum Plan-
     ning Guide. Rockville: National Institute on Alcohol Abuse
     and Alcoholism, 1978.

Signaling publication information that is unknown

If a document fails to state place or date of publication or the name of the publisher, indicate this lack of information in your entry by using the appropriate abbreviation.

Missing, Andrew. Things I Forgot or Never Knew. N.p.: n.p., n.d.

In the above example, the first *n.p.* stands for "no place of publication." The second *n.p.* means "no publisher given," and *n.d.* stands for "no date."

An edition subsequent to the first

Books of continuing importance may be revised substantially before reissue. Cite the edition you have consulted just after giving the title.

Scrignar, C. B. Post-Traumatic Stress Disorder: Diagnosis, Treat-
     ment, and Legal Issues. 2nd ed. New Orleans: Bruno, 1988.

A book in a series

If the book you are citing is one in a series, include the series name (no quotation marks or underline) followed by the series number and a period before the publication information. You need not give the name of the series editor.

Schuckit, Marc A., ed. <u>Alcohol Patterns and Problems</u>. Series in

Psychological Epidemiology 5. New Brunswick: Rutgers UP, 1985.

An introduction, preface, foreword, or afterword

When citing an introductory or concluding essay by a "guest author" or commentator, begin with the name of that author. Give the type of piece—Introduction, Preface—without quotation marks or underline. Name the author of the book after giving the book title. At the end of the listing, give the page numbers for the essay you are citing. If the author of the separate essay is also the author of the complete work, repeat that author's last name, preceded by *By*, after the book title.

Fromm, Erich. Foreword. <u>Summerhill: A Radical Approach to Child

Rearing</u>. By A. S. Neill. New York: Hart, 1960. ix-xiv.

An unpublished dissertation or essay

An unpublished dissertation, even of book length, has its title in quotation marks. Label it as a dissertation in your entry. Naming the university and year will provide the necessary publication facts.

Reiskin, Helen R. "Patterns of Alcohol Usage in a Help-Seeking

University Population." Diss. Boston U, 1980.

Listing periodicals in the MLA "Works Cited" format

A *periodical* is any publication that appears regularly over time. A periodical can be a daily or weekly newspaper, a magazine, or a scholarly or professional journal. As with listings for books, a bibliographical listing for a periodical article includes information about authorship, title, and facts of publication. Authorship is treated just as for books, with the author's first and last names reversed. Citation of a title differs in that the title of an article is always enclosed in quotation marks rather than underlined; the title of the periodical in which it appears is always underlined. Notice that the articles *a, an,* and *the,* which often begin the name of a periodical, are omitted from the bibliographical listing.

The facts of publication are the trickiest of the three elements because of the wide variation in how periodicals are dated, paginated, and published. For journals, for example, the publication information generally consists of journal title, the volume number, the year of publication, and the page numbering for the article cited. For newspapers, the listing includes name of the newspaper, full date of publication, and full page numbering by both section and page number(s) if necessary. The following examples show details of how to list different types of periodicals. With the exception of May, June, and July, you should abbreviate the names of months in each "Works Cited" entry.

A journal with continuous pagination through the annual volume

A continuously paginated journal is one that numbers pages consecutively throughout all the issues in a volume instead of beginning with page 1 in each issue. After the author's name (reversed and followed by a period and two typed spaces), give the name of the article in quotation marks. Give the title of the journal, underlined and followed by two typed spaces. Give the volume number, in arabic numerals. After a typed space, give the year, in parentheses, followed by a colon. After one more space, give the page number(s) for the article, including the first and last pages on which it appears.

```
Kling, William. "Measurement of Ethanol Consumed in Distilled
    Spirits." Journal of Studies on Alcohol 50 (1989): 456-60.
```

In a continuously paginated journal, the issue number within the volume and the month of publication are not included in the bibliographical listing.

A journal paginated by issue

```
Latessa, Edward J., and Susan Goodman. "Alcoholic Offenders: In-
    tensive Probation Program Shows Promise." Corrections Today
    51.3 (1989): 38-39+.
```

This journal numbers the pages in each issue separately, so it is important to identify which issue in volume 51 has this article beginning on page 38. The plus sign following a page number indicates that the article continues after the last-named page, but after intervening pages.

A monthly magazine

This kind of periodical is identified by month and year of issue. Even if the magazine indicates a volume number, omit it from your listing.

```
Waggoner, Glen. "Gin as Tonic." Esquire Feb. 1990: 30.
```

Some magazines vary in their publication schedule. *Restaurant Business* publishes once a month or bimonthly. Include the full date of publication in your listing. Give the day first, followed by an abbreviation for the month.

```
Whelan, Elizabeth M. "Alcohol and Health." Restaurant Business 20
    Mar. 1989: 66+.
```

A daily newspaper

In the following examples, you see that the name of the newspaper is underlined. Any introductory article (*a, an,* and *the*) is omitted. The complete date of publication is given—day, month (abbreviated), year. Specify the edition if one appears on the masthead, since even in one day an article may be located differently in different editions. Precede the page number(s) by a colon and one typed space. If the paper has sections designated by letter (A, B, C), include the section before the page number.

If the article is unsigned, begin your entry with the title, as in the second example ("Alcohol Can Worsen . . .").

```
Welch, Patrick. "Kids and Booze: It's 10 O'Clock--Do You Know How
     Drunk Your Kids Are?" Washington Post 31 Dec. 1989: C1.
```

The following entry illustrates the importance of including the particular edition of a newspaper.

```
"Alcohol Can Worsen Ills of Aging, Study Says." New York Times 13
     June 1989, natl. ed.: 89.
"Alcohol Can Worsen Ills of Aging, Study Says." New York Times 13
     June 1989, late ed.: C5.
```

A weekly magazine or newspaper

An unsigned article listing would include title, name of the publication, complete date, and page number(s). Even if you know a volume or issue number, omit it.

```
"A Direct Approach to Alcoholism." Science News 9 Jan. 1988: 25.
```

A signed editorial, letter to the editor, review

For these entries, first give the name of the author. If the piece has a title, put it within quotation marks. Then name the category of the piece—Letter, Rev. of (for Review), Editorial—without quotation marks or underline. If the reference is to a review, give the name of the work being reviewed with underline or quotation marks as appropriate.

```
Fraser, Kennedy. Rev. of Stones of His House: A Biography of Paul
     Scott, by Hilary Spurling. New Yorker 13 May 1991: 103-10.
James, Albert. Letter. Boston Globe 14 Jan. 1992: 61.
Stein, Norman. "Traveling for Work." Editorial. Baltimore Sun 12
     Dec. 1991: 82.
```

Listing other sources in the MLA "Works Cited" format

An abstract of an article

Libraries contain many volumes of abstracts of recent articles in many disciplines. If you are referring to an abstract you have read rather than to the complete article, list it as follows.

```
Corcoran, K. J., and M. D. Carney. "Alcohol Consumption and Look-
     ing for Alternatives to Drinking in College Students." Jour-
     nal of Cognitive Psychotherapy 3 (1989): 69-78. Abstract. Ex-
     cerpta Medica Sec. 32 Vol. 60 (1989): 40.
```

A government publication

Often, a government publication will have group authorship. Be sure to name the agency or committee responsible for writing a document.

```
United States. Cong. Senate. Subcommittee to Investigate Juvenile
     Delinquency of the Committee on the Judiciary. Juvenile Alcohol
     Abuse: Hearing. 95th Cong., 2nd sess. Washington: GPO, 1978.
```

An unpublished interview

A listing for an unpublished interview begins with the name of the person interviewed. If the interview is untitled, label it as such, without quotation marks or underlining. Name the person doing the interviewing only if that information is relevant. An interview by telephone or e-mail can be noted as part of the interview citation.

```
Bishop, Robert R. Personal interview. 5 Nov. 1987.
Bly, Robert. Telephone interview. 10 Dec. 1993.
```

An unpublished letter

Treat an unpublished letter much as you would an unpublished interview. Designate the recipient of the letter. If you as the writer of the paper were the recipient, refer to yourself as "the author."

```
Bishop, Robert R. Letter to the author. 8 June 1964.
```

If a letter is housed in a library collection or archive, provide full archival information.

```
Bishop, Robert R. Letter to Jonathan Morton. 8 June 1964. Carol K.
     Morton papers. Smith College, Northampton.
```

A film or videotape

Underline the title, and then name the medium, the distributor, and the year. Supply any information that you think is useful about the performers, director, producer, or physical characteristics of the film or tape.

```
Alcoholism: The Pit of Despair. Videocassette. Gordon Jump. AIMS
     Media, 1983. VHS. 20 min.
```

A television or radio program

If the program you are citing is a single episode with its own title, supply the title in quotation marks. State the name and role of the foremost participant(s). Underline the title of the program, identify the producer, and list the station on which it first appeared, the city, and the date.

```
"Voices of Memory." Li-Young Lee, Gerald Stern, and Bill Moyers.
     The Power of the Word with Bill Moyers. Exec. prod. Judith
     Davidson Moyers and Bill Moyers. Public Affairs TV. WNET, New
     York. 13 June 1989.
```

An interview that is broadcast, taped, or published

Treat a published interview as you would any print source. A broadcast or taped interview can be treated as a broadcast program.

```
"The Broken Cord." Interview with Louise Erdrich and Michael Dor-
     ris. Dir. and prod. Catherine Tatge. A World of Ideas with
     Bill Moyers. Exec. prod. Judith Davidson Moyers and Bill Moy-
     ers. Public Affairs TV. WNET, New York. 27 May 1990.
```

A live performance, lecture

Identify the "who, what, and where" of a live performance. If the "what" is more important than the "who," as in a performance of an opera, give the name of the work before the name of the performers or director. In the following example, the name of the speaker, a cofounder of AA, comes first.

```
Wilson, Bill. "Alcoholics Anonymous: Beginnings and Growth." Pre-
     sented to the NYC Medical Society. New York, 8 Apr. 1958.
```

A work of art

Underline the title of a work of art referred to, and tell the location of the work. The name of the museum or collection is separated from the name of the city by a comma.

```
Manet, Edouard. The Absinthe Drinker. Ny Carlsberg Glyptotek,
     Copenhagen.
```

A separately issued map, chart, or graph

Even a free-standing map or poster generally tells something about who published it, where, and when. Give the title, underlined, and any identifying information available. Use the abbreviation *n.d.* any time a date is lacking in publication information.

```
Roads in France. Map. Paris: National Tourist Information Agency,
     n.d.
```

3   **Listing electronic sources in the MLA "Works Cited" format**

Electronic source materials are available to writers in a variety of delivery systems; the Modern Language Association (MLA) documentation style varies slightly, depending on whether the material is delivered via the Internet or a CD-ROM (or diskette). The guidelines here are based on the 1998 *MLA Style Manual and Guide to Scholarly Publishing* and the 1999 *MLA*

WWW
http://www.mla.org/set_stl.htm

Although the complete *MLA Style Manual* is not online, the guidelines for documenting electronic sources are online.

Handbook for Writers of Research Papers, 5th ed. As electronic media evolve, conventions for listing digital sources in a "Works Cited" list will also change. Whatever formats may emerge, researchers will always need to give clear, consistent, and specific directions for locating every source used in a paper.

Online sources

The MLA offers some general notes regarding publication dates, uniform resource locators (URLs), and page numbering:

- **Publication dates:** Because the content of Web-based sources may change from one user's access to another's, provide readers with at least *two* dates in your citation, if possible—the date the Web document was created or last modified (often located at the bottom of the Web page) and your date of access. If the Web document is a digitized version of an earlier print edition, you can cite that date as well.

- **Uniform Resource Locators:** The MLA recommends including URLs when citing Web-based sources. When fitting a lengthy URL into a citation, break the URL at the end of a line *only* after a forward slash. Do not add a hyphen at the line break (as readers could mistake the hyphen for part of the electronic address). Enclose the URL in angle brackets, as in this example: <http://www.studentadvantage.com>.

- **Page numbering:** Web pages (or paragraphs within Web pages) may or may not be numbered. When they are provided, record paragraph or page numbering in order to help readers locate information. Use the following models as a guide in creating citations for online sources. Cite as much of the requested information as is available.

A scholarly project

Underlined Title of Project. Database editor. Specifics on electronic publication, including date of creation or revision,
versions, organizations. Date of access <URL>.

The Life and Works of Herman Melville. Ed. J. Madden. 10 Apr. 1997.
Multiverse. 3 June 1998 <http://www.melville.org/melville.htm>.

A short work within a scholarly project

Last name, First name. "Title of Short Work." Specifics on print information if any. Underlined Title of Project. Database editor.
Specifics on electronic publication, including date of creation
or revision, versions, organizations. Date of access <URL>.

O'Brien, Fitz-James. "Our Young Authors--Melville." Putnum's Monthly
Magazine Feb. 1853. The Life and Works of Herman Melville. Ed.
J. Madden. 10 Apr. 1997. Multiverse. 3 June 1998 <http://www.
melville.org/obrien.htm>.

An online book published independently

```
Last name, First name. Title of Work. Editor or translator if any.
    Specifics on print information if any. Specifics on electronic
    publication, including date of creation or revision, versions,
    organizations. Date of access <URL>.
Twain, Mark. The Adventures of Tom Sawyer. Ed. Internet Wiretap.
    1993. 15 Jan. 1998 <http://www.cs.cmu.edu/People/rgs/
    sawyr-table.html>.
```

An online book within a scholarly project

```
Last name, First name. Title of Work. Editor or translator if any.
    Specifics on print information if any. Underlined Title of
    Scholarly Project. Editor of Project. Specifics on electronic
    publication, including date of creation or revision, ver-
    sions, organizations. Date of access <URL>.
DuBois, W. E. B. The Souls of Black Folk. Chicago: A. C. McClurg,
    1903. Project Bartleby. Apr. 1995. Columbia U. 12 May 1998
    <http://www.columbia.edu/acis/bartleby/dubois/100.html>.
```

Personal or professional site

```
Last name, First name of creator. Title of Site. Institutional af-
    filiation of site. Date of access <URL>.
Hylton, Jeremy. Shakespeare Resources on the Internet. MIT. 14
    Oct. 1998 <http://the-tech.mit.edu/Shakespeare/other.html>.
Q-Corp. Home page. 5 Feb. 1998 (http://www.qcorp.com).[1]
```

An article in a scholarly journal

```
Last name, First name. "Title of Work." Name of Periodical Print in-
    formation such as volume and issue number (Year of publication):
    Number of paragraphs or pages if given. Date of access <URL>.[2]
Badt, Karin Luisa. "The Roots of the Body in Toni Morrison: A Matter
    of 'Ancient Properties.'" African American Review 29.4 (1995):
    11 pp. 5 Mar. 1998 <http://thunder.northernlight.com/cgi-bin/
    pdserv?cbrecid=LW19970923040189466&cb=0>.
```

---

[1] If the personal or professional site has no title, write "Home page" (no underline or quotation marks).

[2] Use the abbreviation "pp." for pages and "pars." for paragraphs. If no paragraph or page numbers are given for the article, use a period instead of a colon after the year of publication and follow with the date of access.

An article in a magazine

Connolly, Brian. "Puzzling Pastimes." <u>IntellectualCapital.com</u> 28
      May 1998. 2 Aug. 1998 <http://www.intellectualcapital.com/
      issues/98/0528/iccyberrep.asp>.

Gray, Paul. "Paradise Found." <u>Time</u> 19 Jan. 1998. 5 Feb. 1998 <http://
      www.pathfinder.com/time/magazine/1998/dom/980119/cover1.html>.

An article in a newspaper

Meyers, Laura. "Britain Backs U.S. on Iraq." <u>Los Angeles Times</u> 3
      June 1998. 17 June 1998 <http://www.latimes.com/HOME/NEWS/
      AUTOAP/tCB00V0294.1.html>.

An unsigned editorial

"Flirting with Disaster." Editorial <u>New York Times on the Web</u> 3
      June 1998. 18 July 1998 <http://www.nytimes.com/yr/mo/day/
      editorial/03wed3.html>.

A signed editorial

Klayman, Larry. "No Special Treatment." Editorial. <u>USA Today</u> 3
      June 1998. 3 June 1998 <http://www.usatoday.com/news/comment/
      ncoppf.htm>.

A letter to the editor

Fletcher, Anthony Q. Letter. <u>New York Times on the Web</u> 3 June
      1998. 3 June 1998 <http://www.nytimes.com/yr/mo/day/letters/
      lfletc.html>.

A review

Lipschutz, Neal. "Buchanan's Anti-Trade Tirade." Rev. of <u>The Great
      Betrayal</u>, by Patrick Buchanan. <u>IntellectualCapital.com</u> 3.21
      (1998): 2 pp. 28 Aug. 1998 <http://www.intellectualcapital.com/
      bibliotech/rev-052898.asp>.

Electronic mail

Chadima, Steve. "Re: Business as Poker." E-mail to Leonard J.
      Rosen. 14 Aug. 1998.

Online postings

      You may want to cite a contribution to an e-mail discussion list or a
posting to an online news group or listserv. Generally, follow this format:

```
Last name, First name. "Title of Posting from Subject Line." On-
     line posting. Date of electronic posting. Name of online
     group. Date of access <URL or, if none, e-mail address of
     group's moderator>.
Nostroni, Eric. "Collaborative Learning in a Networked Environ-
     ment." Online posting. 8 Sept. 1997. Electronic Forum. 9 Nov.
     1997 <eforum@cgu.edu>.
```

Synchronous communications: MOOs, MUDs, IRC

```
Richardson, Lea. Online debate. "The Politics of Recycling." 16
     Aug. 1997. EnviroMOO. 16 Aug. 1997 <telnet://enviro.moo.
     greenearth.org:42557>.
```

Computer software

```
Q-Notes for Windows 95. Vers. 1.0.1A. 15 Nov. 1997. Brookline: Q-
     Corp, Inc. 1997.
```

Online service

You may locate and use source materials from an online service, such as America Online (AOL) or Lexis-Nexis. If you do so, and the service provides a URL for the source, follow the format above for citing online sources. When you access a source through a keyword or a path and no URL is provided, use the following format—recording as much information as is provided:

```
Author's Last name, First name. "Name of article" Underlined title
     of source in which the article appears. Version or date of
     creation including page numbers. Name of Online Service. Date
     of access. Keyword or Path (no italics, followed by a colon):
     Write the keyword, followed by a period, or the pathway (sep-
     arating items with a semicolon).
Fenwick, Ben. "Oklahoma Twister Survivors Face Long Recovery."
     Reuters. 9 May 1999. America Online. 10 May 1999. Path: News;
     U.S. and World.
```

If you are citing material found on a premium search service such as UMI's ProQuest Direct or Lexis-Nexis, present as much of the following information as is available: Begin with information from the print edition—author, title, publication date, and page(s). Follow with the name of the database, underlined; the name of the search service; the abbreviated name of the library and its location (with state, if needed for clarification); date of access; and URL of the service.

Targett, Simon. "Oxford to Offer Degree Courses over Internet." Financial Times 20 July 1998: 1. Proquest Direct. Bentley Coll.
   Lib., Waltham, MA. 20 May 1999 <http://proquest.umi.com/pqdweb>.

CD-ROMs and diskettes

CD-ROMs and diskettes issued as a single publication
(analogous to the publication of a book)

Last name, First name. "Title of Article." Title of Specific Collection. Editor of collection if given. Publication information for printed text if given. Title of CD-ROM or Diskette.
   Publication medium--i.e., CD-ROM or Diskette. Edition or ver-
   sion number if given. Place of publication: Name of pub-
   lisher, year of publication.
Chin, Jeffrey. "The Role of Impermanence in American Dating Rit-
   ual." Sociological Review of Dating and Marriage: 1990-1998.
   Ed. Ellen Markham. Dating and Marriage: A Cross-Disciplinary
   Approach. CD-ROM. Rel.1.2. Newton, MA: Westhill Wired, 1999.
"Industrial Revolution." Concise Columbia Encyclopedia. CD-ROM.
   Redmond: Microsoft, 1994.

CD-ROMs and diskettes updated periodically
(analogous to the publication of a magazine or journal)

Last name, First name. "Title of Article." Publication information
   for printed text if given. Title of CD-ROM or Diskette. Pub-
   lication medium--i.e., CD-ROM or Diskette. Name of publisher.
   Month and year of electronic publication.
Bureau of the Census. "Exports to Germany, East: Merchandise Trade-
   Exports by Country." National Trade Statistics (1995): 85-96.
   National Trade Databank. CD-ROM. U.S. Bur. of Census. Aug. 1995.

7b   Using the APA system of documentation

The American Psychological Association's *Publication Manual* has set documentation style for psychologists. Writers in other fields, especially those in
which researchers report their work fairly frequently in periodicals and edited
collections of essays, also use the APA system of documentation. Whichever
style of documentation you use in a given research paper, use only one; do not
mix features of APA and MLA (or any other format) in a single paper.

   APA documentation is similar to the MLA system in coupling brief in-
text citations, given in parentheses, with a complete list of information about

the sources at the end of the paper. In the APA system this list is called "References." In the in-text citation itself, APA style differs by including the date of the work cited. The publication date is often important for readers in psychology and related fields, in which researchers may publish frequently, often modifying conclusions reached in prior publications. Date of publication also serves to distinguish readily among publications by authors who have many titles to their name.

1   Making in-text citations in the APA format

In the sample paragraphs that follow, you will find variations on using APA in-text citation. Notice that, wherever possible, reference information is incorporated directly into the text, and parentheses are used to supplement that information. Supply the parenthetical date of publication immediately after an author's name in the text. If you refer to a source a second time within a paragraph, you need not repeat the information if the reference is clear. If there is any confusion about which work is being cited, however, supply the clarifying information. If in your entire paper you are citing only one work by a particular author, you need give the date only in the first reference. If the page number for a subsequent reference differs from the earlier page number, supply the number. Separate items within a parenthetical reference by commas.

Dardis's study (1989) examines four twentieth-century American writers--three of them Nobel Prize winners--who were alcoholics. Dardis acknowledged (p. 3) that American painters, too, include a high percentage of addicted drinkers. Among poets, he concludes (p. 5) that the percentage is not so high as among prose writers.

However, even a casual reading of a recent biography of poet John Berryman (Mariani, 1990) reveals a creative and personal life dominated by alcohol. Indeed, "so regular had [Berryman's] hospital stays [for alcoholism] become . . . that no one came to visit him anymore" (Mariani, p. 413). Berryman himself had no illusions about the destructive power of alcohol. About his friend Dylan Thomas he could write, "Dylan murdered himself w. liquor, tho it took years" (qtd. in Mariani, p. 274). Robert Lowell and Edna St. Vincent Millay were also prominent American poets who had problems with alcohol (Dardis, p. 3).

A work by two authors

To join the names of two authors of a work, use *and* in your text, but use the ampersand (&) in a parenthetical reference. Notice how the parenthetical information immediately follows the point to which it applies.

```
Roebuck and Kessler (1972) summarized the earlier research
(pp.21-41).
```

```
A summary of prior research on the genetic basis of alcoholism
(Roebuck & Kessler, 1972, pp. 21-41) is our starting point.
```

Two or more works by the same author

If the work of the same author has appeared in different years, distinguish references to each separate work by year of publication. If, however, you refer to two or more works published by the same author(s) within a single year, you must list the works in alphabetical order by title in the list of references, and assign each one an order by lowercase letter. For example,

```
(Holden, 1989a)
```

could represent Caroline Holden's article "Alcohol and Creativity," and

```
(Holden, 1989b)
```

would refer to the same author's "Creativity and Craving," published in the same year.

A work by three to five authors

Use names of all authors in the first reference, but subsequently give only the first of the names followed by *et al.* Use the *et al.* format for six or more authors.

```
Perls, Hefferline, and Goodman (1965) did not focus on the addic-
tive personality. Like other approaches to the study of the mind
in the '50s and '60s, Gestalt psychology (Perls et al.) spoke of
addiction only in passing.
```

A work by a corporate author

Give a corporate author's whole name in a parenthetical reference. If the name can be readily abbreviated, supply the abbreviation in brackets in the first reference. Subsequently, use the abbreviation alone.

```
Al-Anon Faces Alcoholism (Alcoholics Anonymous [AA], 1974) has
been reissued many times since its initial publication.
```

```
One of the books most widely read by American teenagers (AA, 1974)
deals with alcoholism in the family.
```

Distinguishing two authors with the same last name

Distinguish authors with the same last name by including first and middle initials in each citation.

(J. Williams, 1990)

(C. K. Williams, 1991)

Two or more sources in a single reference

Separate multiple sources in one citation by a semicolon. List authors alphabetically within the parentheses.

We need to view the alcoholic in twentieth-century America from many perspectives (Bendiner, 1962; Dardis, 1989; Waggoner, 1990) in order to understand how people with ordinary lives as well as people with vast creative talent can appear to behave identically.

2 Preparing a "References" list in the APA format

Entries in the "References" list should be alphabetized by the author's last name. Within an entry, the date is separated from the other facts of publication. The list should include only those works referred to in your paper.

Listing books in the APA format

Leave two typed spaces to separate items in an entry. Double-space the list throughout. Start each entry at the left margin; if the entry runs beyond one line, indent subsequent lines three spaces. **Note that these formatting instructions are for preparing student papers. If you are preparing a paper for publication in a journal, refer to the APA manual for guidelines.**

Dardis, T. (1989). The thirsty muse: Alcohol and the American writer. New York: Ticknor & Fields.

A book with two authors

Invert both names; separate them by a comma. Use the ampersand (&).

Roebuck, J. B., & Kessler, R. G. (1972). The etiology of alcoholism: Constitutional, psychological and sociological approaches. Springfield, IL: Charles C. Thomas.

A book with three or more authors

List *all* authors, treating each author's name as in the case of two authors. Use the ampersand before naming the last. (This book was first published in 1951, then reissued without change.)

Perls, R., Hefferline, R. F., & Goodman, P. (1951/1965). Gestalt psychology: Excitement and growth in the human personality. New York: Delta-Dell.

A selection from an edited book or anthology

Underline the title of the book. The selection title is not underlined or enclosed in quotation marks. (In APA style, spell out the name of a university press.)

```
Davies, P. (1985). Does treatment work? A sociological perspec-
     tive. In N. Heather (Ed.), The misuse of alcohol (pp.
     158-177). New York: New York University Press.
```

A corporate author

Alphabetize the entry in the references list by the first significant word in the name, which is given in normal order.

```
National Center for Alcohol Education. (1978). The community
     health nurse and alcohol-related problems: Instructor's cur-
     riculum planning guide. Rockville, MD: National Institute on
     Alcohol Abuse and Alcoholism.
```

An edition subsequent to the first

Indicate the edition in parentheses, following the book title.

```
Scrignar, C. B. (1988). Post-traumatic stress disorder: Diagnosis,
     treatment, and legal issues (2nd ed.). New Orleans: Bruno.
```

A dissertation

In contrast with MLA style, the title of an unpublished dissertation or thesis is underlined.

```
Reiskin, H. R. (1980). Patterns of alcohol usage in a help-seeking
     university population. Unpublished doctoral dissertation,
     Boston University.
```

If you are referring to the abstract of the dissertation, the style of the entry differs because the abstract itself appears in a volume (volume number underlined).

```
Reiskin, H. R. (1980). Patterns of alcohol usage in a help-seeking
     university population. Dissertation Abstracts International,
     40, 6447A.
```

Listing periodicals in the APA format

A journal with continuous pagination through the annual volume

The entry for a journal begins with the author's last name and initial(s), inverted, followed by the year of publication in parentheses. The title of the article has neither quotation marks nor an underline. Only the first word of the title and subtitle are capitalized, along with proper nouns. The volume number, which follows the underlined title of the journal, is also underlined. Use the abbreviation *p.* or *pp.* when referring to page numbers in a magazine or newspaper. Use no abbreviations when referring to the page numbers of a journal.

Kling, W. (1989). Measurement of ethanol consumed in distilled
        spirits. Journal of Studies on Alcohol, 50, 456–460.

A journal paginated by issue

In this example, the issue number within volume 51 is given in parentheses. Give all page numbers when the article is not printed continuously.

Latessa, E. J., & Goodman, S. (1989). Alcoholic offenders: Inten-
        sive probation program shows promise. Corrections Today,
        51(3), 38–39, 45.

A monthly magazine

Invert the year and month of a monthly magazine. Write the name of the month in full. (For newspapers and magazines use the abbreviations *p.* and *pp.*)

Waggoner, G. (1990, February). Gin as tonic. Esquire, p. 30.

A weekly magazine

If the article is signed, begin with the author's name. Otherwise, begin with the article's title. (You would alphabetize the following entry under *d*.)

A direct approach to alcoholism. (1988, January 9). Science News,
        p. 25.

A daily newspaper

Welch, P. (1989, December 31). Kids and booze: It's 10 o'clock--Do
        you know how drunk your kids are? The Washington Post, p. C1.

A review or letter to the editor

Treat the title of the review or letter as you would the title of an article; do not use quotation marks. Use brackets to show that the article is a review or letter. If the review is untitled, place the bracketed information immediately after the date.

Fraser, K. (1991, May 13). The bottle and inspiration [Review of
        the book Stones of his house: A biography of Paul Scott]. The
        New Yorker, pp. 103–110.

Two or more works by the same author in the same year

If you refer to two or more works published by the same author(s) within a single year, list the works in alphabetical order by title in the list of references, and assign each one an order by lowercase letter.

Chen, J. S., & Amsel, A. (1980a). Learned persistence at 11-12 days but not at 10-11 days in infant rats. Developmental Psychobiology, 13, 481-492.

Chen, J. S., & Amsel, A. (1980b). Retention under changed-reward conditions of persistence learned by infant rats. Developmental Psychobiology, 13, 469-480.

Listing other sources in the APA format

An abstract of an article

Show where the abstract may be found, at the end of the entry.

Corcoran, K. J., & Carney, M. D. (1989). Alcohol consumption and looking for alternatives to drinking in college students. Journal of Cognitive Psychotherapy, 3, 69-78. (From Excerpta Medica, 1989, 60, Abstract No. 1322)

A government publication

U.S. Senate Judiciary Subcommittee. (Hearing, 95th Congress, 2nd sess.). (1978). Juvenile Alcohol Abuse. Washington, DC: U.S. Government Printing Office.

A film or videotape

For nonprint media, identify the medium in brackets just after the title.

Jump, G. (Producer). (1983). Alcoholism: The pit of despair [Videocassette, VHS and Beta]. New York: AIMS Media.

A television or radio program

Erdrich, L., & Dorris, M. (Interviewees). (1990, May 27). The broken cord. A world of ideas with Bill Moyers [Television program]. New York: Public Affairs TV. WNET.

An information service

Weaver, D. (1988). Software for substance abuse education: A critical review of products (Report No. NREL-RR-88-6). Portland, OR: Northwest Regional Educational Lab. (ERIC Document Reproduction Service No. ED 303 702)

Computer software

Begin your reference to a computer program with the name of the author or other primary contributor, if known.

```
Cohen, L. S. (1989). Alcohol testing: Self-help [Computer pro-
    gram]. Baltimore, MD: Boxford Enterprises.
```

Listing electronic sources in the APA format

Conventions for citing electronic sources in APA format begin with the same information on author, date, and title as citations for print sources. Then follow with a reference to the electronic source, making a distinction between Web-based sources and CD-ROM sources.

For information found on a CD-ROM, follow the initial information—author, date, title—with the listing *CD-ROM* placed in brackets as the medium of electronic transmission.

Reference to a work on CD-ROM

```
NCTE. (1987). On writing centers [CD-ROM]. Urbana: ERIC Clearing-
    house for Resolutions on the Teaching of Composition. Silver
    Platter.
```

Reference to part of a work on CD-ROM

```
Peterson, C. L. (1995). Further lifting of the veil: Gender,
    class, and labor in Frances E. W. Harper's Iola Leroy. In New
    essays in feminist criticism [CD-ROM]. Silver Platter.
```

Reference to an Internet source

The APA has not updated its 1994 *Publication Manual* to reflect current scholarly practice regarding the citing of sources found on the Internet. Instead of announcing a standard, APA has elected to let a standard emerge from the scholarly community—which means that, for the moment, anyway, no firm standard exists. Still, the expectation remains that every citation provide clear pointers to a particular source. A Web site being monitored by the APA—Web Extension to American Psychological Association Style (WEAPAS) <http://www.beadsland.com/weapas/>—offers a clear and sensible format for citing Internet sources. The format is as follows.

Begin the entry with bibliographic information just as for a print source: author, date, title. Follow immediately with bracketed information

WWW
http://www.apa.org/journals/
webref.html

The most recent statement of the APA on how to cite documents retrieved from the World Wide Web.

that lists the type of online material you are citing. For a serial publication (for example, a journal), write *Online serial* in brackets. For documents published as a Web page but not as part of an online journal or a Web-based version of a newspaper, write *WWW document* in brackets. Place a period after this bracket and write *URL.* Follow immediately with the URL of the document you have retrieved. Do not enclose the URL in brackets and do not follow the URL with any punctuation. In this presentation of the APA style for citing electronic sources, note that you do *not* list the date you accessed an electronic source (as you do in MLA format). Note that the Li and Tent citation examples, below, appear on the WEAPAS Web site.

Online book

Landow, G. (1997). Hypertext 2.0: The convergence of contemporary
    critical theory and technology [Online]. URL http://www.stg.
    brown.edu/projects/hypertext/landow/ht/contents.html

Article in an edited online work

Keegan, J. (1999). Normandy: The invasion conceived, 1941–43. In
    Encyclopedia Britannica [Online]. URL http://normandy.eb.com/
    normandy/week1/buildup.html

World Wide Web document

Dice, R. (1998, June 15). Web Database Crash course--Lesson 1 [WWW
    document]. URL http://www.hotwired.com/webmonkey/98/24/
    index0a.html?tw=frontdoor
Li, X., & Crane, N. (1996a, May 20). Bibliographic formats for cit-
    ing electronic information [WWW document]. URL http://www.uvm.
    edu/~ncrane/estyles

Online newspaper

McDowell, R. (1999, April 21). Colorado students struggle to un-
    derstand rampage. The Boston Globe [Online newspaper]. URL
    http://www.globe.com/news/daily/21/school.htm

Online magazine article

Dubow, C. (1999, April 21). Turning acorns into trees. Forbes [On-
    line magazine]. URL http://www.forbes.com/tool/html/99/apr/
    0421/feat.htm

Online article in a journal paginated by issue

```
Tent, J. (1995, February 13). Citing e-texts summary.
     Linguist list, 6(210) [Online serial]. URL
          http://www.lam.man.deakin.edu.au/citation.txt
```

Abstract of an online article in a journal with continuous pagination

```
Jacobs, D. R., Hisashi, A., Mulder, I., Kromhout, D., Menotti, A.,
     Nissinen, A., & Blackburn, H. (12 April 1999). Cigarette
     smoking and mortality risk: Twenty-five year follow-up of
     the seven countries study. Archives of internal medicine,
     159, 733-740. Abstract [Online serial]. URL http://www.
     medstudents.com.br/jornal/index.htm
```

For more information on citing electronic sources using APA style, see Li and Crane (1996), *Electronic Styles: An Expanded Guide to Citing Electronic Information.* Li and Crane advise a slightly different format—one that ends with the date of access. (See the Web site associated with their *Guide* in the Li citation, above.) Check with your instructor to determine his or her preference regarding date of access.

7c Using the CMS style of documentation

In some social sciences (including economics, communication, and political science), as well as in most business-related disciplines, many writers have long preferred the system of endnotes or footnotes developed in *The Chicago Manual of Style,* fourteenth edition, and the closely related system that is offered as an alternate in the *MLA Handbook for Writers,* fourth edition. (The MLA footnote/endnote system differs from CMS in some details of punctuation and spacing, as noted below.) To use footnotes or endnotes, signal a citation in the text by a raised numeral (superscript) at the appropriate point, preferably after a comma or period. The citation information signaled with this numeral is placed in a separate note numbered to match the one in the text. Both the CMS and the MLA systems prefer citation information to be collected as *endnotes* at the end of your paper, though some publications continue to use *footnotes* placed at the bottom of pages where in-text citations are signaled.

Place endnotes in double-spaced form at the end of your paper on a separate page, with the heading "Notes." Indent the start of each note three spaces (the MLA convention asks for five spaces), and continue the note on subsequent lines with a return to the left margin. The full-sized number preceding each endnote should be aligned with the text (not a superscript), followed by a period and a space. If footnotes are used, they are placed at the bottom of a page, four line spaces below the text, in single-space format, with a double space to separate footnotes on the same page. The old MLA style and other traditional formats specify that footnotes be numbered with superscript numerals like those in the text. Many word processing programs are able to handle these formatting conventions automatically, and also to place footnotes at the bottom of a page.

There are two key features of the CMS footnote or endnote format: (1) an author's name appears in normal (not inverted) order and is followed by a comma, and (2) publishing information is contained in parentheses and follows the book title with no intervening period.

1 Making the first and subsequent references in CMS notes

The first time you cite a source in a CMS paper, give complete information about it. If you refer to that source again, you need give only the briefest identification. Usually, this is the author's name and a page reference.

In the following sample paragraph, the first CMS note refers to an entire book. The second note cites a particular passage in a review, and refers to that page only. The third note refers to a work already cited in note 2.

Alcohol has played a destructive, painful role in the lives of numerous twentieth-century writers. Among poets, Dylan Thomas is often the first who comes to mind as a victim of alcoholism. John Berryman, too, suffered from this affliction.[1] Among novelists who battled alcohol was the great British writer Paul Scott, author of the masterpiece The Raj Quartet. A reviewer of a new biography of Scott faults the biographer for not understanding fully the effect of alcoholism on Scott and his wife and daughters.[2] Scott's own mother, out of a kind of bravado, encouraged Paul to drink gin at the age of six.[3]

1. Paul Mariani, Dream Song: The Life of John Berryman (New York: Morrow, 1990).

2. Kennedy Fraser, review of Stones of His House: A Life of Paul Scott, by Hilary Spurling, New Yorker 13 May 1991, 110.

3. Fraser, 108.

Compare the format of these CMS footnotes with their corresponding entries in the MLA "Works Cited" list.

Fraser, Kennedy. Rev. of Stones of His House: A Biography of Paul Scott, by Hilary Spurling. New Yorker 13 May 1991: 103-10.

Mariani, Paul. Dream Song: The Life of John Berryman. New York: Morrow, 1990.

2 Following the CMS note style in citing books

A book with two or three authors

1. Julian B. Roebuck and Raymond G. Kessler, <u>The Etiology of</u> <u>Alcoholism: Constitutional, Psychological and Sociological Ap-</u> <u>proaches</u> (Springfield, IL: Thomas, 1972), 72.

A book with four or more authors
　　　Name each author, or use the *et al.* format.

2. Norman Stein et al., <u>Family Therapy: A Systems Approach</u> (Boston: Allyn, 1990), 312.

A corporate author

3. National Center for Alcohol Education, <u>The Community Health</u> <u>Nurse and Alcohol-Related Problems: Instructor's Curriculum Plan-</u> <u>ning Guide</u> (Rockville: National Institute on Alcohol Abuse and Alcoholism, 1978), 45–49.

A multivolume work

4. G. M. Trevelyan, <u>Illustrated English Social History</u> (Har- mondsworth, Eng.: Pelican-Penguin, 1964), 3:46.

Two sources cited in one note

5. Joy Williams, <u>Escapes</u> (New York: Vintage, 1990), 57–62; C. K. Williams, <u>The Bacchae of Euripides: A New Version</u> (New York: Farrar, 1990), 15.

An edition subsequent to the first

6. C. B. Scrignar, <u>Post-Traumatic Stress Disorder: Diagnosis,</u> <u>Treatment, and Legal Issues</u>, 2nd ed. (New Orleans: Bruno, 1988), 23–28.

A selection in an edited book or anthology

7. Emil Bendiner, "The Bowery Man on the Couch," in <u>Man Alone:</u> <u>Alienation in Modern Society</u>, ed. Eric Josephson and Mary Joseph- son (New York: Dell, 1962), 408.

An introduction, preface, foreword, or afterword

8. Erich Fromm, foreword to <u>Summerhill: A Radical Approach to</u> <u>Child Rearing</u>, by A. S. Neill (New York: Hart, 1960), xii.

A journal with continuous pagination through the annual volume

9. William Kling, "Measurement of Ethanol Consumed in Distilled Spirits," Journal of Studies on Alcohol 50 (1989): 456.

A monthly magazine

10. Glen Waggoner, "Gin as Tonic," Esquire, February 1990, 30.

A weekly magazine

11. "A Direct Approach to Alcoholism," Science News, 9 January 1988, 25.

A daily newspaper

12. "Alcohol Can Worsen Ills of Aging, Study Says," New York Times, 13 June 1989, late edition, p. C5.

A dissertation abstract

13. Helen R. Reiskin, "Pattern of Alcohol Usage in a Help-Seeking University Population" (Ph.D. diss., Boston University, 1980), abstract in Dissertation Abstracts International 41 (1983): 6447A.

Computer software

14. Alcohol and Pregnancy: Protecting the Unborn Child, computer software, Student Awareness Software, 1988.

A government document

15. United States Senate Judiciary Subcommittee, Juvenile Alcohol Abuse: Hearing, 95th Cong., 2nd sess. (Washington, DC: GPO, 1978), 3.

Internet sources

WWW

http://www.msoe.edu/gen_st/style/stylguid.html

Since *The Chicago Manual of Style* has not been revised since 1993, citation of electronic sources is inadequate. This guide is based on *The Chicago Manual of Style* with extensions to cover electronic sources.

For up-to-date guidance on citing Internet sources in CMS format, consult "A Brief Citation Guide for Internet Sources in History and the Humanities," which you can find at http://www.h-net.msu.edu/~africa/citation.html. The site is maintained by Melvin Page (Professor of History at East Tennessee State University) and has been endorsed by H-Net (Humanities and Social Sciences Online).

    16. Laura Meyers, "Britain Backs U.S. on Iraq," Los Angeles Times, (http:// www.latimes.com/HOME/NEWS/ AUTOAP/tCB00V0294.1.html), 17 June 1998.

7d Using the CBE systems of documentation

The Council of Biology Editors (CBE) systems of documentation are standard for the biological sciences and, with minor or minimal adaptations, are also used in many of the other sciences. You will find many similarities between the CBE styles of documentation and the APA style, which was derived from the conventions used in scientific writing. As in APA and MLA styles, any in-text references to a source are provided in shortened form in parentheses. For complete bibliographic information, readers expect to consult the list of references at the end of the document.

1 Making in-text citations in the CBE formats

The *CBE Style Manual* presents three formats for citing a source in the text of an article. Your choice of format will depend on the discipline in which you are writing. Whatever format you choose, remain consistent within any one document.

The name-and-year system

The CBE convention that most closely resembles the APA conventions is the name-and-year system. In this system, a writer provides in parentheses the name of an author and the year in which that author's work was published. Note that, in contrast to the APA system, no comma appears between the author's name and the year of publication.

Slicing and aeration of quiescent storage tissue induces a rapid metabolic activation and a development of the membrane systems in the wounded tissue (Kahl 1974).

If an author's name is mentioned in a sentence, then only the year of publication is set in parentheses.

Jacobsen et al. found that a marked transition in respiratory substrate occurs in sliced potato tissue that exhibits the phenomenon of wound respiration (1974).

If your paper cites two or more works published by the same author in the same year, assign a letter designation (a, b, etc.) to inform the reader of precisely which piece you have cited. This form of citation applies both to journal articles and to books.

Chen and Amsel (1980a) obtained intermittent reinforcement effects in rats as young as eleven days of age. Under the same conditions, they observed that the effects of intermittent reinforcement on perseverance are long lived (Chen and Amsel 1980b).

When citing a work by an organization or government agency with no author named, use the corporate or organizational name in place of a reference to an individual author. Provide the year of publication following the name, as indicated previously.

Style guides in the sciences caution that the "use of nouns formed from verbs and ending in -tion produces unnecessarily long sentences and dull prose" (CBE Style Manual Committee 1983).

The number system

The briefest form of parenthetical citation is the number system, a convention in which only an arabic numeral appears in parentheses to identify a source of information. There are two variations on the number system. With references *in order of first mention,* you assign a reference number to a source in the order of its appearance in your paper. With references *in alphabetized order,* you assign each source a reference number that identifies it in the alphabetized list of references at the end of the paper.

Citation for a reference list in order of first mention

According to Kahl et al., slicing and aeration of quiescent storage tissues induces a rapid metabolic activation and a development of the membrane systems in the wounded tissue (1). Jacobsen et al. found that a marked transition in respiratory substrate occurs in sliced potato tissue that exhibits the phenomenon of wound respiration (2).

Citation for a reference list in alphabetized order

According to Kahl et al., slicing and aeration of quiescent storage tissues induces a rapid metabolic activation and a development of the membrane systems in the wounded tissue (2). Jacobsen et al. found that a marked transition in respiratory substrate occurs in sliced potato tissue that exhibits the phenomenon of wound respiration (1).

These numbered text citations are linked to corresponding entries in a list of references. The reference list may be numbered either in the order of first mention or alphabetically.

Preparing a list of references using CBE systems

In the sciences the list of references appearing at the end of the paper is often called "Literature Cited." If you adopt the name-and-year system for in-text citation (see 7d-1), the entries in your "Literature Cited" section should be alphabetized rather than numbered. Like the list of references in the APA system, the "Literature Cited" list is double-spaced; each entry starts at the left margin, and the second or subsequent lines are indented three typewriter spaces.

If you adopt one of the numbered systems for in-text citation, you will number entries either alphabetically or in order of appearance in the paper. A numbered entry, beginning with the numeral, starts at the left margin. Place a period after the number, skip two spaces, and list the author's last name followed by the rest of the entry. For the spacing of the second or subsequent lines of a numbered entry, there are two conventions: either align the second line directly beneath the first letter of the author's last name, or indent the second and subsequent lines five spaces from the left margin. Select a convention depending on the preference of your instructor. The following are some of the basic formats for listing sources in the CBE systems.

Listing books in the CBE format

In preparing a list of references in the CBE format, leave two typed spaces between each item in an entry.

If you refer to more than one work published by the same author(s) in the same year, list the works in alphabetical order by title in the list of references, and assign each one a lowercase letter according to its order.

Books by individual or multiple authors

For a book with one author, follow the conventions immediately above. For a book with multiple authors, place a semicolon after each coauthor.

1.   Beevers, H. Respiratory metabolism in plants. Evanston, IL: Row, Peterson and Company; 1961.

2.   Goodwin, T. W.; Mercer, E. I. Introduction to plant biochemistry. Elmsford, NY: Pergamon Press; 1972.

Books by corporate authors

3.   CBE Style Manual Committee. CBE style manual. 5th ed. Bethesda, MD: Council of Biology Editors; 1983.

Books by compilers or editors

4.   Smith, K. C., editor. Light and plant development. New York: Plenum Press; 1977.

Dissertation or thesis

5. Reiskin, H. R. Patterns of alcohol usage in a help-seeking university population. Boston: Boston Univ.; 1980. Dissertation.

Listing periodicals in the CBE format

Leave two typed spaces between each item in an entry. Sequence the items as follows:

- Number: Assign a number to the entry if you are using a numbered system.
- Author's name: Use the last name, followed by a comma and the initials of the first and middle names. For multiple authors, see the convention for books above.
- Title of the article: Do not use underlining or quotation marks. Capitalize the first letter of the first word only.
- Journal name: Abbreviate the name, unless it is a single word, without underlining. For example, The Journal of Molecular Evolution would be abbreviated as J. Mol. Evol.
- Publication information: Use the volume number, followed by a colon, followed by page numbers (use no abbreviations), followed by a semicolon and the year of publication.

Articles by individual and multiple authors

6. Kling, W. Measurement of ethanol consumed in distilled spirits. J. Stud. Alcohol. 50:456-460; 1989.

7. Coleman, R. A.; Pratt, L. H. Phytochrome: immunological assay of synthesis and destruction in plants. Planta 119:221-231; 1974.

Newspaper articles

8. Welch, P. Kids and booze: it's 10 o'clock--do you know how drunk your kids are? The Washington Post. 1989 Dec. 21:C1.

Listing other references in the CBE format

Media materials

9. Jump, G. Alcoholism: the pit of despair [Videocassette]. New York: AIMS Media; 1983. VHS; Beta.

Electronic materials

10. Alcohol and pregnancy: protecting the unborn child [Computer program]. New York: Student Awareness Software; 1988.

PART III
Other Types of Writing

CHAPTER 8
Writing and Arguing in the Disciplines

This chapter opens with a general discussion of argument, then introduces the more specific approaches you are likely to take as you write arguments in the humanities, the social sciences, and the sciences. In terms of research and writing, each discipline has different purposes and goals and different approaches to making claims and presenting evidence. You must think carefully about these differences both in terms of the kind of research you do and the way you structure your writing. Using the information presented here and in the previous chapters in Part II, you will be able to approach your research writing assignments across the curriculum with confidence.

CRITICAL DECISIONS

Focusing Claims

When addressing a general audience, writers often make broad claims about social, political, and even moral issues. Most academic argument, however, has a much narrower focus. Based on careful reading of one or more texts, objective gathering of specific data, or closely observed experimentation, academic writers tend to make claims that expand our knowledge incrementally rather than wholesale claims that ask readers to look at a subject in a completely new light. There are exceptions to this, of course—critics who set forth radically new interpretations of texts, researchers who discover new ways of looking at human behavior or the physical world. But, as a student, realize that the more sweeping your claim, the stronger your evidence must be to support that claim. A narrowly focused claim that is well argued will be more successful than a broadly original claim that is not.

8a Understanding the elements of argument

An *argument* is a process of influencing other people, of changing their minds through reasoned discussion. Arguments consist of three parts: claim, support, and reasoning. No argument is possible unless these components work together to make a persuasive whole.[1]

CLAIM A claim is an argument's thesis, a statement about which people will disagree. There are three types of claims; whichever one you use, you need to define terms with care.

- Claims about facts
- Claims about what is valuable
- Claims about policy

SUPPORT Support consists of facts, opinions, and examples that you present to readers so that they will accept your claim. Usually, you will present several types of support for a claim.

REASONING Reasoning is the pattern of thought that connects support to a claim. Each type of support involves a corresponding form of reasoning. Reasoning is based on appeals to a reader's logic, respect for authority, or emotion.

The arguments you write will usually be longer than the one below, but the same principles apply. Note the three kinds of support, each connected to the claim by a specific type of reasoning.

Sample Argument

1st statement of support (Appeal to logic)

Do not expect your undergraduate college education to prepare you for a *specific* job. Seventy percent of college graduates take jobs unrelated to their majors, and what is true of them is likely to be true of you. What, then, should you be learning in college? No single answer could satisfy everyone, but most would accept this *partial* answer: You should learn to think critically in college. Develop your capacity to think critically. Robert Ornstein of the Institute for the Study of Human Knowledge put it this way: "Solutions to the significant problems facing modern society demand a widespread, qualitative improvement in thinking and understanding. [. . .] We need a breakthrough in the *quality* of thinking employed both by decision-makers at all levels of society and by each of

Claim

2nd statement of support (Appeal to authority)

---

[1] The approach to argument taken here is based on the work of Stephen Toulmin, as developed in *The Uses of Argument* (Cambridge: The University Press, 1958). In the discussion here, *reasoning* is substituted for the term *warrant*.

us in our daily affairs." Effective, strategic thinkers are needed urgently in all fields. Job advertisements in fields ranging from retailing to software design specify "clear-headed, analytical thinking" as a qualification. If you do not make clear thinking an explicit goal of your studies, then you may have difficulty succeeding in your career. Specifically, you should learn to identify and solve problems; to plan strategically; to challenge others and yourself; and to generate new ideas and information.

3rd statement of support (Appeal to emotion)

Key term defined

ANALYSIS The example paragraph consists of three sets of statements that support the claim. Each is based on a corresponding type of reasoning. Claim, support, and reasoning function as one persuasive whole:

(1) **Support:** Fact (most students take jobs unrelated to their majors)
Reasoning: Appeal to logic (a generalization—what's true of most will be true of you)
Claim (about policy):

> You should learn to think critically in college.

(2) **Support:** Opinion (statement by Robert Ornstein)
Reasoning: Appeal to authority (Ornstein is an expert on thinking and learning; his testimony is valuable)

(3) **Support:** Opinion (you should make clear thinking a goal of college)
Reasoning: Appeal to emotion (self-interest will lead you to agree)

Key term defined: Critical thinking is the ability to identify and solve problems; to plan strategically; to challenge others and yourself; and to generate new ideas and information.

While writing an argument, you should aim to pull claim, support, and reasoning together so that you construct a persuasive whole. As you will see, each discipline (and very often subgroups within a discipline) defines what counts as an acceptable claim, as reasonable support, and as convincing logic.

8b | Making a claim (an argumentative thesis)

You should learn to think critically in college.

Any persuasive paper that you write in college will have a claim, a single statement that crystallizes your purpose for writing and governs the logic and development of the paper. The claim, also called an **argumentative**

thesis, will provide answers to one of three types of questions: questions of *fact, value,* or *policy.* A *question of fact* can take the following forms: *Does X exist? Does X lead to Y? How can we define X?* A *question of value* takes another form: *What is X worth?* The writer determines value based on standards called *criteria* that are explicitly stated and then used to judge the worth of the object being reviewed. A *question of policy* takes a different form: *What action should we take?* Politics and business are major arenas for arguments of policy. Answers to these (and related) questions will lead you to the claims you will make in your arguments.

Defining terms in the claim

Specifically, you should learn to identify and solve problems; to plan strategically; to challenge others and yourself; and to generate new ideas and information.

In order to provide the basis for a sound argument, all words of a claim must be carefully defined so that people are debating the same topic. Consider this claim, which answers a question of policy: *The United States should not support totalitarian regimes.* Unless the term *totalitarian regimes* is clearly defined (and distinguished from, say, authoritarian regimes), the argument could not succeed.

Examine your claims and, if one term or another requires it, write a paragraph of definition into your argument. If you suspect that your audience will not accept your definition, then you will need to argue for it. Entire arguments are sometimes needed to define complex terms, such as *honor.* If a key term in your claim is not complicated, a paragraph or even a sentence of definition will suffice. Then, with terms well defined, argumentation can begin.

8c   Supporting the claim

FACT   Seventy percent of college graduates take jobs unrelated to their majors.

OPINION   Effective, strategic thinkers are needed urgently in all fields.

EXAMPLE   Job advertisements in fields ranging from retailing to software design specify "clear-headed, analytical thinking" as a qualification.

You can offer facts, opinions, and examples as support for your claims. A *fact* is a statement that can be verified, proven to be true. As a writer you should be able to verify facts on demand, and often you will do this by referring to an authoritative source.

An **opinion** is a statement of interpretation and judgment. Opinions are themselves arguments and should be based on evidence in order to be convincing. Opinions are not true or false in the way that statements of fact are. Rather, opinions are more or less well supported. You can strengthen your own argument by referring to the opinions of experts who agree with you. An *example* is a particular instance of a statement you are trying to prove. The statement is a generalization; by offering an example you are trying to demonstrate that the generalization is correct.

The Critical Decisions box on this page will help you assemble material to support your claims.

8d Reasoning: Connecting support to the claim

The type of reasoning you use in an argument must convince readers of a clear connection between your claim and your support. You can convince readers by appealing to their sense of logic, their respect for authority, or their emotions.

1 Appeals to logic

> Do not expect your undergraduate college education to prepare you for a *specific* job. Seventy percent of college graduates take jobs unrelated to their majors, and what is true of them is likely to be true of you.

In the academic world, appeals to logic are the most common. Strategies for these appeals include generalization, cause-and-effect, and parallel case. When making a generalization, you examine several representative examples of a group (people, animals, paintings—whatever) and then infer a general pattern that you think will apply to all other examples in that group, even ones you have not examined. Based on your close study of the examples, you are able to make a convincing claim.

CRITICAL DECISIONS

What Will Convince Your Readers?

Once you have decided on a claim, turn your attention to gathering support. Question your claim vigorously: What will readers need to see in order to accept your view as true, probable, or desirable? Assemble support from the categories available to you:

- **Facts and statistics:** Find sources on your topic. Take notes on any facts or statistics that you think are pertinent. Remember that the facts you gather should accurately represent the available data. The U.S. Government Printing Office publishes volumes of statistics on life in the United States. These are often the source for statistics used in other studies.

- **Expert opinions:** Locate experts by reviewing source materials and checking for people whose work is referred to repeatedly.

continued

> **What Will Convince Your Readers, *continued***
>
> Also compare bibliographies and look for names in common. Within a week or so of moderately intensive research, you will identify acknowledged experts on a topic. Quote experts when their language is particularly powerful or succinct; otherwise, summarize or paraphrase.
>
> ■ **Examples:** Examples give you the opportunity to discuss in real and practical terms the points you wish to make in an argument. When you argue, make your points *through* particular details of a well-chosen example. The details demonstrate your argument, and concrete, understandable terms may be more memorable than your abstract claim. Readers will recall your example and then your point—and you will have communicated effectively.

When you use cause-and-effect reasoning to link the support you've gathered to your argument's claim, you try to establish that an action created by a person, object, or condition leads to a specific result (or effect). For example, you could argue that smoking causes lung cancer. You can also approach cause-and-effect from the opposite direction, beginning with the presumed effect—for instance, numerous accidents at a particular intersection. You can then ask: What causes this? Working in either direction, you can conduct research and construct a cause-and-effect argument.

You can also link your support to your claim with a parallel case that presents a relationship between directly related people, objects, events, or conditions. The logic that underlies this approach assumes that the way things turned out in a closely related situation is the way things will (or should) turn out in the situation you are focusing on. Reasoning with parallel cases requires that situations presented as parallel be alike in essential ways; if they are not, then the argument loses force.

These are but three strategies for appealing to readers' sense of logic in your effort to show that a claim is valid or reasonable. There are others. The point to remember is that an appeal to logic is a sound approach that you should rely on extensively when making arguments in academic or business settings.

2 Appeals to authority

Robert Ornstein of the Institute for the Study of Human Knowledge put it this way: "Solutions to the significant problems facing modern society demand a widespread, qualitative improvement in thinking and understanding. . . . We need a breakthrough in the *quality* of thinking employed both by decision-makers at all levels of society and by each of us in our daily affairs."

As a writer, you greatly help your cause when you can appeal to your readers' respect for authority by quoting experts on a subject who support your point of view. You should realize, though, that experts are likely to disagree. Facts usually lend themselves to multiple interpretations, and you should not be discouraged when authorities seem to contradict one another. Whether you find contradictions or not, however, the sources you use must be authoritative. The Critical Decisions box on this page provides a number of general guidelines that should help you make a determination.

3   Appeals to emotion

> If you do not make clear thinking an explicit goal of your studies, then you may have difficulty succeeding in your career.

Appeals to reason are based on the force of logic; appeals to authority are based on the reader's respect for the opinions of experts. By contrast, appeals to *emotion* are designed to tap into the audience's needs and values. Arguments based on appeals to reason and authority may well turn out to be valid; but validity does not guarantee that readers will *endorse* your position.

CRITICAL DECISIONS

Determining Whether a Source Is Authoritative

1. Prefer acknowledged authorities to self-proclaimed ones.
2. Prefer an authority working within his or her field of expertise to one who is reporting conclusions about another subject.
3. Prefer first-hand accounts over those from sources who were separated by time or space from the events reported.
4. Prefer unbiased and disinterested sources over those who can reasonably be suspected of having a motive for influencing the way others see the subject under investigation.
5. Prefer public records to private documents in questionable cases.
6. Prefer accounts that are specific and complete to those that are vague and evasive.
7. Prefer evidence that is credible on its own terms to that which is internally inconsistent or demonstrably false.
8. In general, prefer a recently published report to an older one.
9. In general, prefer works by standard publishers to those of unknown or "vanity" presses.

continued

> *Determining Whether a Source Is Authoritative, continued*
>
> 10. In general, prefer authors who themselves follow [standard] report-writing conventions. [. . .]
> 11. When possible, prefer an authority known to your audience to one they have never heard of. [. . .]
>
> Source: Thomas E. Gaston and Bret H. Smith, *The Research Paper: A Common-Sense Approach* (Englewood Cliffs: Prentice Hall, 1988) 31–33.

To succeed, you may need to appeal to the readers' emotions in an effort to make them feel the same urgency to act that you feel. Here is a simple method for constructing an effective emotional appeal.

1. List the needs of your audience with respect to your subject: these needs might be physical, psychological, humanitarian, environmental, or financial.
2. Select the category of needs best suited to your audience and identify emotional appeals that you think will be persuasive.
3. Make the reader feel responsible for finding a solution or taking action.
4. Call on the reader to agree with you on a specific course of action.

8e Making rebuttals

By definition, arguments are subject to challenge, or to counterarguments. Because reasonable people will disagree, you must be prepared, when arguing, to acknowledge differences of opinion and to address them.

Once you acknowledge opposing views, respond with a **rebuttal**, an argument that addresses and then rejects these views. If you can, point out the faulty logic behind them. If you do not raise objections, your readers inevitably will; better that you raise them on your terms so that you can control the debate.

Of course, one response to an opposing argument is *to let it change you*. When arguing, you should be open to accepting the views of others. Readers will appreciate your ability to concede at least some of your opposition's points, and they will take it as a sign of your reasonableness.

8f Presenting your argument

Although the particular discipline in which you are writing research-based arguments will have its own preferred methods of organization, there are two time-honored strategies for arranging arguments that will serve you well in many situations: the "problem–solution" structure and the classic "five-part" structure are summarized in the following box. In these structures, each part of the argument may consist of either one paragraph or a section that contains several paragraphs.

Inductive and deductive arrangements

Inductive and deductive arrangements have to do with where you place your claim in an argument. Induction moves from support—particular facts, examples, and opinions—to a claim. A great deal of scientific and technological argument proceeds this way. The writer makes certain observations, finds patterns in those observations, and then makes a claim about those observations.

Deduction moves from a claim to support—to particular facts, opinions, and examples. A good deal of writing in the humanities, in politics, and in law proceeds this way. The writer begins with a general principle or claim, then proves the truth, likelihood, or desirability of that principle or claim.

8g Making arguments in the humanities

The *humanities*—traditionally considered as the disciplines of literature, history, and philosophy—address many puzzles of life and human nature, frequently by posing "large," difficult questions to which there are seldom definite answers. Those who study the humanities ask in distinctive ways such questions as these: Who are we? What are our responsibilities to ourselves? To others? What is a *good* life? How do we know what we know? Difficult questions like these lend themselves to difficult and varied answers.

Writing an Argument
The Problem–Solution Structure

I. There is a serious problem.
   A. The problem exists and is growing. (Provide support.)
   B. The problem is serious. (Provide support.)
   C. Current methods cannot cope with the problem. (Provide support.)

II. There is a solution to the problem. (Your claim goes here.)
   A. The solution is practical. (Provide support.)
   B. The solution is desirable. (Provide support.)
   C. We can implement the solution. (Provide support.)
   D. Alternate solutions are not as strong as the proposed solution. (Review—and reject—competing solutions.)

continued

Writing an Argument, continued

The Classic Five-Part Structure

I. Introduce your topic and its importance.
II. Provide background information.
III. State and support your claim.
  A. Provide reason #1 for accepting the claim.
  B. Provide reason #2.
  C. Provide reason #3, etc.
      (In providing reasons, appeal to logic, authority, and emotion.)
IV. Introduce counterarguments.
  A. Summarize each counterargument fairly and respectfully.
  B. Reject, or reject partially, the argument's evidence or logic. As an alternative to discussing counterarguments in a separate section, you can also merge sections III and IV: As you present each reason for accepting your claim, pair it with a reason not to accept a counterargument.
V. Conclude your argument.
  A. Summarize the main points.
  B. Remind readers of what you want them to believe or do.

Source: Adapted from Richard D. Rieke and Malcolm O. Sillars, *Argumentation and the Decision Making Process* (Glenview: Scott, Foresman, 1984) 163.

Students of humanities are concerned with discovering or recreating relationships among three elements: (1) the world as it has been observed by or commented on by someone; (2) a *text* that somehow reflects the facts about or the observer's impressions of that world; and (3) an audience—a reader, listener, or viewer. Texts provide the occasion to learn how others have investigated the large questions and to investigate these questions ourselves. A text could be a novel, a philosophical treatise, a letter, a film, a symphony, a song, a poem, a sculpture, or a painting. It is any creation that records one person's response to, or accounting of, what he or she sees, and that later can be read, viewed, or listened to by someone else.

1 **Purpose and goals**

The purpose of making an argument in the humanities is usually to *interpret* a text and to *defend* that interpretation as reasonable.[2] The purpose of puzzling through the large questions raised by a particular text is not to ar-

_____
[2] This discussion is based directly on the work of Stephen Toulmin, Richard Rieke, and Allan Janik in *Introduction to Reasoning* (New York: Macmillan, 1979).

rive at agreement (as in the sciences), but rather to deepen our individual perception and to affirm our ties with the larger human community. The goal of an argument in the humanities is reached when readers can make this sort of acknowledgment: "I understand your point of view, and I find it reasonable." You should therefore not expect to read—or write—a single, correct interpretation of a play. History professors will urge you to reject single, apparently definitive versions of the past. Philosophy professors will urge you to reject the notion that any one answer to the question, *What is a good life?* could satisfy all people.

Although consensus is not the goal of arguments in the humanities, not all arguments are equally valid. They can be plainly wrong. They can also be irresponsible, as when someone insists: "Since discussions in this course are based on personal opinions, my opinion is as good as anyone else's." Not true. One interpretation, argued well, can be clearly superior to and more compelling than another.

2   Claims and evidence

In making a *claim* in the humanities, a writer usually interprets a text. That is, the writer attempts to explain how the text is meaningful—how, for instance, a poem's images direct the reader's attention to certain themes, how an essay confirms or contradicts our understanding of a particular problem, how the content of a letter or diary suggests a revised understanding of some historical event. The process for making and supporting claims in the humanities typically follows these steps:

1. Read a text and discover in it a pattern that helps to make the text meaningful.
2. Reread and confirm that the pattern exists, and then make a claim: a formal statement in which you interpret some element of the text, its relationship to the reader, or its relationship to the writer and the times in which it was written.
3. Refer to the text as evidence for your claim.
4. Comment on or discuss these references (optional).

3   Sample student paper: "The Role of Color in Kate Chopin's 'A Shameful Affair'"

Following is an excerpt from a student paper that demonstrates how claims and evidence are used to construct arguments in the humanities—in this case, in a literature course. This paper is typical in that it requires the student to conduct research and do independent analysis. It is presented in standard MLA (Modern Language Association) format.

↕ 1/2"
Brooks 1

↕ 1"

Brandy H. M. Brooks

Dr. Glenn Adelson

English 16

25 October 2001 ┃ **Double space**

The Role of Color in Kate Chopin's

**Indent
5 spaces** "A Shameful Affair"

1"

←→ Kate Chopin is a writer of self-discoveries--

of characters who awaken to desires buried deep

1" within and only dimly understood (if understood at

all). In leading the reader through a character's

discovery, Chopin often prefers powerful descriptive

images to explicit speeches or action. The setting

in which a character finds herself, for instance,

can reflect or influence her development of self-

awareness. In "A Shameful Affair," Chopin communi-   **The thesis
                                                        (claim)**
cates Mildred Orme's sexual awakening through de-

scriptions of a farm and, particularly, through the

colors one finds there.

        Mildred Orme is a twenty-year-old sophisticated

beauty who seeks simple country life for a summer of

quiet reading and reflection. With the rest of her

family vacationing at Narragansett Bay, Mildred ar-

rives at Kraummer's farm as a mature young woman

who's temporarily free of her parents' restrictions   **Plot sum-
                                                        mary (pres-
and fully aware that she's placed herself in the   ent tense)**

company of strong, young men. Mildred sees the

farmhands every day as she sits reading on the

Kraummers' porch. While at first "she never look[s]

at them" (31), one day one of the men returns a slip

of paper blown from her side by a gust of wind. She

notices him. And "that," writes Chopin, is "the be-

ginning of the shameful affair" (32).

        At the farm, Mildred finds herself immersed in

a rich, fertile natural world that distracts her

from the "exalted lines of thought" (33) she had in-

↕ 1"   **(to bottom
        of page)**

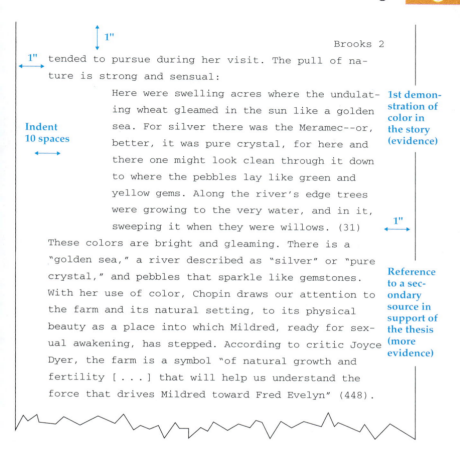

1"

tended to pursue during her visit. The pull of nature is strong and sensual:

> Here were swelling acres where the undulat-
> ing wheat gleamed in the sun like a golden
> sea. For silver there was the Meramec--or,
> better, it was pure crystal, for here and
> there one might look clean through it down
> to where the pebbles lay like green and
> yellow gems. Along the river's edge trees
> were growing to the very water, and in it,
> sweeping it when they were willows. (31)

Indent 10 spaces

1st demonstration of color in the story (evidence)

1"

These colors are bright and gleaming. There is a
"golden sea," a river described as "silver" or "pure
crystal," and pebbles that sparkle like gemstones.
With her use of color, Chopin draws our attention to
the farm and its natural setting, to its physical
beauty as a place into which Mildred, ready for sexual awakening, has stepped. According to critic Joyce
Dyer, the farm is a symbol "of natural growth and
fertility [. . .] that will help us understand the
force that drives Mildred toward Fred Evelyn" (448).

Reference to a secondary source in support of the thesis (more evidence)

The writer continues by making three more demonstrations of
Chopin's use of color in "A Shameful Affair." The conclusion restates the argumentative thesis, or claim. The writer and her readers understand that this
is not the only claim that can be made about the short story. If the argument
is effective, however, the reader will accept the claim as reasonable. Here is
the final paragraph of the essay, along with the "Works Cited" list (see Chapter 7 for details on MLA citation forms).

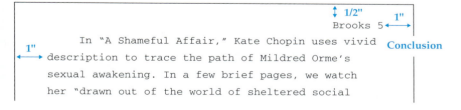

1/2" 1"

In "A Shameful Affair," Kate Chopin uses vivid
description to trace the path of Mildred Orme's
sexual awakening. In a few brief pages, we watch
her "drawn out of the world of sheltered social

Conclusion

1"

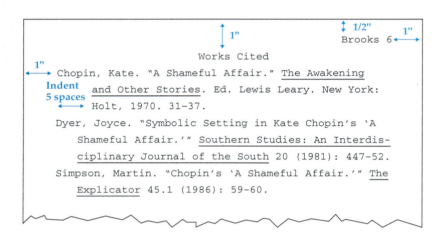

convention and into a natural world that is rich with sensuous physical surroundings" (Simpson 59). Chopin carefully, and subtly, uses color to heighten the drama of each moment in which Mildred grows in sexual awareness.

Reference to a secondary source in support of the thesis (concluding evidence)

↕ 1/2"
Brooks 6 ←→ 1"
↕ 1"

Works Cited

1" ←→ Chopin, Kate. "A Shameful Affair." The Awakening
Indent 5 spaces ←→ and Other Stories. Ed. Lewis Leary. New York:
←→ Holt, 1970. 31-37.

Dyer, Joyce. "Symbolic Setting in Kate Chopin's 'A Shameful Affair.'" Southern Studies: An Interdisciplinary Journal of the South 20 (1981): 447-52.

Simpson, Martin. "Chopin's 'A Shameful Affair.'" The Explicator 45.1 (1986): 59-60.

Making arguments in the social sciences

Social scientists—psychologists, sociologists, economists, political scientists, and anthropologists—attempt to discover patterns in human behavior that illuminate the ways in which we behave as members of groups: as members of family or community groups; as members of racial, ethnic, or religious groups; and as members of political or economic groups.[3]

The belief that behavior is patterned suggests that a person's actions in his or her social setting are not random but instead are purposeful—whether or not the actor explicitly understands this. Social scientists do not claim that

---

[3] Some historians also consider themselves to be social scientists because they use procedures such as statistical analysis to find meaningful patterns in the past. In this book, however, history is discussed as one of the humanities.

human behavior can be known absolutely—that, for instance, given enough information we can plot a person's future. They speak, rather, in terms of how and why a person or group is likely to behave in one set of circumstances or another. Social science is not mathematically precise in the manner of the natural sciences, and yet it is similar to those disciplines in the way that claims are based on what can be observed. Social scientists share the following broad theories:

- Human behavior is patterned, rule-governed behavior that can be described and explained.
- Individuals exist in a complex array of social systems, large and small. Individuals within systems interact; systems themselves interact and are dynamic, evolving entities.
- Individuals and social systems evolve—they change over time. Present behaviors can be traced to prior causes.

1 Purpose and goals

When social scientists report their findings in journals, they make arguments, but they acknowledge the complexity of human behavior by avoiding cause-and-effect explanations. They prefer, instead, to estimate the *probability* that a finding is correct—in terms of its "significance level." A level of .05, for instance, signifies that there is a less than 5 out of 100 possibility that the researcher's findings occurred by chance.

2 Claims and evidence

In his book *Philosophy of Social Science,* David Braybrooke notes that claims in the social sciences are often based on observations of individuals or groups. The claims state how these actions are significant for those observed.[4] The variety of human behavior is, of course, vast, and researchers have developed methods for gathering data both in controlled laboratory settings and in field settings. The interview and the survey are two widely used techniques that allow researchers to observe aspects of behavior that are usually invisible, such as attitudes, beliefs, and desires. Researchers carefully develop questionnaires, trying not to skew responses by the way questions are framed. If successfully developed and administered, questionnaires yield information about behavior that can be quantified and grouped into categories. These categories, in turn, can be analyzed statistically so that logical and reliable comparisons or contrasts can be drawn. Statistics can then

---

[4] Braybrooke, David. *Philosophy of Social Science.* Prentice-Hall Foundations of Philosophy Series. (Englewood Cliffs: Prentice Hall, 1987) 11.

be used as *evidence* in social scientific arguments to show whether a proposed connection between behaviors is significant.

The logic by which social scientists argue and connect evidence to claims will also depend on the method of investigation. Following are sketches of two social scientific arguments. You will see in each the interplay of method of observation, type of evidence, and logic that connects evidence to a claim.

Study 1   "Factors Influencing the Willingness to Taste Unusual Foods" [5]

PURPOSE   Psychologist Laura P. Otis investigates the factors that influence a person's willingness to taste unusual foods.

METHOD   Laboratory experiment—Otis showed students at a Canadian university various unusual foods (e.g., octopus), which they were led to believe they might eat. At various points during the experiment, subjects responded to questionnaires.

EVIDENCE   Statistical, based on frequency of responses to a questionnaire.

LOGIC   An argument from correlation or sign; one pattern of responses is shown to be closely associated with another pattern—one pattern indicates the presence of another.

CLAIM   The older a person is, the more likely it is that he or she will experiment with unusual foods. Food preference is generally unrelated to an individual's willingness to engage in novel or risky activities.

Study 2   "The Story of Edward: The Everyday Geography of Elderly Single Room Occupancy Hotel Tenants" [6]

PURPOSE   Ethnographer Paul A. Rollinson "seeks to provide a rich description of the everyday geography of an often overlooked population in contemporary urban America: elderly tenants of Single Room Occupancy Hotels" (188).

METHOD   Participant observation—Rollinson spends extended periods of time visiting run-down hotels in a section of Chicago where elderly tenants rent rooms. He tape records his conversations with tenants and forms a close and trusting relationship with one such man, seventy-year-old Edward.

EVIDENCE   Personal observations.

LOGIC   An argument from generalization (see 8d-1); the observations made are shown to form a pattern. The observer suggests that this pattern may form a general principle describing conditions for other individuals in similar circumstances.

---

[5] Otis, Laura P. "Factors Influencing the Willingness to Taste Unusual Foods." *Psychological Reports* 54 (1984): 739–45.

[6] Rollinson, Paul A. "The Story of Edward: The Everyday Geography of Elderly Single Room Occupancy (SRO) Hotel Tenants." *Journal of Contemporary Ethnography* 19 (1990): 188–206.

CLAIM   "The problems faced by elderly tenants of SRO hotels are numerous and often life-threatening. Their treasured independence is encumbered by their poverty-level incomes, their wide range of chronic disabilities, and their inappropriate housing environments."

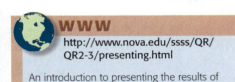

WWW

http://www.nova.edu/ssss/QR/
QR2-3/presenting.html

An introduction to presenting the results of qualitative research.

These two studies represent two distinct strains of social scientific argumentation and research—one quantitative (a researcher's number-based analysis of experiments in a laboratory setting) and the other qualitative (a researcher's perceptions of life lived in its natural social setting). When you take courses in a social science, you may be required to develop one or both types of argument.

3   Sample student paper: "Women Alcoholics: A Conspiracy of Silence"

The following library research paper, written by a student for her sociology class, investigates why women alcoholics in this country are largely an unrecognized population. Kristy Bell read several sources in order to support her thesis that the denial surrounding the problems of women alcoholics "amounts to a virtual conspiracy of silence and greatly complicates the process of diagnosis and treatment." Notice that Bell organizes her material by *idea*, not by source—as indicated by headings in the paper. Each heading develops one part of her thesis. Her work clearly demonstrates that she is thinking and arguing like a social scientist. Note how she discusses alcoholic women *in relation* to the people around them. Finally, notice as well her use of the American Psychological Association's (APA's) format for documenting sources (see Chapter 7).

Title Page

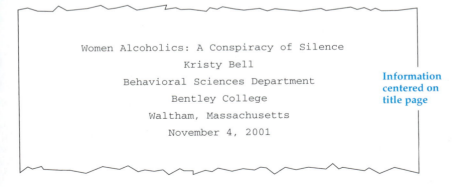

Women Alcoholics: A Conspiracy of Silence
Kristy Bell
Behavioral Sciences Department
Bentley College
Waltham, Massachusetts
November 4, 2001

Information centered on title page

Bell 1

Currently, in the United States, there are an estimated seven million women alcoholics (Women for Sobriety, 1997). Americans are largely unaware of the extent of this debilitating disease among women and the problems it presents. Numerous women dependent on alcohol remain invisible largely because friends, family, coworkers, and the women themselves refuse to acknowledge the problem. This denial amounts to a virtual conspiracy of silence and greatly complicates the process of diagnosis and treatment.

Silence: The Denial of Family, Friends, and Employers

Although the extent of the problem of alcoholism among women is slowly being recognized, research is still very limited, and a tremendous stigma still accompanies the disease for women. The general public remains very uncomfortable in discussing the topic. A primary reason that women alcoholics remain invisible is that they are so well protected. Family and friends, even if aware of the seriousness of the addiction, suffer pain and embarrassment and generally protect their loved one rather than suggesting that she seek professional counseling. By not confronting the issue, family and friends hope the problem will correct itself. According to Turnbull (1988), "The initial response of those close to the alcoholic woman is usually to deny the problem right along with her" (p. 366). Spouses, friends, relatives, and even employers tend to protect the alcoholic rather than help her initiate treatment. "A husband will nervously protect his wife's illness from friends and neighbors" (Sandmaier, 1980, p. 8). Family and friends experience a great deal of guilt and responsibility that, in turn, causes them to deny or hide the problem (Grasso, 1990, p. 32).

Intro-duction: women alcoholics will be studied in their social context.

Thesis (claim)

Denial by others. (evidence)

References to social science literature. (evidence)

APA format for documenting sources.

Bell 2

The needs of women dependent on alcohol are also ignored by employers, who are unable to confront the problem, in part, due to their having no prior experience with alcoholic women. The conspiracy of silence thus extends to the workplace. Employers tend generally to dodge confrontation by simply firing the alcoholic woman on an unrelated charge rather than steering her to an employee assistance program (Sandmaier, p. 131).

Silence: Self-Denial among Women Alcoholics

Women fail to seek treatment not only because they are ignored and abandoned, but also because they deny the extent of the problem themselves. Sandmaier believes that in "responding to survey questions, women may be more likely than men to minimize alcohol-related problems because of more intense guilt and shame" (p. 73). Thus, statistics published concerning women's dependence upon alcohol understate the extent of the problem. Once again, guilt and pain can be directly related to unfamiliarity with the issue--this time the woman alcoholic's own awareness that alcoholism among women is a debilitating and growing problem. Women alcoholics suffer from the same feelings of guilt and embarrassment felt by family members and friends. Obviously, these feelings are incredibly more intense in the actual alcoholic and tend to force the woman to be driven underground by her drinking problem. Unterberger observes that "[m]ore often than men, female alcoholics turn their anger on themselves rather than others, with anxiety and guilt being the result" (p. 1150).

Specialists in the field of alcoholism believe that there is an inherent trait among women to ignore the value of their own lives. Unfortunately,

Denial by alcoholic, herself. (evidence)

At second and subsequent references to an author, no date needed in citation.

Examination of reasons alcoholic women deny their problems.

Making Arguments in the Social Sciences   **175**

Bell 3

a woman today is rarely taught nor is she able to
properly take care of herself first (Grasso, p. 40).
As soon as she marries, in most cases, she is expected to "take care" of her husband. With the ar-
rival of children she is required to take care of
them. Often, if parents are aged, she will feel responsible for their well-being. Grasso firmly believes that women not only ignore and deny their
problem, but never really think enough about themselves to realize that they are in trouble with and
becoming very dependent on alcohol. Sandmaier says
this feeling is especially true among housewives due
to the close identification with their dual roles of
wife and mother.

Difficulties in Treatment and Diagnosis

    Many women avoid treatment because of concern
for the well-being of their children. A rehabilita-
tion program including hospital care cannot be considered because the woman is unable to be absent
from home for an extended period. Feelings of obligation to a husband and children are extremely powerful for a woman, especially one whose emotions are
intensified by alcohol. Turnbull (1988) believes
that "child-care services need to be provided to allow women to seek and remain in treatment" (p. 369).
Treatment would be considerably easier and progress
much more quickly if the woman was confident that
her children would receive proper care.

    Professionals in the field of social work are
not yet experienced enough to recognize alcoholism
by its preliminary characteristics. Because female
alcoholism has never really been a well-defined
problem, health specialists do not have the experience needed to detect it when a woman approaches
them with an alcohol-related problem. Frequently,

New heading signals development of second part of thesis.

Date continues to be cited in this reference since Turnbull has written two articles that are referred to in this paper.

Social work professionals need help in detecting alcoholism among women. (extension of claim)

Bell 4

the alcoholic woman is dismissed as being "just depressed" or under stress (Turnbull, 1989, p. 291).

Conclusion

    Society is now realizing that there is and has
been a definite alcohol problem among women. The
problem now lies in learning to recognize the symp-
toms and help women to seek treatment. Many believe
that women should be screened routinely at the onset
of any kind of treatment program. This would allow
for identification of alcohol problems much earlier
and would facilitate treatment before problems grow
out of control. Social workers, as well, should include screening for drinking problems in all female
clients. Some specialists believe that routine
screening for substance abuse should become a manda-
tory part of all gynecological examinations as well
as job orientations (Turnbull, 1988, pp. 366-68).

    As the recognition of alcoholism among women
grows, changes are being initiated to help make
these women more visible to themselves, to health
care professionals, and to society at large.

Conclusion: the paper *has* estab- lished that a problem exists.

Two solutions explored.

Self- perception of women alcoholics encour- aged.

Bell 5

References

Grasso, A. (1990). Special treatment needs of the
    chemically dependent woman. Syracuse: Crouse-
    Irving Memorial School of Nursing.
Sandmaier, M. (1980). The invisible alcoholics. New
    York: McGraw-Hill.

Bell 6

Turnbull, J. (1988). Primary and secondary alcoholic
        women. Social Casework: The Journal of Contem-
        porary Social Casework, 36, 290-298.

Turnbull, J. (1989). Treatment issues for alcoholic
        women. Social Casework: The Journal of Contem-
        porary Social Casework, 47, 364-370.

Unterberger, G. (1989, December 6). Twelve steps for
        women alcoholics. The Christian Century, pp.
        1150-1152.

Women for Sobriety. "Introducing . . . Women for So-
        briety." http://www.mediapulse.com/wfs/wfs_
        history.html (25 July 1997).

8i   Making arguments in the sciences

Scientists work systematically to investigate the world of nature—at scales so small that they are invisible to the naked eye and at scales so vast that they are equally invisible. A scientist's investigations are always built on observable, verifiable information, known as *empirical evidence.* Scientific investigations often begin with questions like these:

- What kinds of things are in the world of nature?
- What are these things composed of, and how does this makeup affect their behavior or operation?
- How did all these things come to be structured as they are?
- What are the characteristic functions of each natural thing and/or its parts? [7]

At one point or another, we have all asked these questions and speculated on answers. Scientists do more than speculate. They devise experiments in order to gather information and, on the basis of carefully stated predictions, or **hypotheses,** they conduct analyses and offer explanations. A study conducted by the American Association for the Advancement of

---

[7] Much of the discussion in this section is based directly on the work of Stephen Toulmin, Richard Rieke, and Allan Janik in *Introduction to Reasoning* (New York: Macmillan, 1979). See, particularly, Chapter 12, "Introduction" to fields of argument, pages 195–202, and Chapter 14, "Argumentation in Science," pages 229–63.

Science found that all scientists share two fundamental assumptions about the world and the way it works: first, that "things and events in the universe occur in consistent patterns that are comprehensible through careful, systematic study"; and second, that "[k]nowledge gained from studying one part of the universe is applicable to other parts."[8] On the strength of these assumptions, scientists pose questions and conduct experiments in which they observe and measure. Then they make claims (usually) of fact or definition, about *whether* a thing exists and, if it does, *what* it is or *why* it occurs. Questions that cannot be answered by an appeal to observable, quantifiable fact may be important and necessary to ask (for example, "What makes *Moby Dick* a great novel?" or "What are a society's responsibilities to its poor?"), but these are not matters for scientific investigation.

1 Purpose and goals

A scientist's efforts to inform readers are very often part of a larger attempt to *persuade*. In every discipline, arguments are built on claims, evidence, and the logical relationships that connect them. But the characteristics of these elements change from one discipline to the next and also *within* disciplines as theoretical perspectives change. Geneticists working on techniques of tissue analysis argue differently from astronomers. Each discipline uses different methods and different tools of investigation. Each asks different questions and finds meaning in different sorts of information. Within any one discipline you will find that multiple perspectives give rise to competing communities or schools of thought. Within any one scientific community the purpose of argument will be to achieve agreement about the way in which some part of the universe works.

Scientific inquiry typically proceeds in a fixed order within the scientific community. Once investigators make their observations in a laboratory or in a natural setting, they report their findings to colleagues in articles written for scientific and technical journals. The scientific community will not accept these reports as dependable until independent researchers can recreate experiments and observe similar findings. As scientists around the world try to replicate the experiments and confirm results, a conversation—an argument —develops in which researchers might publish a challenge or addition to the original findings. In this way, a body of literature on a particular topic grows.

2 Claims and evidence

Scientific arguments often involve two sorts of claims. The first takes the form *X is a problem* or *X is somehow puzzling*. This claim establishes some

---

[8] American Association for the Advancement of Science. *Project 2061: Science for All Americans.* (Washington: AAAS, 1989) 25.

issue as worthy of investigation, and it is on the basis of this claim (which must be supported) that experiments are designed. Recognizing what counts as a problem or a puzzle requires both experience and creativity. Assume it is early October. One evening the temperature drops and you have the first hard frost of the season. The following day you notice that most of the flowers and vegetables in your garden have wilted—but one particular grouping of flowers (your mums) and one vegetable (your turnips) seem as healthy as ever. You and your neighbor both notice this fact. Your neighbor passes it by with a shrug, but you wonder *why*. You have noticed a *difference,* an anomaly. If you were scientifically inclined, you might begin an investigation into why a certain plant or flower is frost resistant.

Recognizing a difference or anomaly often begins the process of scientific investigation. The process continues when you make a second claim that attempts to explain the anomaly. Such a claim takes this form: *X can be explained as follows.* If in a book on horticulture you did not find an answer to your puzzle about resistance to frost, you might conduct a study in which you examined the leaf and root structures of the various plants in your garden. Based on your research you might develop an educated guess, or hypothesis, to explain why certain plants are frost resistant. To test your hypothesis you might design an experiment in which you exposed several plants to varying temperatures. Based on your results, you might claim that frost resistance in plants depends on two or three specific factors.

3   Sample student paper: "Comparison of Two Strains of Wine-Producing Yeasts"

Following is a student lab report on the fermentation of wine. The microbiological processes involved in wine production have been known for nearly 150 years, and the student writing this report has added no new knowledge to our understanding of how wine is made. But creating new knowledge was not the purpose of the assignment. Clarence S. Ivie met his professor's objectives by successfully planning and carrying out an experiment, by making careful observations, and by arguing like a biologist.

Notice that the writer demonstrates the logic of a scientific investigation. Ivie bases claims on measurable observations—with an important exception at the end of the paper, in which he makes what he calls "subjective observations" of the two wines he is comparing. In the context of a laboratory experiment, Ivie is careful to distinguish subjective impressions from objective measurements. He follows a standard format for reporting lab results. He also documents sources appropriately for a scientific paper, using CBE conventions (see Chapter 7). Note that he does not actually state his claim (that wine yeast produces better wine than baker's yeast) until he has presented all the evidence. By this time, readers will have reached the same conclusion on their own.

Title Page

Comparison of Two Strains of
Wine-Producing Yeasts
Clarence S. Ivie III
Microbiology 314
Department of Biological Sciences
University of South Alabama
Mobile, Alabama 36688
Professor Burke Brown
4 March 2001

Information centered on title page.

1

Comparison of Two Strains of
Wine-Producing Yeasts

The purpose of this experiment was to determine which strain of yeast produced the most favorable wine. Wine yeast, Saccharomyces cerevisiæ var. ellipsoideus, and Fleischmann's baker's yeast, Saccharomyces cerevisiæ, were used to make two samples of wine. The wines were then compared with one another to determine which yeast created the best wine based on smell, taste, and alcohol content. The results of the experiment indicated that the wine yeast produced a better wine.

The abstract consists of one-sentence summaries of the report's major sections.

Fermentation is a process whereby a strain of yeast metabolizes sugar to produce alcohol. Wine is most commonly produced from grape juice by the process of fermentation. Grapes are crushed to acquire the juice. Sugar is then added to the grape juice. The grape juice, or

In some disciplines, "Introduction," as a heading is omitted from the lab report.

<u>must</u>, is then inoculated with yeast and allowed to ferment, a process that takes around fourteen days. <u>The end product is an alcoholic beverage that has been valued for centuries. It is not known when the first wines were created. However, throughout the history of wine making, people have constantly made attempts at improving the quality of the wine (2)</u>. In this experiment, the strain of yeast that produced the best wine was determined on the basis of smell, taste, and alcohol content.

> The introduction sets the study in a larger context and establishes the research perspective: microbiology.

Materials and Methods

Two 1.9L bottles were used. Each bottle contained 1.7L of grape juice. Two hundred thirty (230) grams of table sugar were added to each bottle of grape juice. Bottle #1 was then inoculated with one package of <u>Saccharomyces</u> var. <u>ellipsoideus</u>. Bottle #2 was inoculated with one package of Fleischmann's baker's yeast. The mixtures were then shaken to dissolve their contents. Initial measurements were immediately taken, including: pH, specific gravity, and temperature. Subjective observations, such as the mixture's color, were also made. A pH meter was used to measure pH, a hydrometer was used to measure specific gravity, and a thermometer was used to measure temperature. After initial measurements, both bottles were then sealed and allowed to ferment. Periodically CO_2 gas production rates were measured for each experimental wine fermentation procedure. This was done by measuring the volume of displacement, due to the gas production. As the wine continued to ferment, these measurements were made daily throughout the twenty-day duration of the experiment. On the eighteenth day of the experiment, both bottles were inoculated with a bisulphite to stop the fermentation process.

> The author provides exact information so that readers can replicate the study.

Ivie 3

Results

After the fermentation process was halted, the specific gravity changes of bottles 1 and 2 were compared. The specific gravities of both wine experiments decreased, but the most substantial decrease occurred in bottle #1. These results indicated that the wine yeast metabolized the sugar more efficiently than the Fleischmann's baker's yeast (Fig. 1).

> The author provides a specific criterion, or test, by which to analyze the two samples.

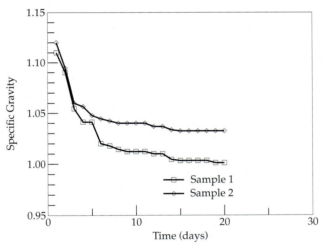

> The graph is given a title; its elements are clearly labeled; its information is self-contained.

Fig. 1. Comparison of specific gravity versus time between Saccharomyces var. ellipsoideus, the wine yeast, and Saccharomyces cerevisiæ, the baker's yeast.

The results of the pH change, in each case, fluctuated daily. There was, however, an overall increase in both samples.

The temperatures of both samples remained more or less constant at 22.5 degrees Celsius throughout the entire fermentation process.

> The author provides three additional criteria by which to analyze the samples.

Ivie 4

The gas production measurements showed that
the wine yeast produced more carbon dioxide than the
baker's yeast. Gas production is directly related
to yeast growth. Because of this fact, it was not a
surprise to find that the graph of the gas production rate of the yeast was quite similar to a typical growth curve (Fig. 2).

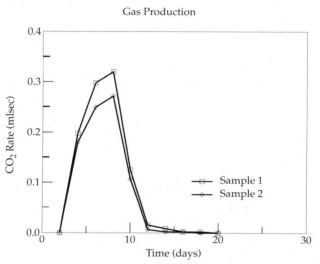

The graph is given a title; its elements are clearly labeled; its information is self-contained.

Fig. 2. Comparison of CO_2 production between
Saccharomyces var. ellipsoideus and Saccharomyces cerevisiæ.

     To calculate the % alcohol content of wine,
data from table 1 was used in the following equation
(1): % alc. = (Initial % potential alc.) - (Final %
potential alc.).

     The wine produced from Saccharomyces var. el-
lipsoideus was 14.9% alcoholic, while the wine produced from Saccharomyces cerevisiæ was only 12.3%
alcoholic.

Ivie 5

<u>Subjective observations of smell and taste fa-</u>
<u>vored the wine yeast.</u> The wine made from the baker's
yeast smelled like bread and tasted bitter. The wine
made from the wine yeast smelled like wine and
tasted sweet.

Discussion

Wine is the product of yeast fermentation. The
purpose of this experiment was to determine which
type of yeast produced the best wine. The basis by
which the wines made in the experiment were judged
included taste, smell, and alcohol content. It was
clearly evident that the wine yeast created a more
pleasant smelling and tasting wine than did the
baker's yeast. The wine produced by the baker's
yeast had a harshly overpowering smell that resem-
bled the smell of bread. Its taste was extremely
bitter. Overall, on the basis of taste and smell,
the baker's yeast created an undesirable wine, while
the wine yeast created a pleasant smelling and more
desirable tasting wine. <u>On the basis of alcohol con-</u>
<u>tent, it is clearly seen from the results of this</u>
<u>experiment that the wine yeast produced a more alco-</u>
<u>holic wine than the baker's yeast. The wine yeast</u>
<u>proved to be more efficient in the metabolism of</u>
<u>sugar than the baker's yeast. Evidence of this is</u>
<u>seen in the specific gravity measurements, which</u>
<u>ranged from 0 percent potential alcohol for samples</u>
<u>with a specific gravity of 1.00 to 17.7 percent po-</u>
<u>tential alcohol for samples with a specific gravity</u>
<u>of 1.130. The wine yeast also achieved a greater</u>
<u>rate of fermentation as seen in the gas production</u>
<u>measurement.</u> From this experiment, it can be con-
cluded that the use of wine yeast, <u>Saccharomyces</u>
var. <u>ellipsoideus</u>, is far more advantageous than the
use of baker's yeast in making wine.

Subjective observations are clearly distinguished from objective measurements.

The discussion does more than merely repeat results: it reviews the purpose of the experiment, sets the results in relation to the purpose, and succinctly states a conclusion.

Each of the author's claims is supported by evidence gathered during the experiment.

```
                                          Ivie 6
                    Literature Cited
1.   Case, J.; Johnson, L.   Laboratory experiments in
     microbiology.  Reading: The Benjamin/  Cummings
     Publishing Company; 1984.
2.   Prescott, A.; Harley, J.; Klein, P.  Microbiol-
     ogy.  Dubuque: Wm. C. Brown Publishers; 1990.
3.   Stryer M.; Lubert, A.   Biochemistry.  New York:
     W. H. Freeman and Company; 1988.
```

CHAPTER 9

Writing in a Business Environment

In a business environment, you need to appreciate that your readers have many pressing matters to attend to. In letters and memos, you should try to get your readers' attention immediately and hold their attention by staying on point. Otherwise, they are likely to turn to other concerns.

CRITICAL DECISIONS

Writing Letters and Memos that Succeed

In writing for busy people in the professional world, make sure that your work is direct, concise, and clearly organized. A *direct* letter or memo will state in its opening sentence your purpose for writing. A *concise* letter or memo will state your exact needs in as few words as possible. A *well-organized* letter or memo will present only the information that is pertinent to your main point, in a sequence that is readily understood. Keep this in mind as you plan, draft, and revise.

Standard formats

Use unlined, white bond paper (8½ × 11 inches) or letterhead stationery for your business correspondence. Prepare your letter on a typewriter or word processor, and print on one side of the page only. Format your letter according to one of three conventions: full block, block, and semi-block—terms describing the ways in which you indent information. The six basic elements of a letter—return address, inside address and date, salutation, body, closing, and abbreviated matter—begin at the left margin in the *full block* format. Displayed information such as lists begins five spaces from the left margin. In the *block* format, the return address and the closing are aligned just beyond the middle of the page, while the inside address, salutation, new paragraphs, and abbreviated matter each begin at the left margin. (See the "Letter of Inquiry" on page 190 for an example of block format.) The *semi-block* format is similar to the block format except that each new paragraph is indented five spaces from the left margin and any displayed information is indented ten spaces. (See the "Letter of Application" on page 192 for an example of a semi-block format.)

Standard spacing

Maintain a one-inch margin at the top, bottom, and sides of the page. Use single spacing for all but very brief letters (two to five lines), the body of which you should double-space. Skip one or two lines between the return address and the inside address; one line between the inside address and the salutation (which is followed by a colon); one line between the salutation and opening paragraph; one line between paragraphs; one line between your final paragraph and your complimentary closing (which is followed by a comma); four lines between your closing and typewritten name; and one line between your typewritten name and any abbreviated matter.

Standard information

RETURN ADDRESS AND DATE

Unless you are writing on letterhead stationery (with a preprinted return address), type as a block of information your return address—street address on one line; city, state, and zip code on the next; the date on a third line. If you are writing on letterhead, type the date only, centered one or two lines below the letterhead's final line.

INSIDE ADDRESS

Provide as a block of information the full name and address of the person to whom you are writing. Be sure to spell all names—personal, company, and address—correctly. Use abbreviations only if the company abbreviates words in its own name or address.

SALUTATION

Begin your letter with a formal greeting, traditionally *Dear* ____: Unless another title applies, such as *Dr.* or *Senator,* address a man as *Mr.* and a woman as *Miss* or *Mrs.*—or as *Ms.* if you or the person addressed prefer this. When in doubt about a woman's marital status or preferences in a salutation, use *Ms.* If you are not writing to a specific person, avoid the gender-specific and potentially insulting *Dear Sirs.* Open instead with the company name, *Dear Acme Printing,* or with a specific department name or position title: *Dear Personnel Department* or *Dear Personnel Manager.* See the discussion at 26a for the conventions on abbreviating titles in a salutation or an address.

BODY OF THE LETTER

Develop your letter in paragraph form. State your purpose clearly in the opening paragraph. Avoid giving your letter a visually dense impression. When your content lends itself to displayed treatment (if, for instance, you are presenting a list), indent the information. You may want to use bullets, numbers, or hyphens. (See, for example, the "Letter of Inquiry" on page 190.)

CLOSING

Close with some complimentary expression such as *Yours truly, Sincerely,* or *Sincerely yours.* Capitalize the first word only of this closing remark and follow the remark with a comma. Allow four blank lines for your signature, then type your name and, below that, any title that applies.

ABBREVIATED MATTER

Several abbreviations may follow at the left-hand margin, one line below your closing. If someone else has typed your letter, indicate this as follows: the typist should capitalize your initials, place a slash, then place his or her initials in lowercase—*LR/hb.* If you are enclosing any material with your letter, type *Enclosure* or *Enc.* If you care to itemize this information, place a colon and align items as in the example letter on page 192. If you are sending copies of the letter to other readers (known as a *secondary audience*), write *cc:* (for *carbon copy*) and list the names of the recipients of the copies.

THE SECOND PAGE

Begin your letter's second page with identifying information so that if the first and second pages are separated the reader will easily be able to match them again. The blocked information should consist of your name, the date, and the page number presented in a block at the upper left-hand corner of the page.

```
Jon Lipman
January 7, 2001
Page 2


and in the event of your coming to Worcester, I would be
happy to set up an interview with you here. Perhaps the week
of May 20 would be convenient, since I will be traveling to
eastern Massachusetts.
```

ENVELOPE

Single-space all information. If you are not using an envelope with a preprinted return address, type your return address at the upper left-hand corner. Center between the right- and left-hand sides the name and address of the person to whom you are writing. Vertically, type the address just below center.

```
Jon Lipman
231 Gray Street
Worcester, Massachusetts 01610



                    Ms. Hannah Marks
                    Equipment Design, Inc.
                    1254 Glenn Avenue
                    Arlington, MA 02474
```

9b   Letters of inquiry

A letter of inquiry is based on a question you want answered. Presumably, you have done enough research to have identified a person knowledgeable in the area concerning you. Do not ask for too much information or for very general information that you could readily find in a library. If you are inquiring about price or product information, simply ask for a brochure.

- Begin the letter with a sentence that identifies your need. State who you are, your general project, and your reason for writing.
- Follow with a sentence on how you have learned of the reader or the reader's company and how this person or company could be of help.
- Pose a few *specific* questions. Frame questions in a way that demonstrates you have done background research.
- State any time constraints you may have. Do not expect your reader to respond any sooner than two or three weeks.
- Close with a brief statement of appreciation. If you feel it would expedite matters, include a self-addressed, stamped envelope.

The example on page 190 conforms with these guidelines.

9c   Letters of application

Whether you are applying for summer work or for a full-time job you will need to write a letter of application to accompany your résumé. Limit

Letter of Inquiry
Block Format

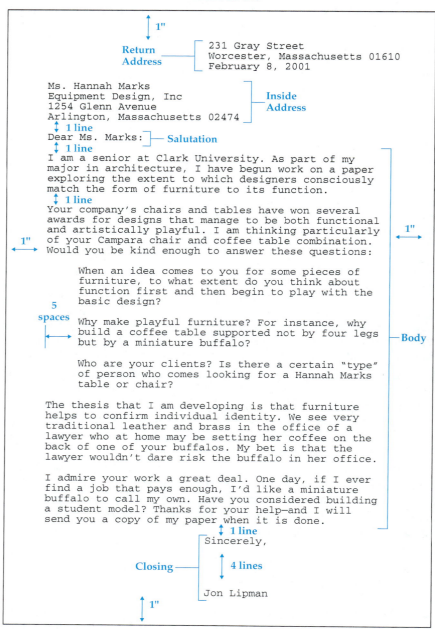

Return Address

231 Gray Street
Worcester, Massachusetts 01610
February 8, 2001

Ms. Hannah Marks
Equipment Design, Inc
1254 Glenn Avenue
Arlington, Massachusetts 02474

Inside Address

↕ 1 line
Dear Ms. Marks: ⎯ Salutation
↕ 1 line
I am a senior at Clark University. As part of my
major in architecture, I have begun work on a paper
exploring the extent to which designers consciously
match the form of furniture to its function.
↕ 1 line
Your company's chairs and tables have won several
awards for designs that manage to be both functional
and artistically playful. I am thinking particularly
of your Campara chair and coffee table combination.
Would you be kind enough to answer these questions:

5 spaces

When an idea comes to you for some pieces of
furniture, to what extent do you think about
function first and then begin to play with the
basic design?

Why make playful furniture? For instance, why
build a coffee table supported not by four legs
but by a miniature buffalo?

Who are your clients? Is there a certain "type"
of person who comes looking for a Hannah Marks
table or chair?

The thesis that I am developing is that furniture
helps to confirm individual identity. We see very
traditional leather and brass in the office of a
lawyer who at home may be setting her coffee on the
back of one of your buffalos. My bet is that the
lawyer wouldn't dare risk the buffalo in her office.

I admire your work a great deal. One day, if I ever
find a job that pays enough, I'd like a miniature
buffalo to call my own. Have you considered building
a student model? Thanks for your help—and I will
send you a copy of my paper when it is done.

Body

↕ 1 line
Sincerely,

Closing

↕ 4 lines

Jon Lipman

your letter to one page, and present yourself as a dependable person who can be counted on for steady work, creative thinking, and effective teamwork. Remember that skills grow dated as new technologies become available. You want to suggest that your ability to learn and to adapt will never grow dated.

- State which job you are applying for and where you learned of it.
- Review specific skills and work experience that qualify you for the job.
- Review the personal qualities (in relation to work experience, if appropriate) that make you well suited for the job.
- Express your desire for an interview, noting any constraints on your time: exams, jobs, and other commitments. Avoid statements like "you can contact me at . . . ." Your address and phone number are on your résumé.
- Close with a word of appreciation.

When you have written a second draft of your letter, seek advice from people who have had experience applying for jobs and particularly from those who often read letters of application and set up interviews. Ask them to respond to these questions: Am I emphasizing my skills and abilities in the right way? How do you feel about the tone of this letter? Am I direct and confident without being pushy? Then, based on their feedback, revise. Proofread two or three times so that your final document is direct, concise, well organized, and letter-perfect with respect to grammar, usage, and punctuation. Write your letter in a block or semi-block format on bond paper and use an envelope of matching bond paper. The example on page 192 conforms with these guidelines.

9d   Résumés

A résumé highlights information that you think employers will find useful in considering you for a job. Typically, résumés are written in a clipped form. Although word groups are punctuated as sentences, they are, strictly speaking, fragments. For instance, instead of writing "I supervised fund-raising activities" you would write "Supervised fund-raising activities." Keep these fragments parallel. Keep all verbs in either the present or the past tense; begin all fragments with either verbs or nouns.

WWW

http://leo.stcloudstate.edu/résumés/index.html

Hypertext guide to writing a résumé, from the Write Place at St. Cloud State U.

A résumé works in tandem with your letter of application. Written in your voice, the letter will suggest intangible elements such as your habits of mind and traits of character that make you an attractive candidate. The

Letter of Application
Semi-Block Format

231 Gray Street
Worcester, Massachusetts 01610
March 30, 2001

Ms. Hannah Marks
Equipment Design, Inc.
1254 Glenn Avenue
Arlington, Massachusetts 02474

Dear Ms. Marks:

5 spaces

⟵⟶ I would like to apply for the marketing position you advertised in <u>Architectural Digest</u>. As you know from our previous correspondence, I am an architecture major with an interest in furniture design. As part of my course work I took a minor in marketing, with the hope of finding a job similar to the one you have listed.

For the past two summers I have apprenticed myself to a cabinet maker in Berkshire County, Massachusetts. Mr. Hiram Stains is 70 years old and a master at working with cherry and walnut. While I love working in a shop, and have built most of the furniture in my own apartment (see the photographic enclosures), I realize that a craftsman's life is a bit too solitary for me. Ideally, I would like to combine in one job my woodworking skills, my degree in architecture, and my desire to interact with people.

Your job offers precisely this opportunity. I respect your work immensely and am sure I could represent Equipment Design with enthusiasm. Over time, if my suggestions were welcomed, I might also be able to contribute in terms of design ideas.

I would very much like to arrange an interview. Final exams are scheduled for the last week of April. I'll be preparing the week before that, so I'm available for an interview anytime aside from that two-week block. Thank you for your interest, and I hope to hear from you soon.

Sincerely,

Jon Lipman

Jon Lipman

enc.: photographs
writing sample

**Align
itemized
enclosures**

Résumé

Jon Lipman
231 Gray Street
Worcester, Massachusetts 01610
Tel/Fax: 508-555-8212
e-mail: jlipman@tiac.net

Objective: Marketing position in an arts-related company

Education: Clark University, Worcester, Massachusetts
Bachelor of Arts in Architecture, May 2001
Minor in Marketing, May 2001
Grade point average (to date) 3.3/4.0

Work Experience: September 1999-present: Directed
marketing campaign for campus-based artists'
collective and supervised fund raising. Spoke
at three area meetings on the "Entrepreneurial
Side of the Art World." Generated community
interest in the work of campus artists by organizing a fair and a direct mail program.

May 1999-August 1999: Studied cabinet making
with Hiram Stains, master cabinetmaker in
Berkshire County, Massachusetts. Prepared
wood for joining, learned dove-tail technique, and applied design principles learned
in school to cabinet construction.

September 1998-April 1999: Organized
artists' collective on campus and developed
marketing plan.

May 1998-August 1998: Studied cabinet making
with Hiram Stains. Learned tool use and
maintenance.

Related Activities: Supervised set design for theater
productions on campus. Donated services as
carpenter to local shelter for the homeless.
Designed and built virtually all furniture
in my apartment.

References: Mr. Hiram Stains
Route 16
Richmond, Massachusetts 01201

Ms. Amanda Lopez
Center Street Shelter
Worcester, Massachusetts 01610

Dr. Edward Bing
Department of Architecture
Clark University
Worcester, Massachusetts 01610

On-line Résumé

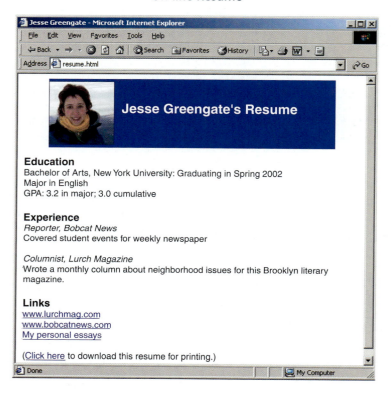

Jesse Greengate's Resume

Education
Bachelor of Arts, New York University: Graduating in Spring 2002
Major in English
GPA: 3.2 in major; 3.0 cumulative

Experience
Reporter, Bobcat News
Covered student events for weekly newspaper

Columnist, Lurch Magazine
Wrote a monthly column about neighborhood issues for this Brooklyn literary magazine.

Links
www.lurchmag.com
www.bobcatnews.com
My personal essays

(Click here to download this resume for printing.)

---

résumé, by contrast, works as a summary sheet or catalog of your educational and work experience. The tone of the résumé is neutral and factual. Center your name, address, telephone and fax numbers, and e-mail address at the top of the page. Then, provide headings as follows (see page 193):

- *Position Desired* or *Objective.* State the specific job you want.
- *Education.* Provide the full name of your college (and graduate school). List degrees earned (or to be earned); major; classes taken, if pertinent; and your grade point average, if you are comfortable sharing this information.
- *Work Experience.* List your jobs, including titles, chronologically, beginning with your most recent job.
- *Related Activities.* List any clubs, volunteer positions, or activities that you feel are indicative of your general interests and character.
- *References.* Provide names and addresses if you expect the employer to contact references directly. If you are keeping references on file at a campus office, state that your references are available upon request.

Principles for writing an online résumé

Increasingly, job applicants are creating résumés for view on the World Wide Web, where the résumé is one hyperlink on the applicant's Home page. While the goal of any résumé is to introduce the applicant in a favorable light, Web-based résumés differ from traditional paper résumés in important ways. Most of these differences, you'll find, will work to your advantage. Some tips:

1. Adhere to basic strategies and design principles for creating Web sites. See Chapter 10 for advice.

2. Include links to your work. Whether you have posted writing samples or other efforts online, here is a superb opportunity to show-case your work. Add hyperlinks within the body of your résumé, or create a special links area.

3. Because readers may not have the patience to click through multiple pages on the Web, try to keep your key information—contact information, education, and work experience—well organized and on one page.

4. Place the most important items of your résumé in the topmost 300 pixels of the screen—the area that every Web user should be able to read without scrolling down the page. It is the area of highest impact.

5. Include an e-mail link on the page (if you are comfortable doing so).

6. Incorporate relevant graphics into your résumé: showcase projects (such as artwork) with scanned photographs or images from a digital camera.

7. Give your page an informative title, such as "Marie Hobahn's Résumé," so that users who bookmark it will recognize that this your résumé.

8. Include the date that you have most recently updated the page. Users will want to know that your résumé is current.

9. **The Scannable Résumé:** Provide a non-Web version of your résumé in downloadable form for readers who want to print the résumé or scan it into a résumé database. (You might, at an employer's request, attach a scannable résumé to an e-mail message.) Prepare a résumé for scanning as follows:

   - Eliminate design elements: avoid boldface and italics; remove photos and hyperlinks; remove boxes, underlining, and tab spaces; run text flush to the left margin.

   - Use a standard type face (such as Times Roman), with a 12-point font.

   - Use standard résumé headings, including Education, Work experience, References.

   - Separate categories of information with one line of white space.

   - Add a "keywords" section (after your contact information) with nouns that represent your achievements: for example, biology major, student representative, field hockey player, hospice volunteer, dean's list member. Make sure to use the individual keywords throughout the résumé, so that database search engines will produce your name when a prospective employer searches on a particular keyword.

Memoranda: Print and electronic

Memoranda, or memos, are internal documents written from one employee to another in the same company to announce or summarize a meeting, set a schedule, request information, define and resolve a problem, build consensus, and so on. Memos tend to be less formal in tone than business letters; they also differ in the following ways:

- Memos have no return address, no inside address, and no salutation. Instead, they begin with a set format: Date; To; From; Subject (or Re). Some companies also place a *cc:* line under the *To:* line or add a *Distribution:* line.
- Memos use a full block format; all information is flush with the left margin.
- Memos often use headings to divide the document into parts, and they often contain bulleted or numbered lists. All of these devices help busy readers understand your message quickly.

If you are sending the memo electronically, the "To:" line will be an e-mail address, as will the "From:" and "cc:" lines.

Memorandum

```
Date: 4/4/01

To: Jon Lipman

From: Hannah Marks <marksh@equip.com>

Re: Interview

Jon:

I've contacted your references, who all had good things to say
about your abilities. Why don't you come to Equipment Design for
an interview when the semester is over. Call soon. We'll compare
schedules and set a date and time. (I've got to warn you: I'm
constantly traveling, so be patient and we'll get to talk.)

Regards,

HM
```

CHAPTER 10

Writing for the Web

The World Wide Web is a radically democratic publishing forum. Anyone can create and post Web sites, spreading points of view and information across town and across continents. This chapter will introduce you to the basic elements of Web publishing so that you can take the first steps necessary to post your work.

CRITICAL DECISIONS

Planning and Writing a Document for the Web

In one key respect, Web-based documents differ fundamentally from print-based documents: in the print world, both you and your audience assume that an essay, letter, or report will make sense only if read linearly—that is, from start to finish. You can make no such assumption about the ways in which computer users read a Web page. Given the development of hyperlinks that enable readers to jump from a document on one Web page to related topics on others at the click of a mouse, readers will likely not work through long Web documents, from start to finish, without taking detours (if these are offered). Bear these suggestions in mind as you prepare to post documents on the Web:

WWW

http://info.med.yale.edu/caim/manual/contents.html

The Yale Web Style Guide—the king of online web design guides.

1. *Anticipate multiple audiences.* Even though you may post a document that you believe only your classmates or teacher might read, other people may find your work online. You should therefore provide a context for your work: links to your home page and to course and university information.

2. *Prepare brief units of thought.* You cannot assume in a document embedded with hypertext links that readers will read multiple paragraphs in the order you've presented. Therefore, keep "thought units" brief—a paragraph or two at most—and link to other thought units.

3. *Anticipate a nonlinear development of ideas.* Readers *will* jump
   (continued)

Planning and Writing a Document for the Web, continued

between sections of a page and, if you provide links, off your site to other pages, so the organization of your page must make sense in whatever order readers choose.

4. *Make navigation easy.* Be sure to provide a site map that will facilitate navigating to the various parts of your document.

5. *Design your documents.* Design your Web-based documents for legibility, both on the screen and on the printed page. Also, design your documents with the awareness that browsers and computers may display Web pages differently.

10a Creating documents for the Web

1 Content planning

As the author of an essay, you are the content expert: You have done the research and the writing. Identify items that will serve as hyperlinks to other Web pages.

You can link citations in an essay to their online sources, not only in the formal bibliography but also within the text of the essay. You can also incorporate other materials not included in the print-based version of the essay. You might allocate a separate Web page for each such element and then link to it where appropriate, using an icon within the essay text.

2 Site maps

A Web site consists of many, sometimes dozens (or more) individual Web pages. The site map is a logistical illustration of all of the pages in a site, the content that is contained on each page, and where links exist. On page 199 you'll find an illustration of a site map created by student Marie Hobahn as she prepared to make a Web-based version of her essay, "Women and Computing: Beyond the Glass Ceiling."

From a home page that includes her introduction and thesis, Marie creates links that will take readers to all the major "thought units" of her essay. Also, each thought unit is linked to others, so that readers may navigate to different parts of the essay as they please.

Some site maps consist of pencil scrawling on a single sheet of paper, while others are the size of conference-room tables and contain color-coded areas, elaborate illustrations, and hundreds of link-arrows marching back

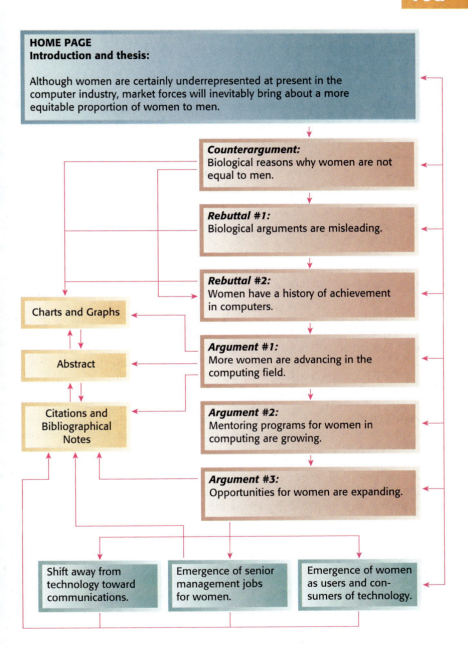

HOME PAGE
Introduction and thesis:

Although women are certainly underrepresented at present in the computer industry, market forces will inevitably bring about a more equitable proportion of women to men.

Counterargument:
Biological reasons why women are not equal to men.

Rebuttal #1:
Biological arguments are misleading.

Rebuttal #2:
Women have a history of achievement in computers.

Charts and Graphs

Abstract

Argument #1:
More women are advancing in the computing field.

Citations and Bibliographical Notes

Argument #2:
Mentoring programs for women in computing are growing.

Argument #3:
Opportunities for women are expanding.

Shift away from technology toward communications.

Emergence of senior management jobs for women.

Emergence of women as users and consumers of technology.

The Process of Web-Page Design and Production

Every page of a well-designed Web site is built on sketches, maps, and megabytes of digital revisions. The process of Web-page design and construction involves a good deal of planning and a commitment to iterative design.

Iterative design is the process of creating a rough estimate of what something (in this case, a Web page) ought to be, presenting the work to others for critique, revising based on feedback, and re-presenting—to revise again and again until a finished, polished product is created. Typically, Web sites are built up and partially torn down, only to be rebuilt and repeatedly torn down during the production of a single page. Constant refinement (along with continual updating of site maps and storyboards) improves the end product.

and forth. Regardless of how complex or simple the site map, creating it is the most important step in building a Web site.

3 Storyboards

In a Web developer's office you will find elaborate sketches, called "storyboards," for all pages in a project, with each sketch indicating what photographs will be used, what illustrations will be needed, and where links will be. Creating detailed sketches early in the process helps designers anticipate the amount of content—text *and* images—that can realistically fit on a page. If an image is central to your plan for a particular Web page, then you should integrate this image into your site map and storyboard very early in the process.

On page 201 is the first page of Marie Hobahn's Web-based essay, which incorporates these reader-friendly elements. Note: the following example page from Marie Hobahn's essay is shown *out* of a browser window so that the entire page is viewable. On a computer monitor, the reader would need to use the scroll bar to see the full page as presented.

4 Production

WWW

http://www.ncsa.uiuc.edu/General/Internet/WWW/HTMLPrimerPI.html

Though it's easiest to create your pages with a Web page editor, this Beginner's Guide to HTML from NCSA may help with fine-tuning your pages.

To create a Web file, you need to learn a bit about HTML, **H**yper**T**ext **M**arkup **L**anguage. The basic process of creating a Web page involves taking a page of text that you want to present online and adding to it

HOME PAGE: Women and Computing: Beyond the Glass Ceiling

For Comp 101 @ New York University

By Marie Hobahn (marie.hobahn@nyu.edu)

Introduction and Thesis

How well are women doing in the professional world of computing? There's no use denying it: the numbers don't look good. None of the top 50 computer companies boasts a female CEO, even though women make up about a third of the high-tech workforce (DeBare, "High-tech" 1). Women fill less than 30% of programming, engineering, and management jobs at high-tech companies. Companies created or run by women received just 1.6% of the venture capital invested in high-tech firms from 1991 to 1996 (Crain; Hamm). The glass ceiling that keeps women from advancing seems real. According to D.J. Young, a software quality assurance manager at the software firm Intuit, "More women are [. . .] reaching that first level of management, but [. . .] the higher [they] go, the harder it is to get to the next level" (qtd. in DeBare, "Voices" 1). Considering this discouraging news, it might seem a hopeless act of faith to believe that things will get better anytime soon. But that faith would, in fact, be justified. Although women are certainly underrepresented at present in the computer industry, cultural and market forces will inevitably bring about a more equitable proportion of women to men.

Home Page: Introduction and Thesis
Counterargument: Biological reasons why women are not equal to men.
  Rebuttal #1: Biological arguments are misleading.
  Rebuttal #2: Women have a history of achievement in computers.
Argument #1: More women are advancing in the computer field.
Argument #2: Mentoring programs for women are growing.
Argument #3: Opportunities for women are expanding.
  A: Shift away from technology towards communications.
  B: Emergence of senior management jobs for women.
  C: Emergence of women as users and consumers of technology.
Charts and Graphs
Abstract

a few lines of code, or instructions to the computer on how to "read" your text. The world's simplest Web page looks like this:

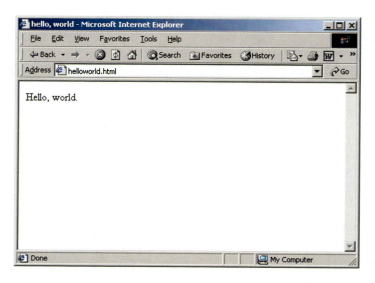

Here is the HTML coding that makes this page viewable as a Web document. Note that instructions to the browser, or code, are enclosed in angle brackets, called tags:

<HTML>
<HEAD>
<TITLE> Hello, world.</TITLE>
</HEAD>
<BODY>
Hello, world.
</BODY>
</HTML>

HTML code instructs browsers on how to interpret and display information. Content without proper tagging will not be displayed when a browser opens that page. Let's examine each HTML tag involved in the creation of the example Web page:

■ **<HTML>** This tag announces to the browser that the content that follows is formatted in HTML.

■ **<HEAD>** This tag announces that key, global information will follow about the Web page, for example, the document's title, author, subject matter, and date of publication. The forward slash character

(/) marks the ending for all tagged elements that occur in pairs, such as </HEAD> and </TITLE>. Information within the <HEAD> tags will not appear in the browser page itself, but will be indexed by search engines.

■ **<TITLE>** All text between the opening tage <TITLE> and the closing tag </TITLE> will be regarded as the title of the document, which will appear at the top of the browser window when the page loads.

■ **<BODY>** This tag opens the body of the document. All text and graphics following this tag will appear on the Web page, provided these elements are followed by the ending tag </BODY>. The entire document is completed with the ending tag </HTML>.

■ **Some miscellaneous tags:**

– **</B>** and **</B>** Everything between these tags will appear as **bold type.**

– **</I>** and **</I>** Everything between these tags will appear as *italicized type.*

– **</U>** and **</U>** Everything between these tags will appear as underlined type.

– **<P>** This tag (no closing tag required) makes a paragraph break.

– **
** This tag (no closing tag required) creates a line break.

– **<FONT SIZE=+1>** and **</FONT>** placed around words make them one size larger than other type on the page. Likewise, **<FONT SIZE=–1>** and **</FONT>** make words one size smaller than other words.

Rather than learning HTML coding, you can create your Web pages using one of several commercially available HTML programs that make creating HTML much easier than coding by hand. Word processing programs such as Microsoft Word allow writers to save documents in HTML format. More advanced programs for Web developers include "HomeSite" (PC only), "Dreamweaver" (Mac and PC), "Cyberstudio" (Mac only), and "BBBEdit" (Mac only).

5   Hyperlinks

Readers will move from one page in your Web site to related pages by means of hyperlinks. You add links to a page by using HTML tags, as in this example:

This is a sample sentence from a Web page. When users click
<A HREF="page2.html">here**</A>**, they will go to another Web page.

Here is how this tagged example text would look on a Web page:

This is a sample sentence from a Web page. When users click here, they will go to another Web page.

A page from Marie Hobahn's Web-based essay.

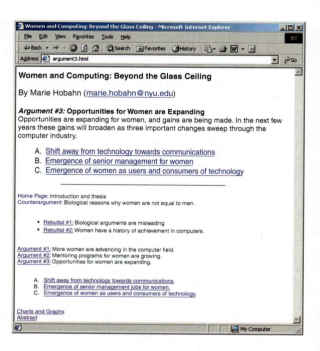

The underlined <u>here</u> is now a hyperlink. In HTML coding, the tag <A "HREF="page2.html"> tells the browser that all text until the closing tag </A> is a hyperlink. Anchored words appear as a link in the browser (typically underlined in blue), and clicking on the link will take the user to another HTML page, called "page2.html," which has been placed after the equal sign (=) in the hypertext reference. To make the link work, you'll need to create two HTML pages: "page1.html," on which the link is featured, and "page2.html," the page to which the link is attached.

There are two other kinds of hyperlinks. The jump link enables the user to skip down a page, for instance, to a footnote at the bottom of a page. The last type of link brings a user to another site entirely on the World Wide Web. As a Web author, you can link elements on your pages to any site in the world, from the Library of Congress to your nephew's kindergarten site.

10b   Images, page design, and launching on the Web

1   Images

An all-text Web page will probably look bland to readers. When possible, try including an image related to your content and plan the presentation of your content with images in mind.

Most computer stores sell CD-ROM collections of thousands of clip-art images that you can use royalty free. Images are also available wherever you find them on the Web (but see the note on citing sources, below). And you will find a multitude of Web sites that specialize in stock photography. Here are four:

http://www.digitalstock.com/
http://www.picturequest.com/
http://www.corbis.com/
http://www.photostogo.com/

You can also scan photographs and illustrations into your computers or create new art in programs such as Photoshop or Illustrator.

Once you select an appropriate image, you will need to position it on the page you are designing. Special tags exist to mark images in the source code of a Web page. For instance, if you wanted to place your image on a Web-based résumé, you would code the image as follows:

<IMG SRC="myimage.gif" height=200 width=300 border=0 align=left>

IMG is short for "image" and alerts the browser to the existence of the image and its source (SRC) in a file called "myimage.gif." Almost all of the images you see on the Web are either GIF (pronounced "jiff" or "giff") or JPG (pronounced jay-peg) files.

Remember to Cite Sources

An image on the Web is likely to be the property of the person who made the page, unless that material is clearly labeled as available for anyone's use. You should credit your source, at least, and, depending on your intended use, you may need to secure written permission from the copyright holder.

2 Page design

In laying out pages for the Web, you should be aware of both design principles in general (see Chapter 12) and the constraints that technology places on you. Not everyone with an Internet connection has the same computer and monitor that you have. Some people, for example, have huge monitors capable of displaying high resolution graphics, while others have small screens that can only display half a page at a time. Still, there are several design principles to follow that will give your Web pages the highest probability of being viewed in the way you intend them to be, by the widest possible audience.

1. Use high contrast between type and background colors.
2. Keep your core content on a solid (preferably light) background. Before finalizing your Web site, check your use of background

colors on different computers (PC and Mac) and with different browsers (Internet Explorer and Netscape).

3. Text is often easier to read when formatted into narrow columns, a layout that allows the eye to skip down the screen easily.

4. Use the power of images as navigational aids. Many users find it easier to navigate from graphic representations on a Web site than from hotlinked words or phrases. An example: If you're building a travel Web site, why not use a clickable image of the world as a way of navigating through the Web site?

3   Launching

Web pages live on a server, a computer specially designed to hold thousands of HTML files, images, and other materials that comprise Web sites. These computers are connected to the Internet, where any browser can find the HTML files and request pages. A demand for a Web page must be phrased in HyperText Transfer Protocol, otherwise known as http. This is the language your Web browser speaks and the language that you use when specifying a Web address (or URL), such as <http://www.mypage.com>.

Many universities maintain servers on which students can post Web sites. If your university has not provided you with server space, you can rent your own space from an Internet Service Provider (ISP). There are thousands of ISPs around the world, and you can search for an inexpensive one on the Web. As an alternative, you might consider posting your pages on a free commercial Web site hosting service such as Geocities.com, Tripod.com, or theglobe.com.

CHAPTER 11
Writing about Literature

WWW
http://www.uky.edu/ArtsSciences/
Classics/Harris/rhetform.html

A searchable and browsable site offering definitions of literary and rhetorical terms.

To write knowledgeably about a literary work—about a poem, a play, a short story, or a novel—you need to understand, generally, how arguments are made in the humanities. In 8g you saw that arguments in the humanities depend on a cycle of claim, reference to a text, and comment. The discussion here assumes your familiarity with the terms *claim, text, refer/reference,* and *comment.*

CRITICAL DECISIONS

Tailoring Your Purpose to Your Assignment

In some cases, you will be asked by your instructor simply to analyze or interpret a single literary work based on your own response to that work. At other times, though, you will be expected to analyze and compare two or more works, or to consider a work or several works within a historical context, or to research and synthesize the responses of various critics to a particular work or author. You need to clearly understand what is expected of you and read, plan, and draft with those goals in mind.

11a First reading: Respond

Personal response is fundamental to the critical reading of *any* text. Developing a personal response requires that you read a text closely, in such a way that you are alert to details that make the text meaningful. At the risk of stating the obvious, you should prepare for a close reading by finding a block of uninterrupted time when you are feeling alert and able to concentrate on what you read. Realize that close reading involves *multiple* readings. Expect that you will read a full text twice and selected parts of the text three or more times. On your first reading, disregard for the moment the paper you intend to write and read to be engaged, even moved. Read for the same reasons people have read or listened to stories and poetry or watched dramas for centuries: to be fascinated, to learn something of other lives, to wonder, and to question. If you have not thought about what you have read, if you have not responded to it personally, you can hardly expect to write about it with conviction.

Questions to prompt a personal response on a first reading

- What do I feel when reading this material? Why do I feel this way?
- Does this text make me *want* to read? Why or why not?
- What about this text is worth reading a second time?
- How am I challenged by or changed in response to this text?
- With what questions does this text leave me?
- What differences do I see between the author's observations of the world and my own? How can I explain these differences?

Personal responses based on these and related questions can make you want to know more about what you have read. For instance, if on completing a story, drama, or poem you find yourself *moved, offended, challenged, saddened, confused, needled,* or *intrigued,* you will have an immediate and even pressing reason to return for a second reading. And it is the second reading in which you will discover the patterns that will enable you to write a worthwhile paper. Sometimes, you may need to brainstorm after a first reading in order to understand your particular response to a text.

11b Second reading: Analyze the text

You can approach a second reading of a text by working with the response that most interested you in your first reading. Convert that response into a pointed question by asking *Why? How? What are some examples?* Guided by this question, return to the text and analyze it. If your analysis succeeds, it will yield insights into how the text works, how you think it achieves its meaning in one particular way (with respect to your question). As you read a second time, make notes in the margin wherever you feel the text provides details that can help you answer your guiding question. These notes, considered in light of your question, can suggest a pattern that makes the text meaningful.

11c Construct a pattern of meaning: Making claims and providing evidence

Based on your first and second readings of a text, you are ready to make a claim: to state for your readers the pattern you have found and your reasons for believing this pattern is worth your time pursuing and your reader's time considering. A literary work lends itself to countless interpretations. The point to remember is that whatever pattern you find in a text, you are obliged to show readers why, given all the patterns that *could* be found, this one is reasonable and worth the reader's consideration. A writer demonstrates the worthiness of a pattern, or claim, by repeatedly referring the reader to the text—a primary source, and when pertinent, to secondary sources.

1 Plot summaries

A **plot summary** is a brief description of characters and events that provides readers, some of whom may be unfamiliar with the story, context enough to follow a discussion. Plot summaries are written in the historical present tense. Consider this sentence from a plot summary (present-tense verbs are underlined):

```
Mildred Orme is a 20-year-old sophisticated beauty who seeks simple
country life for a summer of quiet reading and reflection. [ . . . ]
```

Remember that the purpose of the plot summary is to allow the writer to refer to a text and in this way support a claim. Typically, the writer's observation about the text immediately follows the plot summary, sometimes in the same sentence.

2 Posing more formal questions

You may find yourself writing papers for literature courses in which you approach the study of literature according to the viewpoints of various schools of literary criticism. Without naming these schools here and introducing you to complicated terminologies and methods, following are some additional questions you might pose to a text. These questions assume that you have already completed a first close reading.

- What circumstances of the author's life does the text reflect?
- In what ways does the text exist in a relationship with other texts by the same author and with other texts from the same time period?
- How might the text shift its meaning from one reader to the next? from one audience to the next, over time?
- What is the reader's role in making this text meaningful?
- How does the text reflect certain cultural assumptions (about gender or culture, for instance) in the author's and the readers' times?
- What psychological motives underlie the characters' actions?
- What are the economic or power relationships among the characters?

When you want to maintain your focus on a poem, play, or work of fiction itself, you can pose the following questions, arranged by category.

- **Characterization**   Who are the main characters? What are their qualities? Is each character equally important? Equally well developed?
- **Language**   What devices, such as rhyme (identical sounds), meter (carefully controlled rhythms), and pauses does the author use to create special emphasis? How does the author use metaphors and choose words to create visual images? In what ways are these images tied to the meaning of the text?
- **Narrator, Point of View**   Who is speaking? What is the narrator's personality and how does this affect the telling? Is the narrator omniscient in the sense that he or she can read into the thoughts of every character? If not, how is the narrator's vision limited?
- **Plot**   How does the writer sequence events so as to maintain the reader's attention? Which actions are central? How are other, subsidiary actions linked to the central ones? What patterning to the plot do you see? Are there ways in which the plot's structure and theme are related?
- **Structure**   In what ways can you (or does the author) divide the whole poem or story into component parts—according to theme? plot? setting? stanza? How are these parts related?

- **Setting**   Where does the story take place? How significant is the setting to the meaning of the text?
- **Symbolism**   Are any symbols operating, any objects that (like a flag) create for readers emotional, political, religious, or other associations? If so, how do these symbols function in the poem, story, or play?
- **Theme**   What large issues does this text raise? Through which characters, events, or specific lines are the questions raised? To what extent does the text answer these questions?

11d   Synthesize the details you have assembled.

The goal of a paper in a literature course is to show that your interpretation, the pattern of meaning you have found, is reasonable and can help others understand the text. Your observations about the text and, if you use them, the observations of others, are the details that you will *synthesize* into a coherent argument. See 2d for a discussion on writing syntheses. An excerpt from a sample student paper analyzing a short story begins on page 168.

CHAPTER 12

Manuscript Form and Document Design

12a   Preparing your manuscript

A clean, well-prepared, typed manuscript is a sign of respect for your readers and the mark of a skillful writer.

Style guides in the disciplines recommend slightly different conventions for preparing manuscripts. The recommendations here follow the guide commonly used in the humanities, the *MLA [Modern Language Association] Handbook for Writers of Research Papers*, 5th ed.

1   Paper and binding

Prepare your work on plain white, twenty-pound paper that measures $8\frac{1}{2} \times 11$ inches. Make a copy of your final paper to keep for your files, and submit the original to your instructor. In binding pages, affix a single paper clip to the upper left-hand corner. To ease your reader's handling of your paper, do *not* place multiple staples along the left margin, and avoid plastic folders unless otherwise directed.

2 Page layout

Whether you adopt conventions for page layout suggested by the *MLA Handbook* or by other style guides, maintain consistent margins and spacing. Print on one side of a page with standard typefaces. Avoid typefaces that give the appearance of script, since these are difficult to read.

Very few instructors accept handwritten papers. If yours does, use lined, white 8½ × 11 inch paper. Do not use spiral-bound notebook paper with its ragged edges. Write neatly and legibly in pen on one side of the page, using dark blue or black ink. Consult your instructor, who may ask you to skip every other line to allow room for editorial comments.

3 Alterations

In a final review of your paper, when you are working away from your typewriter or word processor, you may find it necessary to make minor changes to your text—perhaps to correct a typographical error or to improve your wording. Make corrections *neatly*. When striking out a word, do so with a single line. Use a caret (^) to mark an insertion in the text, and write your correction or addition above the line you are altering. Retype or reprint a page when you make three or more handwritten corrections on it. If your typewriter or computer keyboard lacks a particular symbol or mark that you need, handwrite that symbol on the page.

4 Punctuation and spacing

Observe the following standard conventions for spacing before and after marks of punctuation.

ONE SPACE BEFORE

beginning parenthesis or bracket
beginning quotation mark
period in a series denoting an omission

NO SPACE BEFORE (EXCEPT AS NOTED)

comma	question mark	semicolon
period[1]	apostrophe	end quotation mark
exclamation point	colon	hyphen or dash

NO SPACE AFTER (EXCEPT AS NOTED)

hyphen[2] or dash
beginning parenthesis or bracket
apostrophe[3]

ONE SPACE AFTER (EXCEPT AS NOTED)

comma
semicolon
colon[4]
apostrophe denoting the possessive form of a plural
end parenthesis or bracket that does not end a sentence
end quotation within a sentence
period in a series denoting an omission—see ellipses, 32e
period marking an abbreviated name or an initial

TWO SPACES AFTER THE FOLLOWING MARKS WHEN THEY CONCLUDE A SENTENCE[5]

period	closing quotation
question mark	end parenthesis or bracket
exclamation	

EXCEPTIONS (AS NOTED ABOVE)

[1]Unless the period occurs in a series denoting omission—see 32e.

[2]Unless the hyphen denotes one in a pair or series of delayed adjectives, as in *a first-, second-, or third-place finish.*

[3]Unless the apostrophe denotes the possessive form of a plural, as in *boys',* in which case skip one space.

[4]Unless the colon denotes a ratio, as in *3:2.*

[5]This is always true for typewritten documents. In word-processed documents, a single space is commonly used after these elements.

---

5   Punctuation and mechanics in the electronic world

■ When writing an e-mail address or a World Wide Web address (a Uniform Resource Locator—or URL) in a sentence, set the address in angle brackets. Note the upper- and lower-case letters in the original address, and reproduce the address exactly in your writing. If possible, keep the URL on a single line:

Anyone interested in reading the report should request a copy from Brian Kelliher <kelliherbr@mail.tula.edu>

You can locate an overview of educational Web sites at <http://www.xula.edu/Administrative/cat>

- If you must break a URL or e-mail address into segments, do so after the double slashes (//) that begin the address or before a mark of punctuation within the address. Do *not* introduce a hyphen into the address to indicate a break:

    You can locate an overview of educational Web sites at <http://www.xula.edu/Administrative/cat>

    You can request a copy of the report from Brian Kelliher <kelliherbr@mail.tula.edu>

- When preparing a Works Cited or Reference entry, do *not* underline or italicize the e-mail address or URL.

```
Badt, Karin Luisa. "The Roots of the Body in Toni Morrison: A Matter
    of 'Ancient Properties.'" African American Review 29.4 (1995):
    11 pp. 5 Mar. 1998 <http://thunder.northernlight.com/cgi-bin/
    pdserv?cbrecid=LW19970923040189466&cb=0>.
```

12b Designing your manuscript

The effective use of art, graphics, typeface, and format can make your content more accessible to readers. A single principle underlies this discussion:

> Every design element in a document should help readers to understand your content.

Without content, you have no reason for writing. Therefore, understand your content first. Articulate it as clearly as you can, with words; then look to the ways effective design can help you to deliver that content.

1 Effective headings and typography emphasize content

Begin with clear, concise writing. Well-chosen typography will improve readability and reduce confusion. Clearly worded, brief headings will communicate the logic of your document's organization. The combination of clear typeface and carefully worded headings will bring a visual coherence to your work that suggests coherent ideas.

Typeface

A type "face" is the name given to the distinctive design and shape of a family of lettering used for text. A face or design usually includes several "fonts," or lettering of different sizes and styles, including italics or boldface. As a general principle, the fewer the typefaces in one document, the better.

Word processing typefaces

If you write with a word processor, you will likely have many choices of typefaces. Your most basic consideration, for anything simpler than an advertising brochure, is whether to use a typeface that features "serif" lettering, or "sans serif" lettering. Serif lettering, as used throughout this book, is the family of typefaces most commonly seen in North America for basic text. If you closely observe the two samples below, you will notice an important difference. The text sample on the left features fine horizontal lines, called "serifs," at the top and bottom of each vertical stroke in the lettering. But the sample on the right, lacking these horizontal serifs, has a plainer look and (using the French term for "without") is called a "sans serif" or sometimes "gothic" family of lettering.

This is serif lettering.   [This is sans serif lettering.]

For most North American readers the difference is more than stylistic; the serifs are thought to act like a horizontal ruler, leading the eye smoothly across a long line of type on a page. For this reason serif type is commonly considered effective for lengthy documents featuring long lines of text. Sans serif, with its clean, emphatic appearance, is often considered useful for headings or brief messages presented in short lines.

Type size

Your word processor will be able to vary emphasis and readability by expanding or contracting type sizes. These sizes are commonly designated with numbers from as low as 6 or 8 "points" (a typesetter's unit of measure) to 10, 11, or 12, commonly used for basic text in books or magazines, up to point sizes as large as the 30-, 40-, or even 50-point headings used in advertising.

If you vary type size in your document, again bear in mind the principle of orderliness. Assign specific type sizes to specific functions. Relative to the size of the standard type size you are using in your document, you may want to assign section headings a larger size and chapter titles an even larger size, while footnotes and index entries might receive a smaller size. This book uses several varieties of type size, each for a distinct purpose.

Formatting the margins

If you work with a word processor, another decision you need to make for basic text is how to treat the margins. It is standard to see the left margin in straight alignment for documents other than advertising brochures, where centering or right-alignment of type is sometimes used. The left-aligned convention helps the eye begin each line at the same place on the page.

For the right margin you need to decide whether or not to "justify"—that is, to align letters on both left and right exactly in a vertical line. Right-justified documents are common in professionally prepared documents and are possible with most word processors, often without complex hyphenation for line breaks. (Hyphenation, available on many word processors, is often avoided because it slows scrolling and processing.) Unless the software is very sophisticated, right-justified documents without hyphenation may create uneven spacing, or "holes" on the page, making reading erratic and difficult. To avoid this problem, and to help readers follow individual lines more smoothly without hyphenation, many professional documents prefer to show the typewriter's standard "ragged right" format, with which most readers are quite comfortable.

Highlighting with boldface, italics, and boxes

Again, the principle of restraint holds: less is usually more. If you want boldfaced, italicized, or boxed words and phrases to receive special emphasis, then use these tools sparingly. Maintain a "base" of plain text that contrasts clearly with any emphatic type, and try to establish a convention for its use. For instance, you could reserve boldfaced words for headings; you could reserve italics for words that are being defined; you could draw a box around material that you consider crucially important. Overuse of these tools will quickly diminish their effectiveness and disorient your readers with a cluttered document.

Overall format and heading structure

A coherent, overall plan

Plan an overall structure for your document in such a way that its internal logic, and its key points, are quickly communicated to anyone who takes a few minutes to scan the pages. To communicate structure and idea, divide your content into well-connected chunks of varying sizes: major units, sections, subsections, paragraphs. Communicate these chunks of material with format elements such as these:

- Table of contents—For longer, formal presentations, a listing of titles or topics can provide a map and overview of your document's plan. Schematic overviews or charts can also be used.
- Unit or chapter titles—Units that begin on new pages will focus attention on the main elements of your presentation.
- Unit or chapter openings—Brief overviewing paragraphs can set out the unit's plan.
- Section titles—Headings at different levels of emphasis can focus the reader's attention on broad ideas and specifics. (See the next section.)

■ Unit summaries—When clearly marked and located at the end of a unit, or possibly at the opening and called an "abstract," summary restatements can distill key points.

When you choose format elements for your document, be consistent in structure, heading scheme, and typeface. Readers will understand these visual elements and will come to depend on them as cues to your content.

Headings

Headings—words or brief phrases or sentences—announce the content of your presentation. An effective scheme for headings will communicate your overall idea to readers who scan a long document, but a clear scheme is also important for newsletters, brochures, or Web pages. By assigning a particular typestyle and heading structure to each element of your document, you can enhance its clarity, interest, and visual coherence.

The wording of headings should forecast the main issues or thesis ideas to come in each section. Frame your headings with enough white space to give the full visual emphasis you desire. Here is a checklist of questions to help you to plan a heading scheme:

■ How many levels of heads will you use? Consult your outline and try to reduce the number of hierarchical levels to a simple scheme.

■ Will you number the heads? Numbering is normally to be avoided except in complex reference or technical works, where numbered heads make it easy to cross-reference, as in this book.

■ What typographical emphasis will you give the hierarchy of headings? For each level, make a consistent scheme for distinctive treatment of size, typeface, boldface, italics, or color, with all headings made distinct from your text.

■ Will you use color in headings or in type? If so, keep the color scheme simple. Too many colors used unsystematically may confuse readers and make your scheme harder to follow.

■ In addition to heads, will you use software to make "headers" or "footers"—brief identifying phrases that appear at the top or bottom of pages, usually on the line with page numbers? If yes, use these as brief locating labels, not as a way to convey detailed information. Will headers and footers be different on the left and right pages? If so, it is common for the left header or footer to give a brief version of the unit or chapter heading, and for the right side to give a label for lesser sections or subsections.

A warning   When your final document is laid out in pages, survey it to make sure that headings at the bottom of a page are not left alone ("widowed"), but have at least two or three lines of text following. If need be, break pages to run a short page and push the lone heading to the top of a new page.

Itemized lists

Lists, outlines, and bullet points are effective visual tools for concentrating the reader's attention on the content you deem important. A list of brief items can compress ideas and connect them in a series that forecasts a direction or a pattern you want readers to see. Lists are a frequent feature of newsletters, brochures, and Web pages. For lists and bullet points, bear these considerations in mind:

■ List items that you can express in a sentence or two.

■ Use a bullet (•), a dash (—), or an asterisk (*) for briefer material that you can express in one or two indented lines.

■ Keep listed and bulleted items grammatically parallel. The rules of parallelism for outlining apply especially to lists, and often to a series of headings as well.

■ Indent the listed numbers or bullet points to set them off from your text.

■ Use bullet points if the order of items is unimportant; otherwise, use numbers.

■ For the left margins of lists, use either the list format on your word processor or the "hanging indent" form, with second and subsequent lines indented back from the initial word, number, or bullet and aligned as in this example.

If your list or your bullet points run longer than seven or eight items, consider regrouping material and presenting two lists or sets of bullet points, each with its own heading. As with other formatting elements, it is important to make a consistent plan for functional use of itemized or bulleted lists, avoiding visual confusion from inconsistency or overuse.

Using white space

Too much text on a page tires readers' eyes as they scan the page looking for important information. Some experts on page design (especially for documents intended for nonacademic audiences) suggest that writers devote no more than 60 percent of a page to text. The remainder of the page should consist of graphical elements and white space. The use of white space on a page creates a frame for information you have already highlighted with type styles and thus doubly emphasizes it.

2 Graphic material in reports, presentations, or proposals

Quite aside from the visual variety graphics contribute to a document, the use of flowcharts, tables, charts, graphs, photographs, and art can actually be "worth a thousand words" as the clearest and most compact way of delivering information. As with your use of headings and

WWW

http://writing.colostate.edu/references/graphics.htm

A guide to using illustrations, graphics, tables, and figures in document design.

typography to focus a reader's attention, you should strive in your use of graphics for a simple, consistent, and clean design framed by plenty of white space.

Graphic elements and their functions

Ideally, your use of graphics will complement—but not repeat—the material you've already written. To achieve an effective visual balance in your documents, plan the document's layout in advance. Understand in broad terms the balance you want to achieve between text and graphics. When you do incorporate graphical elements, refer in your text to these elements at the earliest opportunity. Try to not wait until your reader has completed reading your text to present related graphics. Consider using these graphical forms for the following specific purposes:

TO review, preview, emphasize, prioritize	USE a flowchart, table list, outline list
TO orient readers in terms of space or sequences	USE a chart, diagram, map, photo views
TO show flow of functions or actions	USE a flowchart, diagram, photo
TO add emphasis to key relationships	USE a bar graph, pie chart, simple table
TO analyze or summarize key data	USE a complex graph, table, diagram
TO illustrate original data and sources	USE a facsimile recreating your source
TO help motivate	USE a photo, image, drawing, cartoon

For a detailed look at how to organize and present the types of graphical materials just mentioned, see the following recent texts: K. W. Houp et al., *Reporting Technical Information*, 9th edition, Chapter 10, "Graphical Elements" and M. J. Killingsworth, *Information in Action: A Guide to Technical Communication*, Chapter 3, "Developing Purposeful Graphics" (both Boston: Allyn & Bacon).

Tables, charts, graphs

Tables present data that usually shows a relationship between at least two sets of varying quantities, listed in columns. To show a table's relationships clearly, each set of quantities in each column or section of data is labeled. The often dense, complex data in tables needs simple, direct labels. Any qualifying or complex elements should be explained in footnotes.

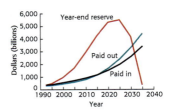

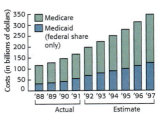

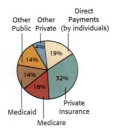

Tables are the best vehicle for displaying large blocks of dense quantitative data. When you need a vivid display of critical changes or patterns of relationships in the table, a graph is the next option. Using software packages, you can convert tabular data into line, bar, or circle graphs.

Consider the examples above showing similar material displayed in a line graph, a bar graph, and a circle graph. All three graphs compress a great deal of numerical information into a readily understood visual format. While the graphs show similar material relating to Medicare/Medicaid finances, each type offers a different emphasis and different options for the presentation best suited to your data and the points you wish to emphasize.

Note that in all three presentations there is a brief label, similar to those for tables, that identifies the significance of the quantities in each dimension of the graph. In constructing line or bar graphs, it is very important to plan the proportions you attach to the vertical and horizontal scale of quantities being displayed. If either dimension appears too short or too long, readers are likely to challenge the relationship you are showing between the graphed quantities, especially if the graph looks steeper or flatter than seems warranted by the data.

A line graph can show complex relationships, trends, and changes over space or time—in this case money paid into and out from federal Medicaid/Medicare funds, with surpluses and projected deficits shown. The scales on both axes of the graph are proportionally chosen to represent the abruptness of change.

When your message consists of simpler, less dense information, consider converting line graphs to bar graphs or pie charts. A bar graph emphasizes simple contrastive relationships among distinct units being compared, rather than the continuous trend relationships of line graphs. A pie chart is good for showing proportional parts of a whole entity—especially percentages.

Diagrams and images

Use diagrams, photographs, and images to help readers focus on your content and to amplify its meaning. Use graphical elements with care, positioning them where you think they will best enhance the reader's understanding of your content.

Writers working on computers now have thousands of images available for use from clip-art programs. Clip-art images can sometimes direct a reader's attention effectively and thus have a place in document design. But take care to match clip-art images with your content. Do not decorate documents with images that can't be justified on the basis of content.

3 Newsletters

Organizations of all sorts use newsletters to disseminate information both internally, to employees, and externally, to the public. The newsletter is often presented in an 8½ × 11 inch format that takes advantage of the various design tools discussed in this section. One distinctive feature is the newsletter's newspaper-like column width for text, which you see in the example below from the New England office of the Environmental Protection Agency. Notice the use of typeface and size, headers, a box, and white space to achieve unity, balance, and proportion. Attractively designed, this first page of the newsletter invites readers to continue reading inside.

PART IV
Sentence Decisions

CHAPTER 13

Constructing Sentences

If you are a lifelong speaker of English, then you are an expert in the language. You may not realize this, however, because in all likelihood your knowledge of the language is *implicit.* For example, even though you correctly use participles every day, you may not know the textbook definition of *participle.* Yet understanding the basic terminology of English grammar can help you make sentence-level decisions that will improve your writing.

CRITICAL DECISIONS

Conveying Meaning Clearly

The sentence is our basic unit of communication. Sentences, of course, are composed of words, each of which can be classified as a part of speech—a noun, a verb, an adjective, and so forth. Remember, though, that these are parts of a whole: meaning in language is based on the *relationship* among words. As a writer, you must make careful decisions not only about individual words, but also about their arrangement, in order to convey your intended meaning.

13a Understanding sentence parts

1 Recognizing subjects and predicates

The fundamental relationship in a sentence is the one between a subject and its predicate. Every sentence has a **subject:** a noun or noun-like word group that engages in the main action of the sentence or is described by the sentence. In addition, every sentence has a **predicate:** a verb, and other words associated with it, that state the action undertaken by a subject or the condition of the subject.

Subject   Predicate

In small doses, alcohol acts as a stimulant.

2   Nouns

A **noun** (from the Latin *nomen,* or name) is the part of speech that names a person, place, thing, or idea.[1] Only nouns can be introduced by an **article** or a **determiner.** The **indefinite article** *a* appears before a noun or an adjective describing a noun when these begin with a consonant: *a* book, *a* large book, *a* small egg. Also, words that begin with the letter *u* when it's pronounced *yoo* are preceded by *a:* *a* unit, *a* useful device. The word *an* is placed before a noun beginning with a vowel or unpronounced *h*—as in *hour: a* book, *an* hour, *an* ant. If an adjective appears before the noun and begins with a consonant, use the article *a: a* small ant. The **definite article,** *the,* denotes a specific noun: *the* book.

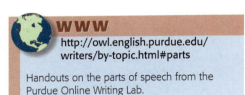

WWW

http://owl.english.purdue.edu/
writers/by-topic.html#parts

Handouts on the parts of speech from the
Purdue Online Writing Lab.

Nouns change their form to show **number;** they can be made singular or plural: *boy/boys, child/children, herd/herds.* They also undergo limited change in form to show **possession.** Unlike pronouns, however, they do this only with the addition of an apostrophe and usually an *s: girl's, children's, herd's.* Finally, nouns can be classified according to categories of meaning that affect the way they are used:

Proper nouns, which are capitalized, name particular persons, places, or things:

> *Sandra Day O'Connor, Chevrolet, "To His Coy Mistress"*

Common nouns refer to general persons, places, or things and are not capitalized:

> *judge, automobile, poem*

Count nouns can be counted:

> *cubes, cups, forks, rocks*

Mass nouns cannot be counted:

> *sugar, water, air, dirt*

Concrete nouns name tangible objects:

> *lips, clock, dollar*

Abstract nouns name an intangible idea, emotion, or quality:

> *love, eternity, ambition*

---

[1] The discussions on the parts of speech are adapted from Hulon Willis, *Modern Descriptive English Grammar* (San Francisco: Chandler, 1972).

Animate versus **inanimate nouns** differ according to whether they name something alive:

fox and *weeds* versus *wall* and *honesty*

Collective nouns are singular in form but plural in sense:

crowd, family, group, herd

3 Verbs

A **verb,** the main word in the predicate of a sentence, expresses an action, describes an occurrence, or establishes a state of being.

ACTION   Eleanor *kicked* the ball.

OCCURRENCE   A hush *descended* on the crowd.

STATE OF BEING   Thomas *was* pious.

Verbs change form on the basis of their **principal parts.** Building from the **infinitive** or **base form** (often accompanied by **to**), these parts are the **past tense,** the **present participle,** and the **past participle.**

BASE FORM	PAST TENSE	PRESENT PARTICIPLE	PAST PARTICIPLE
to escape	escaped	am escaping	escaped
to ring	rang	am ringing	rung

The principal parts of a verb have a major role in how the verb shows **tense,** the change in form that expresses the verb's action in time relative to a present statement.

There are four varieties of verbs in English; each establishes a different relationship among sentence parts:

Transitive verbs transfer action from an actor—the subject of the sentence—to a person, place, or thing receiving that action.

buy, build, kick, kiss, write
Wanda *built* a snowman.

Intransitive verbs show action; yet no person, place, or thing is acted on.

fall, laugh, sing, smile
Stock prices *fell.*

Linking verbs allow the word or words following the verb to complete the meaning of a subject.

be (am, is, are, was, were, has/have been), look, remain, sound, seem, taste
Harold *seems* happy.

Helping or **auxiliary verbs** help to show the tense and mood of a verb.

be (am, is, are, was, were), has, have, had, do, did, will, may, might, can, could
I *am* going. I *will* go. I *have* gone. I *did* go.

4   Verbals

A **verbal** is a verb form that functions in a sentence as an adjective, an adverb, or a noun. There are three types of verbals: gerunds, participles, and infinitives. A **gerund,** the *-ing* form of a verb without its helping verbs, functions as a noun.

> *Editing* is both a skill and an art. [The gerund is the subject of the sentence.]

A **participle** is a verb form that modifies nouns and pronouns.

> The *edited* manuscript was 700 pages. [The past participle modifies the noun *manuscript.*]

An **infinitive,** often preceded by *to,* is the base form of the verb (often called its *dictionary form*). An infinitive can function as a noun, adjective, or adverb.

> *To edit* well requires patience. [The infinitive functions as the noun subject of the sentence.]

The following Critical Decisions box provides a list for checking key relationships in your sentences.

CRITICAL DECISIONS

Checking Key Elements of Your Sentences

When rereading sentences you have written, check three key relationships:

1. Does the sentence have a subject and a verb? A word grouping that lacks a subject, a verb, or both is considered a fragment. See Chapter 14 on fragments.

   INCOMPLETE   At the beginning of the meeting. [no verb]

   REVISED   At the beginning of the meeting, the treasurer reported on recent news.

2. Does the sentence have a subject and verb that *agree in number*? A subject and verb must both be singular or plural.

INCONSISTENT	The treasurer are a dynamic speaker. [The plural verb does not match the singular subject.]
REVISED	The treasurer is a dynamic speaker.

3. Does the sentence have a subject close enough to the verb to ensure clarity? Meaning can be confused if the subject/verb pairing is interrupted with a lengthy modifier. See Chapter 19 for a discussion of misplaced modifiers.

INTERRUPTED	We because of our dire financial situation have called this meeting.
REVISED	We have called this meeting because of our dire financial situation.

5   Adjectives

By modifying or describing a noun or pronoun, an **adjective** provides crucial defining and limiting information in a sentence. It can also provide information to help readers see, hear, feel, taste, or smell something named. The single-word adjectives in the following sentence are italicized.

Climate plays an *important* part in determining the *average* numbers of a species, and *periodical* seasons of *extreme* cold or drought I believe to be the most *effective* of *all* checks.

—CHARLES DARWIN, *On the Origin of Species*

Adjectives can be intensified or qualified with words like *very* and *hardly: very important part.* See 18b for a discussion on using adjectives with the verb *to be.*

6   Adverbs

An **adverb** can modify a verb, an adjective, an adverb, or an entire sentence. Adverbs describe, define, or otherwise limit, generally answering these questions: *when, how, where, how often, to what extent,* and *to what degree.* Many adverbs in English are formed by adding the suffix *-ly* to an adjective.

The poor *unwittingly* subsidize the rich. [The adverb modifies the verb *subsidize.*]

Poverty *almost* always can be eliminated at a higher cost to the rich. [The adverb modifies the adverb *always.*]

Widespread poverty imposes an *increasingly* severe strain on our social fabric. [The adverb modifies the adjective *severe.*]

Conjunctive adverbs establish adverb-like relationships between whole sentences. These words—*moreover, however, consequently, thus, therefore,* *furthermore,* and so on—play a special role in linking ideas and sentences. See the Critical Decisions box on pages 302 and 303 for more information.

7 Pronouns

Pronouns substitute for nouns. The word that a pronoun refers to and renames is called its **antecedent.** Like a noun, a pronoun shows **number**—it can be singular or plural. Depending on its function in a sentence, a pronoun will change form—that is, its **case:** it will change from **subjective,** to **objective,** to **possessive.**

Subjective   Objective   Possessive

He reads the book. Joan gave *him* a book. It was *his* book.

There are eight classes of pronouns.

Personal pronouns refer to people and things.

SINGULAR   *I, me, you, he, him, she, her, it.*

PLURAL   *we, us, you, they, them.*

Relative pronouns begin dependent clauses and refer to people and things: *who, whose, which, that, whom.*

Demonstrative pronouns point to the nouns they replace: *this, these, that, those.*

Interrogative pronouns form questions: *who, which, what, whose.*

Intensive and reflexive pronouns repeat and emphasize a noun or pronoun or rename a noun or pronoun: *herself, themselves,* and other compounds formed with *-self* or *-selves.*

Indefinite pronouns refer to general, or nonspecific, persons or things: *one, anyone, somebody, nobody, everybody, anything, both, each, neither, none, no one, several, some, someone, all, another.*

Reciprocal pronouns refer to the separate parts of a plural noun: *one another, each other.*

See Chapters 17 and 20 for more discussion of pronouns.

8 Prepositions

A **preposition** links a noun (or word group substituting for a noun) to other words in a sentence—to nouns, pronouns, verbs, or adjectives. *In, at, of, for, on, by,* are all prepositions. Along with the words that follow them, prepositions form **prepositional phrases,** which function as adjectives or adverbs. In the following sentence, an arrow leads from each prepositional phrase to the words it modifies.

The theory *of evolution* was proposed *in the 1850s.*

9   Conjunctions

Conjunctions join sentence elements or entire sentences in one of two ways: either by establishing a coordinate or *equal* relationship among joined parts or by establishing a subordinate or *unequal* relationship.

Coordinating conjunctions join grammatically equivalent elements, from words to phrases to whole sentences: *and, but, or, nor, for, so, yet.*

> Infants only cry at birth, *but* within a few short years they speak in complete sentences. The infant's cooing *and* babbling is a form of communication.

Conjunctive adverbs create special logical relationships between the clauses or sentences they join: *however, therefore, thus, consequently.*

> Infants can only cry at birth. Within a few short years, *however,* they can speak in complete sentences.

Correlative conjunctions are pairs of coordinating conjunctions that place extra emphasis on the relationship between the parts of the coordinated construction: *both/and, neither/nor, not only/but also.*

> Three-year-olds *not only* speak in complete sentences *but also* possess vocabularies of hundreds or even thousands of words.

Subordinating conjunctions connect subordinate clauses to main clauses: *when, while, although, because, if, since, whereas.*

> *When* children reach the age of three, they can usually carry on complete conversations with their peers and with adults.

See the Critical Decisions box on pages 302 and 303 for more on using conjunctions.

10   Interjections

An **interjection** is an emphatic word or phrase. When it stands alone, it is frequently followed by an exclamation point. As part of a sentence, the interjection is usually set off by commas.

> Oh, they're here.   Never!

11 Expletives

An **expletive** is a word that fills a slot left in a sentence that has been rearranged. *It* functions as an expletive—as a filler word without meaning of its own—in the following example.

BASIC SENTENCE   A sad fact is that too few Americans vote.

WITH EXPLETIVE   It is a sad fact that too few Americans vote.

13b Understanding basic sentence patterns

English has five basic sentence patterns. Virtually all of the sentences you read in any book will be built on these patterns:

┌─ Predicate ─┐
Pattern 1:   Subject   verb
              We   *look.*

SUBJECT   a noun or noun-like word group that produces the main action of the sentence or is described by the sentence.

PREDICATE a verb, and other words associated with it, that state the action undertaken by the subject or the condition of the subject.

┌──── Predicate ────┐
Pattern 2:   Subject   verb (tr.)   direct object
              Stories   *excite*   *the imagination.*

DIRECT OBJECT   a noun, or group of words substituting for a noun, that receives the action of a transitive verb (tr.). A direct object answers the question *What or who is acted on?*

┌────── Predicate ──────┐
Pattern 3:   Subject   verb (tr.)   indirect object   direct object
              Stories   *offer*   *us*   *relief.*

INDIRECT OBJECT   a noun, or group of words substituting for a noun, that is indirectly affected by the action of a verb. Indirect objects typically follow transitive verbs such as *buy, bring, do, give, offer, teach, tell, play,* or *write.* The indirect object answers the question *To whom or for whom has the main action of this sentence occurred?*

┌────── Predicate ──────┐
Pattern 4:   Subject   verb (tr.)   direct object   object complement
              They   *make*   *us*   *tense.*

OBJECT COMPLEMENT   an adjective or noun that completes the meaning of a direct object by renaming or describing it. Typically, object complements follow verbs such as *appoint, call, choose, consider, declare, elect, find, make, select,* or *show.*

Predicate

Pattern 5: Subject   verb (linking) subject complement
            We   *are*   *readers.*

Subject **complement** a noun or adjective that completes the meaning of a subject by renaming or describing it. Subject complements follow linking verbs such as *appear, feel, seem,* and *remain,* as well as all forms of *be.* (See 18b for more on subject complements.)

<hr>

13c   Modifying and expanding sentences with phrases

A **phrase** is a grouping of related words without a subject or a complete verb. Since a phrase does not express a complete thought, it cannot stand alone as a sentence. Phrases function in a sentence as modifiers and as objects, subjects, or complements. They can be integrated into any of the five sentence patterns (see 13b) to add detail.

Together with its *object,* a preposition forms a **prepositional phrase,** which functions in a sentence as a modifier.

Adjective   Stories can excite the imaginations *of young people.*

Adverb   Paul reads *in the evening.*

Infinitives and the various words associated with them form **infinitive phrases** that can function as subjects, objects, adjectives, and adverbs. An infinitive is the base form of a verb preceded by the word *to.*

Subject   *To read in the evening* is a great pleasure.

Object   Some children start *to read at an early age.*

Adjective   Stories offer us a chance *to escape dull routines.*

Adverb   We read *to gain knowledge.*

A **noun phrase** consists of a noun or pronoun accompanied by all of its modifying words. A noun phrase can function as a subject, direct object, or subject complement.

Subject   *Even horror stories with their gruesome endings* can delight readers.

Direct **object** A tale of horror will affect *anyone who is at all suggestible.*

Complement   Paul is *someone who likes to read horror stories.*

When the present participle, or -*ing* form of a verb, is used without a helping verb, it can function either as a noun in a **gerund phrase** or as an adjective in a **participial phrase** or an **absolute phrase**. In a gerund phrase, a noun or pronoun appearing before the gerund must be in possessive form. See 20c for additional information.

FAULTY	We did not approve of *him* reading all night.
REVISED	We did not approve of *his* reading all night.

Participial phrases used as adjectives should be placed near the word or phrase they are modifying in order to avoid confusion. See Chapter 19 for more information on correct placement for modifiers.

FAULTY	*Clambering* over the rocks, *Marion* was pelted by the monkey's discarded banana peels. [Implies that Marion, not the monkey, was clambering.]
REVISED	*Clambering* over the rocks, the *monkey* pelted Marion with discarded banana peels.

Absolute phrases modify entire sentences and consist of a subject and incomplete predicate. They are formed either by changing the main verb of a sentence to its *-ing* form or by deleting the linking verb *be* from the sentence. In both instances, you must then combine the absolute phrase with another sentence.

ORIGINAL SENTENCE	His hands *were* weak with exhaustion.
ABSOLUTE PHRASE COMBINED WITH NEW SENTENCE	His hands weak with exhaustion, Paul lifted the book from the shelf. [*Be* verb eliminated.]
ORIGINAL SENTENCE	His hands *trembled* with exhaustion.
ABSOLUTE PHRASE COMBINED WITH NEW SENTENCE	His hands *trembling* with exhaustion, Paul lifted the book from the shelf. [Verb changed to *-ing* form.]

Appositive phrases, which rename nouns, are typically formed by using the predicate part (minus the verb) of Sentence Pattern 5.

		Predicate	
Pattern 5:	Subject	verb (linking)	subject complement
	Paul	*is*	*an old college friend.*

APPOSITIVE PHRASE	an old college friend
NEW SENTENCE	Paul, an old college friend, is an avid reader.

13d Modifying and expanding sentences with dependent clauses

A **clause** is any grouping of words that has both a subject and a predicate. There are two types of clauses. An **independent** (or **main**) **clause** can stand alone as a sentence. A **dependent** (or **subordinate**) **clause** cannot stand alone as a sentence because it is usually introduced either with a subordinating conjunction (e.g., *while*) or with a relative pronoun (e.g., *who*). Writers typically use three types of dependent clauses: adverb, adjective, and noun clauses.

Dependent **adverb clauses** that modify verbs, adjectives, and other
adverbs begin with subordinat-
ing conjunctions and answer
the question *when, how, where,
how often, to what extent,* or *to
what degree.* Like adjectives, **adjective clauses** modify nouns.
The clauses usually begin with
the relative pronoun *which, that,
who, whom,* or *whose.*

WWW

http://www.quiknet.com/
~jukes/sentenc1.htm

http://www.quiknet.com/~jukes/
sentenc2.htm

These two pages provide practice combining
sentence parts for more sophistication.

People *who lived through the Depression of the 1930s* remember it well.

Noun clauses function exactly as single-word nouns do in a sentence:
as subjects, objects, complements, and appositives. Noun clauses are introduced with the pronoun *which, whichever, that, who, whoever, whom, whomever,*
or *whose* or with the word *how, when, why, where, whether,* or *whatever.*

SUBJECT	*That ozone holes have already caused blindness and skin cancer in graz-ing animals* suggests the need for immediate legislative action.
OBJECT	Apparently, few inhabitants of populous northern cities are aware of *how the depletion of ozone can harm living organisms.*
COMPLEMENT	The looming danger that ozone depletion poses is *why researchers have sounded an alarm.*

13e Classifying sentences

1 Functional definitions

Sentences are classified by structure and by function. There are four
functional types:

DECLARATIVE	The driver turned on the ignition.
INTERROGATIVE	Was the engine flooded?
EXCLAMATORY	What an awful fire! How terrible!
IMPERATIVE	Get back! Don't you go near that!

2 Structural definitions

There are four structural classes of sentences in English: simple, compound, complex, and compound-complex.

Each of the five basic sentence patterns discussed in 13b qualifies as
a **simple sentence:** each has a single subject and a single predicate. The

designation "simple" refers to a sentence's structure, not its content. A simple sentence, with all its modifying words and phrases, can be long.

> Vampirism figures prominently in two major works of literary criticism from the first half of this century—Mario Praz's *The Romantic Agony* and D. H. Lawrence's *Studies in Classical American Literature*. [This sentence consists of one subject, *vampirism,* and one simple predicate, *figures.*]

Compound sentences have two subjects and two predicates. They are created when two independent clauses are joined with a coordinating or correlative conjunction or with a conjunctive adverb. For details on how coordination can be used to create sentence emphasis, see 25a.

> As the Undead, the vampire casts no shadow and has no reflection, but he (or she) manifests prominent canine teeth. [The conjunction *but* joins two independent clauses.]

Complex sentences consist of an independent clause and one or more dependent clauses.

> Stoker's *Dracula* is dignified and still *until* he explodes into ravenous action. [The subordinating conjunction *until* signals a dependent adverb clause.]

Compound-complex sentences consist of at least two independent clauses and one subordinate, dependent clause.

> Anne Rice's vampires seem to regard vampirism amorally, *and* whatever scruples they feel about their predatory nature gradually subside *as* they become increasingly inhuman. [The coordinating conjunction *and* signals a compound sentence, and the subordinating conjunction *as* signals a dependent clause in a complex sentence.]

One way to maintain a reader's interest is to vary sentence types as well as sentence lengths. The more you write, the more you will develop a relationship between your goals as a writer and the sentence types you choose.

CHAPTER 14

Correcting Sentence Fragments

A central goal of writing is to keep readers focused on clearly stated ideas. Few errors are more disruptive of this goal than the sentence fragment. In drafting and editing your work, it is important that you determine how best to spot and correct this error.

CRITICAL DECISIONS

Keeping the Needs of Readers in Mind

One way to spot sentence fragments is to think carefully about your readers. With a critical eye, read every group of words you have set off as a complete sentence. Individually, is the intended meaning of each complete and clear? Is the relationship among ideas easy to follow? If not, use the tests for determining sentence fragments discussed in this chapter.

The **sentence fragment** is a partial sentence punctuated as if it were a complete sentence. Because it is only a partial sentence, a fragment leaves readers confused, trying to guess at what claims or statements are being made. To be a sentence, a group of words must first have a subject and a predicate. A sentence fragment may lack either a subject or a predicate—and sometimes both. A fragment may also be a dependent clause that has not been joined to an independent (or main) clause.

WWW

http://leo.stcloudstate.edu/punct/
fragmentcauses.html

A succinct bottom-up view of the causes of sentence fragments, from LEO: Literacy Education Online.

FRAGMENT Like scratching an itch [The clause lacks both a subject and a verb.]

REVISED Using profanity can be like scratching an itch in that both tend to relieve tension. [A subject and a verb are added to create a sentence.]

 14a Eliminate fragments: Revise dependent clauses set off as sentences.

A dependent clause functions as a modifier—as an adverb, an adjective, or a noun. A dependent clause that has been used incorrectly as a sentence can be corrected in one of two ways: by converting the clause to an independent clause or by joining the clause to another independent clause.

The Critical Decisions box on page 234 shows ways to test for sentence fragments.

CRITICAL DECISIONS

Testing for Sentence Fragments

Apply a three-part test to confirm that a grouping of words can stand alone as a sentence.

Test 1:   Locate a verb: A sentence must have a verb.

> FRAGMENT   A leader of great distinction. [No verb]
>
> REVISED   Churchill *was* a leader of great distinction. [Verb—*was*]

Note: Be sure the word selected as a verb is not a verbal, which looks like a verb but actually serves as a subject, object, or modifier.

> FRAGMENT   After serving his country in the First World War. [*Serving* is an object in the prepositional phrase beginning with *after*.]
>
> REVISED   After serving his country in the First World War, he *became* Prime Minister. [Verb—*became*]

Test 2:   Locate the verb's subject: A sentence must have a subject.

> FRAGMENT   Became prime minister. [No subject]
>
> REVISED   *Churchill* became prime minister. [Subject—*Churchill*]

Test 3:   Be sure that words such as *when, while, because* or *who, which, that* do not prevent the word group from being a sentence.

> FRAGMENTS   *When* he became   *Who* became prime
>   prime minister.   minister.

[*When* (a subordinating conjunction) and *who* (a relative pronoun) prevent these word groups from standing alone as sentences.]

> REVISED   He became prime minister.

---

1   Convert the dependent clause to an independent clause.

If the dependent clause begins with a subordinating conjunction, delete the conjunction and you will have an independent clause—a sentence.

FRAGMENT   While Americans keep recycling the same old clichés.

REVISED   ~~While~~ Americans keep recycling the same old clichés.

If a dependent clause uses a relative pronoun, eliminate the relative pronoun. Replace it with a noun or personal pronoun to form an independent clause.

FRAGMENT   Many students, who might read more often.

REVISED   Many students ~~who~~ might read more often.

      OR

REVISED   ~~Many students~~ *They* might read more often.

---

2   Join the dependent clause to a new sentence.

A dependent clause introduced by a subordinating conjunction can be made to function as an adverb by joining it to an independent clause.

FRAGMENT   If our culture did not portray reading as an almost antisocial activity.

REVISED   *Many students might read more often* if our culture did not portray reading as an almost antisocial activity.

A dependent clause fragment that uses a relative pronoun can be made to function as an adjective (a relative clause) by attaching it to an independent clause. If the new relative clause is not essential to defining the noun it modifies, set off the clause with a *pair* of commas. If the new relative clause *is* essential to the definition, do not use commas (see 28d-1).

FRAGMENT   Verdenal Johnson, a president of the Association for the Encouragement of Correct Pronunciation, Spelling and Usage in Public Communications, who has used a felt-tipped marker to correct errors on public signs. [The subject, *Verdenal Johnson,* has no verb.]

REVISED   Verdenal Johnson, who has used a felt-tipped marker to correct errors on public signs, served as president of the Association for the Encouragement of Correct Pronunciation, Spelling and Usage in Public Communications. [The *who* clause functions as an adjective in a sentence with the new verb *served.*]

14b   **Eliminate fragments: Revise phrases set off as sentences.**

Phrases consist either of nouns and the words associated with them or of verb forms not functioning as verbs (*verbals*) and the words associated with them. Phrases function as sentence parts—as modifiers, subjects, objects, and complements—but never as sentences. The various kinds of phrases are defined in 13c. To correct a phrase fragment, you may either convert it to a complete sentence by adding words or join it to an independent clause.

1 Revising verbal phrases

Participial and gerund phrases (functioning as modifiers or nouns)

FRAGMENT   Crossing out the word *very*.

REVISED   Verdenal Johnson ~~crossing~~ crosses out the word *very*. [The phrase is converted into a sentence.]

REVISED   Crossing out the word *very*, the copyeditor Verdenal Johnson encourages writers to use more specific words—for example, *crimson* for *very red*. [The phrase fragment is now joined to an independent clause to form a sentence.]

Infinitive phrases (functioning as nouns)

FRAGMENT   To delete the word *very*.

REVISED   Johnson prefers to delete the word *very* when she works as a copyeditor. [The phrase is converted into a sentence.]

2 Revising prepositional phrases (functioning as modifiers)

FRAGMENT   With its ready-made expressions and terse, imprecise phrases.

REVISED   With its ready-made expressions and terse, imprecise phrases, American English is truly the language of people in a hurry. [The phrase fragment is now joined to an independent clause to form a sentence.]

3 Revising absolute phrases (modifying an entire sentence)

FRAGMENT   Our shorthand style of speech mirroring our fast-paced existence.

REVISED   Our shorthand style of speech mirrors our fast-paced existence. [The phrase is converted into a sentence.]

4 Revising appositive phrases (renaming or describing other nouns)

FRAGMENT   A mix of words and pictures characterized by immediacy and by visual appeal.

REVISED   "Electronic Literacy" is a mix of words and pictures characterized by immediacy and visual appeal. [The phrase is converted into a sentence.]

REVISED   Many deplore the loss of print literacy and decry the rise of "electronic literacy," a mix of words and pictures characterized by immediacy and visual appeal. [The phrase now renames the final noun in the independent clause.]

SPOTLIGHT 4

14c   Eliminate fragments: Revise repeating structures or compound predicates set off as sentences.

Repetition can be an effective stylistic tool. Repeated elements, however, are not sentences but sentence parts and should not be punctuated as sentences. Use a comma or dashes to set off repeated elements.

FRAGMENT   Adolescents want to know they belong in the social order. An order shaped by forces they barely understand.

REVISED   Adolescents want to know they belong in the social order—an order shaped by forces they barely understand.

Compound predicates consist of two sentence verbs (and their associated words) joined with a coordinating conjunction, such as *and* or *but*. The two predicates share the same subject and are part of the same sentence. When one half of the compound predicate is punctuated as a sentence, it becomes a fragment. To correct the fragment either join it to a sentence that contains an appropriate subject or provide the fragment with its own subject.

FRAGMENT   The process of maturation is lifelong. *But is most critical during the adolescent years.* [The last unit has no subject.]

REVISED   The process of maturation is lifelong. But *the process* is most critical during the adolescent years. [The unit is given its own subject.]

REVISED   The process of maturation is lifelong but is most critical during the adolescent years. [The unit is joined to the preceding sentence.]

14d   Use fragments intentionally on rare occasions.

Whose business was it? No one's.

The speaker made his point. Barely.

Experienced writers will occasionally use sentence fragments by design. These intentional uses are always carefully fitted to the context of a neighboring sentence, sometimes answering an implied question or completing a parallel structure that has been separated for emphasis. Such intentional uses occur mainly in personal or expressive essay writing or in fiction. A fragment should be used rarely if at all in academic prose, where it will probably be regarded as a lapse, not as a stylistic flourish.

CHAPTER 15

Correcting Comma Splices and Fused Sentences

Fused sentences and comma splices can disrupt sentence meaning. In the **fused** (or **run-on**) **sentence,** the writer fails to recognize the end of one independent clause and the beginning of the next. The writer of a **comma splice** recognizes the end of one independent clause and the beginning of the next, but marks the boundary between the two incorrectly with a comma, as you will see in the examples that follow.

CRITICAL DECISIONS

Recognizing Independent Clauses

In order to avoid creating comma splices and fused sentences, it is essential that you be able to recognize independent clauses. An independent clause is a complete unit of thought that contains one subject (or a compound subject) and one verb (or a compound verb) and is not introduced by a subordinating conjunction or relative pronoun. Check your sentences for the presence of a second subject following the verb; if it is not the subject of a subordinate clause, then it is likely the start of a new independent clause. See Chapter 13 for more definitions.

15a Identify fused sentences and comma splices.

SPOTLIGHT
5

Before submitting a draft of your work to be read or reviewed by others, reread—and be alert for the following three circumstances in which fused sentences and comma splices are common.

1. **A sentence of explanation, expansion, or example** is frequently fused to or spliced together with another sentence that is being explained, expanded on, or illustrated. Even if the topics of the two sentences are closely related, the sentences themselves must remain distinct.

   FUSED   The Pre-Raphaelite Brotherhood was a group of painters, poets, and painter-poets their artistic aims varied widely.

   COMMA   The Pre-Raphaelite Brotherhood was a group of painters,
   SPLICE   poets, and painter-poets, their artistic aims varied widely.

REVISED   The Pre-Raphaelite Brotherhood was a group of painters, poets, and painter-poets. Their artistic aims varied widely.

2. **The pronouns** *he, she, they, it, this,* and *that,* when renaming the
   subject of a sentence, can signal a comma splice or a fused sentence.
   Even when the same subject is named or renamed in adjacent sentences, the sentences themselves must be kept distinct.

   FUSED   Dante Gabriel Rossetti was a poet he was also a painter.

   COMMA   Dante Gabriel Rossetti was a poet, he was also a painter.
   SPLICE

   REVISED   Dante Gabriel Rossetti was a poet, and he was a painter.

3. **Conjunctive adverbs** (words such as *however, furthermore, thus,*
   therefore, and *consequently*) **and transitional expressions** (phrases
   such as *for example* and *on the other hand*) are commonly found
   in fused or spliced clauses. Conjunctive adverbs and transitions
   should always link complete sentences. Reflect this linkage with appropriate punctuation: a period or semicolon.

   FUSED   Ninety percent of the Hispanic vote is concentrated in nine
   SENTENCE   states that cast 71 percent of all electoral ballots conse-
                quently Hispanics have emerged as a nationally influential
                group of voters.

   COMMA   Ninety percent of the Hispanic vote is concentrated in nine
   SPLICE   states that cast 71 percent of all electoral ballots, consequently,
                Hispanics have emerged as a nationally influential group of
                voters.

   REVISED   Ninety percent of the Hispanic vote is concentrated in nine
             states that cast 71 percent of all electoral ballots. Conse-
             quently, Hispanics have emerged as a nationally influential
             group of voters.

   SPOTLIGHT
   5

15b   Correct fused sentences and comma splices in one of five ways.

1   Separate independent clauses with a period.

FUSED   Logging is often the first step in deforestation it may be followed by
SENTENCE   complete clearing of trees and a deliberate shift to unsound land
             uses.

COMMA   Logging is often the first step in deforestation, it may be followed
SPLICE   by complete clearing of trees and a deliberate shift to unsound land
             uses.

REVISED   Logging is often the first step in deforestation. It may be followed by
          complete clearing of trees and a deliberate shift to unsound land uses.

2   Link clauses with a comma and a coordinating conjunction.

WWW

http://parallel.park.uga.edu/~sigalas/
Commas/2ic.html

Here's an upbeat page with a handy mnemonic
device for curing comma splices.

FUSED	January may be the coldest month it is a month of great productivity.
COMMA SPLICE	January may be the coldest month, it is a month of great productivity.

CLEAR   January may be the coldest month**, but** it is a month of great
productivity.

3   Link clauses with a semicolon.

Use a semicolon in place of a comma and a coordinating conjunction to
link sentences that are closely related and equally important. The semicolon
links independent clauses without making the relationship between them
explicit. You might choose a semicolon to repair a fused or spliced construction either when the relationship between clauses is crystal clear and a conjunction would be redundant or when you wish to create anticipation—leaving your readers to discover the exact relationship between clauses.

FUSED   Wind is one cause of erosion water is another cause.

COMMA   Wind is one cause of erosion, water is another cause.
SPLICE

CLEAR   Wind is one cause of erosion**;** water is another cause.

4   Link clauses with a semicolon (or period) and a conjunctive adverb.

Use conjunctive adverbs—words such as *however, furthermore, thus,*
therefore, and *consequently*—to link closely related, equally important clauses.
As with most adverbs, a conjunctive adverb can shift its location in a sentence. Wherever you place the adverb, be sure to use a period or a semicolon
between the two clauses you have linked. Place a period between clauses
when you want a full separation of ideas. Place a semicolon between clauses
when you want to emphasize the links between ideas.

FUSED   Deforestation is not irreversible once a forest is cleared regeneration
SENTENCE   takes a lifetime.

COMMA   Deforestation is not irreversible, once a forest is cleared regeneration
SPLICE   takes a lifetime.

REVISED   Deforestation is not irreversible**;** however**,** once a forest is cleared, regeneration takes a lifetime. [The semicolon emphasizes the link be-
tween ideas.]

REVISED   Deforestation is not irreversible. However, once a forest is cleared, regeneration takes a lifetime. [The period makes a full separation.]

CRITICAL DECISIONS

Choosing a Method to Link Independent Clauses

Sentence boundaries clearly marked with a period help readers focus on, and understand, one thought at a time. When you want to
show the relationship *between* thoughts, then you should consider
linking clauses. You have various options for doing so; which option
you choose depends on the relationship you want to establish between independent clauses.

■ **Do you want one independent clause to announce another?**
If so, use a colon to make the announcement.

> **SEPARATED**   The race was postponed for one reason. The spon-
> sors withdrew their support.
>
> **LINKED**   The race was postponed for one reason: the sponsors
> withdrew their support.

■ **Do you want to relate but maintain equal emphasis between
two independent clauses?** If so, use a coordinating conjunction with a comma, a conjunctive adverb with a semicolon or
period, or a semicolon to link the clauses.

Coordinating conjunction with a comma

> **SEPARATED**   Runners had already arrived. They were angry with the
> postponement.
>
> **LINKED**   Runners had already arrived, and they were angry with
> the postponement.

Conjunctive adverb with a semicolon or a period

> **SEPARATED**   The sponsors cited financial worries. They had political
> concerns as well.
>
> **LINKED**   The sponsors cited financial worries; however, they had
> political concerns as well.

Semicolon

> **SEPARATED**   One faction of runners wanted to boycott all future races
> in that city. Another faction wanted to stage a protest
> march.
>
> **LINKED**   One faction of runners wanted to boycott all future races
> in that city; another faction wanted to stage a protest
> march.   *(continued)*

Choosing a Method to Link Independent Clauses, continued

■ **Do you want to link two independent clauses but emphasize one more than the other?** If so, use a subordinating conjunction.

SEPARATED	The press was embarrassing. The sponsors canceled the race permanently.
LINKED	**Because** the press was embarrassing, the sponsors canceled the race permanently.

---

5   Link clauses with a subordinating conjunction or construction.

Use a subordinating conjunction or construction to join fused or spliced independent clauses. By placing a subordinating conjunction at the beginning of an independent clause, or by using a relative pronoun such as *who, whom, which,* or *that,* you can make that clause dependent and then join it to another independent clause. The new dependent clause will function as a modifier.

FUSED SENTENCE	International development-assistance agencies have begun to lend help a number of governments are now strengthening their forest-management programs.
COMMA SPLICE	International development-assistance agencies have begun to lend help, a number of governments are now strengthening their forest-management programs.
REVISED	Because international development-assistance agencies have begun to lend help, a number of governments are now strengthening their forest-management programs.

CHAPTER 16

Using Verbs

WWW
http://cctc2.commnet.edu/grammar/verbs.htm

A resource on verbs, including quizzes and graphics.

The decisions you make about verb forms will convey three important messages that are the focus of this chapter: *tense*—an indication of when the action or state of being described in your sentence occurred; *voice*—your judgment about the relative importance of the actor versus the object acted on in your sentence; and *mood*—your judgment as to whether a statement is a fact, a command, or an unreal or hypothetical condition contrary to fact.

CRITICAL DECISIONS

Making Other Decisions about Verbs

Although this chapter focuses on decisions about tense, voice, and mood, using verbs effectively requires care in other areas as well. For example, you must make sure that verbs agree with their subjects (see Chapter 17) and that verbs are near enough to their subjects and objects so that readers don't get confused (see pages 250–251). You also need to choose verbs that are precise and that lend vigor to your writing; using strong verbs is discussed on pages 299–301.

Verb Forms

16a Using the principal parts of regular verbs consistently

Most verbs in the dictionary are **regular.** They follow the simple, predictable pattern shown in the box below. Note that the past tense and past participle are identical. (For regular verbs, only base forms appear in most dictionaries.)

The Principal Parts of Regular Verbs

BASE FORM	PRESENT TENSE (-S FORM)	PAST TENSE	PAST PARTICIPLE	PRESENT PARTICIPLE
share	shares	shared	shared	sharing
start	starts	started	started	starting
climb	climbs	climbed	climbed	climbing

1 Recognizing the forms of regular verbs

The **base** (or infinitive) **form** of a verb is its **dictionary form**—the form that would appear with the word *to.* Use the base form of a verb to indicate action in the present for plural nouns or for the personal pronouns *I, we, you,* or *they.*

> Alaska's Pacific mountains *create* a region of high peaks, broad valleys, and numerous island fjords.

Use the **-s *form*** of a verb (creates, tries, loves) with third-person, singular subjects when an action is in the present and with the personal pronouns *he, she,* or *it* (or with a subject that can be replaced by one of these).

> Alaska's north slope *consists* of the plateaus and coastal regions north of the Brooks mountain range.

The **past tense** of a verb indicates that an action has been completed in the past. Regular verbs form the past tense by taking the suffix *-ed* or *-d.*

> Secretary of State William H. Seward *arranged* for the purchase of Alaska from Russia in 1867.

Irregular verbs do not follow this pattern: the spelling of the base form changes to show the past tense (see 16b).

---

2   **Revising nonstandard verb forms by using standard -*s* and -*ed* forms**

In rapid conversation, many people skip over -*s* and -*ed* endings. In some dialects, the base (or infinitive) form of the verb is used in place of verbs with -*s* and -*ed* endings. Writers of standard academic English, however, need to observe the regular forms.

NONSTANDARD   She was *ask* to read this assignment. She *like* to stay up late, and she *be* still wide awake.

REVISED   She was *asked* to read it. She *likes* to stay up late, and she *is* still wide awake. [Base forms have been replaced by standard verb forms with -*s* and -*ed* endings.]

16b   **Learning the forms of irregular verbs**

An irregular verb forms its past tense and past participle by altering the spelling of the base verb, as in *build/built.* A dictionary entry will show you when a verb is irregular.

The most frequently used verb in our language, *be,* is also the only verb with more than five forms. It functions both as the main verb in a sentence and as a frequently used auxiliary verb. The eight forms of *be* are shown in the box on page 245.

The Principal Parts of be

BASE FORM	PRESENT TENSE	PAST TENSE
(to) be	he, she, it *is*	he, she, it *was*
	I *am*	I *was*
	we, you, they *are*	we, you, they *were*

PAST PARTICIPLE	PRESENT PARTICIPLE
been	*being*

The following box contains the principal parts for a partial list of irregular verbs. Remember that the past participle is the form of the verb used with the helping verb *have:* They *have broken* the bike. Without the helping verb, the past participle functions as an adjective: the *broken* arrow.

Some Irregular Verb Forms

BASE FORM	PAST TENSE	PAST PARTICIPLE
beat	beat	beaten
become	became	become
begin	began	begun
bite	bit	bit, bitten
blow	blew	blown
break	broke	broken
bring	brought	brought
build	built	built
burn	burned, burnt	burned, burnt
buy	bought	bought
catch	caught	caught
choose	chose	chosen
come	came	come
cost	cost	cost
cut	cut	cut
dig	dug	dug
dive	dove, dived	dived
do (does)	did	done

(continued)

Some Irregular Verb Forms, continued

BASE FORM	PAST TENSE	PAST PARTICIPLE
draw	drew	drawn
drink	drank	drunk
drive	drove	driven
eat	ate	eaten
fall	fell	fallen
feed	fed	fed
feel	felt	felt
fight	fought	fought
fly	flew	flown
forbid	forbade, forbad	forbidden *or* forbid
forget	forgot	forgot *or* forgotten
freeze	froze	frozen
get	got	got, gotten
give	gave	given
go	went	gone
grow	grew	grown
hang[1]	hung	hung
have (has)	had	had
hear	heard	heard
hide	hid	hidden
hit	hit	hit
keep	kept	kept
know	knew	known
lead	led	led
leave	left	left
lose	lost	lost
make	made	made
mean	meant	meant
pay	paid	paid
prove	proved	proved *or* proven
read	read	read
ride	rode	ridden
ring	rang	rung
run	ran	run
say	said	said
see	saw	seen
send	sent	sent

---

[1]*Hang* as an irregular verb means to *suspend*. When *hang* means to *execute*, it is regular: *hang, hanged, hanged.*

Some Irregular Verb Forms, continued

BASE FORM	PAST TENSE	PAST PARTICIPLE
shake	shook	shaken
sing	sang	sung
sink	sank	sunk
sleep	slept	slept
speak	spoke	spoken
spend	spent	spent
spring	sprang, sprung	sprung
stand	stood	stood
steal	stole	stolen
stick	stuck	stuck
swear	swore	sworn
swim	swam	swum
take	took	taken
teach	taught	taught
tear	tore	torn
tell	told	told
think	thought	thought
wake	woke, waked	waked, woken
wear	wore	worn
wind	wound	wound
write	wrote	written

16c Using auxiliary verbs

An **auxiliary** (helping) **verb** is combined with the base form of a verb or the present or past participle form to establish tense, mood, and voice in a sentence. This combination of verbs creates a **verb phrase.** The most frequently used auxiliaries are *be, have,* and *do. Be* functions as an auxiliary when it combines with the *-ing* form of a verb to create the progressive tenses (as in I *am going*). *Have* functions as an auxiliary when it combines with the past participle form of a verb to create the perfect tenses (as in I *have gone*). *Do* functions as an auxiliary when it combines with the base form of a verb to form questions, to show emphasis, and to show negation. (*Do* you care? I *do* care. I *don't* care.)

1 Use modal auxiliaries to refine meaning.

When paired with the base form of a verb, a **modal auxiliary** expresses urgency, obligation, likelihood, possibility, and so on:

I must resign.   I ought to resign.   I might resign.

The auxiliaries *will* and *shall* establish the future tense.

> When shall I resign?   She will resign.

Other modal auxiliaries include *can, could, should,* and *would.* (See the Critical Decisions box on page 288.)

2   Revise nonstandard auxiliaries by using standard forms of *be.*

Some dialects form present-tense auxiliary constructions with variations on the base form of *be.* For written academic English, these forms must be revised.

NONSTANDARD She be singing.   **REVISED** She is singing.

16d   Using transitive and intransitive verbs

Action verbs are classified as *transitive* and *intransitive.* A **transitive verb** (marked with the abbreviation **tr.** in the dictionary) transfers an action from a subject to an object; the action of an **intransitive verb** is limited to the subject of a sentence.

1   Distinguish between verbs that take direct objects and those that do not.

A large number of verbs regularly take a direct object and are always transitive; others never take an object and are always intransitive.

TRANSITIVE   The politician kissed the baby. [The transitive verb *kissed* transfers action from *politician* to *baby.*]

INTRANSITIVE   The politician smiled. [An action is performed, but no object is acted on.]

Many verbs can have both a transitive and an intransitive sense.

INTRANSITIVE   She runs every day. [The verb takes no object. *Every day* is an adverb explaining *when* she runs.]

TRANSITIVE   She runs a big business. [The verb has changed meaning and now transfers action to a direct object.]

Note that a transitive verb is the *only* type that can be made passive: The baby was kissed by the politician.

2   Avoid confusion between the verbs *sit/set* and *lie/lay.*

SPOTLIGHT
2

Difficulties in distinguishing between transitive and intransitive verbs lead to misuse of *sit/set* and *lie/lay.* *Sit* is normally an intransitive verb; its action is limited to the subject.

adverb

You sit *on the bench.*

Set is a transitive verb. It transfers action to an object, which must be present in the sentence.

object   adverb

You set *the papers on the bench.*

Lie is an intransitive verb; its action is limited to the subject.

adverb

I lie *on the couch.*

Lay is a transitive verb. It transfers action to an object, which must be present in the sentence.

object   adverb

I lay *the pillow on the couch.*

The following box reviews the principle parts of *sit/set* and *lie/lay.*

The Principal Parts of sit/set *and* lie/lay

BASE FORM	PRESENT TENSE	PAST TENSE	PAST PARTICIPLE	PRESENT PARTICIPLE
sit	sits	sat	sat	sitting
set	sets	set	set	setting
lie	lies	lay	lain	lying
lay	lays	laid	laid	laying

Tense

16e   Understanding the uses of verb tenses

A verb's **tense** indicates when an action has occurred or when a subject exists in a given state. There are three basic tenses in English: *past, present,* and *future.* Each has a **perfect** form, which indicates a completed action; each has a **progressive** form, which indicates ongoing action; and each has a **perfect progressive** form, which indicates ongoing action that will be completed at some definite time.

Present: I start the engine.

Present perfect: I have started the engine.

Present progressive: I am starting the engine.

Present perfect progressive: I have been starting the engine.

Past: I started the engine.

> **Past perfect:** I had started the engine.
>
> **Past progressive:** I was starting the engine.
>
> **Past perfect progressive:** I had been starting the engine.

Future: I will start the engine.

> **Future perfect:** I will have started the engine.
>
> **Future progressive:** I will be starting the engine.
>
> **Future perfect progressive:** I will have been starting the engine.

SPOTLIGHT 2

16f Sequencing verb tenses

Although a sentence will always have a main verb located in its independent clause, it may have other verbs as well. Since every verb shows tense, any sentence with more than one verb may indicate actions that occur at different times. Keep clear the time relationships among two or more verbs in closely linked clauses or sentences, as shown in the Critical Decisions box below.

CRITICAL DECISIONS

Maintaining Clear Time Relationships among Closely Linked Verbs

If you refer to *past events occurring at roughly the same time*, use past-tense verbs:

FAULTY

> Tom *had traveled* where jobs *presented* themselves. [past perfect/past]
> [The different tenses wrongly suggest that the events happened at different times.]

REVISED

>   past event   past event
> Tom *traveled* where jobs *presented* themselves. [past/past]

If you refer to *past events occurring one before the other*, use the past tense for the more recent event and the past perfect for the earlier event.

FAULTY

> I *remembered* Mrs. Smith, who *showed* me kindness. [past/past]
> [The tenses wrongly suggest that actions occurred at the same time.]

Voice

16g   Using the active and passive voices

Voice refers to the emphasis a writer gives to the actor in a sentence or to the object acted on. The **active voice** emphasizes the actor of a sentence.

Brenda scored the winning goal.

In a **passive-voice** sentence, the object acted on is emphasized.

The winning goal was scored by Brenda.

The emphasis on the object of a passive-voice sentence is made possible by a rearrangement of words. A passive-voice construction also requires use of the verb *be (is, are, was, were, has been, have been)* and the preposition *by.*

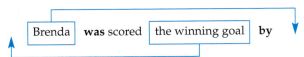

The winning goal was scored by Brenda.

In a further transformation, you can make the original actor/subject disappear altogether by deleting the prepositional phrase.

The winning goal was scored.

Use a strong active voice for clear, direct assertions. In active-voice sentences, people or other agents *do* things. Active-voice sentences create a direct, lively link between the subject and the reader. By contrast, passive-voice sentences are inherently wordy. Use the active voice unless you want to emphasize the object of the verb (by placing it at the head of a passive voice sentence) or to deemphasize the subject (by dropping it *out* of the passive voice sentence). See the Critical Decisions box in 24b-1.

STRONGER   A guidance counselor recommended the book.

WEAKER   A book was recommended by a guidance counselor.

Mood

16h   Understanding the uses of mood

The **mood** of a verb indicates the writer's judgment as to whether a statement is a fact, a command, or an unreal or hypothetical condition contrary to fact. In the **indicative mood,** a writer states a fact, opinion, or question. Most of our writing and speech is in the indicative mood.

The mayor has held office for eight years. [fact]

In the **imperative mood,** a writer gives a command, the subject of which is "you," the person being addressed. Often, the subject of a command is omitted, but occasionally it is expressed directly.

Follow me!
Don't you touch that switch!

By using the **subjunctive mood,** a writer shows that he or she believes an action or situation is unreal or hypothetical. Of the three moods, the subjunctive is the most tricky to master.

1   Use the subjunctive mood with certain *if* constructions.

When an *if* clause expresses an unreal or hypothetical condition, use the subjunctive mood. In a subjunctive *if* construction, the modal auxiliary *would, could, might,* or *should* is used in the main clause.

SUBJUNCTIVE   If Tom *were* more considerate, he *would* have called.

SUBJUNCTIVE   If I *were* elected, I might raise taxes.

NOTE: When an *if* construction is used to establish a cause-and-effect relationship, the writer assumes that the facts presented in a sentence either are true or could very possibly be true. Therefore, the writer uses an indicative ("factual") mood with normal subject–verb agreement.

FAULTY   If I were late, start without me.

REVISED   If I am late, start without me. [The lateness is assumed to be a likely or possible fact.]

2   Use the subjunctive mood with *as if* and *as though* constructions.

When an *as if* or *as though* construction sets up a purely hypothetical comparison that attempts to explain or characterize, use the subjunctive mood.

FAULTY   She swims as if she *was* part fish. [Since the speaker knows she is not part fish, the indicative ("factual") mood is inconsistent.]

REVISED   She swims as if she *were* part fish.

3   Use the subjunctive mood with a *that* construction.

Use the subjunctive mood with subordinate *that* constructions expressing a requirement, request, urging, belief, wish, recommendation, or doubt. In each of these constructions, the word *that* may be omitted.

The rules require that we *be* present.

I wish that I *were* a painter.

CHAPTER 17

Correcting Errors in Subject–Verb Agreement

SPOTLIGHT 3

Subjects and verbs must agree in both number and person. The term **number** indicates whether a noun is singular (denoting one person, place, or thing) or plural (denoting more than one). The term **person** identifies the subject of a sentence as the same person who is speaking (the first person), someone who is spoken to (the second person), or someone or something being spoken about (the third person). Pronouns differ according to person.

WWW
http://Webster.commnet.edu/
grammar/sv_agr.htm

A guide to subject–verb agreement, with quizzes and exercises.

	FIRST-PERSON SUBJECT	**SECOND-PERSON SUBJECT**	**THIRD-PERSON SUBJECT**
SINGULAR	I	you	he, she, it
PLURAL	we	you	they

Agreement between a verb and first- or second-person pronoun subject does not vary. The pronouns *I, we,* and *you* take verbs *without* the letter *s.*

I walk.   We walk.   You walk.

I scream, you scream, we scream—for ice cream.

The forms of agreement for third-person subjects and verbs, however, can be confusing.

CRITICAL DECISIONS
Recognizing Singular and Plural

Making correct decisions about agreement requires recognizing whether certain sentence parts are regarded as singular or plural. This is easy enough with nouns because most form the plural with the addition of *-s* or *-es,* although there are exceptions (see 38e). Problems can arise, however, with indefinite pronouns (such as *everyone, none, neither*), collective nouns (*staff, band*), and some other sentence elements, because their form and function are not so clearly singular or plural. This chapter provides information to help you make this crucial distinction.

17a   Make a third-person subject agree in number with its verb.

The suffix *-s* or *-es* serves two functions. When added to a present-tense verb, it signals a singular, third-person subject (The frog *leaps.*); however, when added to a noun subject or third-person pronoun subject, the same suffix changes that subject to a plural, so the verb must also be plural (The *frogs* leap.). You can use these seemingly contradictory functions to advantage by thinking of agreement as a kind of "trade-off" arrangement.

The "trade-off" technique

To remember the basic forms of third-person agreement for most verbs in the present tense (a notable exception is the verb *be*), you may find it helpful to visualize something like a balanced trade-off of *-s* endings between most noun subjects and their verbs: if one ends with an *-s,* then the other does not.

SINGULAR   A boy__ hikes.   A girl__ swims.   A kid__ does it. [Verbs end in *s;* nouns do not.]

PLURAL   The boys hike__.   The girls swim__.   Kids do__ it. [Nouns end in *s;* verbs do not.]

The verb *be*

The *-s* and *-es* suffixes are not used with the verb *be*. Instead, subject–verb agreement operates as follows:

SINGULAR	PLURAL
I *am*	we *are*
you *are*	you *are*
he, she, it *is*	they *are*

Revising nonstandard verb and noun forms to observe *-s* and *-es* endings

In rapid conversation people sometimes skip over the *-s* or *-es* endings for singular verbs. In some English dialects, the base (or infinitive) form of the verb is used with singular nouns. Academic English requires that writers use the standard conventions for subject–verb agreement.

| NONSTANDARD | He read the book. | NONSTANDARD | She do it. |
| STANDARD | He reads the book. | STANDARD | She does it. |

1 A subject agrees with its verb regardless of whether any phrase or clause separates them.

Sheets of thick ice <u>build</u> over time and <u>become</u> a glacier.

Often a subject may be followed by a lengthy phrase or clause that comes between it and the verb, confusing the basic pattern of agreement. To be sure the subject matches the verb, mentally strike out or ignore phrases or clauses separating them.

The words *each* and *every* have a singular sense. When either of these words precedes a compound subject joined by *and,* use a singular verb.

Every city and county in Massachusetts <u>has</u> struggled with the problem of downward mobility.

EXCEPTION: When *each* follows a compound subject, the sense is plural and the plural verb is used.

Boston and New York *each* <u>maintain</u> programs to reeducate workers.

NOTE: Phrases beginning with "in addition to," "along with," "as well as," or "accompanied by" may come between a subject and its verb. Although they add material, these phrases do *not* create a plural subject; they must be mentally stricken out to determine the correct number of the verb.

The anthropologist, as well as social researchers such as statisticians and demographers, <u>looks</u> for indicators of change in status.

2 A compound subject linked by the conjunction *and* is in most cases plural.

When a compound subject linked by *and* refers to two or more people, places, or things, it is usually considered plural.

PLURAL   *Statistical information* and *the analysis based upon it* <u>allow</u> an anthropologist to piece together significant cultural patterns.

EXCEPTION: When a compound subject refers to a single person, place, or thing, it is considered singular.

SINGULAR   Whatever culture she studies, *this anthropologist* and *researcher* <u>concerns</u> herself with the relations among husbands, wives, children, kin, and friends.

3 When parts of a compound subject are linked by the conjunction *or* or *nor*, the verb should agree in number with the part of the subject closer to the verb.

When all parts of the compound subject are the same number, agreement with the verb is fairly straightforward: Either John or *Maria* <u>sings</u> today.

When one part of the compound subject is singular and another plural, there can be confusion. The subject closer to the verb determines the number of the verb. If the closer subject is singular, then the verb is singular.

SINGULAR   According to popular wisdom, either poor habits or *ineptitude* <u>is</u> responsible when an individual fails to succeed in American culture.

When the subject closer to the verb is plural, the verb is plural.

PLURAL   Neither the downwardly mobile individual nor the *people* surrounding him or her <u>realize</u> that losing a job is often due to impersonal economic factors.

17b Identify a third-person subject as singular or plural, and make the verb agree.

1 Most indefinite pronouns have a singular sense and take a singular verb.

Indefinite pronouns rename no particular person, place, or thing, so they often raise questions about subject–verb agreement. The following indefinite pronouns have a singular sense:

another	anything	either	everyone
anybody	each	everybody	everything

much	none, no one	other	someone
neither	nothing	somebody	
nobody	one	something	

SINGULAR *Much* of the law concerning the admissibility or exclusion of evidence <u>involves</u> standards of truth and fairness.

The indefinite pronouns *both, ones, few,* and *others* have a plural sense and take a plural verb.

PLURAL Some critics of the O. J. Simpson trials believe that the verdicts damaged the American jurisprudence system; *others* <u>argue</u> that the system worked splendidly.

The indefinite pronouns *all, any, more, many, enough, some,* and *most* have a singular or plural sense, depending on the meaning of a sentence.

Try substituting *he, she, it, we,* or *they* for the indefinite pronoun. The context of a sentence will give you clues about the number of its subject.

PLURAL Millions of Americans watched the criminal trial. *Most* <u>were</u> tuned in as if to a soap opera.

SINGULAR Some of the public interest in the trial was sparked by the legal maneuverings of well-paid lawyers. But *most* of the interest <u>was</u> rooted in voyeurism.

2 **Collective nouns have a plural or a singular sense, depending on the meaning of a sentence.**

When a collective noun, such as *audience, band, bunch, crew, crowd, faculty, family, group, staff, team,* and *tribe,* refers to a single unit, the sense of the noun is singular, and the noun takes a singular verb. The context of a sentence will give you clues about the number of its subject.

SINGULAR The *jury* <u>hears</u> all the evidence presented by both the prosecution and the defense.

When the collective noun refers to individuals and their separate actions within a group, the sense of the noun is plural and the noun takes a plural verb.

PLURAL The *jury* often <u>have</u> diverse reactions to the evidence they hear. [*Jury* in this case emphasizes the actions of individual members. It has a plural sense and takes a plural verb: *have.*]

If this plural use sounds awkward to you, add a plural noun to the sentence to clarify matters.

PLURAL The *jury members* often <u>have</u> diverse reactions to the evidence they hear.

---

3   Nouns plural in form but singular in sense take singular verbs.

The nouns *athletics, economics, mathematics, news, physics,* and *politics* all end with the letter *-s,* but they denote a single activity.

Economics depends heavily on mathematics.

4   A linking verb agrees in number with its subject, not with the subject complement.

Identify the singular or plural subject when deciding the number of the verb. In addition to striking out mentally any phrases or clauses that interrupt the subject and verb, also disregard the subject complement *following* the linking verb.

SINGULAR   The *reason* for Simpson's acquittal in the criminal trial was the many mistakes made by the police in gathering evidence.

PLURAL   *The many mistakes made by the police in gathering evidence* were the reason for Simpson's acquittal.

5   In sentences with inverted word order, a verb should agree in number with its subject.

The subject of an English sentence is normally placed before a verb. When this order is rearranged, the subject and verb continue to agree in number. Most errors with rearranged sentences occur with the verb *be.*

NORMAL ORDER   Janice and Michael *come* here.

INVERTED ORDER   Here *come* Janice and Michael.

6   The verb of a dependent clause introduced by the pronoun *which, that, who,* or *whom* should agree in number with the pronoun's antecedent.

In such a dependent clause, both the pronoun subject (*which, that,* etc.) and verb are dependent for their number on an antecedent in the main clause.

The *books, which* are old, are falling apart.

7   Phrases and clauses that function as subjects are treated as singular and take singular verbs.

Often a noun clause, or a phrase with a gerund or infinitive, will act as the subject of a sentence. Such a construction is always regarded as a singular element in the sentence.

To swim well <u>is</u> the first prerequisite for scuba diving.
That the child is able to cough <u>is</u> a good sign.

---

8   Titled works, key words used as terms, and companies are treated as singular in number and take singular verbs.

Titles of works, names of companies or corporations, underlined or italicized words referred to as words, numbers, and units of money are regarded as singular entities in a sentence and take singular verbs.

Classics <u>is</u> an overused word.   "The Killers" <u>is</u> a Hemingway story.

CHAPTER 18
Using Adjectives and Adverbs

Adjectives and adverbs are **modifiers**—*descriptive* words, phrases, or clauses that enliven sentences with vivid detail. To make effective decisions about modifiers, you need to understand the differences between the two main types: adjectives and adverbs.

18a   Distinguishing between adjectives and adverbs

The Critical Decisions box below can help you decide whether to use an adjective or an adverb in your sentence.

CRITICAL DECISIONS

Choosing between Adjectives and Adverbs

Ask questions: Adjectives and adverbs answer different questions.

An **adjective** modifies a noun or pronoun and answers these questions:

Which: The *latest* news arrived.
What kind: An *insignificant* difference remained.
How many: The *two* sides would resolve their differences.

(continued)

Choosing between Adjectives and Adverbs, continued

An **adverb** modifies a verb and answers these questions:

When: *Tomorrow,* the temperature will drop.

How: The temperature will drop *sharply.*

How often: Weather patterns change *frequently.*

Where: The weather patterns *here* change frequently.

An **adverb** also modifies adjectives, adverbs, and entire clauses:

Modifying an adjective: An *especially* large group enrolled.

Modifying a clause: *Consequently,* the registrar closed the course.

Modifying an adverb: Courses at this school *almost* never get closed.

When choosing between an adjective and adverb form, identify the word being modified and determine its part of speech. Then follow the conventions presented in this chapter.

Identifying and using adjectives

WWW

http://ccc.commnet.edu/grammar/adjectives.htm

A review of adjectives, with exercises.

An **adjective** modifies a noun or pronoun by answering these questions: **which?** the *tall* child; **what kind?** the *artistic* child; **how many?** *five* children.

Identifying adverbs

An **adverb** modifies a verb by answering several questions: **When?** *Yesterday,* the child sang. **How?** The child sang *beautifully.* **How often?** The child sings *regularly.* **Where?**

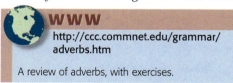

WWW

http://ccc.commnet.edu/grammar/adverbs.htm

A review of adverbs, with exercises.

The child sang *here.* Adverbs modify adjectives: The child sang an *extremely* intricate melody. Adverbs can modify other adverbs: The child sings *almost* continuously. Certain adverbs can modify entire sentences: *Consequently,* the child's voice has improved.

Some adverbs are not derived from other words: *again, almost, always, never, here, there, now, often, seldom, well.* Many adverbs, however, are formed from adjectives. These adverbs may be formed simply by adding the suffix *-ly* to adjectives: *beautiful—beautifully; clever—cleverly.* However, an *-ly* ending alone is not sufficient to establish a word as an adverb, since certain adjectives show this ending: a friend*ly* conversation, a love*ly* afternoon. In any standard dictionary, look for the abbreviations **adj.** and **adv.,** which will distinguish between the forms of a word.

Adverbs are used to modify verbs even when a direct object stands between the verb and its modifier.

FAULTY A *precise* measured object in Denver will weigh somewhat less than the same object measured in Washington. [The adjective *precise* incorrectly modifies the participle *measured*.]

REVISED A *precisely* measured object in Denver will weigh somewhat less than the same object measured in Washington.

In informal or nonstandard usage, adjectives like *real* or *sure* may function as adverbs ("a real bad time"). In standard academic usage, however, adverbs modify adjectives and other adverbs.

NONSTANDARD The scientific community would sure be shocked if evidence were to surface regarding the coexistence of humans and dinosaurs.

REVISED The scientific community would surely be shocked if evidence were to surface regarding the coexistence of humans and dinosaurs.

18b Use an adjective (not an adverb) after a linking verb to describe a subject.

The following verbs are linking verbs: forms of *be* (*is, are, was, were, has been, have been*), *look, smell, taste, sound, feel, appear, become, grow, remain, seem, turn*, and *stay*. A sentence with a linking verb establishes, in effect, an equation between the first part of the sentence and the second:

A LINKING VERB B, OR $A = B$.

The pilots were *thirsty.*

In this construction, the predicate part, B, is called the *subject complement*. The subject complement may be a noun, pronoun, or adjective—but *not* an adverb. (See 13b.)

Good, well, bad, badly

The words *good* and *well, bad* and *badly* are not interchangeable in formal writing (though they tend to be in conversation). The common linking verbs associated with well-being, appearance, or feeling—*looks, seems, appears, feels*—can cause special problems. The rules of usage follow.

1 Good and well

Good is an adjective, used either before a noun or after a linking verb to describe the condition of a subject.

ACCEPTABLE	Kyle looks good. [After a linking verb, *good* describes the subject's appearance.]
	Kyle is a good dancer. [*Good* modifies the noun *dancer.*]
NONSTANDARD	Susan drives good. [*Drives* is an action verb and requires an adverb as modifier.]
REVISED	Susan drives well.

The word *well* can be used as either an adjective or an adverb. It has limited use as an adjective only after certain linking verbs (*looks, seems, be/am/is/are*) to describe the subject's good health.

ACCEPTABLE	Robert looks well. [*Looks* is a linking verb. The sense of this sentence is that Robert seems to be healthy.]

Well functions as an adverb whenever it follows an action verb.

NONSTANDARD	Janet sings good. [*Sings* is an action verb and requires an adverb as modifier.]
REVISED	Janet sings well.

2 Bad and badly

Bad is an adjective, used before a noun and after a linking verb to describe a subject. Again, the linking verbs that involve appearance or feeling—*looks, seems, appears, feels*—can cause special problems.

FAULTY	Marie feels badly. [*Feels* is a linking verb and must tie the subject, *Marie,* to an adjective.]
REVISED	Marie feels bad. [As an adjective, *bad* is linked to the subject to describe *Marie* and her mental state.]

Badly is an adverb, used after an action verb or used to modify an adjective or adverb.

NONSTANDARD	John cooks bad. [*Cooks* is an action verb and must be modified by an adverb.]
REVISED	John cooks badly.

18c Using comparative and superlative forms of adjectives and adverbs

Both adjectives and adverbs change form to express comparative relationships. The base form of an adjective or adverb is called its **positive** form. The **comparative** form is used to express a relationship between two elements, and the **superlative** form is used to express a relationship among three or more elements. Most single-syllable adverbs and adjectives, and many two-syllable adjectives, show comparisons with the suffix *-er* and superlatives with *-est.*

	POSITIVE	COMPARATIVE	SUPERLATIVE
ADJECTIVE	crazy	crazier	craziest
	crafty	craftier	craftiest
ADVERB	near	nearer	nearest
	far	farther	farthest

Adverbs of two or more syllables and adjectives of three or more syllables change to the comparative and superlative forms with the words *more* and *most*. Adjectives and adverbs show downward (or negative) comparisons with the words *less* and *least* placed before the positive form. If you are uncertain of an adjective's or adverb's form, refer to a dictionary.

	POSITIVE	COMPARATIVE	SUPERLATIVE
ADJECTIVE	elegant	more/less elegant	most/least elegant
	logical	more/less logical	most/least logical
ADVERB	beautifully	more/less beautifully	most/least beautifully
	strangely	more/less strangely	most/least strangely

Use *few, fewer, fewest,* or *many* with nouns that can be counted; use *little, less, least,* or *much* with nouns that cannot be counted.

many cups	(not *much* cups)
fewer calories	(not *less* calories)
less caffeine	(not *fewer* caffeine)

 18d | **Express comparative and superlative relationships accurately, completely, and logically.**

Accuracy

Use the comparative form of adverbs and adjectives to show a relationship between two items. Use the superlative form when relating three or more items.

TWO ITEMS   In the winter months, New York is colder than Miami.

TWO ITEMS   First-year students are often more conscientious about their studies than second-year students.

MULTIPLES   America Online was voted by *PC Magazine* as the "Best Choice" of all online services. [*Better* would be incorrect, since there are more than two online services.]

Completeness

If the elements of a two- or three-way comparison are not being mentioned explicitly in a sentence, be sure to provide enough context so that the comparison makes sense.

INCOMPLETE	Jason is more efficient. [More efficient than whom? at what?]
REVISED	Jason is the more efficient runner. [Two runners are being compared.]
	OR
	Jason is a more efficient runner than Dylan.

Logic

Certain adjectives have an absolute meaning—they cannot be logically compared. *Death,* for example, represents an absolute endpoint, as do the words *unique, first, final, last, absolute,* and *infinite.* Once *death* is reached, comparisons literally make no sense.

ILLOGICAL	The story was submitted in its most final form.
REVISED	The story was submitted in its final form.
	OR
	The story was submitted in nearly final form.

18e Avoid double comparisons, double superlatives, and double negatives.

Double comparisons/superlatives

Adjectives and adverbs show comparative and superlative relationships either with a suffix (*-er/-est*) *or* with the words *more, most, less, least.* It is redundant and awkward to use the *-er/-est* suffix with *more/most* or *less/least.*

| FAULTY | The World Trade Center is more taller than the Chrysler Building. |
| REVISED | The World Trade Center is taller than the Chrysler Building. |

Double negatives

Double negatives—two modifiers that say "no" in the same sentence—are redundant and sometimes confusing, though fairly common in nonstandard usage. A clear negation in a sentence should be expressed only once.

NONSTANDARD	I didn't have none.
	I didn't have no cash.
REVISED	I had none.
	I didn't have any cash.

CHAPTER 19

Correcting Misplaced and Dangling Modifiers

A modifier can be a single word: a *sporty* car; a phrase: Joanne drove *a car with racing stripes*; or a dependent clause: *After she gained confidence driving a sporty car,* Joanne took up racing. As you write, you will need to make decisions about where to place modifiers within your sentences. In order to function most effectively, a modifier should be placed directly next to the word it modifies. If this placement disrupts meaning, then the modifier should be placed *as close as possible* to the word it modifies. The Critical Decisions box on pages 266–267 poses three questions you can ask to determine if you have placed your modifiers well.

WWW

http://www.uottawa.ca/academic/
arts/writcent/hypergrammar/
msplmod.html

How not to use misplaced and dangling modifiers in your writing.

Misplaced Modifiers

19a	Position modifiers so that they refer clearly to the words they should modify.

Readers expect a modifier to be linked clearly with the word the writer intended it to modify. When this link is broken, readers become confused or frustrated.

CONFUSING   A truck rumbled down the street, gray with dirt.

CLEAR   A dirty, gray truck rumbled down the street.

OR

A truck rumbled down the gray, dirty street.

If a phrase or clause beginning a sentence functions as an adjective modifier, then the first words after the modifier—that is, the first words of the independent clause—should include the noun being modified.

CONFUSING   A small, Green Mountain town, Calvin Coolidge was born in Plymouth, Vermont. [Who or what is a *Green Mountain town?*]

REVISED   Calvin Coolidge was born in Plymouth, Vermont, a small, Green Mountain town. [*Green Mountain town* now modifies *Plymouth, Vermont.*]

19b Position limiting modifiers with care.

In conversation, **limiting modifiers**—words such as *only, almost, just, nearly, even,* and *simply*—are often shifted within a sentence with little concern for their effect on meaning. When written, however, a limiting modifier literally restricts the meaning of the word placed directly after it:

Nearly 90 percent of the 200 people who served in presidential cabinets from 1897 to 1973 belonged to the social or business elite.

Ninety percent of the *nearly* 200 people who served in presidential cabinets from 1897 to 1973 belonged to the social or business elite.

Placement of the limiting modifier *nearly* fundamentally alters the meaning of these sentences.

19c Reposition modifiers that describe two elements simultaneously.

A **squinting modifier** appears to modify two words in the sentence—the word preceding it and the word following it. To convey a clear meaning, the modifier must be repositioned so it can describe only a *single* word.

CONFUSING   The supervisor conducting the interview thoughtfully posed a final question.

CLEAR   The supervisor conducting the interview posed a final, thoughtful question.

CRITICAL DECISIONS

Questioning Your Placement of Modifiers

Modifiers provide much of the interest in a sentence; but when misused, they confuse readers. You should know precisely *which* word in a sentence you are modifying. Posing three questions should help you to be clear.

■ **What modifiers am I using in this sentence?** To use modifiers effectively and correctly, you should be able to recognize modifiers when you write them. Single words, phrases, and clauses can function as modifiers.

Modifying word

ADJECTIVE   The artist made a *deliberate* effort.

ADVERB   The artist succeeded *brilliantly*.

Modifying phrase

ADJECTIVE   The painting, *displayed on a dark wall*, glowed.

ADVERB   Patrons responded *with an unusual mix of excitement and nervousness*.

Modifying clause

ADJECTIVE   Many attended the opening, *which had become a much anticipated event*.

ADVERB   *After the gallery closed that evening*, the staff celebrated.

■ **What word is being modified?**

The artist made a *deliberate* effort.   The artist succeeded *brilliantly*.
[The noun *effort* is being modified.]   [The verb *succeeded* is being modified.]

Several patrons who returned *repeatedly* called the young artist "a wonder." [Confusing: The single-word modifier *repeatedly* seems to modify two words, *returned* and *called*.]

Having made a commitment of time and money, it was gratifying to see a successful show. [Confusing: The phrase *having made a commitment of time and money* does not modify any specific word.]

■ **Does the modifying word, phrase, or clause clearly refer to this word?**

Upon returning, several patrons *repeatedly* called the young artist "a wonder." [The modifier *repeatedly* now clearly modifies the verb *called*.]

Having made a commitment of time and money, the manager was gratified to see a successful show. [The modifying phrase now clearly modifies the noun *manager*.]

19d   Reposition a modifier that splits the parts of an infinitive.

Move an adverb to a position before or after an infinitive, or rewrite the sentence and eliminate the infinitive.

SPLIT   Many managers are unable *to* with difficult employees *establish* a moderate and reasonable tone.

REVISED   Many managers are unable *to establish* a moderate and reasonable tone with difficult employees.

Occasionally, a sentence with a split infinitive will sound more natural than a sentence rewritten to avoid the split. This will be the case when the object of the infinitive is a long phrase or clause and the adverbial modifier is short.

SPLIT   Some managers like to *regularly* interview workers from different departments in order to identify potential problems.

Avoiding the split may become somewhat awkward.

NO SPLIT   Some managers like to interview *regularly* workers from different departments in order to identify potential problems.

Some readers do not accept split infinitives, no matter what the circumstances of a sentence. The safe course is to avoid the split by eliminating the infinitive or changing the modifier.

MODIFIER   *On a regular basis,* some managers like to interview workers from
CHANGED   different departments in order to identify potential problems.

Dangling Modifiers

19e   Identify and revise dangling modifiers.

A modifier is said to "dangle" when the word it modifies does not appear in the same sentence. Correct the error by rewriting the sentence, making sure to include the word that is being modified.

1   Give introductory clauses or phrases a specific word to modify.

First-draft sentences beginning with long phrases or clauses often contain dangling modifiers. Revision involves asking what the opening clause or phrase modifies and then rewriting the sentence to provide an answer.

DANGLING   Dominated though they are by a few artists who repeatedly get the best roles, millions of people flock to the cinemas. [Who or what are dominated? The main clause lacks a word to be modified.]

REVISED   Dominated though they are by a few artists who repeatedly get the best roles, *movies* continue to attract millions of people. [Now, the opening phrase is immediately followed by a noun it can modify.]

DANGLING   After appearing in *The Maltese Falcon,* it was clear that Warner Brothers had a box-office star. [Who appeared in the film?]

REVISED   After appearing in *The Maltese Falcon,* Humphrey Bogart became Warner Brothers' box-office star.

2   Rewrite passive constructions to provide active subjects.

Often a modifying phrase that begins a sentence will dangle because the independent clause is written in the passive voice. Missing from this passive-voice sentence is the original subject (see example), which would have been modified by the introductory phrase or clause. Correct the dangling modifier by rewriting the independent clause in the active voice.

DANGLING   After considering these issues, the decision was postponed.
                  [Who postponed the decision? The subject does not appear in this passive-voice sentence.]

REVISED WITH   After considering these issues, the candidate postponed his
ACTIVE VOICE   decision.

CRITICAL DECISIONS

Revising to Maintain Passive Constructions

Occasionally, the original subject of a passive construction—either stated directly or implied—is not what a dangling modifier is meant to modify. In such cases, revise the modifier itself.

DANGLING   After complaining to the authorities, the debris was cleared.

REVISED   After I complained to the authorities, the debris was cleared.

CHAPTER 20

Using Nouns and Pronouns

The primary decision you will need to make in using nouns and pronouns is which *case* to use with these words. The term **case** refers to a noun or pronoun's change in form, depending on its function in a sentence. Such decisions are more troublesome with pronouns than with nouns because nouns change form only to show possession, whereas pronouns change form both to show possession and to show a change in function from subject to object.

CRITICAL DECISIONS

Determining the Function of Personal Pronouns

The personal pronouns are *I, we, you, he, she, it,* and *they,* along with their other forms. As personal pronouns (except *you* and *it*) change their function in a sentence, they also change their form. (For example: *I* am happy. Pass *me* the salad.) The relative pronouns *who* and *whoever* also change form to *whom* and *whomever* when their function changes from subject to object. You need to be alert to the function of these pronouns in order to decide whether to use the subjective or the objective case. Most of this chapter is devoted to personal and relative pronouns.

20a Using pronouns as subjects

1 Use the subjective case when a pronoun functions as a subject.

She speaks forcefully. The speaker is *she.*
The executive officers—and only *they*—can meet here.

SUBJECT OF AN INDEPENDENT CLAUSE	In September 1908, Orville Wright began demonstration flights of the "Signal Corps Flyer"; *he* invited a young officer to be a passenger.
SUBJECT OF A DEPENDENT CLAUSE	When *they* attempted a fourth circuit of the parade grounds, the Flyer's right propeller hit a bracing wire and cracked.
APPOSITIVE THAT RENAMES A SUBJECT	Thomas Selfridge—*he* alone—bears the title of first person killed in the crash of a powered airplane.

The following box lists pronouns used as subjects.

Pronouns Used as Subjects

	SINGULAR	PLURAL
1ST PERSON	I	we
2ND PERSON	you	you
3RD PERSON	he, she, it	they

2 Use the subjective case for pronouns with the linking verb *be*.

This is *she*.   These are *they*.   It is *I*.

The linking verb *be* links the subject of the sentence to a completing or "complement" word. When pronouns function as subject complements, they take the subjective form.

Roosevelt *was* president.   It was *he*, the president, who spoke.

In informal usage it is fairly common to hear a linking-verb construction using an objective form: as in "It's me" or "This is her." But in academic English these constructions should be revised using a subjective pronoun that maintains sentence logic and consistency: "It's I" and "This is she."

20b Using pronouns as objects

1 Use the objective forms for pronouns functioning as objects.

WWW
http://www.uottawa.ca/academic/
arts/writcent/hypergrammar/
prntrcky.html

Explanations of some tricky points of pronoun usage.

The governor handed *her* the report. The job appealed to *me*. We enjoyed taking *them* to dinner. Pressing *her* for information, the reporter asked another question.

Pronouns functioning as the object of a preposition, as the direct object or indirect object of a verb, or as the object of a verbal take the objective form. The following box lists pronouns used as objects.

Pronouns Used as Objects

	SINGULAR	PLURAL
1ST PERSON	me	us
2ND PERSON	you	you
3RD PERSON	him, her, it	them

2 Use the objective form before an infinitive.

Study enabled *us* to reach the goal.

When a pronoun appears between a verb and an infinitive, the pronoun takes the objective form. In this position, the pronoun is called the subject of the infinitive.

20c Using nouns and pronouns to show possession

Use a possessive noun or pronoun before a noun to indicate ownership of that noun.

Give the child *his* toy.

Eleanor Roosevelt gave the Civil Works Administration *her* support for hiring 100,000 women by the end of 1933.

The following box lists the possessive forms of pronouns.

Possessive Forms of Pronouns

	SINGULAR	PLURAL
1ST PERSON	my, mine	our, ours
2ND PERSON	your, yours	your, yours
3RD PERSON	his, her, hers, its	their, theirs

---

1 Certain possessive pronouns are used as subjects or subject complements to indicate possession.

Yours are the first hands to touch this. These are *theirs*.

The possessive pronouns *mine, ours, his, hers* can also be used in place of a noun as subjects or subject complements.

2 Use a possessive noun or pronoun before a gerund to indicate possession.

The group argued for Wanda's getting the new position.

Be careful not to mistake a gerund for a participle, which has the same *-ing* form but functions as an adjective. A participle is often preceded by an objective pronoun.

PARTICIPLE WITH OBJECTIVE PRONOUN	Clinton quickly tried to do damage control. One account describes *him circling* the room, trying to extricate himself from his verbal blunder. [*Him*, an objective pronoun, is modified by the participle *circling*.]
GERUND WITH POSSESSIVE PRONOUN	One account describes *his circling* the room in an attempt to do damage control as the instinctive move of a politician.

The focus in this last sentence is no longer on *him* (on Clinton) but on *circling*—a difference in meaning.

20d   Compound constructions: Using pronouns in the objective or subjective form according to their function

Sally and *I* went to the movies. Tom went with Sally and *me.*

The coordinating conjunction *and* is used to create compound sentences with two subjects or two objects. When a personal pronoun (such as *I, me, you, he, she, it*) follows the word *and,* choose the pronoun's form as if the pronoun were alone in the sentence. When a personal pronoun follows the word *between,* use the objective case.

FAULTY	REVISED
Sally and me went to the movies.	Sally and **I** went to the movies. [TEST: I went to the movies.]
She and me went. (*or*) Her and me went.	She and **I** went. [TEST: She went. I went.]
Tom went with Sally and I.	Tom went with Sally and **me.** [TEST: Tom went with me.]
It's a secret between you and I.	It's a secret between you and **me.**
That's between he and Sally.	That's between **him** and Sally.

20e   Pronouns paired with a noun take the same case as the noun.

1   When choosing between *we* and *us* to pair with a noun, choose the pronoun whose case matches the noun.

We first-year *students* face important challenges. [students = subject]
Transitions can be challenging for *us* first-year *students.* [students = object]

The first-person plural pronoun *we* or *us* is sometimes placed before a plural noun to help establish the identity of the noun. Use the subjective-case *we* when the pronoun is paired with a noun subject and the objective-case *us* when the pronoun is paired with an object of a verb, verbal, or preposition.

2   In an appositive, a pronoun's case should match the case of the noun it renames.

The executive officers—and only *they*—can attend.
Give this report to Linda—*her* and no one else.

Pronouns may occur in an **appositive**—a word or phrase that describes, identifies, or renames a noun in a sentence. If so, the pronoun must take the same case as the noun being renamed.

COMPUTER TIPS

Beware of Grammar Checkers

Avoid using a grammar checker, no matter how tempted you are by the concept of a software program that will "correct" your grammar mistakes. The technology required to support such a function effectively is still years away. Unfortunately, today's grammar checkers literally make more mistakes than they correct: they might tell you that a certain sentence is a run-on, for example, when it's not; or they might advise you to use a plural verb to agree with a singular subject that happens to be spelled like a plural one. Software programs for desktop computers are simply not powerful enough to capture the complexities of grammar and usage in any language, let alone the sometimes illogical, erratic English language. If your mastery of grammar is already nearly perfect, then grammar software may have some value; you can test your writing decisions against the recommendations of the program and then decide whether your approach is valid. However, remember to proceed cautiously.

20f Choose the appropriate form of the pronouns *whose, who, whom, whoever,* and *whomever* depending on the pronoun's function.

The basic forms of the pronouns *whose, who, whom, whoever,* and *whomever* are shown in the following box. A pronoun's form depends on its function within its own clause.

Forms of the Relative Pronoun Who(m)/Who(m)ever

SUBJECTIVE	OBJECTIVE	POSSESSIVE
who	whom	whose
whoever	whomever	—

1 In a question, choose a subjective, objective, or possessive form of *who(m)* or *who(m)ever* according to the pronoun's function.

Who is going? To *whom* are you writing? *Whose* birthday is it?

To test the correct choice for these pronouns at the beginning of a question, mentally *answer* the question, substituting a personal pronoun for the word *who, whom,* or *whose.* Your choice of the subjective or objective form will likely be quite clear.

QUESTION   (Who/whom) are you addressing?

ANSWER   You are addressing (he/*him*). [The choice of the objective form is clear.]

REVISED   *Whom* are you addressing? [The objective form is correct.]

To determine whether the possessive pronoun *whose* is correct for a sentence, replace the initial pronoun in the question with *what,* and then mentally answer that question. If the answer requires that you use *his, her, their,* or *its* in place of the relative pronoun, then choose the possessive form, *whose.*

QUESTION   What name goes on the envelope? [Is a pronoun in the possessive case—his/her/their/its—needed?]

POSSESSIVE   *Whose* name goes on the envelope?

2   In a dependent clause, choose *who, whom,* or *whose* according to the pronoun's function within the clause.

Henry Taylor, *who* writes poems, lives in Virginia. Taylor, *whom* critics have praised, has a new book. The poet, *whose* book *The Flying Change* won a Pulitzer Prize, lives on a farm.

Apply this test to choose the correct case for a relative pronoun in a dependent clause: If the relative pronoun beginning a dependent clause needs to show possession, use the possessive-case *whose.* To confirm the choice, substitute the word *his, her, their,* or *its* for the relative pronoun. A sentence should result when the dependent clause is considered by itself.

POSSESSIVE   The poet, *whose* book *The Flying Change* won a Pulitzer Prize, lives on a farm. [Substituting *his* yields a sentence: *His* book *The Flying Change* won a Pulitzer Prize.]

The Critical Decisions box on page 276 provides further information about choosing the correct relative pronoun.

20g   Choose the case of a pronoun in the second part of a comparison depending on the meaning intended.

I studied Keats more than *him* (more than I studied Arnold—him).
I studied Keats more than *she* (more than Margo—she—studied Keats).

CRITICAL DECISIONS

Choosing Correctly between Who *and* Whom

Choosing between *who* and *whom* requires that you see that pronoun in relation to the words immediately following. Two questions should help you to choose between *who* and *whom* correctly.

- **Is the relative pronoun followed by a verb?**

  –"Yes": choose the subjective-case *who* or *whoever.*

  If a relative pronoun is followed by a verb, then the pronoun functions as a subject. To confirm this choice, substitute *I, we, you, he,* or *she* for the pronoun.

  > Clinton, *who* won by a landslide in the electoral college, did not win as convincingly in the popular vote. [*Who* is followed by a verb, and when it is converted to *he,* it yields a sentence: "*He* won by a landslide. . . ."]

  –"No": choose the objective-case *whom* or *whomever.* See the next test.

- **Is the relative pronoun followed by a noun or by any of these pronouns:** *I, we, you, he, she, few, some, many, most, it, they*?

  –"Yes": choose the objective-case *whom* or *whomever.*

  If a relative pronoun is followed by a noun or one of the listed pronouns, then it functions as an object. To confirm your choice of *whom* or *whomever,* consider the pronoun and the words immediately following. Rearrange these words and substitute *him, her,* or *them* for the relative pronoun.

  > Clinton, *whom* most analysts counted out of the presidential race, surprised supporters and detractors alike. [*Whom* is followed by *most,* and when it is converted to *him* it yields a sentence: "Most analysts counted *him* out."]

If the pronoun in the second part of a comparison takes the place of a noun subject, use the subjective form: *he, she, we.*

> Some think that Prospero is a more perplexing figure than *Hamlet* (is perplexing). [noun subject]
>
> Some think that Prospero is a more perplexing figure than *he.* [pronoun subject]

If the pronoun in the second part of a comparison takes the place of a noun object, use the objective form: *him, her, us.*

> Many critics are more intrigued by Prospero than by *Hamlet.* [noun object]
>
> Many critics are more intrigued by Prospero than by *him.* [pronoun object]

CHAPTER 21

Correcting Errors in Pronoun-Antecedent Agreement and Reference

CRITICAL DECISIONS

Recognizing Antecedents

An **antecedent** is a word—usually a noun, sometimes a pronoun—that is renamed by a pronoun. To correct problems of pronoun agreement or reference, you need to identify each pronoun's antecedent and then make decisions about pronoun form and placement. If you're not sure of a pronoun's antecedent—that is, if you can't easily substitute a noun for the pronoun—then your sentence is likely faulty.

Pronoun–Antecedent Agreement

A pronoun and antecedent must agree in *number, person,* and *gender.* Pronouns in the following examples are underlined, and antecedents are italicized.

Mary flies planes.	She flies planes.
Bob rides trolleys.	He rides trolleys.
A trolley runs on tracks.	It runs on tracks.

In cases such as these, a pronoun is easily matched to its antecedent in terms of person (first, second, or third), number (singular or plural), and gender (masculine, feminine, or neuter). At times, however, the choice of the right pronoun requires careful attention.

SPOTLIGHT
3

21a Pronouns and their antecedents should agree in number.

The *number* of a noun (either as subject or antecedent) is not always clear. The following conventions will help you to determine whether an antecedent is singular or plural.

1 A compound antecedent linked by the conjunction *and* is usually plural.

Watson and Crick were awarded a Nobel prize for <u>their</u> achievement.

Exceptions: When a compound antecedent with parts joined by the conjunction *and* has a singular sense, use a singular pronoun.

SINGULAR *An English naturalist and writer,* Thomas Blythe, used <u>his</u> classification scheme to identify more than 18,000 different <u>types</u> of plants.

The words *each* and *every* have a singular sense. When either of these words precedes an antecedent joined by *and,* use a singular pronoun.

SINGULAR Every *visible organism* and *microscopic organism* has <u>its</u> own distinctive, two-word Latin name.

Exception: When *each* follows an antecedent joined by *and,* the sense is plural and the plural pronoun is used.

PLURAL Daly and Blythe have *each* made <u>their</u> contribution to our understanding of classification systems.

2 When parts of a compound antecedent are linked by the conjunction *or* or *nor,* a pronoun should agree in number with the nearer part of the antecedent.

The pattern of agreement for *or* or *nor* follows the same convention as does subject–verb agreement.

SINGULAR Neither the traditional two-kingdom systems nor the recent five-kingdom *system* is complete in <u>its</u> classification of organisms.

Note: Avoid awkward pronoun use by revising to place the plural part of the compound antecedent nearer to the pronoun.

REVISED Neither the five-kingdom system nor the traditional two-kingdom *systems* are complete in <u>their</u> classifications.

3 Make pronouns agree in number with indefinite pronoun antecedents.

When an indefinite pronoun such as *each, anyone,* or *everyone* has a singular sense, rename it with a singular pronoun.

SINGULAR *Each* of the millions of organisms now living has <u>its</u> own defining features.

When an indefinite pronoun (such as *both* or *others*) functions as an antecedent and has a plural sense, rename it with a plural pronoun.

PLURAL   Some organisms are readily classified as animal or plant; *others,* most often the simplest single-cell organisms, find <u>themselves</u> classified in different ways, depending on the classification <u>system used</u>.

A few indefinite pronouns (such as *some, more,* or *most*) can have a singular or a plural sense, depending on the context of a sentence. Determine the number of an indefinite pronoun antecedent before selecting a pronoun replacement. (See 17b-1.)

4   Make pronouns agree in number with collective noun antecedents.

Collective nouns will be singular or plural depending on the meaning of a sentence. When a collective noun such as *audience, band, group,* or *team* refers to a *single unit,* the sense of the noun as an antecedent is singular and takes a singular pronoun. When a collective noun refers to individuals and their *separate actions* within a group, the sense of the noun as an antecedent is plural and takes a plural pronoun.

A well-informed group, the *faculty* is outspoken in <u>its</u> opinions.

The *faculty* at the gathering shared <u>their</u> thoughts on the issue.

The Critical Decisions box on page 280 provides guidelines for avoiding unintentional sexism in maintaining pronoun agreement.

Pronoun Reference

A **pronoun** substitutes for a noun, allowing you to talk about someone or something without having to repeat its name. To serve this function, a pronoun must take on meaning from a specific noun; the pronoun must make a clear and unmistakable reference to the noun for which it substitutes—called its **antecedent.** When the reference is not clearly made to a specific noun, the meaning of the whole sentence can become vague or confused.

21b   Maintain clear pronoun reference.

1   Make pronouns refer clearly to their antecedents.

Revise a sentence whenever a pronoun can refer to more than one antecedent. Use a noun in place of a pronoun, if needed for clarity; or reposition a pronoun so that its antecedent is unmistakable.

CONFUSING   When Mark and Jay return home, *he* will call.

CLEAR   When Mark and Jay return home, *Mark* will call.

Describing a person's speech indirectly can lead to unclear pronoun reference. You can convert indirect quotations to direct ones in order to clarify a pronoun's reference. Otherwise, you can restate the sentence carefully to avoid confusion.

CONFUSING   One of the astronomers told the reporter that *she* didn't know where the comets' home base was located. [Who is *she*?]

DIRECT
STATEMENT   "I don't know where the comets' home base is located," one of the astronomers told the reporter.

2   Keep pronouns close to their antecedents.

Even when pronoun choice is correct, too many words between a pronoun and its antecedent can confuse readers. If in a long sentence or in adjacent sentences several nouns appear between a pronoun and its proper antecedent, these nouns will incorrectly claim the reader's attention as the word renamed by the pronoun.

CONFUSING   The *statement* that Dr. Parker made and that she issued as a formal warning infuriated the mayor, who knew *it* would alarm the public.

CLEAR   Issued as a formal warning, Dr. Parker's *statement* alarmed the public, and *it* infuriated the mayor.

The relative pronouns *who, which,* and *that,* when introducing a modifying adjective clause, should be placed close to the nouns they modify.

CONFUSING   Prehistoric peoples used many organic substances difficult to find at archaeological sites, which included bone and antler. [Does *which* refer to *sites* or *substances*?]

CLOSER
ANTECEDENT   Prehistoric peoples used many organic substances, including bone and antler, which survive at relatively few archaeological sites.

CRITICAL DECISIONS

Understanding Gender Messages Implied by Your Pronouns

A physician must respect his patients' privacy.

The gender-specific pronoun in this example (his) is both inaccurate and offensive. To avoid unintentional sexism, use five techniques, either alone or in combination.

1. **Use the constructions** *he or she, his or her,* **and** *him or her* **in referring to an indefinite pronoun or noun.** Choose this option when the antecedent of a pronoun must have a singular sense.

WWW
http://dlc.tri-c.cc.oh.us/wt/docs/
mech/agreement.htm

A primer on avoiding gender-biased pronouns.

Realize, however, that some readers object to the *he or she* device as cumbersome.

AWKWARD	To some extent, *a biologist* must decide for <u>him- or her-self</u> which system of classification <u>he or she</u> will use.
REVISED	To some extent, *a biologist* must decide which system of classification <u>he or she</u> will use.
REVISED	To some extent, *a biologist* must decide which system of classification to use. [The infinitive *to use* avoids the <u>he</u> or *she* difficulty.]

2. **Make a pronoun's antecedent plural.**

PLURAL	To some extent, *biologists* must decide for <u>themselves</u> which system of classification *they* will use.

3. **Use the passive voice to avoid gender-specific pronouns—but only if it is appropriate to deemphasize a subject.** Remember that using the passive voice creates its own problems of vague reference.

NEUTRAL	It is every biologist's responsibility to specify which system of classification *is being used.*

4. **Reconstruct the entire statement so as to avoid the problem.**

NEUTRAL	When choosing among competing systems of classification, the biologist makes a choice that greatly affects later work both in the field and in the lab.

5. **Link gender assignments to specific indefinite antecedents.** Some writers will arbitrarily assign a masculine identity to one indefinite antecedent and a feminine identity to another. The gender assignments are then maintained throughout a document.

ALTERNATE GENDER ASSIGNMENTS	A *biologist* must decide which system of classification <u>she</u> will use. An *anthropologist* must also choose when selecting the attributes <u>he</u> will use in distinguishing ancient objects from one another.

3 Make a pronoun refer to a specific noun antecedent, not to a modifier that may imply the antecedent.

Although an adjective may imply the antecedent of a pronoun, an adjective is not identical to and thus cannot serve as that antecedent. Revise sentences so that a *noun* provides the reference for a pronoun. You can also (simply) use the intended noun instead of the pronoun.

CONFUSING   Two glass rods will repel each other when they are electrified. *It* is created from a buildup of positive and negative charges in the rods. [What does *it* refer to?]

NOUN
ANTECEDENT   Two glass rods will repel each other when they carry *electricity*. *It* is created from a buildup of positive and negative charges in the rods.

OR

Two glass rods will repel each other if they are electrified. *Electricity* is created from a buildup of positive and negative charges in the rods.

4 Make a pronoun refer to a noun, not the possessive form of a noun.

Although the possessive form of a noun may imply the noun as the intended antecedent of a pronoun, this form is not identical to, and thus is not clear enough to serve as, that antecedent. Revise sentences so that a *noun* provides the reference for a pronoun. Alternately, change the pronoun so that it, too, is in the possessive form.

CONFUSING   *Sally's* case is in trouble. Does *she* know that?

CLEAR   *Sally* is in trouble with this case. Does *she* know that?

5 Give the pronouns *that, this, which,* and *it* precise reference.

The pronouns *that, this, which,* and *it* should refer to specific nouns. Avoid having them make vague reference to the overall sense of a preceding sentence.

CONFUSING   The paper proposed to link cancer and secondary smoke. *This* was established.

CLEAR   The paper proposed to link cancer and secondary smoke. *This connection* was established.

6   Avoid indefinite antecedents for the pronouns *it, they,* and *you.*

Expressions such as "you know," "they say," and "it figures" are common in speech and informal writing. The pronouns in these expressions do not refer to particular people or objects and are said to have *indefinite* reference. In academic writing, pronouns should refer to specific antecedents. *You* should be used either to address the reader directly or for a direct quotation; *it* and *they* should refer to particular things, ideas, or people.

NONSTANDARD   *It* will rain tomorrow.

STANDARD   *We* are expecting rain tomorrow.

7   Avoid mixing uses of the pronoun *it.*

The word *it* functions both as a pronoun and as an expletive—that is, as a space filler in a rearranged sentence. Avoid using the word *it* both as an expletive and as a pronoun in the same sentence.

CONFUSING   *It* is clear that *it* is shirking *its* responsibilities.

WEAK   *It* is clear that the committee is shirking *its* responsibilities.

CLEAR   Clearly, the committee is shirking *its* responsibilities.

8   Use the relative pronouns *who, which,* and *that* appropriately.

Relative pronouns introduce dependent clauses that usually function as adjectives. The pronouns *who, which,* and *that* rename and refer to the nouns they follow. The pronoun *who* can refer to people or to divinities or personified animals.

> The most highly respected baseball player in the year 1911 was Ty Cobb, *who* had joined the Detroit Tigers in 1905.

That refers to animals, things, or people (when not referring to a *specific* person, in which case the pronoun *who* is used).

> For decades, Cobb held a record *that* remained unbroken—until Pete Rose stroked his 4192nd career hit in 1985.

Which refers to animals and things.

> Cobb's career, *which* lasted 24 years, was marked by extraordinary statistics—for example, a batting average of .367, 2244 runs, and 892 stolen bases.

CRITICAL DECISIONS

Tests for Choosing Who, Which, or That—with or without Commas

Writers can be unsure of themselves when choosing relative pronouns (*who, which*, and *that*) and when using commas with relative clauses. Relative pronouns begin relative clauses, and these function in a sentence as if they were adjectives: they modify nouns. You can apply three tests for deciding which pronoun to use and whether or not to use commas.

Identify the noun being modified.

■ **Is this a proper noun—the name of a *specific* person (George), place (Baltimore), or thing (Levis)?** If yes, then use the pronoun *who, whom*, or *whose* (for a person) or *which* (for a place or thing) *with* commas. The noun does not need the modifying clause to specify its meaning. This clause is *nonessential*.

My friend George, *who* is constantly angry, has developed a stress disorder.

The Levis, which fit me well, were on sale.

■ **Is the noun being modified a common noun—an unspecified person (people), place (city), or thing (pants)?** If yes, then it is quite likely that the modifying information of the clause is essential for specifying the noun's identity. Use *who, whom*, or *whose* (for a person) and *which* or *that* (for a place or thing) *without* commas. The modifying clause is *essential*.

People *who* are constantly angry often develop stress disorders.

The pants *that* fit me best were on sale.

■ **Is the identity of the common noun being modified made clear and specific to the reader in the context of the paragraph?** If yes, then treat the common noun in the same way that you would a proper noun: use a relative clause, with commas.

Over a year ago, I met the woman *who* is seated at that table in the corner. The woman, *whose* name I can't remember, is a friend of Joan's.

[In the first sentence, the relative clause *who is seated* . . . is needed to identify which woman, presumably in a room full of people. In the second sentence, the reader knows who is being referred to, so the relative clause in that sentence (*whose name* . . .) is nonessential and takes commas.]

CHAPTER 22

Correcting Errors in Consistency

Consistency is an essential quality of language, and we expect that within sentences writers will adhere to certain patterns or conventions. This means that the decisions you make in writing one part of a sentence must be in line with the decisions you make subsequently. If not, clear communication suffers.

CRITICAL DECISIONS

Recognizing Grammatical Inconsistency

Decisions regarding grammatical consistency can be challenging and quite complex. Careful rereading will generally help you spot shifts, which are discussed in the first section of this chapter, but recognizing mixed constructions and incomplete sentences (discussed in the second section) is often more complicated. To do so, you will need to understand how sentence elements can—and cannot—function. For example, a prepositional phrase cannot function as a subject, but a gerund phrase can (Playing an instrument well requires practice.). You will also need to read every sentence with a fresh eye, as if you were another reader trying to make sense of it for the first time. If there is any possibility of confusion, then you will need to make the changes necessary to clarify your ideas.

Shifts

Aside from the content it communicates, a sentence expresses other important information: person, number, tense, voice, and tone. Once writers make a decision about these matters, they should follow their decision conscientiously within any one sentence.

1 Revise shifts in person by keeping all references to a subject consistent.

INCONSISTENT	A person who is a nonsmoker can develop lung troubles when you live with smokers.
CONSISTENT THIRD PERSON	A person who is a nonsmoker can develop lung troubles when *he* or *she* lives with smokers.
CONSISTENT SECOND PERSON	If you are a nonsmoker, *you* can develop lung troubles if *you* live with smokers.

2 Revise shifts in number by maintaining consistent singular or plural forms.

INCONSISTENT	At the turn of the century, it was common for a man to come to the United States alone and work to raise money so that family members could later join them.
CONSISTENT SINGULAR	At the turn of the century, it was common for a man to come to the United States alone and work to raise money so that family members could later join *him*.

22b Revise shifts in tense, mood, and voice.

1 Revise shifts in tense by observing the appropriate sequence of verb tenses.

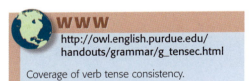

WWW
http://owl.english.purdue.edu/
handouts/grammar/g_tensec.html

Coverage of verb tense consistency.

INCONSISTENT   The road climbed from the Montezuma Castle National Monument, and the vegetation changes from desert scrub to scrub pines and finally to thick forests of Ponderosa Pine.

CONSISTENT PAST TENSE	The road climbed from the Montezuma Castle National Monument, and the vegetation *changed* from desert scrub to scrub pines and finally to thick forests of Ponderosa Pine.

The "historical present tense" is often used in academic writing to refer to material in books or articles or to action in a film.

INCONSISTENT	In her article, Karen Wright referred to Marshall McLuhan's global village and asks rhetorically, "Who today would quarrel with McLuhan's prophecy?"
CONSISTENT PRESENT TENSE	In her article, Karen Wright *refers* to Marshall McLuhan's global village and asks rhetorically, "Who today would quarrel with McLuhan's prophecy?"

2   Revise for shifts in mood.

A verb's **mood** indicates whether a writer judges a statement to be a fact, a command, or an occurrence contrary to fact. When mood shifts in a sentence, readers cannot be sure of a writer's intentions.

INCONSISTENT	If he were more experienced, he will be able to help us. [The sentence shifts from the "doubtful" subjunctive to the "factual" indicative, leaving readers unsure about what is intended.]
CONSISTENT SUBJUNCTIVE	If he were more experienced, he would be able to help us.

3   Revise for shifts in voice.

If writers shift from one voice to the other in a single sentence, both emphasizing and deemphasizing a subject, then readers will be confused. Choose an active *or* a passive voice in any one sentence.

INCONSISTENT	Columbus arrived in the New World, and it was believed he had found the coast of Asia. [The shift from active voice to passive leaves doubt about who believed this.]
CONSISTENT ACTIVE VOICE	Columbus arrived in the New World and believed he had found the coast of Asia.

22c   Maintain consistent use of direct or indirect discourse.

Direct discourse reports exactly, with quotation marks, spoken or written language. **Indirect discourse** approximately reproduces the language of others, capturing its sense, though not its precise expression. The Critical Decisions box on page 288 provides help in distinguishing between direct and indirect discourse.

Mixing direct and indirect discourse in one sentence can disorient a reader by raising doubts about what a speaker has actually said. Avoid the problem by making a conscious choice to refer to another's speech either directly or indirectly.

CRITICAL DECISIONS

Distinguishing between Direct and Indirect Discourse

Reported speech, or indirect discourse, is very different from directly quoted speech, which gives the exact verb tense of the original. Most often, reported speech has occurred sometime before the time of the main verb reporting it. An indirect quotation therefore requires changes in verb tense and pronouns.

The following table shows the patterns for changing verb tenses, verb forms, and modal auxiliaries in reported speech or indirect discourse.

DIRECT SPEECH	REPORTED SPEECH
TENSES:	
present Ellie said, "I like horses."	→ **past** Ellie said [that] she liked horses.
past Ellie said, "I rode the horse."	→ **past perfect** Ellie said [that] she had ridden the horse.
present progressive Ellie said, "I'm going riding."	→ **past progressive** Ellie said [that] she was going riding.
present perfect Ellie said, "I have ridden there."	→ **past perfect** Ellie said [that] she had ridden there.
past progressive She said, "I was out riding."	→ **past perfect progressive** She said [that] she had been out riding.
***past perfect** She said, "I had ridden there."	→ **past perfect** She said [that] she had ridden there.
AUXILIARY VERBS:	
can She said, "I can show him."	→ **could** She said [that] she could show him.
will She said, "I will ride again."	→ **would** She said [that] she would ride again.
***could** She said, "I could ride."	→ **could** She said [that] she could ride.
***would** She said, "I would go."	→ **would** She said [that] she would go.

Note: The asterisked verbs do not change form as they undergo tense shifts.

Mixed Constructions

A **mixed construction** occurs when a sentence takes a reader in one direction by beginning with a certain grammatical pattern and then concludes as if the sentence had begun differently. The resulting mix of incompatible sentence parts invariably confuses readers.

22d | Establish clear, grammatical relations between sentence parts.

Mixed constructions are common in speech. We can compensate for grammatically inconsistent thoughts in speech with gestures or intonation, and listeners usually understand. More so than listeners, readers are likely to be sensitive to and confused by mixed constructions.

"If/then"

MIXED If a stage set is poorly designed is when a set looks and "feels" absolutely complete even without the presence of the actors.

REVISED If a stage set is poorly designed, then it will look and "feel" absolutely complete even without the presence of the actors. [An independent clause beginning with *then* now completes the introductory *if* construction.]

REVISED A stage set that is poorly designed looks and "feels" absolutely complete even without the actors. [The mixed construction is avoided by eliminating the *if* construction.]

"The fact that"

MIXED The fact that design elements are as important to a play's success as actors. [Even though *are* is a verb and *design elements* functions as a noun, this string of words is not a sentence. It is a noun clause that could take the place of a noun in another sentence, as below.]

REVISED The fact that design elements are as important to a play's success as actors is often overlooked by beginning students of theater. [The noun clause *The fact that . . . actors* functions as the subject of the sentence.]

A prepositional phrase

MIXED By creating a functional set design can help the audience believe the "place" on the stage is real. [The prepositional phrase *by creating a functional set design* operates incorrectly as the subject of the sentence.]

REVISED Creating a functional set design can help the audience view the stage as a believable other world. [*Creating . . . design* now functions only as the subject of the sentence. The preposition *by* has been cut.]

A second type of mixed construction occurs when the predicate part of a sentence does not logically complete its subject. The error is known as **faulty predication.**

INCONSISTENT   The electron microscope is keenly aware of life invisible to the human eye. [Can a microscope be keenly aware?]

REVISED   The electron microscope helps us to be keenly aware of life invisible to the human eye. [Now it is people (*us*) who have been made aware.]

Avoiding *is when, is because*

Faulty predication occurs in other constructions. Do not write a sentence of definition using a form of the verb *to be* and follow that verb with word groupings beginning with *when, where,* or *because.* The structure of such a sentence requires that you follow *be* with a noun or an adjective (or word groups substituting as these).

FAULTY   The reason electron microscopes have become essential to research is because their resolving power is roughly 500,000 times greater than the power of the human eye.

REVISED   Electron microscopes have become essential because their resolving power is roughly 500,000 times greater than the power of the human eye.

Incomplete Sentences

An **incomplete sentence** lacks certain important elements. A fragment (see Chapter 14), the most extreme case of an incomplete sentence, lacks either a subject or a predicate. In less extreme cases, a sentence may lack a word or two, which you can identify and correct with careful proofreading.

22f Edit elliptical constructions to avoid confusion.

Both in speech and in writing, we frequently omit certain words in order to streamline communication. These "clipped" or shortened sentences are called **elliptical constructions,** and, when used with care, they can be concise and economical. But elliptical constructions may confuse readers if a writer omits words that are vital to sentence structure.

1   Use *that* when necessary to signal sentence relationships.

You can omit *that* to create an elliptical construction if the omission does not confuse readers. If omitting *that* alters the relationship among words in a sentence, then restore *that* to the sentence.

UNCLEAR   Thoughtful people honestly fear an implant of miniature ID tags in cats is a precursor to implants in humans. [The wording incorrectly points to *an implant* as the object of *fear.*]

CLEAR   Thoughtful people honestly fear *that* an implant of miniature ID tags in cats is a precursor to implants in humans. [The word *that* now indicates that an entire noun clause will serve as the object of *fear.*]

2   Provide all the words needed for parallel constructions.

Elliptical constructions are found in sentences where words, phrases, or clauses are joined by the conjunction *and* or are otherwise made parallel. Grammatically, an omission is legitimate when a word or words are repeated *exactly* in all compound parts of the sentence. An incomplete sentence results when words omitted in one part of an elliptical construction do not match identically the words appearing in another part.

NOT   Sensory and short-term memory *last* seconds or minutes, whereas
PARALLEL   long-term memory years or decades.

PARALLEL   Sensory and short-term memory *last* seconds or minutes, whereas long-term memory *lasts* years or decades.

Special care is needed with a preposition that functions idiomatically as part of a complete verb phrase: believe *in*, check *in*, handed *in*, hope *in*, hope *for*, looked *up*, tried *on*, turned *on*. When a parallel construction has two of these expressions doubled by the conjunction *and*, and you wish to omit the second preposition, be sure this preposition is identical to the one remaining in the sentence.

In 1914, Henry Ford opened an auto manufacturing plant that relied and ultimately thrived on principles of assembly-line production. [The parallel construction is relied *on* and thrived *on.*]

If the prepositions are not identical, then *both* must appear in the sentence so that the full sense of each idiomatic expression is retained.

FAULTY   Henry Ford believed and relied *on* the assembly line as a means to revolutionize American industry.

REVISED   Henry Ford believed *in* and relied *on* the assembly line as a means to revolutionize American industry.

22g Make comparisons consistent, complete, and clear.

To make comparisons effective, you should compare logically consistent elements and state comparisons completely and clearly. (In 18c you will find more on comparative forms of adjectives and adverbs.)

1 Keep the elements of a comparison logically related.

ILLOGICAL   Modern atomic theory provides for fewer types of atoms than Democritus, the ancient Greek philosopher who conceived the idea of atoms. [Atoms are being compared with Democritus, a person. The comparison must be made logical.]

LOGICAL   Modern atomic theory provides for fewer types of atoms than did Democritus, the ancient Greek philosopher who conceived the idea of atoms.

2 Complete all elements of a comparison.

Comparisons must be made fully, so that readers understand which elements in a sentence are being compared.

INCOMPLETE   Democritus believed there existed an infinite variety of atoms each of which possessed unique characteristics—so that, for instance, atoms of water were smoother. [Smoother than what?]

COMPLETE   Democritus believed there existed an infinite variety of atoms each of which possessed unique characteristics—so that, for instance, atoms of water were smoother than atoms of fire.

3 Make sure comparisons are clear and unambiguous.

Comparisons that invite alternate interpretations must be revised so that only one interpretation is possible.

UNCLEAR   Scientists today express more respect for Democritus than his contemporaries. [Two interpretations: (1) Democritus's contemporaries had little respect for him; (2) scientists respect the work of Democritus more than they respect the work of his contemporaries.]

CLEAR   Scientists today express more respect for Democritus than they do for his contemporaries.

CLEAR   Scientists today express more respect for Democritus than his contemporaries did.

CHAPTER 23

Correcting Faulty Parallelism

In writing, **parallelism** involves matching a sentence's structure to its content. When two or more ideas are parallel (that is, closely related or comparable),

WWW

http://webster.commnet.edu/
grammar/parallelism.htm

Full coverage of parallelism, with examples and quizzes.

a writer can emphasize similarities as well as differences by creating parallel grammatical forms. Parallelism can also help to relate the parts of an *entire paragraph* by highlighting the logic by which a writer moves from one sentence to the next. Parallel structures bind a paragraph's sentences into a coherent unit.

PARALLEL SENTENCES WITHIN A PARAGRAPH

A house divided against itself cannot stand. I believe this government cannot endure, permanently half slave and half free. I do not expect the Union to be dissolved. I do not expect the house to fall. But I do expect it will cease to be divided. It will become all one thing, or all the other.

—ABRAHAM LINCOLN, 1858

CRITICAL DECISIONS

Using Parallelism Effectively

To use parallelism effectively, you must make logical decisions about how to present parallel ideas for your readers. The parallel structures you choose should be those that most clearly suit your purpose and style. Consider the following:

> They enjoy <u>dining</u> out, <u>going</u> to clubs, and <u>attending</u> concerts.
> They like going out <u>to restaurants</u>, <u>to clubs</u>, and <u>to concerts</u>.
> They frequent <u>restaurants</u>, <u>clubs</u>, and <u>concerts</u>.

Each of these constructions is parallel. What works best in a particular sentence would be up to the writer.

23a | Use parallel words, phrases, and clauses with coordinating conjunctions: *and, but, for, or, nor, so, yet.*

Whenever you present ideas as a series or as a pair, you are likely to use coordinating conjunctions to join words, phrases, or clauses into *compound*

elements: compound subjects, objects, verbs, modifiers, and clauses. For sentence parts to be parallel in structure, the compound elements must share an equivalent grammatical form. The following Critical Decisions box shows you how to apply logic to identify and correct nonparallel compound elements.

Words that appear in a pair or a series are related in content and should be parallel in form.

NOT PARALLEL	Psychologist Howard Gardner identifies specific and a variety of types of intelligence, rather than one monolithic "IQ" score.
PARALLEL	Psychologist Howard Gardner identifies *specific* and *varied* types of intelligence, rather than one monolithic "IQ" score.

As with parallel elements in a sentence, parallel elements in a list or outline will highlight the logical similarities that underlie parallel content. Keep elements of lists and outlines in equivalent grammatical form.

CRITICAL DECISIONS
Understanding the Logic of Parallel Structures

Learning to recognize situations that call for parallel structures and to correct sentences with faulty parallelism is an exercise in logic.

Recognize situations that call for parallel structures.

Any time you use a coordinating conjunction (*and, but, or,* or *nor*), you are combining elements from two or more sentences into a single sentence.

> The children are fond of ice cream.
> The children are fond of salty pretzels.

Combined elements are logically comparable, and they should share a single grammatical form; otherwise, they are not parallel.

NOT PARALLEL	The children are fond of ice cream and eating salty pretzels.
PARALLEL	The children are fond of ice cream and salty pretzels.
	The children are fond of eating ice cream and salty pretzels.

Correct faulty parallelism.

1. *Recognize a sentence that is not parallel.*

NOT PARALLEL	Before they had horses, Native Americans hunted buffalo by chasing them over blind cliffs, up box canyons, or *when they went* into steep-sided sand dunes.

To revise a sentence with faulty parallelism, *determine which elements should be parallel* (that is, logically comparable), and then *revise the sentence so that these elements share an equivalent grammatical form*. Think of parallel elements as word groupings that complete slots in a sentence. The same grammatical form that you use to complete any one slot in a parallel structure must be used to complete all remaining slots.

2. *Determine the parallel elements.*

by chasing them *Slot 1*, *Slot 2*, and *Slot 3*.

by chasing them *over blind cliffs*, *Slot 2*, and *Slot 3*.

Because Slot 1 is completed with a prepositional phrase (*over blind cliffs*), Slots 2 and 3 should be filled with prepositional phrases. The series *over blind cliffs, up box canyons, or* when they went *into steep-sided sand dunes* lacks parallel structure because the third element in the series introduces a *when* clause, which is not consistent with the grammatical form of Slot 1.

3. *Revise so that parallel elements have equivalent grammatical form.*

PARALLEL   Before they had horses, Indians hunted buffalo by chasing them *over blind cliffs, up box canyons*, or *into steep-sided sand dunes.*

Using this "slot" analysis will help you to understand all of the examples in this chapter.

To echo the idea expressed in a *phrase* in one part of a sentence, use a phrase with the same grammatical structure in another part.

NOT PARALLEL   The judge had an ability to listen to conflicting testimony and deciding on probable guilt.

PARALLEL   The judge had an ability to listen to conflicting testimony *and* to decide on probable guilt.

A *clause* is a grouping of words that has a complete subject and predicate. Both independent clauses (that is, sentences) and dependent clauses can be set in parallel, provided they are parallel in content.

NOT PARALLEL   Before the storm's end but after the worst was over, the captain radioed the Coast Guard. [The opening of the sentence is not parallel: a phrase is joined to a clause.]

PARALLEL   Before the storm had ended *but* after the worst was over, the captain radioed the Coast Guard. [Two dependent clauses are now joined by the conjunction *but*; the sentence opening is now parallel.]

23b Use parallelism with correlative conjunctions: *either/or, neither/nor, both/and, not only/but also.*

Whenever you join parts of a sentence with *correlative conjunctions,* use the same grammatical form in both parts.

NOT PARALLEL After defeating Custer at Little Bighorn, Crazy Horse managed both to stay ahead of the Army and he *escaped.*

PARALLEL After defeating Custer at Little Bighorn, Crazy Horse managed both *to stay* ahead of the Army and *to escape.*

23c Use parallelism in sentences with compared and contrasted elements.

When words, phrases, or clauses are compared or contrasted in a single sentence, their logical and grammatical structures must be parallel. Expressions that set up comparisons and contrasts include *rather than, as opposed to, on the other hand, not, like, unlike,* and *just as/so too.*

NOT PARALLEL The staff approved the first request for funding, not the second presenter who requested funds.

PARALLEL The staff approved the first request for funding, *not* the second request.

PART V
Style Decisions

CHAPTER 24

Being Clear, Concise, and Direct

WWW

http://www.wisc.edu/writefest/ Handbook/ClearConciseSentences. html

A resource for writing clear and concise sentences.

Writing with clarity and directness involves making choices about wording that will help your audience understand your ideas. In most cases, you will achieve clear, concise, and direct expression through revision.

CRITICAL DECISIONS

Understanding the Need to Be Clear, Concise, and Direct

I have made this letter longer than usual, only because I have not had time to make it shorter.

—Blaise Pascal

Over three hundred years ago, the French mathematician and philosopher Blaise Pascal knew what writers know today: Writing concisely is a challenge that takes time. The time spent in revising for clarity, conciseness, and directness is well spent—both for you and your readers.

Be clear, concise, and direct for yourself.

Writing becomes clearer as you revise to eliminate wordiness and to increase your use of active verbs. Revise for clarity, conciseness, and directness in order to be confident and satisfied that you have produced your best work.

Be clear, concise, and direct for your readers.

Revising for clarity, conciseness, and directness also has practical benefits. Readers can more clearly understand the points you want to make. Rather than wasting time trying to understand your meaning, they can respond directly to your points.

24a Revise to eliminate wordiness.

1 Combine sentences that repeat material.

WORDY   The high *cost* of multimedia presentations is due to the combined *cost* of studio shoots and *expensive* video compression. The *costs* of graphic design and programmers are also high.

COMBINED   Studio shoots, video compression, graphic design, and programmers' work all contribute to the high cost of multimedia presentations.

WWW
http://leo.stcloudstate.edu/style/sentencev.html

Combining sentences for variety and clarity.

2 Eliminate redundancy.

REDUNDANT   Historically, immigrants *who came to this country* arrived in America expecting to work long hours.

REVISED   Historically, immigrants arrived in America expecting to work long hours.

3 Eliminate relative pronouns and reduce adjective clauses to phrases or single words.

COMPLEX   Josephine Baker, *who was* the first black woman to become an international star, was born poor in St. Louis in 1906.

CONCISE   Josephine Baker, the first black woman to become an international star, was born poor in St. Louis in 1906.

COMPLEX   Many were drawn by her vitality, *which was* infectious.

CONCISE   Many were drawn by her infectious vitality.

4 Revise sentences that begin with *it is, there is, there are, there were.*

WORDY   *There were many reasons why* Josephine Baker was more successful in Europe than in America.

DIRECT   Josephine Baker was more successful in Europe than in America for several reasons.

5   Eliminate vague words and phrases.

Buzzwords are vague, often abstract expressions that add little but sound to your sentence. Buzzwords can be nouns: *area, aspect, case, character, element, factor, field, kind, sort, type, thing, nature, scope, situation, quality.* Buzzwords can be adjectives, especially those with broad meanings: *nice, good, interesting, bad, important, fine, weird, significant, central, major.* Buzzwords can be adverbs: *basically, really, quite, very, definitely, actually, completely, literally, absolutely.*

WORDY   *Those types of major* disciplinary problems are *really quite* difficult to solve.

CONCISE   Disciplinary problems are difficult to solve.

Substitute concise, direct language for wordy, imprecise expressions. Use the examples in the box to guide you.

Avoiding Long-winded Expressions

LONG-WINDED	DIRECT
at this moment (point) in time	now, today
at the present time	now, today
due to the fact that	because
in order to utilize	to use
in view of the fact that	because
for the purpose of	for
in the event that	if
until such time as	until
is an example of	is
would seem to be	is
the point I am trying to make*	—
in a very real sense*	—
in fact, as a matter of fact*	—

* These expressions are fillers and should be eliminated.

24b   Use strong verbs.

Strong verbs move sentences forward with precision and vigor. Try improving your drafts by circling all verbs, revising as needed to ensure that each helps to make a crisp, direct statement. Use the three following strategies.

1 Give preference to verbs in the active voice.

Sentences with verbs in the active voice emphasize the actor of a sentence rather than the object that is acted on. (See the Critical Decisions box below for help in deciding when to use the passive voice.) When the actor needs to be named, use active-voice sentences.

CRITICAL DECISIONS

Deciding When to Use the Passive Voice

Emphasize an object with a passive construction.

When the subject/actor of a sentence is relatively unimportant compared with what is acted on, use the passive voice both to deemphasize the subject/actor and to emphasize the object.

ACTIVE	We require twelve molecules of water to provide twelve atoms of oxygen.
PASSIVE (ACTOR RETAINED)	Twelve molecules of water are required by us to provide twelve atoms of oxygen.
PASSIVE (ACTOR DELETED)	Twelve molecules of water are required to provide twelve atoms of oxygen.

Deemphasize an unknown subject with the passive voice.

Instead of writing an indefinite subject/actor (such as *someone* or *people*) into a sentence, use the passive voice to shift the subject/actor to a prepositional phrase. You may then delete the phrase.

ACTIVE	People mastered the use of fire some 400,000 years ago.
PASSIVE (ACTOR RETAINED)	The use of fire was mastered by people some 400,000 years ago.
PASSIVE (ACTOR DELETED)	The use of fire was mastered some 400,000 years ago.

2 Use forms of *be* and *have* as main verbs only when no alternatives exist.

When possible, replace the verb *be* with a strong, active-voice verb.

WEAK   Many health care professionals *are of the opinion* that health information on the Internet is not an appropriate vehicle for teaching people about serious health issues.

STRONGER   Many health care professionals *claim* that health information on the Internet is not the appropriate vehicle for teaching people about serious health issues.

When possible, replace forms of *have* that are used alone as the main verb of a sentence.

WEAK   The easy accessibility of medical information *has* the effect of getting patients more involved in planning their treatment programs.

STRONGER   The easy accessibility of medical information *enables* patients to become more involved in planning their treatment programs.

3   Revise nouns derived from verbs.

Adding suffixes to some verbs can create nouns: dismiss/dismiss*al*, repent/repent*ance,* devote/devo*tion,* develop/develop*ment*. When possible, transform these nouns into the original, strong verbs.

WORDY   Many patients *made the discovery* that communication with other patients via the Internet *was helpful* in providing emotional support to everyone.

DIRECT   Many patients *discovered* that communicating with other patients via the Internet *helped* everyone emotionally.

CHAPTER 25

Building Emphasis with Coordination and Subordination

To emphasize a thought, you can assign special weight or importance to particular words in a sentence and to particular sentences in a paragraph. Make decisions about emphasis once you have written a draft and have your main points clearly in mind. Then you can manipulate words, phrases, and clauses to create the effects that will make your writing memorable.

SPOTLIGHT 5

25a   Use coordinate structures to emphasize equal and related ideas.

The guidelines in the Critical Decisions box on page 302 will help you make decisions about when to use coordination.

CRITICAL DECISIONS

Why Choose Coordinate Relationships?

The following sentences can be joined in various ways to establish coordinate relationships. Presently, each sentence—*because* it is a sentence—receives equal emphasis.

> (1) A complete suit of armor consisted of some 200 metal plates. (2) The armor of the fifteenth century offered protection from crossbows. (3) Armor offered protection from swords. (4) Armor offered protection from early muskets. (5) A suit of armor weighed 60 pounds. (6) A suit of armor would quickly exhaust the soldier it was meant to protect.

Choosing when to link sentences with coordination requires that you be clear about (1) the level of emphasis you want to give particular information and (2) the specific logical relationships you want to establish.

Coordinating conjunctions and the relationships they establish:

To show addition: *and*
To show choice: *or, nor*
To show consequences: *so*

To show contrast: *but, yet*
To show cause: *for*

A related group of coordinating conjunctions, called correlative conjunctions, are used in pairs to strengthen these relationships:

To show choice: *either/or, neither/nor, whether/or*
To show addition: *both/and, not only/but also, not only/but*

Use coordinating conjunctions to link sentences by giving equal emphasis to specific words (in this case, words from sentences 2, 3, and 4).

> The armor of the fifteenth century offered protection from crossbows, swords, *and* early muskets.

Use coordinating conjunctions to link sentences by giving equal emphasis to specific phrases (in this case, verb phrases from sentences 1 and 5).

> A complete suit of armor consisted of some 200 metal plates *and* weighed 60 pounds.

Use coordinating conjunctions to link and give equal emphasis to whole sentences, in this case sentence 6 and the combination of sentences 2, 3, and 4.

> The armor of the fifteenth century offered protection from crossbows, swords, and early muskets; *but* the armor would quickly exhaust the soldier it was meant to protect.

> **Conjunctive adverbs and the relationships they establish:**
>
> **To show contrast:** *however, nevertheless, nonetheless,* and *still*
> **To show cause and effect:** *accordingly, consequently, thus,* and *therefore*
> **To show addition:** *also, besides, furthermore,* and *moreover*
> **To show time:** *afterward, subsequently,* and *then*
> **To show emphasis:** *indeed*
> **To show condition:** *otherwise*
>
> Use conjunctive adverbs to link and give equal emphasis to two sentences. Conjunctive adverbs can be shifted from the beginning to the middle or to the end of the second sentence (which is not possible with coordinating conjunctions).
>
> The armor of the fifteenth century offered protection from crossbows, swords, *and* early muskets; *however,* the armor would quickly exhaust the soldier it was meant to protect.

Elements in a coordinate relationship signaled by a coordinating conjunction or a conjunctive adverb share equal grammatical status and equal emphasis. Watch for ineffective use of coordinate elements.

Avoid excessive coordination

Study your use of coordinating and correlative conjunctions and of conjunctive adverbs. You should use coordinate structures only when you are equating main ideas.

FAULTY   Because the young princess Marie Antoinette of Austria was to be handed over by the Austrian government to the care of the French monarchy, she had to cross the national boundary line all alone and she had to remove all her articles of Viennese clothing and replace them with French-made ones, and she could retain no trinket or jewelry, no matter what its sentimental value might have been.

REVISED   Because the young princess Marie Antoinette of Austria was to be handed over by the Austrian government to the care of the French monarchy, she had to cross the national boundary line all alone. Next, she had to remove all her articles of Viennese clothing and replace them with French-made ones. She could retain no trinket or jewelry, no matter what its sentimental value might have been.

25b   Use subordinate clauses to create emphasis.

When you use subordination effectively, the logical flow as well as the rhythm of your sentences will improve. Watch for two errors commonly associated with subordination.

The guidelines in the following Critical Decisions box will help you make decisions about when to use subordination.

CRITICAL DECISIONS

Why Choose Subordinate Relationships?

Subordinating conjunctions and the relationships they establish:

To show condition: *if, even if, unless,* and *provided that*
To show contrast: *though, although, even though,* and *as if*
To show cause: *because* and *since*
To show time: *when, whenever, while, as, before, after, since, once,* and *until*
To show place: *where* and *wherever*
To show purpose: *so that, in order that,* and *that*

Subordinating conjunctions link whole clauses. In the process, the clause with the subordinate conjunction becomes *dependent*—it cannot stand as a sentence. Greater emphasis is given to the *independent* clause. Emphasis and logical sequence should determine the placement of the dependent clause.

AT THE BEGINNING

When the Triangle Shirtwaist Factory fire broke out in a rag bin on a quiet Saturday afternoon in 1911, it spread quickly due to the mass of tissue paper and bits of material that littered the workroom floor.

IN THE MIDDLE

The fire, though it claimed 146 lives, did result in the addition of 30 new ordinances to the New York City fire code.

AT THE END

The terrorized, virtually all-female workforce was hampered in its efforts to leave because management had purposefully designed narrow escape passages in an effort to spot and catch pilferers.

Relative pronouns (*who, which, that*) can create dependent clauses that function like adjectives. Begin with two sentences that you think could be combined.

Transylvania qualifies as one of the most fought-over regions in all of Europe.

Transylvania witnessed the bloody clashes of Bulgarians, Magyars, Huns, and other eastern tribes between the fourth and twelfth centuries.

Substitute a relative pronoun for the subject of the clause that will function like an adjective in the new sentence.

which witnessed the bloody clashes . . . centuries,

Join the now dependent clause to the independent clause.

Transylvania, which witnessed the bloody clashes of Bulgarians, Magyars, Huns, and other eastern tribes between the fourth and twelfth centuries, qualifies as one of the most fought-over regions in all of Europe.

1 Illogical subordination

The problem of illogical subordination arises when a dependent clause does not establish a clear, logical relationship with an independent clause.

FAULTY   *Although* she was agitated at being shut up in a matchbox for so long, the female scorpion seized the first opportunity to escape.

The subordinating conjunction *although* fails to establish a clear, logical relationship between the dependent and independent clauses. The content of the sentence requires a cause-and-effect relationship, suggesting a different subordinate conjunction.

REVISED   *Because* she was agitated at being shut up in a matchbox for so long, the female scorpion seized the first opportunity to escape.

2 Excessive subordination

Retain subordinate structures when you have deliberately made the ideas of one clause dependent on another. Choose some other sentence structure when the clauses you are relating do not exist in a dependent/independent relationship.

FAULTY   The manatee, which is a very tame beast but extremely unattractive with its dull gray skin, has a hippopotamus-like head and virtually no neck, so that one wonders how the creature could ever have been mistaken for the lovely creature that is supposed to be the mermaid, although there are those who claim that if the animal is seen from sufficiently far away as it sits on the rocks, the lines of its head could convey the impression of flowing hair.

REVISED   The manatee, which is a very tame beast but extremely unattractive with its dull gray skin, has a hippopotamus-like head and virtually no neck. One wonders how the creature could ever have been mistaken for the lovely creature that is supposed to be the mermaid. Some claim that if the animal is seen from sufficiently far away as it sits on the rocks, the lines of its head could convey the impression of flowing hair.

COMPUTER TIPS

Limited Use for a Grammar/Style Checker

As noted in the box on page 274, you should avoid relying on grammar checkers to evaluate and correct your usage. However, a grammar/style checker can help you identify with a high degree of accuracy style problems such as sexist language, repeated words, overly long or overly short sentences, clichés, and the use of passive voice. Of course, once you have found the problem, you still have to be the judge of what action to take.

25c Use coordination and subordination for sentence variety.

By controlling the use of subordination and coordination, you can improve sentence variety and the interest level of your paragraphs. To do so, you need to think in terms not of individual sentences, but of groups of sentences and their structures. Try to vary sentence structures, alternating short sentences with longer ones; mix sentences that open with subordinating structures with those that do not.

Here is a paragraph that is correct technically, but stylistically, it lacks variety and shows a writer who makes no attempt to interest readers:

> College sports has a problem. Commercialization is a problem. Student-athletes are exploited. Many student-athletes come to school on athletic scholarships. This happens frequently. The student-athletes may not deserve to be admitted to these schools. Many colleges lower admission requirements for their ball players. Some schools will even waive requirements for the exceptional athlete. This athlete might not have had a place on a college campus. Some kids are not interested in academics. These kids would normally shun a college education. College might be the road to the pros for gifted athletes. Or so they think.

Effectively used, coordination and subordination will help you to emphasize key points, eliminate redundancy, and improve the interest-level of your paragraphs. Here is the preceding paragraph revised primarily through the use of coordination and subordination. Notice how the sentences vary in length and structure:

> One major problem with the commercialization of college sports is the exploitation of student-athletes, many of whom come to school on athletic scholarships. Frequently, student-athletes don't deserve to be admitted to a school. Many colleges routinely lower admissions requirements for their ball players, and some schools will even waive requirements for that exceptional athlete, who without his sports abilities might not have had a place

on a college campus. Most kids not interested in academics would normally shun a college education. But for gifted athletes, college appears to be a road that leads to the pros. Or so they think.

—JENAFER TRAHAR

Refer to the following box for advice on improving sentence variety using subordination and coordination.

How to Eliminate Monotonous Sentences

Variety in sentence structures and rhythms creates stylistically strong writing. While no rules govern exactly how a writer should vary rhythm from sentence to sentence, you may find the following general principles helpful.

- Decide first the key points you want to emphasize. Use the techniques that follow to help you create emphasis.
- Use subordinate structures to vary sentence beginnings.
- Consciously shift the location of phrase- and clause-length modifiers in a paragraph: locate modifiers at the beginning of some sentences, in the middle of others, and at the end of others.
- Use coordination to combine sentence elements and eliminate redundancies.
- Use short sentences to break up strings of long, heavily modified sentences.
- Limit your subordinate structures to one and possibly two locations in a sentence. Heavily modifying a sentence at the beginning, middle, *and* end will create a burden stylistically.
- Vary sentence types.

CHAPTER 26
Choosing the Right Word

Your purpose as a writer and your intended audience profoundly affect your **diction**—your choice of words. The English language usually gives you options in selecting words. The larger your vocabulary, the easier it is to select the right word.

CRITICAL DECISIONS

Expanding Your Vocabulary

As you read or while you are in class, jot down unfamiliar words. Collect them as follows.

- Make a set of flash cards with a new word and the sentence in which it appears on one side of each card; place the definition on the other side.

- Review the cards regularly. Categorize them by discipline or by part of speech. Practice changing the vocabulary word's part of speech with suffixes.

- Expand entries in your file when you find a previously filed word used in a new context.

- Consciously work one or two new words into each paper that you write, especially when the new words allow you to be precise in ways you could not otherwise be.

26a Understanding dictionary entries

Dictionaries give us far more than a list of words and their meanings. They not only define a given word, but also provide a brief description of its etymology, spelling, division, and pronunciation, as well as related words and forms. Here is a typical set of entries:

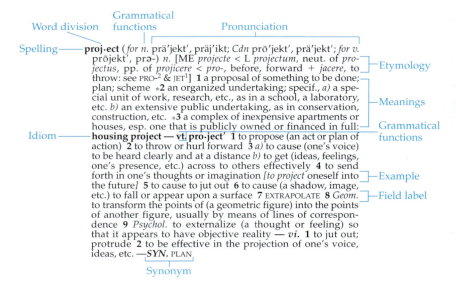

Some entries also contain usage labels that indicate the word is not accepted in standard, formal English usage. You would probably decide not to use such a word in formal writing. These usage labels are generally listed and explained in the frontmatter of most dictionaries:

- *Colloquial:* used conversationally and in informal writing
- *Slang:* in-group, informal language; not standard
- *Obsolete:* not currently used (but may be found in earlier writing)
- *Archaic:* not commonly used; more common in earlier writing
- *Dialect:* restricted geographically or to social or ethnic groups; used only in certain places with certain groups
- *Poetic, literary:* used in literature rather than everyday speech

26b Using the dictionary for building your vocabulary

If a word is mentioned more than twice in something you are reading, then you should know its formal definition. The word's repeated use indicates that it is important. Look the word up and create a personal vocabulary file, using the strategies outlined in the Critical Decisions box on page 308.

Concentrate on building your vocabulary in the discipline you choose as your major. Discipline-specific vocabularies consist of two types of words: those that are unique to the discipline and those that are found elsewhere, though with different meanings. For example, the word *gravity* has one meaning in the physics classroom. In a newspaper article or essay, however, you might find *gravity* used to suggest great seriousness: *The gravity of the accusations caused Mr. Jones to hire a famous attorney.* The dictionary lists both meanings.

26c Beyond the dictionary: Understanding the impact of word choices

In addition to knowing definitions, you should understand other factors that affect the way your audience will interpret your words.

1 Learn a word's denotation and connotation

WWW

http://www.uottawa.ca/academic/arts/writcent/hypergrammar/diction.html

A hyperlinked discussion of denotation, connotation, catch phrases, and clichés.

Your first concern in selecting a word is to be sure that its **denotation,** or dictionary meaning, is appropriate for the sentence at hand. Once you are satisfied that you are using a word correctly according to its denotation, consider its **connotations**—

its implications, associations, and nuances of meaning. Consider these sentences:

His speech was *brief.* His speech was *concise.* His speech was *curt.* His speech was *abbreviated.*

Brief, concise, curt, and *abbreviated:* These adjectives suggest brevity—but only the word "brief" has this single meaning, with no other associations. "Curt" suggests a brief remark, but one made with a degree of rudeness. "Abbreviated" suggests that the speaker has more to say but is being purposely brief. And "concise" suggests mental rigor and discipline, directed at making one's statements as brief and accurate as possible. Your choice among these words with their different connotations will make a difference in how readers react to your writing.

COMPUTER TIPS

Thesauri

Electronic thesauri—both the kind that comes with your word processor and the ones available on the World Wide Web—are subject to the same limitations as printed thesauri. Use them as references only. Never replace a word you've written with a word suggested by a thesaurus unless you're absolutely sure of both its denotations and its connotations.

2   Eliminate vague diction by choosing exact words.

Specific details, illustrations, and observations are more vivid and more memorable than *general* remarks. Read the following sets of sentences.

Genetically engineered organisms can be of great benefit to agriculture.

Scientists have discovered the benefits and uses of genetically engineered organisms in agriculture. One important example is the ice-minus bacterium created by Steve Lindow and Nicholas Panopoulos. Realizing a bacterium commonly found in plants produces a protein that helps ice to form, these scientists removed the unfavorable gene and thereby prevented ice from forming on greenhouse plants.

In the first example, the writer makes a general claim. In the second example, the writer makes the same claim but then provides details that give readers specific information about genetically engineered organisms. Details establish the writer's authority and give readers reasons to accept the writer's claim as true or probable. To produce effective, academic writing, support general claims with specific details.

Like general words, **abstract** words are broad. They name categories or ideas, such as *patriotism, evil,* and *friendship.* **Concrete** expressions (a *throb-*

bing headache, a *lemon-scented* perfume) provide details that give readers a chance to see, hear, and touch—and in this way to understand how an idea or category is made real. Just as with general and specific language, you should seek a balance between the abstract and concrete.

3 Avoid awkward diction.

Awkward diction, or word choice, momentarily stops an audience from reading by calling attention to a word that is somehow not quite right for a sentence. You can minimize awkwardness in your writing by guarding against inappropriate idiom and pretentious language.

An **idiom** is a grouping of words whose meaning may not be apparent based solely on simple dictionary definitions. Unless you are very familiar with the way these groupings are commonly used, your attempts at writing with idioms may be inappropriate and awkward. To avoid awkwardness, either memorize idioms or do not use them at all.

NOT IDIOMATIC   When the intruder left, the manager *got the courage* to call the police. [Idiomatically, we do not normally *get* courage; we either have it or we do not.]

IDIOMATIC   When the intruder left, the manager *got up the courage* to call the police. [The standard idiom implies that courage is summoned from within when needed.]

At times, students straining for sophistication will choose lengthy, pretentious phrasings when simpler ones will do. They will use such language in an attempt to imitate learned writers. In fact, however, the best writers strive for simplicity.

AWKWARD   The eccentricities of the characters could not fail to endear them to this reader.

REVISED   I especially enjoyed the eccentric characters.

4 Use figures of speech with care.

Similes, analogies, and *metaphors* are **figures of speech,** carefully controlled comparisons that clarify or intensify meaning. In academic writing, figurative language is used across disciplines, though in some disciplines more freely than in others. Robert A. Day, the author of a well-respected book on scientific writing, for instance, advises caution in using figures of speech in the life sciences and physical sciences. "Use [them] rarely in scientific writing. If you use them, use them carefully."

There are many techniques for using language figuratively. As you read in the disciplines, you will encounter three figures most often: *simile, analogy,* and *metaphor.*

A **simile** is a figure of speech that explicitly compares two different things—one usually familiar, the other not. Similes often use the word *like* or *as* to set up the comparison.

Plastic is the new protector; we wrap the already plastic tumblers of hotels in more plastic, and seal the toilet seats *like* state secrets after irradiating them with ultraviolet light.

—LEWIS THOMAS
Physician, researcher

As with a simile, the purpose of an **analogy** is to make an explicit comparison that explains an unknown in terms of something known. Analogies most often use direct comparison to clarify a process or a difficult concept.

Just as a trained mechanic can listen to a ping in a car's engine and then diagnose and correct a problem, so too an experienced writer can reread an awkward sentence and know exactly where it goes wrong and what must be done to correct it.

A **metaphor** illustrates or intensifies something relatively unknown by comparison with something familiar. In the case of metaphor, the comparison is implicit. The thing or idea that is relatively unknown is spoken of in terms closely associated with a significant feature of the thing that is known.

In the mirror of his own death, each man would discover his individuality.

—PHILIPPE ARIÈS
Historian

Guard against mixed metaphors and clichés. Metaphors need to match elements that can be compared logically (even if not explicitly). Illogical comparisons result in **mixed metaphors.**

MIXED METAPHOR	This story weaves a web that herds characters and readers into the same camp. [The comparison mixes spider webs with cattle roundups.]
CONSISTENT	This story weaves a web that tangles characters and readers alike.

Clichés such as *play into the hands of, no axe to grind, swan song, hotbed, the game of life, counting chickens before they hatch, water over the dam* or *under the bridge,* and *burning bridges* are trite expressions that can weaken your writing instead of making it more vivid. Work to create your own metaphors; keep them lively and consistent.

26d Maintaining the right tone for your papers

Tone refers to the writer's attitude toward the subject or the audience. Without doubt, tone is a difficult element to revise since so much determines it: choice and quality of description, word selection, sentence structure, and sentence mood and voice.

In papers that you prepare for your courses, your tone should be characterized by writing that is precise, logical, and formal, though not stuffy or filled with jargon.

CRITICAL DECISIONS

Choosing the Right Tone and Register for Your Papers

Choosing an appropriate tone requires that you carefully analyze the writing occasion—the topic, your purpose, and your audience—and that you then make decisions about your document's content, diction, and style.

Formal

- *Likely audience*—specialists or knowledgeable nonspecialists.
- *Content*—choose content that goes beyond introductory material.
- *Diction*—use technical language whenever needed for precision.
- *Style*—adhere to all the rules and conventions expected of writing in the subject area. Use complicated sentences if needed for precision.

Popular or informal

- *Likely audience*—nonspecialists interested in the subject area.
- *Content*—similar to that of a formal presentation, but avoid examples or explanations that require specialized understanding. Emphasize content that will keep readers engaged.
- *Diction*—avoid specialized terms whenever possible.
- *Style*—adhere to all conventions of grammar, usage, and spelling. Use some slang or colloquial language, but keep it to a minimum.

Academic writing is expected to conform to standards of **formal English**—that is, the English described in this handbook. There are many standards, or dialects, of English in this country, all of which are rich with expressive possibilities. The diction of formal English is not better than the diction of other dialects; it *is*, however, the only widely accepted standard for communicating among the many groups of English speakers.

1   Revise most slang, regional, and dialect expressions into standard English.

Slang is the comfortable, in-group language of neighborhood friends, coworkers, teammates, or of any group to which we feel we belong. Slang can be descriptive and precise for those who understand; it can just as readily be confusing and annoying to those who do not. In some cases, slang may mislead: the same expression can have different meanings for different groups. For example, *turbo charged* has distinctly different meanings for computer aficionados and for race-car enthusiasts. In the interest of writing accessibly to as many people as possible, avoid slang expressions in academic papers.

Regionalisms are expressions specific to certain areas of the country. Depending on where you were born, you will use the word *tonic, soda, cola,* or *pop* to describe what you drink with your *sub, hoagie, grinder,* or *hero.* Words that have a clear and vivid reference in some areas of the country may lack meaning in others or have an unrelated meaning.

Dialect expressions are specific to certain social or ethnic groups, as well as regional groups, within a country. Like regionalisms, dialects can use specialized vocabularies and sometimes distinctive grammatical systems that produce correct usages within the dialects they represent, but they address their language to a specific and restricted group rather than to a general audience. Like slang, regionalisms and dialect usages are appropriate for the audience that understands them; however, for general audiences in academic writing, they should be avoided.

2   Revise to restrict the use of colloquialisms and jargon.

Colloquial language is informal, conversational language. Colloquialisms do not pose barriers to understanding in the same way that slang, jargon, and regionalisms do; virtually all long-time speakers of English will understand expressions like *tough break, nitty-gritty,* and *it's a cinch.* In formal English, however, colloquialisms are rewritten or "translated" to maintain precision and to keep the overall tone of a document consistent.

Jargon is the in-group language of professionals, who may use acronyms (abbreviations of lengthy terms) and other linguistic devices to take shortcuts when speaking with colleagues. When writers in an engineering environment refer to RISC architecture, they mean machines designed to allow for **R**educed **I**nstruction **S**et **C**omputing. RISC is an easy-to-use acronym, and it is efficient—as long as one engineer is writing or speaking to another. The moment communication is directed outside the professional group, however, a writer must take care to define terms or to rewrite the concept in terms that outsiders can understand.

26e   Eliminating biased, dehumanizing language

Language is a tool; just as tools can be used for buildings, they can also be used to dismantle. You have heard and seen the words that insensitive people use to denigrate whole groups. Equally repugnant is language used to stereotype. Any language that explicitly or subtly characterizes an individual in terms of a group is potentially offensive. Writers must take care to avoid stereotyping and to show consideration for audiences by referring to any group using the terms that group uses to describe itself.

On one level this principle means understanding the terms currently in use for national, regional, ethnic, and racial groups. Equally important is considering the sensibilities of people who may differ from the writer in terms of gender, sexual orientation, age, disability or illness, religion, and politics. Such condescending or stereotyping modifiers as *old, abnormal, sick, stuffy,* or almost any noun label that ends in *-ist* or *-ism,* will risk offending someone in the writer's audience and should be used only with great care and precision.

Sexism in diction

Especially offensive is sexist, or gender-offensive, language, including such expressions as chair*man,* *man*kind, *man*power, and *mother*ing. Reread late drafts of your writing to identify potentially gender-offensive language. Unless the context of a paragraph clearly calls for a gender-specific reference, follow the suggestions given in the following box to avoid offending your readers.

Avoiding Sexist Language

Avoid gender-specific nouns.

Avoid: stewardess (and generally nouns ending with *-ess*)

Use: flight attendant

Avoid: chairman

Use: chair or chairperson

Avoid: woman driver; male nurse

Use: woman who was driving; driver; nurse; man on the nursing staff

Avoid: mankind

Use: people; humanity; humankind

Avoid: workmen; manpower

Use: workers; workforce; personnel

Avoid: the girl in the office

Use: the woman; the manager; the typist

Avoid: mothering

Use: parenting, nurturing

(continued)

Avoiding Sexist Language, continued

Use equivalent references to the sexes.

Avoid: The *men* and *girls* in the office contributed generously to the Christmas Fund.

Use: The *men* and *women* in the office contributed generously to the Christmas Fund. [In a school setting the reference might be to *boys* and *girls*.]

Make balanced use of plural and gender-specific pronouns.

(See the Critical Decisions box on pages 280–281 for five strategies that will help you to correct gender problems with pronoun use.)

Avoid: A doctor should wash *his* hands before examining a patient.

Use: *Doctors* should wash *their* hands before examining patients.

PART VI
Punctuation Decisions

CHAPTER 27
Using End Punctuation

WWW

http://wwwuttawa.ca/academic/
arts/writcent/hypergrammar/
endpunct.html

All about end punctuation.

The ending of one sentence and the beginning of the next is a crucial boundary for readers. To mark the end-of-sentence boundary in English you have three choices: a period, a question mark, or an exclamation point.

CRITICAL DECISIONS

Choosing End Punctuation

The choice between using a period and a question mark at the end of a sentence is a matter of function. Your main determination will be whether the sentence is a statement or a direct question. The choice of using an exclamation point, however, is more a matter of style and tone. Your main determination here will be whether using an exclamation point will serve your purpose for writing.

The Period

27a Using the period

1 Placing a period to mark the end of a statement

It is conventional to end statements with a period.

For quite some time after the *Titanic*'s collision with the iceberg, the people on board did not believe that they were in danger.

A restatement of a question asked by someone else is called an **indirect question.** Since it is really a statement, it does not take a question mark.

Many of the women who were being urged to board the life rafts asked whether this measure was truly necessary.

Requests, worded as questions, are often followed by periods.

> Would you pour another glass of wine.

2 **Placing periods in relation to end quotation marks and parentheses**

A period is always placed inside (that is, to the left of) a quotation mark that ends a sentence.

> The rule was, at least on the port side of the ship, "Women and children only."

When a parenthesis ends a sentence, place a period outside the end parenthesis if the parenthetical remark is not a complete sentence.

> There was, in fact, enough room on the life rafts for first- and second-class women and children, but no allowance had been made for steerage passengers (that is, economy class—the cheapest fare).

If the parenthetical remark is a separate complete sentence, enclose it entirely in parentheses and punctuate it as a sentence—with its own period.

> No allowance had been made for steerage passengers. (Steerage was defined as economy class, the cheapest fare.)

3 **Using a period with abbreviations**

The following abbreviations conventionally end with a period:

Mr.   Mrs.   Ms.   apt.
Ave.   St.   Dr.

When an abbreviation ends a sentence, use a single period.

> The lawyers addressed their questions to Susan Turner, Esq.

When an abbreviation falls in the middle of a sentence, punctuate as if the abbreviated word were spelled out.

> We presented the award envelope to Susan Turner, Esq., who opened it calmly.

Do not use periods with acronyms.

ABC   CNN   AT&T   USA   ABM   FAA   NATO

The Question Mark

27b Using the question mark

1 Using a question mark after a direct question

It is conventional to end direct questions with a question mark.

Why do children develop so little when they are isolated from others?

Questions in a series inside a sentence will take question marks if each denotes a separate question.

When an automobile manufacturer knowingly sells a car that meets government safety standards but is defective, what are the manufacturer's legal responsibilities? moral responsibilities? financial responsibilities? [Note that in these three "clipped" questions—all incomplete sentences—capitalization is optional.]

When the sense of the questions in a series is not completed until the final question, use one question mark—at the end of the sentence.

Will the agent be submitting the manuscript to one publishing house, two houses, or more?

The following box gives advice on where to position question marks.

CRITICAL DECISIONS

Placing a Question Mark Before or After End Quotation Marks

Placing the question mark *inside* the end quotation mark

When the question mark applies directly to the quoted material, place it inside the quotation mark.

In a dream, Abraham Lincoln remembered a stranger asking, "Why are you so common looking?"

Place the question mark inside the end quotation mark when the mark applies to both the quoted material *and* the sentence as a whole.

Don't you find it insulting that a person would comment directly to a president, "Why are you so common looking?"

(continued)

Placing a Question Mark Before or After End Quotation Marks, continued

Placing the question mark *outside* the end quotation mark

When the sentence as a whole forms a question but the quoted material does not, place the question mark outside the quotation.

Was it Lincoln who observed, "The Lord prefers common-looking people; that's the reason he makes so many of them"?

2 Using a question mark within parentheses to indicate that the accuracy of information is in doubt

A question mark can be used to indicate dates or numerical references known to be inexact. The following are equivalent in meaning:

Geoffrey Chaucer was born in 1340 **(?).**

Chaucer was born about 1340.

Chaucer was born c. 1340. (The c. is an abbreviation for *circa,* meaning "around.")

The Exclamation Point

27c Using the exclamation point

Use exclamation points—sparingly—to mark emphatic statements or commands. Reserve them for unique, memorable statements.

Arlene was shocked by the prices in New York, especially when the street vendor demanded five dollars for a hot dog and a soda!

Use periods or commas to punctuate mild exclamations.

Please, let me do it myself.

CHAPTER 28
Using Commas

One important purpose of punctuation is to help readers identify clusters of related words. *Within* sentences, the most common mark is the

comma, which is used primarily to signal that some element, a word or cluster of related words, is being set off from a main sentence for a reason. The choices you make about punctuating with commas should be tied to the logic of a sentence's structure.

SPOTLIGHT
9

CRITICAL DECISIONS

Avoiding Comma Errors

Five error patterns account for most of the difficulty with comma use. The illustrations in this box will serve as a quick-reference index to the rules for comma use.

■ Use a comma to set off introductory words or word groupings from the main part of the sentence (see 28a).

FAULTY   Once the weather turned cold the faucet stopped working.

REVISED   Once the weather turned cold, the faucet stopped working.

■ Do *not* use a comma to set off concluding words or word groupings from a main sentence (but see 28a-3 for exceptions).

FAULTY   The faucet stopped working, yesterday.

REVISED   The faucet stopped working yesterday.

■ Place a comma before the word *and, but, or, for,* or *so* when it joins two sentences (see 28b).

FAULTY   The faucet stopped working *and* the sink leaks.

REVISED   The faucet stopped working, *and* the sink leaks.

Do not use a comma if the second grouping of words is not a complete sentence.

FAULTY   I'll fix them myself, and save money.

REVISED   I'll fix them myself and save money.

■ Use a comma to separate three or more items in a series (see 28c-1).

FAULTY   I'll need a washer a valve and a wrench.

REVISED   I'll need a washer, a valve, and a wrench.
            or
            I'll need a washer, a valve and a wrench.

■ Use a *pair* of commas to set off a word or word group that adds nonessential information (see 28d).

(continued)

Avoiding Comma Errors, continued

FAULTY   Ahorn Hardware which is just around the corner will have the materials I need.

REVISED   Ahorn Hardware, which is just around the corner, will have the materials I need.

Do not use commas if a word or word group adds essential information needed for identifying some other word in the sentence.

FAULTY   The hardware store, which is just around the corner, will have materials I need.

REVISED   The hardware store which is around the corner will have the materials I need.

[Note that in the case of essential information, many writers insist on using *that* to introduce the information.]

The hardware store **that** is just around the corner will have the materials I need.

Using Commas Correctly

SPOTLIGHT 9

| 28a | **Using commas with introductory and concluding expressions** |

| 1 | **Place a comma after a modifying phrase or clause that begins a sentence.** |

Once the weather turned cold, the faucet stopped working.

The comma after an introductory word or brief phrase is optional.

Yesterday, the faucet stopped working.

When an introductory element consists of two or more phrases, a comma is required.

As a commercial space with a retailing bias, the mall should have a design that does not let the shopper become distracted from buying.

Note: An opening phrase or clause is set off with a comma if it is used as a modifier; an opening phrase used as a subject is *not* set off.

MODIFIER In creating a shopping environment that is too beautiful, commercial designers are failing to serve the needs of the merchants.

SUBJECT   Creating a shopping environment that is too beautiful fails to serve the needs of the merchants.

2 Place a comma after a transitional word, phrase, or clause that begins a sentence.

The division of labor by sex must have produced several immediate benefits for the early hominids. *First of all,* nutrition would have improved owing to a balanced diet of meat and plant foods.

When you move a transitional element to the interior of a sentence, set it off with a *pair* of commas. At the end of a sentence, the transitional element is set off with a single comma.

Lipid molecules, *of course,* and molecules that dissolve easily in lipids can pass through cell membranes with ease.

Lipid molecules can pass through cell membranes with ease, *to cite one example.*

3 Use a comma (or commas) to set off a modifying element that ends or interrupts a sentence *if* the modifier establishes a qualification, contrast, or exception.

A QUALIFICATION

The literary form *short story* is usually defined as a brief fictional prose narrative, *often involving one connected episode.*

A CONTRAST

The U.S. government located a lucrative project for an atomic accelerator in Texas, *not Massachusetts.*

AN EXCEPTION

The children of the rich are the group most likely to go to private preparatory schools and elite colleges, *regardless of their grades.*

When phrases or clauses of qualification, contrast, and exception occur in the middle of a sentence, set them off with a *pair* of commas.

 28b Using a comma before a coordinating conjunction to join two independent clauses

Use a comma before the coordinating conjunctions *and, but, or, nor* to join two independent clauses.

The faucet stopped working, and the sink leaks.

We can fix the problems ourselves, or we can call a plumber.

However, if one or both of the clauses has internal punctuation, change the comma to a semicolon, as shown on the next page.

Several thousand years ago, probably some lines of Neanderthal man and woman died out; but it seems likely that a line in the Middle East went directly to us, *Homo sapiens.*

28c Using commas between items in a series

1 Use a comma to separate three or more items in a series.

One major function of the comma is to signal a brief pause that separates items in a series—a string of related words, phrases, or clauses.

WORDS   We'll need a washer, a valve, and a wrench.

PHRASES   Booms and busts have plagued economic activity since the onset of industrialization, *sporadically ejecting many workers from their jobs, pushing many businesses into bankruptcy,* and *leaving many politicians out in the cold.*

Option: Some writers omit the comma before the *and* that precedes the final item in a series. Whatever your preference, be consistent.

> Exercise appears *to reduce the desire to smoke, to lessen any tendency toward obesity* and *to help in managing stress.*

Note: When at least one item in a series contains an internal comma, use a semicolon to separate items and prevent misreading. For the same reason, use semicolons to separate long independent clauses in a series.

> I believe that the sun is about ninety-three million miles from the earth; that it is a hot globe many times bigger than the earth; and that, owing to the earth's rotation, it appears to rise every morning and set every evening.

2 Place a comma between two or more coordinate adjectives in a series, if no coordinating conjunction joins them.

When the order of two adjectives before a noun can be reversed without affecting the meaning of the noun, the adjectives are called **coordinate adjectives.** Coordinate adjectives can be linked by a comma or by a coordinating conjunction.

SERIES WITH COMMAS

Getting under the sink can be a tricky, messy job.

SERIES WITH *AND*

Getting under the sink can be a tricky *and* messy job.

SERIES WITH COMMAS

The left hemisphere of the brain thinks sequential, analytical thoughts and is also the center of language.

SERIES WITH *AND*

The left hemisphere thinks sequential *and* analytical thoughts and is also the center of language.

Note: The presence of two adjectives beside one another does not necessarily mean that they are coordinate. In the phrase "the wise old lady," the adjectives could not be reversed in sequence or joined by *and*; the adjective *wise* describes *old lady,* not *lady* alone. The same analysis holds for the phrase "the ugly green car." *Green car* is the element being modified by *ugly.* Only coordinate adjectives modifying the same noun are separated by commas.

| 28d | Using commas to set off nonessential elements |

1 Identify essential (restrictive) elements that need no commas.

When a modifier provides information that is necessary for identifying a word, then the modifier is said to be **essential** (or **restrictive**), and it appears in its sentence *without* commas.

The world-renowned architect *Frank Lloyd Wright* was born in 1869.

Without the name *Frank Lloyd Wright,* we would not know which world-renowned architect was born in 1869.

An essential modifier can also be a clause.

The cyclotron is an instrument *that accelerates charged particles to very high speeds.*

The noun modified—*instrument*—could be *any* instrument, and the clause that follows provides information essential to the definition of *which* or *what kind* of instrument.

2 Use a pair of commas to set off nonessential (nonrestrictive) elements.

If a word being modified is clearly defined (as, for instance, a person with a specific name), then the modifying element is nonessential. Use commas to set the modifier apart from the sentence in which it appears.

NONESSENTIAL   Frank Lloyd Wright, *possibly the finest American architect of the twentieth century,* died in 1959. [The subject of the sentence has already been defined adequately by his name, *Frank Lloyd Wright*.]

WWW
http://www.wisc.edu/writetest/
Handbook/Commas.html
#definitions

Punctuating restrictive and nonrestrictive
modifiers: Definitions of nonrestrictive and
restrictive modifiers with sample pairs of
sentences and self-test sentences and answers.

The meaning of a sentence will change according to whether modifying elements are punctuated as essential or nonessential. The two pairs of sentences that follow are worded identically. The commas give them different meanings.

ESSENTIAL   The students *who have band practice after school* cannot attend the game.

The essential modifier precisely defines *which* students will not be able to attend the game—only those who have band practice.

NONESSENTIAL   The students, *who have band practice after school,* cannot attend the game.

The nonessential modifier communicates that *all* of the students have band practice and that none can attend.

One important type of nonessential information is called an **appositive phrase,** the function of which is to rename a noun. Set off appositive phrases with a pair of commas:

The police investigation, a bungled affair from start to finish, overlooked crucial evidence.

When an appositive phrase consists of a series of items separated by commas, set it off from a sentence with a pair of dashes—not commas—to prevent misreading.

Motion sickness—nausea, dizziness, and sleepiness—is a dangerous and common malady among astronauts.

The following Critical Decisions box provides a series of questions to help you distinguish essential and nonessential information.

CRITICAL DECISIONS

Distinguishing between Essential and Nonessential Information

Comma placement regularly depends on a decision you make about whether certain qualifying (or additional) information is or is not essential to the meaning of a particular word. Your decision about this content determines how you punctuate your sentence.

> **A Test to Determine Whether Qualifying Information Is Essential or Nonessential**
>
> 1. Identify the single word in the sentence being qualified by a word group.
> 2. Identify the qualifying word group.
> 3. Drop the qualifying word group from the sentence.
> 4. Ask of the single word from #1, above: Do I understand which one or who?
>
>   a. If you can give a single answer to this question, the qualifying information is nonessential. Set off the information from the sentence with a pair of commas.
>
>   The train arrived early in Baltimore, the birthplace of Babe Ruth.
>
>   b. If you cannot give a specific answer to the question, the qualifying information is essential. Include the information in the main sentence with no commas.
>
>   The cities that have antiquated water systems need to modernize quickly or risk endangering public health.

28e Using commas to acknowledge conventions of quoting, naming, and various forms of separation

1 Use a comma to introduce or to complete a quotation.

Commas set a quotation apart from the words that introduce or conclude the quotation. Commas (and periods) are placed *inside* end quotation marks.

> The prizefighter Rocky Graziano once said, "I had to leave fourth grade because of pneumonia—not because I had it but because I couldn't spell it."

See additional examples of punctuating sentences with quotations in 31a.

2 Use a comma to set off expressions of direct address. If the expression interrupts a sentence, set off the word with a *pair* of commas.

> "Ed, did you bring your computer?"
> "Our business, Ed, is to sell shoes."

3   Use a comma to mark the omission of words in a balanced sentence.

Sentences are balanced when identical clause constructions are doubled or tripled in a series. So that repeating words in the clauses do not become tedious, omit these words and note the omission with a comma.

The first train will arrive at 2 o'clock; the second, at 3 o'clock.

4   Place a comma between paired "more/less" constructions.

The less you smoke, the longer you'll live.

5   Use a comma to set off tag questions that conclude a sentence.

This is the right house, isn't it?

6   Use a comma to set off yes/no remarks and mild exclamations.

"Yes, I'll call him right away."
"Oh, well, I can put it off for another day."

7   Use commas according to convention in names, titles, dates, numbers, and addresses.

Commas with names and titles

Place a comma directly after a name if it is followed by a title.

Mr. Joe Smith, Executive Editor
Lucy Turner, Ph.D.

Set off a title in commas when writing a sentence.

Lucy Turner, Ph.D., delivered the commencement address.

Commas with dates

Place a comma between the day of the month and year. If your reference is to a particular month in a year and no date is mentioned, do not use a comma.

January 7, 1998   but   January 1998

If you include a day of the week when writing a date, use the following convention:

The package will be delivered on Wednesday, January 7, 1998.

Commas with numbers

Place a comma to denote thousands, millions, and so forth.

543   5,430   54,300   543,000   5,430,000   5,430,000,000

Do *not* use commas when writing phone numbers, addresses, page numbers, or years.

Commas with addresses

When writing an address, place a comma between a city (or county) and state. On envelopes use state abbreviations.

Baltimore, Maryland   Baltimore County, Maryland

Place no comma between a state and zip code.

Baltimore, MD 21215

When writing an address into a sentence, use commas to set off elements that would otherwise be placed on separate lines of the address.

The control boards were shipped to Mr. Abe Stein, Senior Engineer, Stein Engineering, 1243 Slade Avenue, Bedford, Massachusetts 01730.

8   Use commas to prevent misreading.

CONFUSING   To get through a tunnel will need to be dug.

REVISED   To get through, a tunnel will need to be dug.

28f   Editing to avoid misuse or overuse of commas

1   Eliminate the comma splice.

The most frequent comma blunder, the **comma splice,** occurs when a writer joins independent clauses with a comma.

FAULTY   Christopher Columbus is considered a master navigator today, he died in neglect.

To revise a comma splice, see the box on the next page and Chapter 15.

> ### *Four Ways to Avoid Comma Splices*
>
> 1. Separate the two clauses with a period or a semicolon.
>
>   Christopher Columbus is considered a master navigator today. He died in neglect.
>
>   Christopher Columbus is considered a master navigator today; he died in neglect.
>
> 2. Join the two clauses with a coordinating conjunction and a comma.
>
>   Christopher Columbus is considered a master navigator today, but he died in neglect.
>
> 3. Join the two clauses with a conjunctive adverb and the appropriate punctuation.
>
>   Christopher Columbus is considered a master navigator today; nevertheless, he died in neglect.
>
> 4. Join the two clauses by making one subordinate to the other.
>
>   Although Christopher Columbus is considered a master navigator today, he died in neglect.

2 Eliminate commas that split paired sentence elements.

Do not place a comma between a subject and verb—even if the subject is lengthy.

FAULTY What has sometimes been dramatically termed the clash of civilizations, is merely the difference in the interpretation given by different societies to the same acts.

REVISED What has sometimes been dramatically termed the clash of civilizations is merely the difference in the interpretation given by different societies to the same acts.

Similarly, do not place a comma between a verb and its object or complement, nor between a preposition and its object.

FAULTY One culture may organize, its social relations around rites of physical initiation. [The comma should not come between the verb and its object.]

REVISED   One culture may organize its social relations around rites of physical initiation.

---

3   Eliminate misuse of commas with quotations.

A comma *is not* used after a quotation that ends with a question mark or an exclamation point.

FAULTY   "Get out**!,**" cried the shopkeeper.

REVISED   "Get out**!**" cried the shopkeeper.

CHAPTER 29

Using Semicolons

WWW

http://www.csc.calpoly.edu/
~ebrunner/GrammatiCat/
Punctuate/SemiColon.html

The semicolon: sophisticated punctuation. Contains a section called "Inspiration" with a number of samples of exemplary uses of the semicolon by professional writers.

Semicolons are used to separate independent sentence elements. They represent a middle choice between commas and periods because they create a partial break while maintaining a relationship between the elements.

SPOTLIGHT
5

29a   **Use a semicolon, not a comma, to join independent clauses that are intended to be closely related.**

FAULTY   In 1852 Mt. Everest was definitively identified as the highest mountain in the world**,** shortly thereafter it was named in honor of Sir George Everest, an early British Survey General of India.

REVISED   In 1852 Mt. Everest was definitively identified as the highest mountain in the world**;** shortly thereafter it was named in honor of Sir George Everest, an early British Survey General of India.

CRITICAL DECISIONS

Separating and Linking Sentences with Punctuation

Why separate sentences with a period?

Use a period to show a full separation between sentences.

> Dante Alighieri was banished from Florence in 1302. He wrote the *Divine Comedy* in exile.

Why link sentences with a semicolon?

Use a semicolon, alone, to join sentences balanced in content and structure. Also use a semicolon to suggest that the second sentence completes the content of the first. The semicolon suggests a link but leaves it to the reader to infer how sentences are related.

> **BALANCED SENTENCE**   Agriculture is one part of the biological revolution; the domestication of animals is the other.
>
> **SUGGESTED LINK**   Five major books and many articles have been written on the Bayeux tapestry; each shows just how much the trained observer can draw from pictorial evidence.

Why link sentences with a conjunctive adverb and a semicolon or period?

Use a semicolon with a conjunctive adverb (*however, therefore,* etc.) to emphasize one of the following relationships: addition, consequence, contrast, cause and effect, time, emphasis, or condition. With the semicolon and conjunctive adverb, linkage between sentences is closer than with a semicolon alone. The relationship between sentences is made clear by the conjunctive adverb.

> Patients in need of organs have begun advertising for them; **however,** the American Medical Association discourages the practice.

Use a period between sentences to force a pause and then to stress the conjunctive adverb.

> Patients in need of organs have begun advertising for them. **However,** the American Medical Association discourages the practice.

Why link sentences with a comma and a coordinating conjunction?

Use a comma and a coordinating conjunction to join sentences in a coordinate relationship that shows addition, choice, consequence, contrast, or cause (see 25a). Since two sentences are fully merged into one following this strategy, linkage is complete.

Robotics has increased efficiency in the automobile industry, **but** it has put thousands of assembly-line employees out of work.

29b Use a semicolon, not a comma, to join two independent clauses that are closely linked by a conjunctive adverb.

FAULTY Historical researchers cannot control the events they want to recreate, indeed, often they cannot even find enough documentation to learn all the facts.

REVISED Historical researchers cannot control the events they want to recreate; indeed, often they cannot even find enough documentation to learn all the facts.

29c Join independent clauses with a semicolon before a coordinating conjunction when one or both clauses contain a comma or other internal punctuation.

After the Shuttle landed, Perkins tried calling the President; but he didn't get through.

29d Use a semicolon to separate items in a series when each item is long or when one or more items contain a comma.

I sent the letters to Baltimore, Maryland; Portland, Oregon; and Dallas, Texas.

29e Place semicolons *after* end quotation marks.

We read "Ode to the West Wind"; we then discussed the poem in detail.
He said, "The check is in the mail"; then he left for Paris.

CHAPTER 30

Using Apostrophes

The **apostrophe** (ʼ) is used to show possession, mark the omission of letters or numbers, and mark plural forms. Decisions about the use of apostrophes involve questions of function and placement.

CRITICAL DECISIONS

Using Apostrophes According to Convention

In almost every case, apostrophes are required by the conventions explained in this chapter. Their use is rarely governed by questions of style. You must, therefore, make sure that you clearly understand when apostrophes are needed (and not needed) and where they are correctly inserted. Many regard misuse of apostrophes as a mark of extreme carelessness if not downright incompetence.

| 30a | Using apostrophes to show possession with nouns and pronouns |

SPOTLIGHT 1

1 For most nouns and for indefinite pronouns, add an apostrophe and the letter *s* to indicate possession.

Bill**'s** braces   the government**'s** solution

history**'s** verdict   somebody**'s** cat

For singular nouns ending with the letter *s, show possession by adding an apostrophe and s if this new construction is not difficult to pronounce.*

Elli**s's** Diner   hostes**s's** menu   Diane Arbu**s's** photographs

WWW

http://www.ex.ac.uk/~SEGLea/
psy6002/apostrophes.html

A one-page guide to the English apostrophe, claiming that "No one born since about 1950 seems to be able to use the apostrophe correctly."

Note: The possessive construction formed with *ʼs* may be difficult to read, particularly if the *s* at the end of the original word is sounded like *z*. If this is the case, you have the option of dropping the *s* after the apostrophe.

ACCEPTABLE   Mr. Stevens**'** store   OR   Mr. Stevens**'s** store

Whichever convention you adopt, be consistent.

The Critical Decisions box below will help you distinguish between plurals and possessives.

CRITICAL DECISIONS

Distinguishing between Plurals and Possessives

Apply the following tests to determine whether you should be using an apostrophe and *s* ('*s*) or the suffix -*s*, with no apostrophe.

Is the noun followed by a noun? If so, then you probably intend to show possession. Use the possessive form '*s*.

noun
government's <u>policy</u>

noun
family's <u>holiday</u>

Is a noun followed by a verb or a modifying phrase? If so, then you probably intend to make the noun plural. Use the suffix -*s*, with *no* apostrophe.

modifying phrase
governments <u>in that part of the world</u>

modifying phrase
fami*lies* <u>having two or more children</u>

But if an omitted word is involved, you may need a possessive form.

Eric's friends attend Central High. Frank's attend Northern.

[In the second sentence, the omitted noun *friends* is clearly intended as the subject of the sentence. The '*s* is needed to show whose friends—*Frank's*.]

2   For a plural noun ending with *s,* add only an apostrophe to indicate possession. For a plural noun not ending with *s,* add an apostrophe and the letter *s.*

bricklayers' union	children's games	men's locker
dancers' rehearsal	teachers' strike	cattle's watering hole

3   To indicate possession when a cluster of words functions as a single noun, add an apostrophe and the letter *s* to the last word.

executive vice president's role
brother-in-law's car

4   To indicate possession of an object owned jointly, add an apostrophe and the letter *s* to the last noun (or pronoun) named.

Mary and Bill**'s** car needs a muffler. [The car belongs jointly to Mary and Bill.]

5   To indicate individual possession by two or more people, add an apostrophe and the letter *s* to each person named.

Judy**'s** and Rob**'s** interview notes are meticulous. [The reference is to two sets of notes, one belonging to Judy and the other to Rob.]

6   Eliminate apostrophes that are misused or confused with possessive pronouns.

Personal pronouns have their own possessive case forms (see 20c); they *never* use apostrophes to show possession (*theirs, its, ours, yours*). When you write, avoid confusing personal pronouns meant to show possession with personal pronouns that are contractions formed with the verb *be,* as shown here.

Personal Pronouns: Contractions Formed with Be

it's	*It is* doubtful he'll arrive.	*It's* doubtful he'll arrive.
who's	*Who is* planning to attend?	*Who's* planning to attend?
you're	*You are* mistaken.	*You're* mistaken.
there's	*There is* little to do.	*There's* little to do.
they're	*They are* home.	*They're* home.

Edit to eliminate apostrophes from personal pronouns that are meant to show possession, not contraction.

FAULTY   You're order has arrived.

REVISED   Your order has arrived.

30b   **Using apostrophes in contractions to mark the omission of letters and numbers**

1   Use an apostrophe to indicate the omission of letters in a contraction.

can**'t** = can not   won**'t** = will not   you**'ve** = you have

2   Use an apostrophe to indicate the omission of numbers in a date.

the '60s   the '80s   the '90s

30c   Using apostrophes to mark plural forms

1   Use an apostrophe and the letter *s* to indicate the plural of a letter, number, or word referred to as a word.

The letter, number, or word made plural should be italicized (or underlined). Do *not* italicize the apostrophe or the letter *s*.

Mind your *p*'s and *q*'s.   How many *5*'s in sixty?
The frequent *in*'s and *with*'s reduced the effectiveness of his presentation.

Exception: When forming the plural of a proper noun (e.g., someone's name), omit the apostrophe but retain the letter *s*. Using an apostrophe in this case would mistakenly suggest possession and thus confuse a reader.

At the convention I met three *Frank***s** and two *Maude***s**.

2   Use an apostrophe and the letter *s* to indicate the plural of a symbol, an abbreviation with periods, and years expressed in decades.

Do *not* underline or italicize the symbol, the abbreviation, or the decade.

Joel is too fond of using &**'s** in his writing.
Computer-assisted software engineering will be important in the 1990**'s**.

Option: Some writers omit the apostrophe before the letter *s* when forming the plural of decades, abbreviations without periods, and symbols.

1900**s** or 1900**'s**   IBM**s** or IBM**'s**   %**s** or %**'s**
Whichever convention you adopt, be consistent.

3   Do not use an apostrophe to form the plural of a regular noun.

Apostrophes are never used to create plural forms for regular nouns.

FAULTY PLURAL   Cat's eat meat.   Idea's begin in thought.
REVISED PLURAL   Cat**s** eat.   Idea**s** begin.

CHAPTER 31

Using Quotation Marks

Correctly using quotation marks involves decisions about when they are (and are not) required and where and how they are placed. This chapter will help you in making such decisions.

CRITICAL DECISIONS

Knowing Not to Substitute Apostrophes for Quotation Marks

Apostrophes and quotation marks do not serve the same functions. While few writers would be likely to substitute quotation marks for apostrophes in error, it is not uncommon for writers to use a single quotation mark, which has the same form as an apostrophe ('), where double quotation marks are required. American usage differs in some respects from English and other British-influenced usage. Be sure that you use quotation marks in all instances described in this chapter.

31a   **Punctuating direct quotations**

1   Use double quotation marks (" ") to set off a short direct quotation from the rest of a sentence.

Short quotations—those that span four or fewer lines of your manuscript—may be incorporated into your writing by running them in with your sentences as part of your normal paragraphing. When quoting a source, reproduce exactly the wording and punctuation of the quoted material.

> According to the director, "By the year 2020, women and minorities will account for 70 percent of the new workers."
> Eric asked, "Can I borrow the car?"

Note: Indirect quotations are never set off with quotation marks:

> Eric asked whether he could borrow the car.

2 Use single quotation marks (' ') to set off quoted material or the titles of short works within a quotation enclosed by double (" ") marks.

WWW

http://owl.English.purdue.edu/
Files/14.html

A page on quotation marks, from the Purdue University Online Writing Lab.

ORIGINAL PASSAGE

The "business" of school for first-grade students is to learn the distinction between intellectual play and playground play.

QUOTATION

As educator Monica Landau says, "The 'business' of school for first-grade students is to learn the distinction between intellectual play and playground play."

3 Use commas to enclose explanatory remarks that lie outside the quotation.

According to Bailey, "Competition was the key term in the formula—remove it and there was no rating, dating, or popularity."

"Rating, dating, popularity, competition," writes Bailey, "were catch-words hammered home, reinforced from all sides until they seemed a natural vocabulary."

"You had to rate in order to date, to date in order to rate," she adds. "By successfully maintaining the cycle, you became popular."

Note: When the word *that* introduces a direct quotation, or when an introductory remark has the sense of a "that" construction but the word itself is omitted, do not use a comma to separate the introduction from the quoted material. In addition, do not capitalize the first letter of the quotation.

Bailey discovered that "the Massachusetts *Collegian* (the Massachusetts State College student newspaper) ran an editorial against using the library for 'datemaking.' "

4 Display lengthy quotations by setting them off from the text. Do *not* use quotation marks.

Quotations of five or more lines should be displayed in block format using a narrower indentation.

In his remarks, Bill Bradley spoke on the impressive economic growth of East Asia:

> East Asia is quickly becoming the richest, most populous, most dynamic area on earth. Over the last quarter century, the East Asian economies grew at an average real growth rate of 6 percent annually, while the economies of the United States and the countries of the European Community grew at 3 percent.

Standard manuscript form for displayed quotations is as follows:

- Double-space the displayed quotation and indent ten spaces from the left margin.
- Punctuate material as in the original text.
- Keep quotation marks inside a displayed quotation, using double (" ") marks.
- Do not indent the first word of the paragraph if one paragraph is being displayed. If multiple paragraphs are being displayed, indent the first word of each paragraph three additional spaces (that is, thirteen spaces from the left). However, if you are quoting multiple paragraphs and the first sentence quoted does not begin a paragraph in the original source, then do not indent the first paragraph in your paper.

A displayed quotation is best introduced with a full sentence, ending with a colon. The colon provides a visual cue to the reader that a long quotation follows.

5   Place periods and commas before the end quotation mark.

"The big question is whether this kind of growth is sustainable," says Bradley.

He adds, "Asian nations can no longer count as heavily on expanding exports to the United States to fuel their growth."

6   Place colons, semicolons, and footnotes after end quotation marks.

COLON   He asserts that "the futures of Asia and the United States are inextricably intertwined": Asian countries profited by U.S. growth, and the United States can profit by Asian growth.

SEMICOLON   He believes the United States and the East must form a "strong, lasting partnership"; moreover, we must do so without condescension.

FOOTNOTE   He believes that the United States and the East must form a "strong, lasting partnership."[4]

7 Place question marks and exclamation points before or after end quotation marks, depending on meaning.

MARK APPLIES TO QUOTED MATERIAL ONLY

Naturalist José Márcio Ayres began his field work with this question: "How do these primates survive when the forests in which they live are flooded much of the year?"

MARK APPLIES BOTH TO QUOTED MATERIAL AND TO SENTENCE AS A WHOLE

How can we appreciate the rigors of field research when even Ayres remarks, "Is the relative protection of the ukaris habitat surprising in light of the swarms of mosquitoes one encounters?"

MARK APPLIES TO SENTENCE AS A WHOLE BUT NOT TO QUOTATION

Ayres reports that fights among monkeys looking for mates are frequent and that "after all this trouble, copulation may last less than two minutes"!

CRITICAL DECISIONS

How Much Should You Quote?

The following examples draw on this passage about shopping malls by Richard Stein (*The New American Bazaar*):

> When they are successful, shopping malls in American cities fulfill the same function as *bazaars* did in the cities of antiquity. The bazaars of the ancient and medieval worlds were social organisms—if we mean by this term self-contained, self-regulating systems in which individual human lives are less important (and less interesting) than the interaction of hundreds, and sometimes thousands, of lives.

Quote other writers when you find their discussions to be particularly lively, dramatic, or incisive or especially helpful in bolstering your credibility. In general, quote as little as possible so that you keep readers focused on *your* discussion.

■ Quote a word or a phrase, if this will do.

Anthropologist Richard Stein refers to the American shopping mall as a "social organism."

■ Quote a sentence, if needed.

Stein sees in shopping malls a modern spin on an ancient institution: "When they are successful, shopping malls in American cities fulfill the same function as *bazaars* did in the cities of antiquity."

■ Infrequently quote a long passage as a "block." Long quotations of five or more lines are set off as a block. Limit your use

(continued)

> *How Much Should You Quote? continued*
>
> of block quotations, which tempt writers to avoid the hard work of selecting for quotation *only* the words or sentences especially pertinent to the discussion at hand. If you decide that a long quotation is needed, introduce the quotation with a full sentence and a colon.
>
> Various commentators have claimed that shopping malls serve a social function. Anthropologist Richard Stein compares the mall to the bazaar in cities of old:
>
> > When they are successful, shopping malls . . .

31b Quoting dialogue and other material

1 Run in brief quotations of poetry with your sentences. Indicate line breaks in the poem with a slash (/). Quote longer passages in displayed form.

A full poem or a lengthy excerpt from a poem is normally displayed in block form.

The Black Riders

42

I walked in a desert.
and I cried:
"Ah, God, take me from this place!"
A voice said: "It is no desert."
"I cried, "Well, but—
The sand, the heat, the vacant horizon."
A voice said: "It is no desert."

—STEPHEN CRANE

When quoting a brief extract—four lines or fewer—you can run the lines into the sentences of a paragraph, using the guidelines for quoting prose; however, line divisions should be shown with a slash (/) with one space before and one space after.

> Stephen Crane's bleak view of the human condition is expressed in lyric 42 of his series "The Black Riders." Walking in a desert, his narrator cries: "'Ah, God, take me from this place!' / A voice said: 'It is no desert.'"

2 Use quotation marks to quote or write dialogue.

When quoting or writing dialogue, change paragraphs to note each change of speaker. Explanatory comments between parts of the quotation are enclosed with two commas. The first, signaling the (temporary) ending of the quoted material, is placed *inside* the end quotation mark. The second comma, signaling the end of the explanatory remark, is placed before the quotation mark that opens the next part of the quotation. When the quotation resumes, its first letter may be capitalized only if a new sentence has been started. In this case (as illustrated below), place a period at the end of the explanatory comment.

> "Nobody sees you any more, Helen," Nat began. "Where've you disappeared to?"
>
> "Oh, I've been around," she said, trying to hide a slight tremble in her voice. "And you?"
>
> "Is somebody there where you're talking that you sound so restrained?"
>
> —Bernard Malamud, *The Assistant*

In a speech of two or more paragraphs, begin each new paragraph with opening quotation marks to signal your reader that the speech continues. Use closing quotation marks *only* at the end of the final paragraph to signal that the speech has concluded.

3   Indicate the titles of brief works with quotation marks: chapters of books, short stories, poems, songs, sections from newspapers, and essays. [1]

I read the "Focus Section" of the *Boston Sunday Globe* every week.

"The Dead" is, perhaps, Joyce's most famous short story.

"Coulomb's Law" is the first chapter in volume two of Gartenhaus's text, *Physics: Basic Principles*.

For your papers, use standard manuscript form. The title of a paper you are submitting to an instructor or peers should *not* be put in quotation marks. Use quotation marks only when you are quoting a title *in* a paper or if a title itself contains a title—a reference to some other work. For example, if the title of your own paper included a reference to a poem, the title would look like this:

Loneliness in Stephen Crane's "The Black Riders"

This same title, referred to in a sentence would look like this:

In his essay "Loneliness in Stephen Crane's 'The Black Riders,'" Marcus Trudeau argues that Crane's universe is unknowable and indifferent.

When a title is included in any other quoted materials, double quotations marks (" ") change to single marks (' ').

---

[1]The titles of longer works—books, newspapers, magazines, and long poems—should be italicized. See 34c.

COMPUTER TIPS

Smart Quotes

Most word processors offer you a set of fancy typesetter's quotation marks and apostrophes. These smart quotes or curly quotes (" " and ' ') are different from the inch and foot marks (" and ') available on typewriters. For material that will ultimately be submitted in print, use the typesetter's quotes, which look more attractive on the page. However, if the material is to be e-mailed or published on the World Wide Web, use the old-style typewriter marks, because the curly quotes use nonstandard characters that are interpreted differently by different computers. For example, if you type *a baker's dozen* in your e-mail message, it may appear on your reader's computer as *a bakerUs dozen.* Most good word-processing programs allow you to turn the curly quotes on or off, and some even allow you to convert the quotes in a piece of text from curly to typewriter style.

---

4 Use quotation marks occasionally to emphasize words or to note invented words.

Use quotation marks sparingly to highlight an uncommon usage of a standard term or a new term that has been invented for a special circumstance. Once you have emphasized a word with quotation marks, you need not use the marks again with that word.

> We can designate as "low interactive" any software title that does not challenge learners to think. Low-interactive titles may be gorgeous to look at, but looking—not thinking—is what they invite learners to do.

31c Avoiding misuse or overuse of quotation marks

1 Do not use quotation marks to highlight worn-out slang or colloquial expressions. Revise the sentence instead.

OVERUSED Kate promised she would "walk that extra mile" for Mark.

REVISED Kate promised to help Mark in any way she could.

2 Do not use quotation marks to create irony. Revise the sentence instead.

MISUSED Dean Langley called to express his "appreciation" for all I had done.

REVISED   Dean Langley called to complain about the accusations of bias I raised with reporters.

3   **Do not use quotation marks to emphasize technical terms.**

MISUSED   "Electromagnetism" is a branch of physics.

REVISED   Electromagnetism is a branch of physics.

4   **Do not use quotation marks to distinguish commonly accepted nicknames.**

MISUSED   "Bob" Dole was a powerful senator.

Reserve quotation marks for unusual nicknames, which often appear in parentheses after a first name. Once you have emphasized a name with quotation marks, do not use the marks again with that name.

ACCEPTABLE   Ralph ("The Hammer") Schwartz worked forty years as a long-shoreman in San Francisco.

CHAPTER 32
Using Other Marks

This chapter reviews the information you need to make decisions about using colons, dashes, parentheses, brackets, ellipses, and slashes.

CRITICAL DECISIONS
Choosing Colons, Dashes, or Parentheses

In some instances, you will have a choice between using a colon or a dash—for example, with an appositive or a summary at the end of a sentence. And in some instances you will have a choice between using dashes and parentheses to set off nonessential elements within a sentence. Keep in mind that the colon and parentheses are generally considered more formal punctuation marks, whereas the dash is somewhat more informal.

The Colon

32a Using the colon

The **colon** is the mark of punctuation generally used to make an

www
http://webster.commnet.edu/
grammar/marks/marks.htm

Coverage of all punctuation marks.

announcement. In formal writing, a colon follows a *complete* independent clause and introduces a word, phrase, sentence, or group of sentences (as in a quotation).

1 Use a colon to announce an important statement or question.

How can it be that 25 years of feminist social change have made so little impression on preschool culture? Molly, now 6 and well aware that women can be doctors, has one theory: children's entertainment is made mostly by men.
—KATHA POLLITT

2 Use a colon to introduce a list or a quotation.

Place a colon at the conclusion of an independent clause to introduce a list or a quotation. The list or quotation can be either run in with the rest of the sentence or set off and indented.

A LIST [RUN IN WITH SENTENCE]

According to Cooley, the looking-glass self has three components: how we think our behavior appears to others, how we think others judge our behavior, and how we feel about their judgments.

A QUOTATION [SET OFF FROM SENTENCE]

A New England soldier wrote to his wife on the eve of the First Battle of Bull Run:

> I know how great a debt we owe to those who went before us through the Revolution. And I am willing, perfectly willing, to lay down all my joys in this life, to help maintain this government, and to pay that debt.

3 Use a colon to set off an appositive phrase, summary, or explanation.

Appositive

In addition to bats, only a few species are known to display food sharing: wild dogs, hyenas, chimpanzees, and human beings.

Summary

Bats create a fluid social organization that is maintained for many years: vampire bats are remarkably social.

Explanation

When Calais surrendered, King Edward (of England) threatened to put the city to the sword, then offered the people a bargain: He would spare the city if six of the chief burghers would give themselves up unconditionally.

---

4   Follow conventions for colon use.

Biblical citation

Fragments of Phoenician poetry have survived in the Psalms, where the mountains are described as "a fountain that makes the gardens fertile, a well of living water" (Song of Songs 4:15).

Hours from minutes

8:15 a.m.   12:01 p.m.

Titles from subtitles or subsidiary material

The New American Bazaar: Shopping Malls and the Anthropology of Urban Life

Salutation in a formal letter and bibliographic citations

Dear Dr. Hart:

Bike, Patricia. "The Phoenicians." *Archaeology* Mar./Apr. 1990: 30.

---

5   Edit to eliminate colons misused within independent clauses.

Colons should never be used as a break inside an independent clause.

FAULTY   For someone who is depressed, the best two things in life are: eating and sleeping.

REVISED   For someone who is depressed, the best two things in life are eating and sleeping.

REVISED   For someone who is depressed, only two things in life matter: eating and sleeping.

The Dash

32b **Using dashes for emphasis**

On the typewritten page, the dash is written as two hyphens (--). The space between these hyphens closes when the dash is typeset (—). Do not put a space before or after a dash.

The Critical Decisions box below gives advice on when to use dashes.

CRITICAL DECISIONS

Determining When to Use Dashes

Sentence constructions rarely *require* the use of dashes. The dash is a stylist's tool, an elective mark that you can use to control the pace with which readers move through your sentence. On seeing the dash, readers pause. They speed up to read the words you have emphasized, then pause once more before returning to the main part of your sentence:

EFFECTIVE   Zoologist Uwe Schmidt discovered that shortly after birth, vampire bat pups are given regurgitated blood—in addition to milk—by their mothers.

Use the single dash to set off elements at the beginning or end of a sentence and a pair of dashes to set off elements in the middle. When elements are set off at the end of a sentence or in the middle, you have the choice of using commas or parentheses instead of dashes. Whatever punctuation you use, take care to word the element you set off so that it fits smoothly into the structure of your sentence. For instance, in the following sentence the nonessential element would be awkward.

AWKWARD   Zoologist Uwe Schmidt discovered that shortly after birth, vampire bat pups are given regurgitated blood—they drink milk, too—by their mothers.

BETTER   Bat pups are given regurgitated blood—in addition to milk—by their mothers.

1   **Use dashes to set off nonessential elements.**

Use dashes to set off brief modifiers, lengthy modifiers, and appositives. Dashes emphasize these nonessential elements set off in a sentence.

Within the past ten years, a new generation of investigators—armed with fresh insights from sociobiology and behavioral ecology—have learned much about social organization in the birds of paradise.

Note: Use dashes to set off appositives that contain commas.

Since the turn of the century, the percentage of information workers—bankers, insurance agents, lawyers, science journalists—has gone from a trickle to a flood.

2   **Use a dash to set off an introductory series from a summary or explanatory remark.**

Pocket change, ball-point pens, campaign buttons—humanity's imprint continues to be recorded on the grassy slopes of the Boston Common.

3   **Use a dash to express an interruption in dialogue.**

Adam studied his brother's face until Charles looked away. "Are you mad at something?" Adam asked.

"What should I be mad at?"

"It just sounded—"

"I've got nothing to be mad at. Come on, I'll get you something to eat."

—JOHN STEINBECK

COMPUTER TIPS

Em Dash and En Dash

You probably already know that the dash is different from the hyphen. On a typewriter, to indicate a dash, you typed two hyphens with no spaces between, before, or after--like this. In addition, there are *two different* dashes that professional typesetters use, and most newer computers can generate both. One is called the "en dash," because it's the width of a capital N; the other is called the "em dash," because it's wider—roughly the width of a capital M. The en dash is used to indicate a span of some sort: 9:30–10:45. It's not a hyphen. It is customarily preceded and followed by very small spaces, but not full spaces. The em dash is used to indicate a break in thought or a parenthetical comment—like this—and it's neither preceded nor followed by spaces. Find out how to type in these special dashes on your particular computer.

Parentheses

32c	Using parentheses to set off nonessential information

Parentheses ( ) are used to enclose and set off nonessential dates, words, phrases, or whole sentences that provide examples, comments, and other supporting information.

1   Use parentheses to set off nonessential information: examples, comments, appositives.

Beetles (especially those species that scavenge) are among the first organisms to invade terrain opened up to them by changing climates.

The information content of a slice of pizza (advertising, legal expenses, and so on) accounts for a larger percentage of its cost than the edible content does.

2   Use parentheses to set off specialized supplementary information or numbers in an itemized series.

Thomas Aquinas (b. 1225 or 1226, d. 1274) is regarded as the greatest of scholastic philosophers.

Lucy Suchman is staff anthropologist of Xerox's Palo Alto Research Center (better known as PARC).

Interactive learning is student-centered two ways: (1) students set the pace of their own learning; and (2) students set the depth of their own learning.

3   Punctuate parentheses according to convention.

When a parenthetical remark forms a sentence, the remark should begin with an uppercase letter and end with an appropriate mark (period, question mark, or exclamation point) placed *inside* the end parenthesis. In all other cases, end punctuation should be placed outside the end parenthesis.

The Bakhtiari think of themselves as a family, the descendants of a single founding-father. (The ancient Jews had a similar belief.)

The Bakhtiari think of themselves as a family, the descendants of a single founding-father (as did the ancient Jews).

Brackets

32d Using brackets for editorial clarification

1 Use brackets to insert your own words into quoted material.

Use brackets [ ] to clarify or insert comments into quoted material. When you alter the wording of a quotation either by adding or deleting words, indicate as much to your reader with appropriate punctuation.

When quoting a sentence with a pronoun that refers to a word in another, nonquoted sentence, use brackets to insert a clarifying reference. Delete the pronoun and add bracketed information; or, if wording permits (as in this example), simply add the bracketed reference.

According to Katherine Payne, "Many [elephant rumbles] are below our range of hearing, in what is known as infrasound."

To show your awareness that an error is the quoted author's, not yours, place the bracketed word *sic* (Latin, meaning "thus") after the error.

"Intense infrasonic calls have been recorded from finback whales, but weather [sic] the calls are used in communication is not known."

2 Use brackets to distinguish parentheses inserted within parentheses.

Katherine Payne reports that "sound at the lowest frequency of elephant rumbles (14 to 35 hertz [cycles per second]) has remarkable properties—it is little affected by passage through forests and grasslands."

3 Use angle brackets to enclose e-mail and Web addresses.

Reach the publisher at <http:www.abacon.com>.

Ellipses

32e Using an ellipsis to indicate a break in continuity

Just as you will sometimes add words in order to incorporate quotations into your sentences, you will also need to omit words. The overall rule to bear in mind when you alter a quotation is to present quoted material in a way that is faithful to the meaning and sentence structure of the original. If your omission of words risks confusing an author's meaning or misrepresenting the author's sentence structure in any way, use a bracketed ellipsis—three spaced periods set in brackets [. . .]—to indicate that you have altered the original. The spaced periods show that you have omitted either words or entire sentences; brackets indicate that *you* have made the omission and that the spaced periods were not set by the author to indicate a pause.[1]

The following passage will be altered to demonstrate several uses of ellipses. For an extended discussion of using quotations in a research paper, see Chapter 31.

> First, for Americans, the human cost of the Civil War was by far the most devastating in our history. The 620,000 Union and Confederate soldiers who lost their lives almost equaled the 680,000 American soldiers who died in all the other wars this country has fought combined. When we add the unknown but probably substantial number of civilian deaths—from disease, malnutrition, exposure, or injury—among the hundreds of thousands of refugees in the Confederacy, the toll of the Civil War may exceed war deaths in all the rest of American history.

1   Know when *not* to use ellipses.

Do *not* use ellipses to note words omitted from the beginning of a sentence if it is obvious that you are quoting a fragment of the original. In the following example, three words are omitted.

FAULTY   James McPherson observes that "[. . .] the human cost of the Civil War was by far the most devastating in our history."

REVISED   James McPherson observes that "the human cost of the Civil War was by far the most devastating in our history."

REVISED (QUOTATION WITH PARENTHETICAL REFERENCE)
              James McPherson observes that "the human cost of the Civil War was by far the most devastating in our history" (42).

Do *not* use an ellipsis if the passage you quote ends with a period and ends your sentence as well. Readers take for granted that the quoted sentence exists in a paragraph in which other sentences follow.

FAULTY   One scholar believes that "the toll of the Civil War may exceed war deaths in all the rest of American history. [. . .]

---

[1]The addition of brackets to the use of three spaced periods is new to the *MLA Style Manual and Guide to Scholarly Publishing,* 2nd edition (1998) and to the *MLA Handbook for Writers of Research Papers,* 5th edition (1999). In earlier editions. MLA editors had recommended the use of spaced periods only.

REVISED One scholar believes that "the toll of the Civil War may exceed war deaths in all the rest of American history."

REVISED (QUOTATION WITH PARENTHETICAL REFERENCE)
One scholar believes that "the toll of the Civil War may exceed war deaths in all the rest of American history" (McPherson 42).

2 Use an ellipsis to indicate words omitted from the middle of a sentence.

According to James McPherson, "When we add the unknown but probably substantial number of civilian deaths [. . .] among the hundreds of thousands of refugees in the Confederacy, the toll of the Civil War may exceed war deaths in all the rest of American history."

Quotation with a parenthetical reference

According to James McPherson, "When we add the unknown but probably substantial number of civilian deaths [. . .] among the hundreds of thousands of refugees in the Confederacy, the toll of the Civil War may exceed war deaths in all the rest of American history" (42).

3 Use an ellipsis to indicate words omitted from the end of a sentence.

When you omit words from the end of a quoted sentence, skip one space after the last quoted word, follow with the bracketed ellipsis, and conclude with a final period. In the example that follows, the bracketed ellipsis shows that the writer has altered the sentence structure of the original.

Official mortality figures for the Civil War do not include the "probably substantial number of civilian deaths—from disease, malnutrition, exposure, or injury [. . .]."

Quotation with a parenthetical reference

Official mortality figures for the Civil War do not include the "probably substantial number of civilian deaths—from disease, malnutrition, exposure, or injury [. . .]" (McPherson 42).

When the altered quotation appears in the middle of your sentence, skip one space after the last quoted word, follow with the bracketed ellipsis, and continue with your own sentence.

Official mortality figures for the Civil War do not include the "probably substantial number of civilian deaths—from disease, malnutrition, exposure, or injury [. . .]" (McPherson 42), which is one reason historians think that the Civil War may be the costliest, in terms of human lives, in American history.

4   Use an ellipsis to indicate the omission of whole sentences
or parts of sentences.

The following passage will be altered to show the use of ellipsis:

> The successful capitalist was a man who could accurately estimate a firm's
> potential profits. The investors who survived were the ones who knew how
> to take "risks" in such a way that there was no actual risk at all. They prof-
> ited through interest and dividends and through the increased value of their
> holdings, which multiplied as the national economy grew. Under Tom Scott's
> tutelage, Carnegie learned to collect interest rather than pay it, and he be-
> came a shrewd judge of the growth potential of investment opportunities.
>
> —HAROLD C. LIVESAY, *Andrew Carnegie and the Rise of Big Business*

When omitting an entire sentence (or sentences), place the bracketed
ellipsis at the spot of the omission. Observe the placement of the sentence-
ending period *before* the bracketed ellipsis:

> As Carnegie's biographer points out, "The investors who survived were
> the ones who knew how to take 'risks' in such a way that there was no ac-
> tual risk at all. [. . .] Under Tom Scott's tutelage, Carnegie learned to collect
> interest rather than pay it, and he became a shrewd judge of the growth
> potential of investment opportunities" (Livesay 48).

When omitting the end of one sentence through to the end of another sentence, follow the convention at 32e-3. Observe the placement of the sentence-
ending period *after* the end of the bracketed ellipsis.

> According to Livesay, "The investors who survived were the ones who
> knew how to take 'risks' [. . .]. Under Tom Scott's tutelage. Carnegie
> learned to collect interest rather than pay it, and he became a shrewd
> judge of the growth potential of investment opportunities" (48).

When omitting the end of one sentence through to the middle of another sentence, place the author's punctuation mark (if any) after the last
word of the initially quoted sentence, follow with a bracketed ellipsis, and
continue with the remainder of the quotation.

> Writing about the railway boom of the mid 1800s, Carnegie's biographer
> observes, "The investors who survived [. . .] profited through interest and
> dividends and through the increased value of their holdings, which multi-
> plied as the national economy grew" (Livesay 48).

5   Use an ellipsis to show a pause or interruption.

When *you* are writing dialogue or prose—that is, when you are *not*
quoting a source, you can use an ellipsis (with *no* brackets) to indicate a brief
pause or delay. Within a sentence, use three spaced periods. Between sentences, end the first sentence with a period and then set the ellipsis—four
spaced periods in all.

IN DIALOGUE THAT YOU WRITE

"No," I said. I wanted to leave. "I . . . I need to get some air."

IN PROSE THAT YOU WRITE

When I left the seminary, I walked long and thought hard about what a former student of divinity might do. . . . My shoes wore out, my brain wore thin. I was stumped and not a little nervous about the course my life would take.

The Slash

1 Use slashes to separate lines of poetry run in with the text of a sentence.

Retain all punctuation when quoting poetry. Leave a space before and after the slash when indicating line breaks.

The narrator of William Blake's "The Tyger" is struck with wonder: "Tyger! Tyger! burning bright / In the forests of the night. / What immortal hand or eye, / Could frame thy fearful symmetry?"

2 Use slashes to show choice.

Use slashes, occasionally, to show alternatives, as with the expressions *and/or* and *either/or*. With this use, do not leave spaces before or after the slash.

Either/Or is the title of a philosophical work by Kierkegaard.

As a prank, friends entered the Joneses as a husband/wife alternate entry in the local demolition derby.

If your meaning is not compromised, avoid using the slash; instead, write out alternatives in your sentence.

3 Use a slash in writing fractions or formulas to note division.

The February 1988 index of job opportunities (as measured by the number of help wanted advertisements) would be as follows:

$(47,230/38,510) \times 100 = 122.6$

1/2   5/8   20 1/4

PART VII
Mechanics and Spelling Decisions

CHAPTER 33

Using Capitals

Capitals give readers cues on how to read: where to look for the begin-

WWW
http://Webster.comment.edu/
grammar/capitals/htm

A brief guide to capitalization.

ning of a new thought, which words form titles or proper names, and so on. Capitals and italics are also very useful for special designations that can be shown only in writing.

CRITICAL DECISIONS

Understanding Conventions for Using Capitals

Decisions about using capitalization are generally based on convention—that is, in order to use capitals appropriately, you simply have to learn and follow the rules for their use. Misuse of capitals can seriously undercut your authority as a writer.

33a Capitalize the first letter of the first word in every sentence.

When a box of mixed-grain-and-nut cereal is shaken, large particles always rise to the top—for the same reason that, over time, stones will rise to the top of a garden lot or field.

1 Reproduce capitalization in a quoted passage.

Capitalize the first word of quoted material when you introduce a quotation with a brief explanatory phrase.

According to archaeologist Douglas Wilson, "Most of what archaeologists have to work with is ancient trash."

2 In a series of complete statements or questions, capitalize the first word of each item.

In a series of numbered phrases run in with a sentence, the phrases are *not* capitalized.

The program for sustainable agriculture has three objectives: (1) to reduce reliance on fertilizer; (2) to increase farm profits; and (3) to conserve energy.

In a displayed series, capitalization of the first word is optional. In the following example, the *t* in *To* could be a lowercase letter.

The program for sustainable agriculture has three objectives:

1. To reduce reliance on fertilizer.
2. To increase farm profits.
3. To conserve energy.

Capitalizing the first word of a sentence following a colon is optional. In the following example, the *t* in *The* could be lowercase.

OPTIONAL The program has two aims: The first is to conserve energy.

33b Capitalize words of significance in a title.

Do not capitalize articles (*a, an, the*) or conjunctions and prepositions that have four or fewer letters, except at the title's beginning. *Do* capitalize the first and last words of the title (even if they are articles, conjunctions, or prepositions), along with any word following a colon or semicolon.

Pride and Prejudice
West with the Night
"The Phoenicians: Rich and Glorious Traders of the Levant"

Do not capitalize the word *the* unless it is part of a title or proper name.

the Eiffel Tower   *The Economist*

The first word of a hyphenated word in a title is capitalized. The second word is also capitalized, unless it is very short.

"The Selling of an Ex-President"
Engine Tune-ups Made Simple

33c Capitalize the first word in every line of poetry.

When quoting traditional poems, retain the capitalization of the original. When writing poetry, be aware that each new line conventionally opens with a capital.

And I would that my tongue could utter
    The thoughts that arise in me.
        —TENNYSON, from *"Break, Break, Break"*

Capitalize proper nouns—people, places, objects; proper adjectives; and ranks of distinction.

1 **Capitalize names of particular people or groups of people.**

Tom Hanks	Martha Washington
Democrats	the Left

Names of family relations—brother, aunt, grandmother—are not capitalized unless they are used as part of a particular person's proper name.

I saw my favorite aunt, Janet, on a trip to Chicago.
We went to visit Aunt Janet.

2 **Capitalize religious titles and names, nationalities, languages, and places or religions.**

Islam	Muslim	the Koran
God	Allah	Buddha
America	Americans	Native Americans
Cascades	England	Asia
English	Arabic	Swahili

Note: The terms *black* and *white,* when designating race, are usually written in lowercase, though some writers prefer to capitalize them (by analogy with other formal racial designations such as Mongolian and Polynesian).

3 **Capitalize adjectives formed from proper nouns, and titles of distinction that are part of proper names.**

English tea	Cartesian coordinates

Capitalize titles of distinction that are not separated from a proper noun. Do not capitalize titles if they are followed by the preposition *of.*

Governor Bush	Jeb Bush, governor of Florida

Note: When titles of the highest distinction are proper names for a specific office—President, Prime Minister—they often remain capitalized, even if followed by a preposition.

Capitalize titles and abbreviations of titles when they follow a comma—as in an address or closing to a letter.

Martha Brand, Ph.D.   David Burns, Executive Vice-President
Sally Roth, M.D.

4   **Capitalize the names of days, months, holidays, and historical events or periods, particular objects, and name brands.**

Saturday   Christmas   December   Middle Ages

Note: When written out, centuries and decades are not capitalized. Seasons are capitalized only when they are personified, as in "Spring's gentle breath."

Mount Washington   USS *Hornet*   Jefferson Memorial
Apple computer   Aswan Dam

5   **Use capitals with certain abbreviations, prefixes, or compound nouns.**

Capitalize abbreviations only when the words abbreviated are themselves capitalized.

Mister James Wolf   Mr. James Wolf
Apartment 6   Apt. 6
Federal Aviation Administration   FAA

Capitalize the prefixes *ex, un,* and *post* only when they begin a sentence or are part of a proper name or title.

an un-American attitude   the Un-American Activities Committee

Capitalize a number expressed in word form if it is part of a name or title.

Third Avenue   the Seventy-second Preakness

CHAPTER 34
Using Italics

A word set in italics calls attention to itself. On a typewritten (or handwritten) page, words that you would italicize can be underlined. However, most word processors do allow you to italicize selected text.

Italicize words if they need a specific emphasis.

Italics can be used to emphasize particular words in your writing. When used sparingly, they can convey an emotional message.

The first astronauts to land on the moon left a plaque signed by Richard Nixon, *not* by his political rival and originator of the Apollo program, John F. Kennedy.

CRITICAL DECISIONS

Italicizing for Emphasis

Decisions about using italics for emphasis require considerable care. Overuse lessens the impact of italics and makes your writing appear overexcited and unconvincing. The best way to create emphasis is not to simulate emotion with typeface, but to make your point with words.

OVERUSED   The narrator of Charles Baxter's short story "Gryphon" is *overcome* with anger after a classmate reports Miss Ferenczi to the principal. He *wants* to believe the substitute teacher's stories no matter how outlandish they may be.

REWORDED   The narrator of Charles Baxter's short story "Gryphon" is furious after a classmate reports Miss Ferenczi to the principal. It is crucial for him to believe the substitute teacher's stories no matter how outlandish they may be.

Italicize words, letters, and numbers to be defined or identified.

1   Use italics for words to be defined.

Words to be defined in a sentence are usually set in italics. Occasionally, such a word is set in quotation marks.

The *operating system* on a computer is a sort of master organizer that can accept commands whenever no specific program is running.

2   Use italics for expressions recognized as foreign.

Italicize foreign expressions that have not yet been assimilated into English but whose meanings are generally understood, such as *e pluribus unum* (Latin) and *hombre* (Spanish).

No italics are used with foreign expressions that have been assimilated into English, such as guru (Sanskrit) and kayak (Eskimo).

3 Use italics to designate words, numerals, or letters referred to as such.

Italicize words, letters, and numerals when you are calling attention to them as such: Many writers have trouble differentiating the uses of *lie* and *lay*. The combination of italics and an apostrophe with the letter *s* is used to make numbers and letters plural: Cross your *t*'s and dot your *i*'s.

COMPUTER TIPS

Don't Underline; Use Italics

Like many conventions left over from the typewriter era, underlining was at one time a way around a typewriter's limitations. But word processors can actually do the italicizing themselves, so you should use that capability whenever you type the title of a book, play, or movie, or at other times italics are called for. Simply highlight the material you want to italicize, and then click on the symbol in the menu bar for italics (an *I* in most programs). Use the underline function only if you are writing instructions or exercises or doing some other kind of work that requires a variety of typographical distinctions.

34c Use italics for titles of book-length works separately published or broadcast, as well as for individually named transport craft.

WWW
http://ec.uvsc.edu/owl/handouts/
quotes.htm

Handout on when to use italics/underlining and when to use quotation marks, from Utah Valley State College's Online Writing Lab.

1 Use italics for books, long poems, and plays.

Love in the Ruins [novel]
The Odyssey [long poem]
Twelfth Night [play]

2 Use italics for newspapers, magazines, and periodicals.

With newspapers, do not capitalize or set in italics the word *the*, even if it is part of the newspaper's title. Italicize the name of a city or town only if it is part of the newspaper's title.

Brookline *Citizen*   *Newsweek*

3 Use italics for works of visual art, long musical works, movies, and broadcast shows. Set in italics the article *the* only when it is part of a title.

As the World Turns   *A Prairie Home Companion*
Mozart's *The Magic Flute*   the *Burghers of Calais*

4 Use italics for individually named transport craft: ships, trains, aircraft, and spacecraft.

USS *Hornet* (a ship)   *Atlantis* (a spacecraft)

Do not italicize USS or HMS in a ship's name.

CHAPTER 35

Using Abbreviations

CRITICAL DECISIONS

Writing in Other Disciplines

Writers working in an unfamiliar discipline should consult the standard manuals of reference, style, and documentation for guidance in using abbreviations in the field. Several such references are described in Chapter 7, Documenting the Research Paper, with conventions shown in Chapter 8, Writing and Arguing in the Disciplines.

35a Abbreviating titles of rank both before and after proper names

The following are usually abbreviated before a proper name. Though not an abbreviation, *Ms.* is usually followed by a period.

Mr.   Mrs.   Ms.   Dr.

Typically, the abbreviations *Gen., Lt., Sen., Rep.,* and *Hon.* precede a full name—first and last.

FAULTY   Gen. Eisenhower   Sen. Kennedy

REVISED   General Eisenhower   Senator Kennedy

REVISED   Gen. Dwight D. Eisenhower   Sen. Ted Kennedy

The following abbreviated titles or designations of honor are placed *after* a formal address or listing of a person's full name.

B.A.	M.A.	M.S.	Ph.D.	C.P.A.
Jr.	Sr.	M.D.	Esq.	

Place a comma after the surname, then follow with the abbreviation. If more than one abbreviation is used, place a comma between abbreviations.

Lawrence Swift Jr., M.D.

Abbreviations of medical, professional, or academic titles are *not* combined with the abbreviation *Mr., Mrs.,* or *Ms.*

FAULTY   Ms. Joan Warren, M.D.

REVISED   Dr. Joan Warren
          or Joan Warren, M.D.

35b Abbreviating specific dates and numbers

With certain historical or archaeological dates, abbreviations are often used to indicate whether the event occurred in the last two thousand years.

Ancient times (prior to two thousand years ago)

B.C.   (before the birth of Christ)
B.C.E.   (before the common era)

Both abbreviations follow the date.

Modern times (within the last two thousand years)

C.E.   (of the common era)
A.D.   (*Anno Domini,* "in the year of the Lord," an abbreviation that precedes the date)

Augustus, the first Roman Emperor, lived from 63 B.C. (*or* B.C.E.) to A.D. 14 (*or* C.E.).

Clock time uses abbreviations in capitals or in lowercase.

5:44 P.M. (or p.m.)
5:44 A.M. (or a.m.)

When numbers are referred to as specific items (such as numbers in arithmetic operations or as units of currency or measure), they are used with standard abbreviations.

No. 23 or no. 23	2 + 3 = 5	54%
$23.01	99 bbl. [barrels]	

You should not use numerical abbreviations unless they are attached to specific years, times, currencies, units, or items. Revise the sentence if you cannot be specific.

FAULTY   We'll see you in the A.M.

REVISED   We'll see you in the morning.

35c Using acronyms, uppercase abbreviations, and corporate abbreviations

An **acronym** is the uppercase, pronounceable abbreviation of a proper noun. Periods are not used with acronyms. If there is any chance that a reader might not be familiar with an acronym or abbreviation, spell out the proper noun and show the acronym in parentheses.

Medical researchers are struggling to understand the virus that causes Acquired Immune Deficiency Syndrome (AIDS).

In subsequent sentences you can use the acronym alone.

Other uppercase abbreviations use the initial letters of familiar persons or groups to form "call letter" designations conventionally used in writing, such as JFK (John Fitzgerald Kennedy) and SEC (Securities and Exchange Commission).

Abbreviations used by individual companies and organizations are a matter of preference. When referring directly to a specific organization, use its own preferred abbreviations for words such as *Incorporated (Inc.)*, *Limited (Ltd.)*, *Private Corporation (P.C.)*, and *Brothers (Bros.)*.

WWW

http://www.ucc.ie/info/net/acronyms/index.html

The World Wide Web Acronym and Abbreviation Server.

35d Using abbreviations for parenthetical references

Abbreviations from Latin are conventionally used in footnotes, documentation, and sometimes in parenthetical comments. They are not underlined or italicized since they are commonplace in English. Avoid these Latin expressions in a main sentence. Use their English equivalents instead:

e.g. (*exempli gratia*)	for example
et al. (*et alii*)	and others
i.e. (*id est*)	that is
etc. (*et cetera*)	and such things; and so on

Avoid the vague abbreviation *etc.* unless you are referring to a specific and obvious sequence, as in *They proceeded by even numbers (2, 4, 6, 8, etc.).* Even here the phrase *and so on* is preferable.

Bibliographical abbreviations (such as p., ch., or abbreviations of months) are commonly used for citations, but they should not be used in sentences of a paragraph.

35e Revising to eliminate most abbreviations from sentences.

In sentences, do not use abbreviations for the names of days or months, units of measure, courses of instruction, geographical names, and page/chapter/volume references. These abbreviations are reserved for specific uses in charts, data presentations, and bibliographic entries. It is acceptable to abbreviate lengthy phrases denoting measurements, such as mph.

CHAPTER 36

Using Numbers in Writing

The use of numbers as part of written work follows patterns and conventions that may vary in different disciplines. Here are the standard usages that apply in the humanities.

CRITICAL DECISIONS

Citing Numbers Accurately

Using numbers in writing—statistics, dates, measurements, monetary amounts—requires precision on the writer's part. Whenever you cite numbers in your work, make sure to check your source, or your own count, for accuracy.

36a Write out numbers that begin sentences and numbers that can be expressed in one or two words.

ONE TO NINETY-NINE

nineteen   seventy-six

FRACTIONS

five-eighths   two and three-quarters

LARGE ROUND NUMBERS

twenty-one thousand   fifteen hundred

WWW
http://webster.commnet.edu/
grammar/numbers.htm

Using numbers and writing lists.

For decades and centuries you may either write out the words or use standard forms of abbreviation. Do not capitalize the initial letters in either case.

the sixties	OR	the '60s
the twenty-first century	OR	the 21st century

In all disciplines, numbers that begin sentences should be written out. When it is awkward to begin a sentence by writing out a long number, re-arrange the sentence.

AWKWARD   Forty-two thousand eight hundred forty-seven was the paid attendance at last night's game.

REVISED   The paid attendance at last night's game was 42,847.

Note: In the sciences and social sciences, spell out numbers from one to nine; use numerals for numbers above nine.

36b   Use figures in sentences according to convention.

NUMBERS LONGER THAN TWO WORDS

1,345   2,455,421

UNITS OF MEASURE

RATES OF SPEED	**TEMPERATURE**	**LENGTH**	**WEIGHT**
60 mph	32° F	24¼ in.	34 grams

MONEY

$.02   2¢ $20.00 $1,500,000 $1.5 million

Amounts of money that can be written in two or three words can be spelled out.

two cents   twenty dollars

SCORES, STATISTICS, RATIOS

The game ended with the score 2–1.

The odds against winning the weekly lottery are worse than 1,000,000 to 1.

ADDRESSES
Apartment 6
231 Park Avenue
New York, New York 10021

TELEPHONE NUMBERS
301-555-1212

VOLUME, PAGE, AND LINE REFERENCES
page 81   act 1, scene 4, line 16

DATES
70 B.C.   A.D. 70   1991–92
from 1991 to 1992   1991–1992

TIME: WRITE OUT NUMBERS WHEN USING THE EXPRESSION *O'CLOCK*.
10:00 a.m.   BUT   ten o'clock in the morning

CHAPTER 37

Using Hyphens

A small but important mark, the **hyphen** (-) has two uses: to join compound words and to divide words at the ends of lines.

CRITICAL DECISIONS

Understanding Where to Hyphenate

You will find advice on word divisions in any dictionary, where each entry is broken into syllables. If you write on a computer, your word-processing software will probably suggest word divisions unless the program is set not to split words at the ends of lines. As for hyphenating compound words, take special care: relocating a simple hyphen can alter meanings entirely.

37a Using hyphens to join compound words

1 Form a compound adjective with a hyphen to prevent misreading when the adjective precedes the noun being modified.

 **WWW**
http://www.superconnect.com/
wordsmit/hyphens.htm

A lighthearted page on "hyphen-phobia," false notions about the use of the hyphen.

A hyphen, as opposed to a dash (see 32b), connects words; a dash separates. Use a hyphen to link words when a compound expression might otherwise confuse a reader.

CONFUSING   Helen's razor sharp wit rarely failed her. [Helen's *razor* is not the subject; Helen's *wit* is.]

CLEAR   Helen's razor-sharp wit rarely failed her.

Note that a **compound adjective** does not need hyphenation either when it is positioned *after* the noun it modifies or when the first word ends with a suffix (like *-ly*) that signals a modifier.

Helen's wit was razor sharp.

Helen's impressively sharp wit rarely failed her.

2 Form compound nouns and verbs with a hyphen to prevent misreading.

Use a hyphen with **compound nouns** and **compound verbs** when the first word of the compound might be read as a separate noun or verb.

cross-reference (n)   cross-examine (v)   runner-up (n)   shrink-wrap (v)

3 Use hanging hyphens in a series of compound adjectives.

Hang—that is, suspend—hyphens after the first word of compound adjectives placed in a parallel series.

The eighth-, ninth-, and tenth-grade classes went on the trip.

4 Follow conventions in hyphenating numbers, letters, and units.

HYPHENATE FRACTIONS AND THE NUMBERS TWENTY-ONE THROUGH NINETY-NINE.

one-fourth   seven-thousandths   forty-six

HYPHENATE FIGURES AND LETTERS JOINED WITH WORDS TO FORM NOUNS OR MODIFIERS.

4-minute mile   R-rated   U-turn

HYPHENATE UNITS OF MEASURE.

light-year   kilowatt-hour

5   Hyphenate compounds formed by prefixes or suffixes according to convention. (Consult a dictionary for specifics.)

ex-President   quasi-serious   self-doubt

Use a hyphen with the prefixes *pro, anti,* and *pre* only when they are joined with proper nouns.

NO HYPHEN	HYPHEN WITH PROPER NOUN
prochoice	pro-Democracy
antimagnetic	anti-Maoist

But use a hyphen with a prefix or suffix that doubles a vowel or that triples a consonant.

NO HYPHEN	HYPHEN WITH DOUBLED OR TRIPLED LETTERS
antiseptic	anti-intellectual
childlike	bell-like

Hyphenate between prefixes and nouns or verbs in compounds to avoid misreading.

re-form (to form an object—such as a clay figure—again)

reform (to overhaul and update a system)

37b Using hyphens to divide a word at the end of a line

Observe these conventions:

- Divide compound words at the hyphen marking the compound.
- Divide words at a prefix or suffix.
- Eliminate hyphenations that hang a single letter at the beginning or end of a line.
- Avoid hyphenating a word the first syllable(s) of which forms another word (man-age, for-tune) and could confuse readers.
- Never hyphenate single-syllable words.
- Do not hyphenate abbreviations, contractions, or multiple-digit numbers.

CHAPTER 38
Making Spelling Decisions

You can improve your spelling by learning a few rules and the exceptions to those rules. If you tend to misspell the same words over and over again, you can overcome these "demons" by recognizing the source of your confusion and memorizing their correct spelling.

CRITICAL DECISIONS

Using a Dictionary to Check Correct Spellings

Marilyn vos Savant, the *Parade* magazine columnist who is said to have the world's highest IQ, once responded to a reader's question about spelling and intelligence. People who make the fewest spelling errors, she said, are generally those who know that when they are not sure of the correct spelling of a word, they should consult a dictionary. She went on to address the question "But if I don't know how to spell a word, how can I look it up?" Her answer was that if you know a word well enough to use it in a sentence, you know enough about how it is spelled to find it in a dictionary. While word-processing programs with spelling checker functions can also help you with correct spellings, it's still a good idea to train yourself to recognize when you're not sure of how to spell a word.

38a Recognize homonyms and commonly confused words.

One of the most common causes of spelling confusion is **homonyms—** words that sound alike, or are pronounced almost alike, but that have different spellings and meanings. The box on page 372 lists a few commonly confused homonyms and near homonyms. Many others are listed in the Glossary of Usage (pp. 399–408).

WWW
http://www.earlham.edu/~peters/
writing/homofone.htm

An English homophone (or homonym) dictionary.

Commonly Confused Homonyms and Near Homonyms

capital [city seat of government]

capitol [legislative or government building]

cite [quote, refer to]

sight [vision, something seen]

site [place, locale]

discreet [respectfully reserved]

discrete [distinct, separate]

eminent [distinguished]

immanent [inborn, inherent]

imminent [expected momentarily]

its [possessive form of *it*]

it's [contraction of *it is*]

lead [guide; heavy metal]

led [past tense of *to lead*]

loose [not tight, unfastened]

lose [misplace, fail to win]

passed [past tense of *to pass*]

past [after; beyond; a time gone by]

than [besides; as compared with]

then [at that time; therefore]

their [possessive form of *they*]

there [opposite of *here*]

they're [contraction of *they are*]

to [toward]

too [also, in addition to]

two [number following *one*]

weather [climatic conditions]

whether [which of two]

whose [possessive form of *who*]

who's [contraction of *who is*]

your [possessive form of *you*]

you're [contraction of *you are*]

yore [the far past]

Many people find particularly troublesome words that appear sometimes as one word and other times as two words: always/all ways, already/all ready, maybe/ may be, everyday/every day, into/in to, altogether/all together. See the Glossary of Usage for the other troublesome words.

WWW
http://www.qconline.com/myword/perfect.html

A lighthearted look at the shortcomings of computer spelling checkers.

Note: *all right* and *a lot* do not vary: they can be written only as two words.

38b   Learn basic spelling rules for *ie/ei*.

The *i* before *e* rule you learned in grammar school still holds true: "*i* before *e* except after *c*, or when pronounced *ay*, as in n*ei*ghbor and w*ei*gh."

COMPUTER TIPS

Spelling Checkers

Spelling checkers are wonderful inventions. They are quick, accurate, and sharper than your own eye at catching mistakes. But use them wisely. First, wait until the end of your writing process. Spell-checking a rough draft or even an intermediate draft filled with words that you may delete later is a waste of time. Also, remember the limitations of spelling checkers: they will catch only words not in their built-in dictionaries. Because *there*, *their*, and *they're* are all spelled correctly, the spelling checker will not tell you if you've chosen the wrong one. When a correction is suggested, make sure you choose the correct one (consult a dictionary if you need to). If you've written *a lot* and your spelling checker offers to substitute *allot*, be careful not to change your intended meaning. Finally, if your word processor has an ongoing spelling checking feature, consider turning it off. Few things are more damaging to the flow of your thoughts than being interrupted by a beep, a warning that you've misspelled a word, or the silent substitution of an incorrect word.

I BEFORE *E*	EXCEPT AFTER *C*
achieve	receipt/receive
belief/believe	deceit/deceive

EI PRONOUNCED *AY*	EXCEPTIONS	
eight(h)	ancient	foreign
neighbor	height	seize
	either	weird

Finally, if the *ie* is not pronounced as a unit, the rule does not apply: science.

38c   Learn rules for using prefixes.

Prefixes are placed at the beginnings of words to qualify or add to their meaning. The addition of a prefix never affects the spelling of the root word: do not drop a letter from or add a letter to the orginal word.

mis	+	statement	=	misstatement
under	+	rate	=	underrate
dis	+	service	=	disservice
de	+	emphasize	=	deemphasize

The following are also used as prefixes: *en, in, ante, inter, pre, per, pro,* and *over.*

38d Learn rules for using suffixes.

A **suffix** is an ending added to a word in order to change the word's function. For example, suffixes can change a present tense verb into a past tense verb (help, help*ed*); make an adjective into an adverb (silent, silent*ly*); make a verb into a noun (excite, excite*ment*); or change a noun into an adjective (force, for*cible*). Spelling difficulties often arise when the root word must be changed before the suffix is added.

Keeping or dropping a final *e*

Many words end with a silent *e* (hav*e*, mat*e*, rais*e*, confin*e*, procur*e*). When adding a suffix to these words, you can use the following rules.

The basic rule: If the suffix begins with a vowel, drop the final silent *e*.

accuse + ation = accusation	sedate + ive = sedative
inquire + ing = inquiring	cube + ism = cubism

Exceptions

The silent *e* is sometimes retained before a suffix that begins with a vowel in order to distinguish homonyms (dyeing/dying); to prevent mispronunciation (*mileage,* not milage); and especially, to keep the sound of *c* or *g* soft: courage + ous = courageous, notice + able = noticeable.

Rule: If the suffix begins with a consonant, keep the final silent *e*.

manage + ment = management	acute + ness = acuteness

Exceptions

When the final silent *e* is preceded by another vowel, the *e* is dropped (*argument,* not arguement; *truly,* not truely).
Other exceptions include:

judge + ment = judgment	awe + ful = awful
acknowledge + ment = acknowledgment	whole + ly = wholly

Keeping or dropping a final *y*

When suffixes are added to words that end in a final *y*, use the following rules.

Rule: When the letter immediately before the *y* is a consonant, change the *y* to *i* and then add the suffix.

beauty + ful = beautiful   study + ous = studious

Exceptions

Keep the final *y* when the suffix to be added is *-ing*.

study + ing = studying   comply + ing = complying

Keep the final *y* for some one-syllable root words.

shy + er = shyer   wry + ly = wryly

Keep the final *y* of a proper name.

Janey/Janeys   Bobby/Bobbylike

Keep the final *y* when it is preceded by a vowel, and then add the suffix.

journey + ing = journeying   play + ful = playful

Doubling the final consonant

A word that ends in a consonant sometimes doubles the final consonant when a suffix is added.

Rule: Double the final consonant when a one-syllable word ends in a consonant preceded by a single vowel.

flat + en = flatten   slip + er = slipper

Rule: Double the final consonant when adding a suffix to a two-syllable word if a single vowel precedes the final consonant and if the final syllable is accented once the suffix is added.

control + er = controller   commit + ing = committing

Rule: Do not double the final consonant when it is preceded by two or more vowels, or by another consonant.

sustain + ing = sustaining   insist + ent = insistent

Rule: Do not double the final consonant if the suffix begins with a consonant.

commit + ment = commitment   fat + ness = fatness

Rule: Do not double the final consonant if the word is *not* accented on the last syllable, or if the accent shifts from the last to the first syllable when the suffix is added.

> beckon + ing = beckoning   prefer + ence = preference

38e Learn rules for forming plurals.

There are several standard rules for making words plural.

Adding -s/-es

Adding -s: For most words, simply add -s.

> gum/gums   automobile/automobiles

Adding -es: For words ending in -s, -sh, -ss, -ch, -x, or -z, add -es.

> bus/buses   watch/watches

For words ending in -o, add -es if the *o* is preceded by a consonant.

> tomato/tomatoes   hero/heroes

Exceptions
> pro/pros, piano/pianos, solo/solos

Add -s if the final *o* is preceded by a vowel.

> patio/patios   zoo/zoos

Words ending in -*f* or -*fe*.

To form the plural of some nouns ending in -*f* or -*fe*, change the ending to -*ve* before adding the -s.

> half/halves   leaf/leaves

Exceptions
> scarf/scarfs/scarves   hoof/hoofs/hooves

Plurals of words ending in -*y*

For words that end in a consonant followed by -*y*, change the *y* to *i* before adding -*es* to form the plural.

enemy/enemies   mystery/mysteries

Exceptions

Add an *s,* only, to proper names such as McGinty/McGintys; Mary/ Marys. For words ending in a vowel followed by *-y,* add *-s.*

monkey/monkeys   delay/delays

Plurals of compound words

When compound nouns are written as one word, add an *-s* ending as you would to make any other plural.

snowball/snowballs   mailbox/mailboxes
breakthrough/breakthroughs

When compound nouns are hyphenated or written as two words, the most important part of the compound word (usually a noun that is modified) is made plural.

sister-in-law/sisters-in-law   head of state/heads of state
nurse-midwife/nurse-midwives   city planner/city planners

Irregular plurals

Some words change internally to form plurals.

woman/women   goose/geese
mouse/mice   tooth/teeth

Some Latin and Greek words form plurals by changing their final *-um, -on,* or *-us* to *-a* or *-i.*

curricul*um*/curricul*a*   syllab*us*/syllab*i*

For some words, the singular and the plural forms are the same.

deer/deer   sheep/sheep   fish/fish

ESL Reference Guide

These chapters are designed to supplement the rest of *Decisions: A Writer's Handbook.* They provide basic information on structural and idiomatic features of the English language that students from an English as a Second Language (ESL) background may need for reference.

These chapters assume that ESL students are now working in a basic English composition course alongside native speakers, and that they have already completed a college-level course of instruction (or its equivalent) in using English as a Second Language.

The material covers topics in the three functional areas of English language usage: nouns and noun-related structures; verbs, verbals, and related structures; and usage for modifiers and modifying structures. Prepositions—perhaps the most troublesome feature of English—are treated in connection with the structures that determine them.

CHAPTER 39

Using English Nouns, Pronouns, and Articles

English nouns name things or people that are considered either countable or not countable in English. English also distinguishes whether a noun names a person or thing that is specific, or something that is generic.

1 Identifying and using count nouns

In English, **count nouns** name things or people that are considered countable. They identify one of many possible individuals or things in the category named. Count nouns have three important characteristics.

- Singular count nouns can be preceded by *one,* or by *a/an*—the indefinite articles that convey the meaning "one (of many)."

  one car   a rowboat   a truck   an ambulance

Singular count nouns can also be preceded by demonstrative pronouns (*this, that*), by possessive pronouns (*my, your, their*), and often by the definite article (*the*).

- Plural count nouns can be preceded by expressions of quantity (*two, three, some, many, a few*) and can use a plural form.

  two cars   some rowboats   many trucks   a few ambulances

- A count noun used as a singular or plural subject must agree with a singular or plural verb form.

  This *car stops* quickly. [A singular subject and verb agree.]
  Other *cars stop* slowly. [A plural subject and verb agree.]

2 Forming plurals with count nouns

Plural count nouns are either regular or irregular. Regular nouns form the plural with *-s* or *-es.* Irregular plural forms—such as *man/men, tooth/teeth, wolf/wolves, medium/media*—follow the models shown in 38e.

3 Identifying and using noncount (mass) nouns

In English, **noncount (mass) nouns** name things that are being considered as a whole, undivided group or category that is not being counted. Noncount (mass) nouns name various kinds of individuals or things that are considered as group categories in English, such as these:

abstractions: courage, grammar
fields of activity: chemistry, tennis
natural phenomena: weather, dew, rain
whole groups of objects: rice, sand, oxygen, wood, oil

Objects that are considered too numerous or shapeless to count are often treated as noncount nouns, as with the word *rock* in this sentence.

We mined dense *rock* in this mountain.

As such objects become individually identifiable, the same word may be used as a count noun.

Four *rocks* fell across the road.

Some nouns name things that can be considered either countable or noncountable in English, depending on whether they name something specific or something generic.

COUNTABLE (AND SPECIFIC)	A *chicken* or two ran off. A *straw* or two flew up.
NONCOUNTABLE (AND GENERIC)	*Chicken* should be cooked well. *Straw* can be very dry.

Nouns that name generalized or generic things often occur in noncountable form, but may also occur in singular form in scientific usage. Three characteristics distinguish noncount (mass) nouns:

- Noncount nouns never use the indefinite article *a/an* (or *one*).
- Noncount nouns are never used in a plural form.
- Noncount nouns always take singular verbs.

4 Using expressions of quantity with count and noncount nouns

Expressions of quantity—such as *many, few, much, little, some,* and *plenty*—are typically used to modify nouns. Some expressions are used to quantify count nouns; some are used with noncount nouns; and others are used with both kinds of nouns.

COUNT NOUNS	NONCOUNT NOUNS	BOTH COUNT AND NONCOUNT NOUNS
many potatoes	*much* rice	*lots of* potatoes and rice
few potatoes	*little* rice	*plenty of* potatoes and rice
		some, any potatoes and rice

When the context is very clear, these expressions can also be used alone as pronouns.

Do you have *any* potatoes or rice?
I have *plenty* if you need *some*.

5 Using nouns in specific and generic senses

English nouns show differences in usage between nouns that name specific things or people and nouns that name generalized or generic things.

A DEFINITE NOUN	The whale migrated thousands of miles. The whales migrated thousands of miles. [Use the **definite article** or a demonstrative pronoun: this or that.]
AN INDEFINITE NOUN	A whale surfaced nearby; then several whales surfaced. [Use the **indefinite article.**]
GENERIC USAGE	Whales are migratory animals. A whale is a migratory animal. [When the reference is to a general group, nouns often use either the **plural with no article** or the **singular with an indefinite article.**]
SCIENTIFIC USAGE	The whale is a migratory animal. Whales are migratory animals. [A generic noun may also be singular or plural with a definite article.]

6 Distinguishing pronouns in specific and indefinite or generic uses

Most pronouns, including personal pronouns, rename and refer to a noun located elsewhere that names a specific individual or thing. However, indefinite pronouns, such as *some, any, one, someone,* or *anyone*, may refer to a noun in an indefinite or generic sense.

PERSONAL PRONOUN	Where are my pencils? I need *them*. [Meaning: I need specific pencils that are mine.]
INDEFINITE PRONOUN	Where are my pencils? I need *some*. [Meaning: I need generic, indefinable pencils; I will use any I can find.]

39b Using articles with nouns

Articles are the most important class of words used in English to show whether nouns are being used as count or noncount nouns, or as specific or generic nouns. There are three articles in English: *a, an,* and *the. Some*, the indefinite pronoun, is occasionally used as if it were an indefinite article.

1 **Nouns sometimes take the indefinite articles *a* and *an*.**

The indefinite articles *a* and *an* are grammatically the same. They are singular indefinite articles that mean "one (of many)," and they are used only with singular count nouns. Pronunciation determines which to use. *A* precedes a noun beginning with a consonant or a consonant sound (a bottle, a hotel, a youth, a user, a xylophone). *An* precedes a noun beginning with a vowel or vowel sound (an egg, an hour, an undertaker).

W W W

http://leo.stcloudstate.edu/grammar/useartic.html

The Use and Nonuse of Articles, from Leo: Literacy Education Online.

A is sometimes used with the quantifiers *little* and *few*. Note the differences in the following examples.

EXAMPLE	MEANING
a little, a few a few onions a little oil	a small amount of something
little, few few onions little oil	a less-than-expected amount of something

2 **Nouns sometimes take the definite article *the*.**

Use *the* with specific singular and plural count nouns and with noncount nouns.

SPECIFIC NOUNS

I need *the tool* and *the rivets*. [one singular and one plural noun]
I need *the equipment*. [a noncount noun]
I need *the tool* on *the top shelf*.
I need *the tools* that are painted orange.
I need *the smallest tool* on *that shelf*.

[Note the modifiers, clauses, and phrases that make the nouns specific.]

GENERIC NOUNS

I need tools for that work. [In this case, no article is used.]

Use *the* in a context where a noun has previously been mentioned or where the writer and the reader both know the particular thing or person being referred to.

I saw a giraffe at the zoo. *The giraffe* was eating leaves from a tree.

I stopped at an intersection. When *the light* turned green, I started to leave. [The sentence assumes the existence of a particular traffic light at the intersection.]

3 Nouns sometimes take no article.

Typically no article is needed with names of unique individuals. In addition, nouns naming generalized persons or things in a generic usage commonly use no article: *Managers often work long hours.* Here are some other situations in which no article is used:

■ Use no article with proper names of continents, states, cities, and streets, and with religious place names.

Europe Alaska New York Main Street heaven hell

■ Use no article with titles of officials when accompanied by personal names; the title effectively becomes part of the proper noun.

President Truman King Juan Carlos Emperor Napoleon

■ Use no article with fields of study.

Ali studied literature. Juan studied engineering.

■ Use no article with names of diseases.

He has cancer. AIDS is a very serious disease.

■ Use no article with names of magazines and periodicals, unless the article is part of the formal title.

Life Popular Science BUT: *The New Yorker* [The article is part of the title.]

39c Using nouns with prepositions

Some of the complex forms of prepositions in English are determined by their use with nouns. Nouns that follow prepositions are called **objects of prepositions**; this grouping forms a modifying **prepositional phrase.** The distinctive function of such modifying phrases often determines which preposition to choose in an English sentence.

1 Using the preposition *of* to show possession

The preposition *of* is often used to show possession as an alternative to the possessive case form (*I hear a man's voice. I hear the voice of a man.*). It is also used informally to show possession for many nouns that do not usually take a possessive form.

INFORMAL   She stood in the *apartment's lobby.*

FORMAL   She stood in the *lobby of the apartment.*

The preposition *of* is not used with proper nouns.

FAULTY   I washed the *car of Luisa.*

CORRECT   I washed *Luisa's car.*

2   Using prepositions in phrases with nouns or pronouns

The distinctive function of a modifying prepositional phrase often determines which preposition to choose in an English sentence. The chart below shows a few typical functions for prepositional phrases.

FUNCTION	PREPOSITION	EXAMPLE/EXPLANATION
Passive voice	*by* the cook	He was insulted *by* the cook.
	with a snowball	I was hit *with* a snowball.
Time expressions	*on* January 1	use for specific dates
	on Sundays	use for specific days
	in January	use for months
	in 1984	use for years
	in spring	use for seasons
	at noon, *at* 5 p.m.	use for specific times
	by noon, *by* 5 p.m.	use to indicate *before* a specific hour
	by April 15	use to indicate *before* a specific date
Locations	*at* 301 South Street	use for an address
	in the house	I waited *in* the house.
	on the floor	The dog lay *on* the floor.
Directions	*onto* the floor	The chandelier dropped *onto* the floor.
	beside the library	Several boxes of books waited *beside* the library.
	through the window	Alex's ball flew *through* the window.
	into the air	As the rain ceased, the puddles evaporated *into* the air.

CHAPTER 40

Using English Verbs

40a **Distinguishing different types of verbs and verb constructions**

A verb, the main word in the predicate of an English sentence, specifies either the action undertaken by the subject or the condition of the subject. The four types of verbs include transitive verbs (which take direct objects), intransitive verbs (which do not take direct objects), linking verbs, and helping or auxiliary verbs (which show tense or mood).

WWW
http://vweb l.hiway.co.uk/ei/
intro.html

The *English Institute's Preliminary Grammar Book* has an extensive discussion with examples of English verbs, aimed at second-language speakers.

1 **Transitive and intransitive verbs work differently.**

A **transitive verb** can take an object. Examples of transitive verbs include *throw* and *take.*

subject verb object
He throws a pass.
  active voice

Because transitive verbs can take an object, most of them can operate in both the active and passive voices. The transitive verbs *have, get, want, like,* and *hate,* however, are seldom used in passive voice.

subject verb modifier
A pass was thrown (by him).
  passive voice

By contrast, an **intransitive verb** never takes an object and can never be used in the passive voice. Examples of intransitive verbs include *smile* and *go.*

subject verb subject verb
The politician smiled. He went into the crowd.

2 Linking verbs are used in distinctive patterns.

Linking verbs, the most common example of which is *be,* serve in sentences as "equals signs" to link a subject with an equivalent noun or adjective. Some other linking verbs are *appear, become,* and *seem.*

> Things *seem* unsettled.
> Shall I *become* a doctor?

Expletives

Linking verbs also serve in a distinctive English construction that uses changed word order with an **expletive** word, *there* or *it.* Expletives are used only with linking verbs, as in these sentences.

> It *is* important to leave now.
> There *seems* to be a problem.

There and *it* form "dummy subjects" or filler words that occupy the position of the subject in a normal sentence; the true subject is elsewhere in the sentence, and the verb agrees with the true subject.

EXPLETIVE IN SUBJECT POSITION	TRUE SUBJECT
There is a cat in that tree.	*A cat* is in that tree.

In complex English sentences, the "dummy subject" expletive obscures the true subject and makes the sentence overly complicated. Try to avoid expletives. Instead, use the true subject and normal word order.

40b Changing verb forms

Verb forms express *tense,* an indication of when an action or state of being occurs in time. The three basic tenses in English are the past, the present, and the future (see Chapter 16). Additional verb tenses and variations of the basic tenses are used to express ongoing actions and other special conditions. This section focuses on forms that ESL students often find challenging.

1 Some verbs rarely use progressive tense forms.

Each of the three basic tenses has a **progressive** form, made up of *be* and the present participle (the *-ing* form of the verb). The progressive tense emphasizes the *process* of doing whatever action the verb asserts. However, certain verbs are generally *not* used in the progressive form, including the following:

think	belong	be	sound
believe	possess	exist	taste
understand	own	seem	surprise
recognize	want	appear	like
realize	need	see	hate
remember	have	smell	love

Often the simple present tense of these verbs is used to express an ongoing activity.

FAULTY   I *am thinking* that Josephine likes sailing.

CORRECT   I *think* that Josephine likes sailing.

This distinction confuses nonnative speakers because most of these verbs do use the progressive tense in special instances. For example, when the verb *think* is used to express consideration, then the progressive tense is appropriate.

CORRECT   I *am thinking* about changing jobs.

Be alert for these special instances as you read and listen to native speakers, and make note of them for future use.

2   Using the perfect forms

The perfect tense is made up of *have* and the past participle (the *-ed* form of the verb). The form of *have* indicates the tense: present perfect (*has* worked), past perfect (*had* worked), and future perfect (*will have* worked). (See Chapter 16.) For uses of verb tenses with reported speech or indirect quotations, see 22c.

Sometimes students confuse the use of the simple past with the use of the present perfect. The present perfect is used when an action or state of being that began in the past continues to the present; it is also used to express an action or state of being that happened at an indefinite time in the past.

PRESENT PERFECT   Linda has worked in Mexico since 1987.

PRESENT PERFECT   Ann has worked in Mexico. [The time is unspecified.]

By contrast, the simple past is used when an action or state of being began *and ended* in the past.

SIMPLE PAST   Linda worked in Mexico last year. [She no longer works there.]

3   Using the varied forms of English future tenses

The following list shows different ways of expressing the future.

VERB FORM	EXPLANATION
She *will call* us soon. She *is going to* call us soon.	These examples have the same meaning.
The movie *arrives* in town tomorrow. The next bus *leaves* in five minutes. The bus *is leaving* very soon.	The simple present and the present progressive are used to express definite future plans, as from a schedule.
Your flight *is taking off* at 6:55. The doctor *is operating* at once. I *am calling* them right now.	The present progressive is sometimes used to make strong statements about the future.
Hurry! The movie *is about to* begin. Finish up! The bell *is about to* ring.	The "near" future is expressed by some form of *be* plus *about to* and a verb.
It's cold. *I'm going to* get a sweater. It's cold. *I'll lend* you a sweater.	This suggests a plan. This suggests a willingness.

Verbs expressing thoughts about future actions, such as *intend* and *hope,* are not used in any future tense, and the verb *plan* uses a future tense only in the idiomatic *plan on* (to make or follow a plan).

4   Using verb tenses in conditional and subjunctive sentences

Conditional sentences talk about situations that are either possible in the future or hypothetical (not proven to be true) in the present or past. Conditional sentences typically contain the conjunction *if* or a related conditional term (*unless, provided that, only if, [only] after, [only] when*). The following are guidelines for using verb forms in conditional sentences.

Possible or real statements about the future

Use the present tense to express the condition in possible statements about the future. In the same sentence, use the future tense to express the result of that condition.

	conditional + present	future (*will* + base form)
REAL STATEMENT	If *I have* enough money,	*I will go* next week.
	When *I get* enough money,	*I will go.*
	[**Meaning:** The speaker may have enough money.]	

Hypothetical or unreal statements about the future

Use the past subjunctive form (which looks like a past tense) with sentences that make "unreal" or hypothetical statements about the future. In the same sentence, use the past form of a modal auxiliary (usually *would, could,* or *might*) to express an unreal result of that stated condition.

	If + past	past form of modal (*would*)
UNREAL STATEMENT	*If you found* the money,	*you would go* next week.

[**Meaning:** The speaker now is fairly sure you will not have the money.]

Hypothetical or unreal statements about the past

Use the subjunctive with appropriate perfect tense verb forms with sentences that make hypothetical or unreal statements about the past. Use the past perfect tense for the unreal statement about the past. In the same sentence, use the past form of the modal auxiliary plus the present perfect to express the unreal result.

	If + past perfect (*had made*)	past modal + present perfect (*would*) (*have gone*)
UNREAL STATEMENT	*If I had made* money,	*I would have gone* last week.

[**Meaning:** At that time the speaker did not have the money.]

For more on the subjunctive, see 16h; for more on modal auxiliaries, see 16c.

5	Expressing a wish or suggestion for a hypothetical event

In stating a wish in the present that might hypothetically occur, use the *past subjunctive* (which looks like the past tense) in the clause expressing the wish. (The object of the wish takes the form of a *that* clause, although the word *that* is often omitted.)

present	[that]	past subjunctive
He *wishes*	[that]	she *had* a holiday.
I *wish*	[that]	I *were* on vacation.

The auxiliaries *would* and *could* (which have the same form in the present and past tenses) are often used to express the object of a wish.

present	[that]	*would/could* + base form
I *wish*	[that]	she *would stay.*
We *wish*	[that]	we *could take* a vacation day.

In stating a wish made in the past or present for something that hypothetically might have occurred in the past, use the past perfect in the *that* clause. (The verb *wish* may be expressed either in the past or in the present tense.)

present OR past   [that]   past perfect *[had worked]*

I wished   [that]   I *had* not *worked* yesterday.

I wish   [that]   it *had been* a holiday.

See 16h-3 for guidelines on using the subjunctive mood with *that* clauses.

Expressing a recommendation, suggestion, or urgent request

In stating a recommendation, suggestion, or urgent request, use the *present subjunctive*—the base form of the verb (*be, do*)—in the *that* clause.

present   [that] present subjunctive = base form

We *suggest* [that]   he *find* the money.

We *advise*   that   you *be* there on time.

(See 16h-3 for comments on the subjunctive in this form.)

40c Changing word order with verbs

1 Invert the subject and all or part of the verb to form questions.

To form a question, you must invert the normal subject and verb order. The following patterns are used with the verb *be*, with modal auxiliaries, with progressive forms, and with perfect forms.

	NORMAL STATEMENT FORM	QUESTION FORM
Be	He *is* sick today.	Is *he* sick today?
Modals	She *can* help us.	*Can she* help us?
Progressive	They *are* studying here.	*Are they* studying here?
Perfect	It *has* made this sound before.	*Has it* made this sound before?

2 Use the base form of the verb for questions (and negatives) with the auxiliary *do/does.*

Verbs other than those shown above use the auxiliary verb *do/does* to form questions, and also to form negatives with *not*. In this form, when the auxiliary verb *do/does* is added, the verb changes to the base form (the dictionary form). Use this pattern for the simple present and simple past.

Question Form / Negative Form: Do + Base Form

QUESTION   *Does* he *get on* this bus?

NEGATIVE   He *does not get on* this bus.

QUESTION   *Did* it *run* better yesterday?
NEGATIVE   It *did not run* better.

40d   Using the helping verbs: Auxiliaries and modal auxiliaries

1   Auxiliary verbs, or helping verbs, are part of basic grammar.

The basic auxiliary verbs (*be, will, have, do*) are used to show tense, to form questions, to show emphasis, and to show negation.

To show tense, or aspect (*be, will, have*): He is driving. She has driven.
To form questions (*do/does*): Do they drive? Why do you drive?
To show negation (*do + not*): I do not drive there.
To show emphasis (*do/does*): She does drive sometimes.

2   Use modal auxiliaries for a wide range of meanings.

Modal auxiliaries include *can, could, may, might, should, would,* and *must*, as well as the four modals that always appear with the particle *to: ought to, have to, able to,* and *have got to*. The base form of the verb (the dictionary form) is always used with a modal auxiliary, whether the time reference is to the future, present, or past. For a past time reference, use the modal plus the past perfect (*have* + the past participle).

MEANING EXPRESSED	PRESENT TIME OR PAST TIME	MODAL + PAST PERFECT
ability and permission	She can drive. She could drive.	She could have driven.
possibility	She may drive. She might drive.	She might have driven.
advisability	She should drive. She ought to drive. She had better drive.	She should have driven. She ought to have driven.
necessity	She must drive. She has to drive.	She had to drive.
negative necessity versus prohibition*	She does not have to drive. [she need not] She must not drive. [she is not allowed]	

*Note that the two negatives above have very different meanings.

40e   Choosing gerunds and infinitives with verbs

There are three types of verbals: infinitives, gerunds, and participles (see 13a-4).

1   Using infinitives and gerunds as nouns

Use an infinitive or a gerund to function either as a subject or as an object.

AS SUBJECTS   *To be one of the leaders here* is not really what I want.
His being one of the leaders here is unacceptable.

AS OBJECTS   I don't really want *to be one of the leaders here.*
I don't accept *his being one of the leaders here.*

Note: The possessive case is used with gerunds; see 20c-2.

2   Learning idiomatic uses of verb/verbal sequences

Sometimes it is difficult to determine which verbs are followed by a gerund, which are followed by an infinitive, and which can be followed by either verbal. This usage is idiomatic and must be memorized; there are no rules to govern these forms. Note in the following examples that verb tense does not affect a verbal.

VERB + GERUND	**VERB + INFINITIVE**	**VERB + EITHER VERBAL**
enjoy	**want**	**begin**
I enjoy swimming.	I want to swim now.	Today I begin swimming.
		Today I begin to swim.
go	**agree**	**continue**
I went swimming.	I agreed to swim.	I continued swimming.
		I continued to swim.
enjoy + gerund	want + infinitive	begin + either verbal
go + gerund	agree + infinitive	continue + either verbal
finish + gerund	decide + infinitive	like + either verbal
recommend + gerund	need + infinitive	prefer + either verbal
risk + gerund	plan + infinitive	start + either verbal

Sentences can differ in meaning depending on whether a gerund or an infinitive follows the verb. This difference in meaning is a function of certain verbs. See the following examples.

EXAMPLE	**MEANING**
They stop *to drink* some water.	They stopped in order to drink.
They stopped *drinking* water.	They didn't drink any more.

Information on idiomatic usage is provided in ESL dictionaries such as the *Longman Dictionary of American English: Your Complete Guide to American English, 1997.*

40f Using two- and three-word verbs, or phrasal verbs, with particles

Phrasal verbs consist of a verb and a *particle*. Note that a particle can be one or more prepositions (off, up, with) or an adverb (away, back). English has many phrasal verbs, often built on verbs that have one basic meaning in their simple one-word form, but different meanings when particles are added.

The coach *called off* the game because of the storm.

He *left out* some important details.

The meaning of a phrasal verb is idiomatic; that is, the words as a group have a different meaning from each of the words separately. Most of these varied meanings are found in a standard English dictionary. Here are some examples of sentences with two-word and three-word verbs.

I *got ready* for work.

She didn't go to the party because she didn't *feel up to* it.

The doctor told him to *cut down on* red meat.

They *did without* a television for a few years.

1 Some phrasal verbs are separable.

With separable phrasal verbs, a noun object either can separate a verb and particle or follow the particle.

          noun object   noun object

CORRECT I *made out* <u>a check</u> to the IRS. OR I *made* <u>a check</u> *out* to the IRS.

However, a pronoun object always separates the verb and the particle. A pronoun never follows the particle.

         pronoun object

FAULTY I *made out* <u>it</u> to the IRS.

REVISED I *made* <u>it</u> *out* to the IRS.

Other separable phrasal verbs include the following:

call off	hand out	prevent from
check out	leave in, out	set up
divide up	look up [research]	sign on, up
find out	pick up	start over, up
fill in	put over	take on
fit in	[present deceptively]	throw out
give back, up		turn on, off,
hang out, up	put up to [promote]	up, down
[suspend: trans.]	put back	wake up
	put off	write down

2   Some phrasal verbs are nonseparable.

With nonseparable phrasal verbs, a noun or pronoun object always follows the particle. For these verbs it is not possible to separate the verb and its particle with a noun or pronoun object.

	noun object		pronoun object
FAULTY	I ran Mary into.	Faulty	I ran her into.
REVISED	I ran into Mary.	Revised	I ran into her.

Other nonseparable phrasal verbs include the following:

bump into	call on	do without
get into	get over	get through
keep on	keep up with	hang out [= stay]
refer to	see about	stop by

Note: An adverb, but not a noun or pronoun, may separate the verb from its particle.

He *apologized* quickly *for* being late.

3   Some phrasal verbs can be either separable or nonseparable.

Some phrasal verbs can be either separable or nonseparable. The meaning of a phrasal verb will change, depending on whether or not the phrase is separated by an object. Note the difference in meaning that appears with the placement of the object in the similar verbs in the following list.

EXAMPLES	MEANING
I *saw through* it. [nonsep.]	I found it transparent.
I *saw* it *through*. [sep.]	I persisted.
She *looked over* the wall. [nonsep.]	She looked over the top of it.
She *looked* the wall *over*. [sep.]	She examined or studied it.

Note: Standard dictionaries usually list verbs with the meanings of most particles (indicating whether or not they are transitive), but they usually do not indicate whether a phrasal verb is separable or nonseparable. However, this information is provided in ESL dictionaries such as the *Longman Dictionary of American English: Your Complete Guide to American English, 1997.*

CHAPTER 41
Using Modifiers in English Sentences

Modifiers expand sentences in a variety of ways. The two types of modifiers are adjectives and adverbs, as well as phrases and clauses that function as adjectives or adverbs. There are two types of adverbs, descriptive and conjunctive. For basic discussions of the types of modifiers, how they function, and how they are placed or located in sentences, see 13a-5 and 6.

41a   Using single-word adjectives and nouns as modifiers of nouns

A modifier of a noun must be placed as close to the noun modified as possible. Single-word adjectives are normally placed before a noun or after a linking verb.

BEFORE A NOUN   The *bored student* slept through the *boring lecture.*

AFTER A LINKING VERB   Jack *is bored.* The lecture he heard *was boring.*

1   Using the present and past participle forms of verbs as adjectives

The present participle and the past participle forms of verbs are often used as single-word adjectives. The choice of form has an important impact on meaning.

Past participle	Meaning
a tired student	Something tired this student.
damaged buildings	Something damaged these buildings.

Present participle	Meaning
a tiring lecture	The lecture causes a feeling of being tired.
a damaging explosion	The explosion caused the damage.

2   Using nouns as modifiers

When two nouns are combined in sequence, the last is considered to be the noun modified; the first is the modifier. (This follows the pattern for single-word adjectives mentioned earlier.) The importance of sequence is evident in the following examples, where the same nouns are combined in different order to produce different meanings.

Modifier	+ Noun modified	Meaning
a car	company	a company whose business involves cars
a company	car	a car provided to someone by the business
a light	truck	a small truck
a truck	light	a light attached to a truck

Avoid overusing nouns as modifiers.

41b   Positioning adverbial modifiers

1   Observe typical locations for adverbs in English sentences.

Adverbs have typical or standard locations in English sentences, although these patterns can be varied for special emphasis. Adverbs are typically located immediately before a transitive or intransitive verb.

Faulty   She finishes cheerfully her homework.

Revised   She cheerfully finishes her homework.

Emphatic   She finishes her homework—cheerfully.

Common adverbs expressing frequency or probability typically come after the verb *be* and helping verbs. In questions, such adverbs can come after the subject.

He was frequently at the gym on Fridays.

She may often discuss politics.

Does she often come here?

However, when sentences are inverted for negatives, these adverbs are usually placed before the helping verb.

FAULTY   They don't frequently talk. It doesn't sometimes matter.

REVISED   They frequently don't talk. It sometimes doesn't matter.

2   Limiting modifiers cannot move without changing meaning.

Although many adverbs can be located at a number of different places in a sentence without changing the meaning, positioning is quite critical with certain **limiting modifiers** such as *only, almost, just, nearly, even, simply* (see 19b).

NO CHANGE IN MEANING	SIGNIFICANT CHANGE IN MEANING
Generally it rains a lot in April.	*Only* Leonid sings those songs.
It *generally* rains a lot in April.	Leonid *only* sings those songs.
It rains a lot in April, *generally*.	Leonid sings *only* those songs.
	[OR . . . sings those songs *only*.]

41c   Arranging cumulative modifiers

1   Observing typical order of cumulative adjectives

Single-word adjective modifiers are placed close to a noun, immediately before a noun, or after a linking verb.

Cumulative adjectives are groups of adjectives that modify the same noun. Cumulative adjectives in an English sentence follow a typical order. A major disruption of this can confuse readers.

FAULTY   a beach French gorgeous tent   red light my small bulb

REVISED   a gorgeous French beach tent   my small red light bulb

Although some stylistic variations from typical order in the location of cumulative adjectives are possible for emphasis, typical locations in an English sentence provide a very strong normal pattern. Here are some guidelines.

Possessives precede numbers. Ordinal numbers follow cardinal numbers.

Jill's first car   my first nine drafts

The typical order of descriptive adjectives is shown below:

(1) OPINION	(2) SIZE	(3) SHAPE	(4) CONDITION	(5) AGE	(6) COLOR	(7) ORIGIN	(8) NOUN
ugly		round			green		fenders
	huge		muddy				spots
lovely				old	red	Turkish	slippers
comfortable			sunny				room

2 Arranging cumulative noun modifiers[1]

Three nouns are often combined, with the first two forming a two-word modifier for the last noun. When this happens, nouns fall into a typical arrangement somewhat comparable to that of adjectives.

NOT TYPICAL   a file steel cabinet

TYPICAL   a steel steel cabinet

The sequence of two nouns to modify a third noun may be classified and arranged in this sequence.

MATERIAL, NUMBER, OR LOCATION	ORIGIN, PURPOSE, OR TYPE	NOUN MODIFIED
chapter	review	questions
slate	roofing	tile
steel	file	cabinet

To maintain clarity in your sentences, avoid accumulating noun modifiers beyond a two-word limit.

---

[1]This discussion on order of modifiers is based on Jean Praninskas, *Rapid Review of English Grammar* (Englewood Cliffs: Prentice-Hall, 1975).

GLOSSARY OF USAGE

This glossary is intended to provide definitions and descriptions of selected word usages current in formal academic writing. In consulting this kind of glossary, writers should be prepared to make informed decisions about the meaning and the level of diction that is most appropriate to their writing project.

Many entries in this glossary consist of commonly confused homonyms —words that are pronounced almost alike but have different meanings and spellings. A comprehensive listing of often-confused homonyms appears in Chapter 38.

a, an   Use *a* when the article precedes a noun beginning with a consonant. For example, *At last we found a hotel.* Use *an* when the article precedes a word beginning with a vowel or an unpronounced *h*. *It was an honor to receive an invitation.* (See 39b-1.)

accept, except   Use *accept* when your meaning is "to receive." Use *except* when you mean an exception, as in *He invited everyone except Thuan.* You can also use *except* as a verb that means "to leave out," as in *The report excepted the two episodes of misconduct.*

advice, advise   Use *advice* as a noun meaning "a recommendation," as in *Longfellow gave excellent military advice.* Use *advise* as a verb meaning "to recommend," as in *Many counselors advise students to declare a double major.*

affect, effect   If your sentence requires a verb meaning "to have an influence on," use *affect*. If your sentence requires a noun meaning "result," use *effect*. *Effect* can also be a verb, however. Use *effect* as a verb when you mean "to make happen," as in *He was able to effect a change in how the city council viewed the benefits of recycling.*

aggravate, irritate   In formal writing, use *aggravate* when you mean "to make worse," as in *The smoke aggravated his cough.* Use *irritate* when you mean "to bother," as in *He became irritated when the drunken driver said the accident was not her fault.*

ain't   Do not use *ain't* in formal writing. Use *is not, are not,* or *am not* instead.

all ready, already   Use *all ready* when you mean "prepared" as in *He was all ready for an expedition to Antarctica.* Use *already* when you mean "by this time," as in *The ushers at Symphony Hall will not seat you if the concert has already started.*

all right   Do not use *alright*. It is simply a misspelling.

all together, altogether   Use *all together* when you mean "as a group" or "in unison," as in *Once we got the family all together, we could discuss the estate.* Use *altogether* when you mean "entirely," as in *Some of the stories about Poe's addictions and personal habits are not altogether correct.* (See 38a.)

allusion, illusion   Use *allusion* when you mean "an indirect reference," as in *The children did not understand the allusion to Roman mythology.* Use *illusion* when you mean "false or misleading belief or appearance," as in *Smith labored under the illusion that he was a great artist.*

a lot   Do not use *a lot* in formal writing. Use a more specific modifier instead. When you use *a lot* in other contexts, remember that it is always two words.

among, between   Use *between* when you are expressing a relationship involving two people or things, as in *There was general agreement between Robb and Jackson on that issue.* Use *among* when you are expressing a relationship involving three or more separable people or things, as in *He failed to detect a link among the blood cholesterol levels, the red blood cell counts, and the T-cell production rates.*

amount, number   Use *amount* when you refer to a quantity of something that cannot be counted, as in *The amount of effort put into finding the cure for AIDS is beyond calculation.* Use *number* when you refer to something that can be counted, as in *The number of people who want to run the Boston Marathon increases yearly.*

an, and   Use *an* when the article precedes a noun beginning with a vowel or an unpronounced *h.* Use *and* when your sentence requires a conjunction that means "in addition to."

and etc.   Avoid using *etc.* in formal writing. When you must use *etc.* in non-formal writing, do not use *and. Et cetera* means "and so forth"; therefore, *and etc.* is redundant.

and/or   Use *and* or *or,* or explain your ideas by writing them out fully. But avoid *and/or,* which is usually too ambiguous to meet the demands of formal writing.

anxious, eager   Use *anxious* when you mean "worried" or "nervous." Use *eager* when you mean "excited or enthusiastic about the possibility of doing something."

anybody, any body; anyone, any one   Use *anybody* and *anyone* when the sense of your sentence requires an indefinite pronoun. Use *any body* and *any one* when the words *body* and *one* are modified by *any,* as in *The teacher was careful not to favor any one student* and *Any body of knowledge is subject to change.*

any more, anymore   Use *any more* to mean "no more," as in *I don't want any more of those plums.* Use *anymore* as an adverb meaning "now," as in *He doesn't work here anymore.*

anyplace   Do not use *anyplace* in formal writing. Use *anywhere* instead.

anyways, anywheres   Do not use *anyways* and *anywheres* in formal writing; use *anyway* and *anywhere* instead.

as, like   Use *as* either as a preposition or as a conjunction, but use *like* as a preposition only. If your sentence requires a preposition, use *as* when you are making an exact equivalence, as in *Edison was known as the wizard of Menlo Park.* Use *like* when you are referring to likeness, resemblance, or similarity, as in *Like Roosevelt, Reagan was able to make his constituency feel optimism.*

a while, awhile   Use *awhile* when your sentence requires an adverb, as in *He swam awhile.* If you are not modifying a verb, but rather want a noun with an article, use *a while,* as in *I have not seen you in a while.*

bad, badly   Use *bad* as an adjective, as in *Bad pitching changed the complexion of the game.* Use *badly* as an adverb, as in *The refugees badly needed food and shelter.* Use *bad* to follow linking verbs that involve appearance or feeling, as in *She felt bad about missing the party.* (See 18b.)

being as, being that   Do not use either *being as* or *being that* to mean "because" in formal writing. Use *because* instead.

beside, besides   Use *beside* as a preposition meaning "next to." Use *besides* as an adverb meaning "also" or "in addition to" as in *Besides, I needed to lose the weight.* Use *besides* as an adjective meaning "except" or "in addition to," as in *Rosa Parks seemed to have nothing besides courage to support her.*

better, had better; best, had best   Do not use *better, had better, best,* and *had best* for *should* in formal writing. Use *ought* or *should* instead.

between, among   See *among, between.*

breath, breathe   Use *breath* as a noun; use *breathe* as a verb.

bring, take   Use *bring* when you are referring to movement from a farther place to a nearer one, as in *The astronauts were asked to bring back rock samples.* Use *take* for all other types of movement.

burst, bust   Use *burst* when you mean "to fly apart suddenly," as in *The pomegranate burst open.* (Notice that the example sentence doesn't say *bursted;* there is no such form of the verb.)

but however, but yet   When you use *however* and *yet,* do not precede them with *but* in formal writing. The *but* is redundant.

but that, but what   When you use *that* and *what,* do not precede them with *but* in formal writing. The *but* is unnecessary.

can, may   Use *can* when you are writing about the ability to do something, as in *He can jump six feet.* Use *may* when you are referring to permission, as in *He may rejoin the team when the period of probation is over.*

censor, censure   Use *censor* when you mean editing or removing from the public eye on the basis of morality. Use *censure* when you mean "to give a formal or official scolding or verbal punishment."

center around   Do not use *center around* in formal writing. Instead, use *center on.*

compare to, compare with   Use *compare to* to note similarities between things, as in *He compared the Chinese wine vessel to the Etruscan wine cup.* Use *compare with* to note similarities and contrasts, as in *When comparing market-driven economies with socialist economies, social scientists find a wide range of difference in the standard of living of individuals.*

complement, compliment   Use *complement* when you mean "something that completes," as in *The wine was the perfect complement for the elegant meal.* Use *compliment* when you mean "praise," as in *The administrator savored the compliment on her organizational skills.*

conscience, conscious   Use *conscience* when your sentence requires a noun meaning "a sense of right or wrong." Use *conscious* as an adjective to mean "aware of" or "awake."

continual, continuous   Use *continual* when you mean "constantly recurring," as in *Continual thunderstorms ruined their vacation days at the beach.* Use *continuous* when you mean "unceasing," as in *The continuous sound of a heartbeat, unceasing and increasing in volume, haunted the narrator.*

could of, would of, should of, might of, may of, must of   In formal writing, avoid combining modal auxiliaries (*could, would, should, might, may,* and *must*) with *of.* Instead, write *could have, would have, should have, might have, may have,* and *must have.*

criteria Use *criteria* when you want a plural word referring to more than one standard of judgment. Use *criterion* when you are referring to only one standard of judgment.

data Use *data* when you are referring to more than one fact, statistic, or other means of support for a conclusion. When you are referring to a single fact, use the word *datum* in formal writing, or use *fact, figure,* or another term that is specific to the single means of support.

different from, different than Use *different from* when an object or phrase follows, as in *Braque's style is different from Picasso's.* Use *different than* when a clause follows, as in *Smith's position on the deficit was <u>different</u> when he was seeking the presidency <u>than</u> it was when he was president.*

differ from, differ with Use *differ from* when you are referring to unlike things, as in *Subsequent results of experiments in cold fusion differed radically from results first obtained in Utah.* Use *differ with* to mean "disagree," as in *One expert might differ with another on a point of usage.*

disinterested, uninterested Use *disinterested* to mean "impartial," as in *An umpire should always be disinterested in which team wins.* Use *uninterested* to mean "bored" or "not interested."

doesn't, don't Do not use *doesn't* and *don't* in formal writing; instead, use *does not* and *do not.* In other contexts, use *don't* with the first and second person singular, as in *I don't smoke* and with the third person plural, as in *They don't smoke.* Use *doesn't* with the third person singular, as in *He doesn't ride the subway.*

done Use *done* when your sentence requires the past participle; do not use done as the simple past. For example, rewrite a sentence such as *Van Gogh done the painting at Arles* to read *Van Gogh did the painting at Arles.*

due to, due to the fact that Use *due to* to mean "because" only when it follows a form of the verb *be,* as in *The sensation of a leg falling asleep is due to pooling of the blood in the veins.* Do not use *due to* as a preposition, however. Also, do not use *due to the fact that* in formal writing because it is wordy.

effect, affect See *affect, effect.*

elicit, illicit Use *elicit* to mean "to draw out," as in *The social worker finally elicited a response from the child.* Use *illicit* to mean "illegal," as in *Illicit transactions on the black market fuel an underground Soviet economy.* (See 38a.)

emigrate, immigrate, migrate Use *emigrate* to mean "to move away from one's country." Use *immigrate* to mean "to move to another country." Use *migrate* to mean "to move to another place on a temporary basis."

enthused, enthusiastic Use *enthusiastic* when you mean "excited about" or "showing enthusiasm." Do not use *enthused* in formal writing.

et al., etc. Do not use *et al.* and *etc.* interchangeably. *Et al.* is generally used in references and bibliographies and is Latin for "and others." *Et cetera* is Latin for "and so forth." Like all abbreviations, *et al.* and *etc.* are generally not used in formal writing, except that *et al.* is acceptable in the context of a citation to a source. Do not use *etc.* in formal writing. Use *and so forth* instead. Or, preferably, be as specific as necessary to eliminate the phrase.

402   Glossary of Usage

everybody, every body   Use *everybody* when you mean "everyone." Use *every body* when you are using *body* as a distinct word modified by *every*, as in *Is every body of water in Canada contaminated by acid rain?*

every day, everyday   Use *everyday* when your sentence requires an adjective meaning "common" or "daily," as in *Availability of water was an everyday problem in ancient Egypt.* Use *every day* when you are using the word *day* and modifying it with the adjective *every*, as in *Enrico went to the art gallery every day.*

except, accept   See *accept, except.*

explicit, implicit   Use *explicit* when you mean "stated outright," as in *The Supreme Court rules on issues that are not explicit in the Constitution.* Use *implicit* when you mean "implied," as in *Her respect for the constitution was implicit in her remarks.*

farther, further   Use *farther* when you are referring to distance, as in *He was able to run farther after eating carbohydrates.* Use *further* when you are referring to something that cannot be measured, such as *Further negotiations are needed between the central government and the people of Azerbaijan.*

fewer, less   Use *fewer* when you are referring to items that can be counted, as in *There are fewer savings accounts at the branch office this year.* Use *less* when you are referring to things that cannot be counted, as in *The East German people have less confidence in the concept of unification than they had one year ago.* (See 18c.)

figure   See *calculate, figure, reckon.*

get   Do not overuse *get* in formal writing. Prefer more precise words. For example, instead of *get better*, write *improve*; instead of *get*, write *receive, catch*, or *become*; instead of *get done*, write *finish* or *end.*

good, well   Use *good* as an adjective, as in *Astaire gave a good performance, but not one of his best.* Use *well* as an adverb, as in *He danced well.* You can also use *well* as an adjective when you refer to good health, as in *She felt well* or *She is well today.* (See 18b.)

got, have; has/have got to   Do not use *got* in place of *have* in formal writing. For example, rewrite a sentence such as *I got to lose weight* to read *I have to* [or *I must*] *lose weight.*

had better, better; had best, best   See *better, had better.*

hanged, hung   Use *hanged* for the action of hanging a person, as in *The innocent man was hanged by an angry mob.* Use *hung* for all other meanings, such as *The clothes were hung on the line* and *The chandelier hung from a golden rope.*

he, she; he/she; his, her; his/her; him, her; him/her   When using a pronoun to refer back to a noun that could be either masculine or feminine, use *he or she* in order to avoid sexist language. *A doctor must be constantly alert; he or she cannot make a single mistake.* Or recast the sentence in the plural: *Doctors must be constantly alert; they cannot make a single mistake.*

herself, himself, myself, yourself   Use pronouns ending in *-self* when the pronouns refer to a noun that they intensify, as in *The teacher himself could not pass the test.* Do not use pronouns ending in *-self* to take the place of subjective- or objective-case pronouns. Instead of writing, for example, *Joan and myself are good friends*, write *Joan and I are good friends.*

his/her   See *he/she.*

hisself   Do not use *hisself* in formal writing. In a context such as *He hisself organized the picnic,* recast the sentence to read *He himself organized the picnic.*

hopefully   Use *hopefully* when you mean "with hope," as in *Relatives watched hopefully as the first miners emerged after the fire.* Avoid using *hopefully* as a modifier for an entire clause or to convey any other meaning. For example, avoid *Hopefully, a cure for leukemia is not far away.*

hung, hanged   See *hanged, hung.*

if, whether   Use *if* to begin a subordinate clause when a stated or implied result follows, as in *If the court rules against the cigarette manufacturers, [then] thousands of lawsuits could follow.* Use *whether* when you are expressing an alternative, as in *Economists do not know whether the dollar will rebound or fall against the strength of the yen.*

illicit, elicit   See *elicit, illicit.*

illusion, allusion   See *allusion, illusion.*

immigrate   See *emigrate, immigrate, migrate.*

impact   Use *impact* when you are referring to a forceful collision, as in *The impact of the cars was so great that one was flattened.* Do not use *impact* as a verb meaning "to have an effect on." Instead of writing *Each of us can positively impact waste reduction efforts,* write *Each of us can reduce waste.*

implicit, explicit   See *explicit, implicit.*

imply, infer   Use *imply* when you mean "to suggest without directly stating," as in *The doctor implied that being overweight was the main cause of my problem.* Use *infer* when you mean "to find the meaning of something," as in *I inferred from her lecture that drinking more than two cups of coffee a day was a health risk.*

incredible, incredulous   Use *incredible* to mean "unbelievable," as in *Some of Houdini's exploits seem incredible to those who did not witness them.* Use *incredulous* to mean "unbelieving," as in *Many inlanders were incredulous when they heard tales of white people capturing men, women, and children who lived on the coast.*

individual, person, party   Use *individual* to refer to a single unique person, as in *Curie was a tireless and brilliant individual.* Use *party* when you mean a group, as in *The party of eight at the next table disturbed our conversation and ruined our evening.* Use *party* in legal documents referring to a single person. Use *person* for other meanings.

infer, imply   See *imply, infer.*

in regards to   Do not use *in regards to* in formal writing. Generally, you can substitute *about* for *in regards to.*

irregardless, regardless   Do not use *irregardless.* Use *regardless* instead.

is when, is where   Do not use *is when* and *is where* when you are defining something. Instead of writing *Dinner time is when my family relaxes,* write *At dinner time, my family relaxes.*

its, it's   Use *its* when your sentence requires a possessive pronoun, as in *Its leaves are actually long, slender blades.* (See 30a-6.) Use *it's* only when you mean "it is." (See 38a.)

kind, sort, type   Do not precede the singular words *kind, sort,* and *type* with the plural word *these.* Use *this* instead. Also, prefer more specific words than *kind, sort,* and *type.* (See 24a.)

kind of, sort of   Do not use these phrases as adjectives in formal writing. Instead, use *rather* or *somewhat*.

lay, lie   Use *lay* when you mean "to put" or "to place," as in *She lays the present on the table.* Use *lie* when you mean "recline," as in *She lies awake at night,* or when you mean "is situated," as in *The city lies between a desert and a mountain range.* Also, remember that *lay* is a transitive verb that takes a direct object. (See 16d.)

learn, teach   Do not use *learn* to mean "teach." For example, rewrite a sentence such as *Ms. Chin learned us Algebra* to read *Ms. Chin taught us Algebra.*

leave, let   Use *leave* to mean "depart." Use *let* to mean "allow." You can use either *leave* or *let* when the word is followed by *alone,* as in *Leave her alone* or *Let him alone.*

less, fewer   See *fewer, less.*

lie, lay   See *lay, lie.*

like, as   See *as, like.*

lose, loose   Use *lose* as a verb meaning "to misplace" or "to fail to win." Use *loose* as an adjective meaning "not tight" or "unfastened." You can also use *loose* as a verb meaning "to let loose," as in *They loosed the enraged bull when the matador entered the ring.* (See 38a.)

lots, lots of   Do not use *lots* or *lots of* in formal writing. Use *many, very many, much,* or choose a more precise word instead.

man, mankind   Do not use *man* and *mankind* to refer to all people in general. Instead, consider using *people, men and women, humans,* or *humankind.* (See 26e.)

may be, maybe   Use *maybe* to mean "perhaps." Use *may be* as a verb (or auxiliary verb), as in *William may be visiting tomorrow.*

may, can   See *can, may.*

may of   See *could of, would of, should of, might of, may of, must of.*

media   Use a plural verb with *media,* as in *The media are often credited with helping the consumer win cases against large companies. Medium* is the singular form.

might of   See *could of, would of, should of, might of, may of, must of.*

migrate   See *emigrate, immigrate, migrate.*

Ms.   Use *Ms.* to refer to a woman when a title is required and when you either know that she prefers this title or you do not know her marital status. An invented title, *Ms.* was intended to address the issue of discrimination or judgment based on marital status. In research writing, use last names alone, without any title, as in *Jenkins recommends. . . .* In this case, do not use a title for either a man or a woman.

must of   See *could of, would of, should of, might of, may of, must of.*

myself   See *herself, himself, myself, yourself.*

nowheres   Do not use *nowheres* in formal writing. Use *nowhere* instead.

number, amount   See *amount, number.*

off of   Do not use *off of* in formal writing. Use *off* or *from* alone instead, as in *She jumped off the bridge* or *He leaped from the rooftop.*

Ok, okay, O.K.   Do not use *Ok, okay,* or *O.K.* in formal writing as a substitute for *acceptable.*

party, individual, person   See *individual, person, party.*

percent (per cent), percentage   Use *percent* (or *per cent*) with a specific number. Use *percentage* with specific descriptive words and phrases, such as *A small percentage of the group did not eat meat.* Do not use *percentage* as a substitute for *part;* for example, rewrite a sentence such as *A percentage of my diet consists of complex carbohydrates* to read *Part of my diet consists of complex carbohydrates.*

person, party, individual   See *individual, person, party.*

plus   Avoid using *plus* as a conjunction joining independent clauses or as a conjunctive adverb. For example, rewrite *Picasso used color in a new way plus he experimented with shape; plus, he brought new meaning to ideas about abstract painting* to read *Picasso used color in a new way and he experimented with shape; moreover, he brought new meaning to ideas about abstract painting.* It is acceptable to use *plus* when you need an expression meaning "in addition to," as in *The costs of day care, plus the costs of feeding and clothing the child, weighed heavily on the single parent's budget.*

precede, proceed   Use *precede* when you mean "come before," as in *The opening remarks precede the speech.* Use *proceed* when you mean "go forward," as in *The motorists proceeded with caution.*

pretty   Do not use *pretty,* as in *pretty close,* to mean "somewhat" or "quite" in formal writing. Use *somewhat, rather,* or *quite* instead.

principal, principle   Use *principal* when you refer to a school administrator or an amount of money. Use *principle* when you are referring to a law, conviction, or fundamental truth. You can also use *principal* as an adjective meaning "major" or "most important," as in *The principal players in the decision were Sue Marks and Tom Cohen.*

quotation, quote   Use *quotation* when your sentence requires a noun, as in *The quotation from Nobel laureate Joseph Goldstein was used to lend credence to the theory.* Use *quote* when your sentence requires a verb, as in *She asked Goldstein whether she could quote him.*

rarely ever   Do not use *rarely ever* in formal writing. Use *rarely* or *hardly ever* instead.

real, really   Use *real* as an adjective and use *really* as an adverb.

reason is because   Do not use *reason is because* in formal writing. Rewrite your sentence to say, for example, *The real reason that the bomb was dropped was to end the war quickly* or *The bomb was dropped because Truman wanted to prevent Soviet influence in the Far Eastern settlement.*

regardless, irregardless   See *irregardless, regardless.*

respectfully, respectively   Use *respectfully* when you mean "with respect," as in *He respectfully submitted his grievances.* Use *respectively* when you mean "in the given order," as in *The chief of police, the director of the department of public works, and the director of parks and recreation, respectively, submitted their ideas for budget cuts.*

seen   Do not use *seen* without an auxiliary such as *have, has,* or *had.* For example, rewrite a sentence such as *I seen the film* to read *I have seen the film.*

set, sit   Use *set* when you mean "to place." *Set* is a transitive verb that requires an object, as in *I set the book on the table.* Do not use *set* to mean "to sit" in formal writing. (See 16d.)

shall, will   Use *shall* instead of *will* for questions that contain the first person in extremely formal writing, as in *Shall we attend the meeting?* In all other cases, use *will*.

should of   See *could of, would of, should of, might of, may of, must of.*

should, would   Use *should* when you are referring to an obligation or a condition, as in *The governor's mansion should be restored.* Use *would* when you are referring to a wish, as in *I would like to see it repainted in its original colors.*

sit, set   See *set, sit.*

some   Do not use *some* to mean either "remarkable" or "somewhat" in formal writing. For example, rewrite a sentence such as *Babe Ruth was some hitter* to read *Babe Ruth was a remarkable hitter,* or use another more precise adjective to modify *hitter.* Also, rewrite a sentence such as *Wright's mother worried some about the kinds of building blocks her young child used* to read *Wright's mother worried a bit [or was somewhat worried] about the kinds of building blocks her young child used.*

somebody, some body; someone, some one   Use the indefinite pronouns *somebody* and *someone* when referring to a person, such as *There is someone I admire.* Use *some body* and *some one* when the adjective *some* modifies the noun *body* or *one,* as in *We will find the answer in some body of information.*

sometime, sometimes, some time   Use *sometime* when you mean "an indefinite, later time." Use *sometimes* when you mean "occasionally" or "from time to time." Use *some time* when *some* functions as an adjective modifying *time,* as in *His eyes required some time to adjust to the darkened room.*

sort   See *kind, sort, type.*

stationary, stationery   Use *stationary* to mean "standing still." Use *stationery* to mean "writing paper."

supposed to, used to   Do not use *suppose to* or *use to* in formal writing. Use *supposed to* or *used to* instead.

sure and, sure to; try and, try to   Do not use *sure and* and *try and* in formal writing. Instead, use *sure to* and *try to.* For example, rewrite the sentence *Be sure and bring your computer* to read *Be sure to bring your computer.*

take, bring   See *bring, take.*

than, then   Use *than* when you mean "as compared with," as in *The violin is smaller than the cello.* Use *then* when you are stating a sequence of events, as in *First, he learned how to play the violin. Then he learned to play the cello.* Also use *then* when you mean "at that time" or "therefore."

that, which   Use *that* or *which* in an essential (or restrictive) clause, or a clause that is necessary to the meaning of the sentence, as in *This is the book that explains Locke's philosophy.* Use *which* in a nonessential (nonrestrictive) clause, or one that is not necessary to the meaning of the sentence, as in *My library just acquired Smith's book on Locke, which is not always easy to find.* (See 28d.)

their, there, they're   Use *their* as a possessive pronoun, as in *Their father prevented William and Henry James from being under the control of any one teacher for more than a year.* (See 20c.) Use *there* to refer to a place, as the opposite of *here.* Use *they're* to mean "they are." (See 30a-6.)

theirselves Do not use *theirselves* in formal writing. Rewrite a sentence such as *They treated theirselves to ice cream* to read *They treated themselves to ice cream.*

then, than See *than, then.*

these kind See *kind, sort, type.*

to, too, two Use *to* as a preposition meaning "toward"; use *too* to mean "also" or "excessively"; and use *two* as a number. (See 38a.)

toward, towards Use *toward* instead of *towards* in formal writing. *Towards* is the British form.

try and, try to See *sure and, sure to; try and, try to.*

uninterested, disinterested See *disinterested, uninterested.*

unique Do not modify *unique* in formal writing. Because *unique* is an absolute, you should not write, for example, *most unique* or *very unique.*

use, utilize When you need a word that means "use," prefer *use. Utilize* is a less direct choice with the same meaning. (See 24a.)

used to See *supposed to, used to.*

very Avoid using *very* as an intensifier. Sometimes you will want to replace more than one word in order to eliminate *very.* For example, in the sentence *It was a very nice painting,* you could substitute more precise language, such as *It was a colorful [or provocative or highly abstract] painting.* (See 24a.)

wait for, wait on Unless you are referring to waiting on tables, use *wait for* instead of *wait on* in formal writing. For example, rewrite *We grew tired as we waited on Sarah* to read *We grew tired as we waited for Sarah.*

ways Do not use *ways* in formal writing to mean "way." Use *way* instead.

well, good See *good, well.*

whether, if See *if, whether.*

which, that See *that, which.*

which, who Use *which* when you are referring to things. Use *who* when you are referring to people.

who, whom Use *who* when a sentence requires a subject pronoun, as in *Who can answer this question?* Use *whom* when a sentence requires an object pronoun, as in *Whom did you invite?*

who's, whose Do not use *who's* in formal writing. Use *who is* instead. (See 30a-6.) Use *whose* to show possession, as in *Whose computer did you use?* (See 20f.)

will, shall See *shall, will.*

would of See *could of, would of, should of, might of, may of, must of.*

would, should See *should, would.*

your, you're Do not use *you're* in formal writing. Use *you are* instead. (See 30a-b.) Use *your* to show possession, as in *Your CD player is broken.* (See 20f.)

yourself See *herself, himself, myself, yourself.*

INDEX

Historical events/periods, capitalization of names of, 360
History resources, 94
Holidays, capitalization of names of, 360
Home pages, 75, 199, 201
Homonyms, 371–372
hopefully, 404
Hours, colons to separate from minutes, 347
HTML coding, 202–204
Humanities, arguments in. *See* Argument(s), in humanities
hung, hanged, 403
Hypertext, 75, 87–88, 204
Hyphens, 211, 212, 213, 368–370
Hypotheses, 178
Hypothetical statement tense for, 388–389

Ideas
    focusing for research, 63–64
    generating, 22–26
    main. *See* Main ideas; Theses; Topic(s)
Idioms, 311, 392
ie/ei spelling rules, 372–373
if, subjunctive mood with, 252
if/then constructions, 289
if, whether, 404
illicit, elicit, 402
Images, 219–220
Imperative mood, 252
imply, infer, 404
Incomplete sentences, 290–292
incredible, incredulous, 404
Indefinite articles, 382
Indefinite pronouns, 226
    as antecedents, pronoun-antecedent agreement and, 278–279
    subject-verb agreement and, 256–257
Independent clauses, 230, 238
    colons used with, 241, 346, 347

coordinating conjunctions joining, commas before, 323–324
linking with commas and coordinating conjunctions, 240, 241
linking with semicolon, 331–333
linking with semicolons and conjunctive adverbs, 240
linking with subordinating conjunctions or constructions, 242
separating with periods, 239
Indicative mood, 252
Indirect objects, 228
individual, person, party, 404
Inductive arrangement, 165
infer, imply, 404
Infinitive(s), 224, 229
    modifiers splitting, 267–268
    as nouns, 392
    objective case for pronouns before, 271
    set off as sentences, 236
Information, generating, 22–26
Informational Web page, 89
Information services, end-of-paper documentation of, 146
Informative writing, 20
-ing form of verbs. *See* Gerund(s); Participles
Inquiry letters, 189, 190
in regards to, 404
Intensive pronouns, 226
Interjections, 227
Internet, 72–76. *See also* E-mail; Listservs; Newsgroups
    bookmarks and, 100
    discussion groups or "listservs," 74–75
    Domain Name System, 80–81
    downloading files from, 75, 106
    effective searches, 76–87
    evaluating sources found on, 87–90
    online résumés, 195–196

online sharing of drafts and materials using, 112
OWLs on, 113
searching *versus* browsing, 74
sources on
    end-of-paper documentation of, 119, 120, 147–148
    note style of, 152–153
    text documentation of, 116
subject directories, 77–78
URLs and. *See* URLs
Usenet newsgroups on, 73–74
World Wide Web. *See* World Wide Web
Internet Explorer, 76
Interrogative pronouns, 226
Interrogative sentences. *See* Question(s)
Interruptions, punctuation indicating, 227
Interviews, end-of-paper documentation of, 133, 134
In-text citations
    APA documentation system for, 141–143
    CBE documentation system for, 153–154
    MLA documentation system for, 123–127
Intransitive verbs, 223, 385
Introductions, end-of-paper documentation of, 131, 151
Introductory clauses
    commas to set off, 322–323
    dangling modifiers, 268
Introductory paragraphs, 57–59
Introductory series, dashes to set off, 349
Invented words, 344
Inverted word order in questions, 390–391
IRC, end-of-paper documentation of, 139
Irony, quotation marks for, 344–345
irregardless, regardless, 404
Irregular plurals, 377

REVISION SYMBOLS

The symbols below indicate a need to make revisions in the areas designated. Boldface numbers and letters refer to handbook sections.

ab	abbreviation **35**
ad	form of adjective/adverb **18**
agr	agreement **21a**
awk	awkward diction or construction **13b, 19, 26**
ca	case form **20**
cap	capitalization **33**
coh	coherence **2e, 3b**
coord	coordination **13e, 23a, 25a**
cs	comma splice **28f, 15a–b**
d	diction, word choice **24a, 26**
dm	dangling modifier **19e**
dev	development needed **2, 3**
emph	emphasis needed **25**
frag	sentence fragment **13b, 14a–d**
fs	fused sentence **15a–b**
hyph	hyphen **37**
inc	incomplete construction **13b, 22e–g**
ital	italics **34**
lc	lowercase letter **33**
log	logic **8**
mm	misplaced modifier **19a–e**
ms	manuscript form **6c,**
mix	mixed construction **22d–e**
no ¶	no paragraph needed **3**
num	number **36**
¶	paragraph **3**

¶ dev	paragraph development needed **3**
ref	unclear pronoun reference **21b**
rep	unnecessary repetition **24a**
sp	spelling error **38**
shift	inconsistent, shifted construction **22a–c**
sub	sentence subordination **13c–d, 25b–c**
t	verb tense error **16e–f, 40b**
trans	transition needed **3a–e**
var	sentence variety needed **13d, 26**
vb	verb form error **16a-b**
w	wordy **24a**
ww	wrong word; word choice **26**
//	faulty parallelism **23**
. ? !	end punctuation **27**
:	colon **32a**
ᵥ	apostrophe **30a–c**
—	dash **32b**
( )	parentheses **32c**
[ ]	brackets **32d**
. . .	ellipsis **32e**
/	slash **32f**
;	semicolon **29**
" "	quotation marks **31**
⋀	comma **28**
◡	close up
^	insert a missing element
ℯ	delete
⌐⌐	transpose order

SPTLIGHT ON COMMON ERRORS

1   FORMS OF NOUNS AND PRONOUNS

Apostrophes can show possession or contraction. Never use an apostrophe with a possessive pronoun.

FAULTY FORMS	REVISED
The scarf is *Chris*. It is *her's*.	The scarf is *Chris's*. It is *hers*.
Give the dog *it's* collar.	Give the dog *its* collar.
Its a difficult thing.	*It's* [it is] a difficult thing.

Choose a pronoun's form depending on its use. For pronouns connected by *and*, or with forms of the verb *be (is/are/was/were)*, decide which forms to use (*I/he/she/they* OR *me/him/her/them*).

FAULTY FORMS	REVISED
This is *him*. It was *me*. Is that *her*?	This is *he*. It was *I*. Is that *she*?
The ball landed between *she* and I.	The ball landed between *her* and *me*.
Her and *me* practice daily.	*She* and I practice daily.

• Also see the following **SPOTLIGHT** sections: **20a, 20d, 20g, 30a–b.**

2   VERBS

Keep verb tenses consistent when describing two closely connected events.

INCONSISTENT	REVISED
She *liked* the work. Still, she *keeps* to herself.	She *likes* the work. Still, she *keeps* to herself.

(a) Choose the right verb forms with an *if* clause expressing an unreal or hypothetical condition. (b) Decide on which of these verb forms to use: *sit* or *set, lie* or *lay, rise* or *raise*.

FAULTY VERB FORM	REVISED
(a) If it *would be* any colder, the pipes *would* freeze.	(a) If it *were* any colder, the pipes *would* freeze.
(b) *Lie* the books here. Then *lay* down.	(b) *Lay* the books here. Then *lie* down.

• Also see the following **SPOTLIGHT** sections: **16d2, 16f, 16h.**

3   AGREEMENT

Match subjects with verbs. Make sure both are either singular or plural.

NOT IN AGREEMENT	REVISED
The *reason* she wins *are* her friends.	The *reason* she wins *is* her friends.

Match pronouns with the words they refer to. (a) Words joined by *and* require a plural pronoun and verb. (b) For words joined by *or/nor*, match the pronoun and verb to the nearer word.

NOT IN AGREEMENT	REVISED
(a) My friends **and** Sue *likes her* pizza hot.	(a) My friends **and** Sue *like their* pizza hot.
(b) Neither her friends **nor** Sue *like their* pizza cold.	(b) Neither her friends **nor** Sue *likes her* pizza cold.

• Also see the following **SPOTLIGHT** sections: **17, 21a**